T0350950

Qualified Appraisals and Qualified Appraisers

Qualified Appraisals and Qualified Appraisers

Expert Tax Valuation Witness Reports, Testimony, Procedure, Law, and Perspective

MICHAEL R. DEVITT
LAWRENCE A. SANNICANDRO

WILEY

Published by John Wiley & Sons, Inc., Hoboken, New Jersey.
Published simultaneously in Canada.

For general information on our other products and services or for technical support, please contact our Customer Care Department within the United States at (800) 762–2974, outside the United States at (317) 572–3993, or fax (317) 572–4002.

Wiley publishes in a variety of print and electronic formats and by print-on-demand. Some material included with standard print versions of this book may not be included in e-books or in print-on-demand. If this book refers to media such as a CD or DVD that is not included in the version you purchased, you may download this material at http://booksupport.wiley.com. For more information about Wiley products, visit www.wiley.com.

Library of Congress Cataloging-in-Publication Data

Names: Devitt, Michael R., author. | Sannicandro, Lawrence A., author.
Title: Qualified appraisals and qualified appraisers : expert tax valuation witness
  reports, testimony, procedure, law, and perspective / Michael R. Devitt,
  Lawrence A. Sannicandro.
Description: Hoboken, New Jersey : Wiley, 2017. | Series: Wiley finance |
  Includes index. |
Identifiers: LCCN 2017041390 (print) | LCCN 2017041873 (ebook) | ISBN
  9781119438205 (pdf) | ISBN 9781119438175 (epub) | ISBN 9781119437574
  (hardback)
Subjects: LCSH: Tax assessment—Law and legislation—United States. |
  Valuation—Law and legislation—United States. | Tax assessment—United
  States—Data processing. | Tax administration and procedure—United
  States. | Forensic accounting—United States. | Evidence, Expert—United
  States. | United States. Internal Revenue Service. | BISAC: BUSINESS &
  ECONOMICS / Accounting / General.
Classification: LCC KF6759.5 (ebook) | LCC KF6759.5 .D48 2017 (print) | DDC
  343.7305/42—dc23
LC record available at https://lccn.loc.gov/2017041390

Cover Design: Wiley
Cover Image: © O.C Ritz /Shutterstock

Printed in the United States of America.
10 9 8 7 6 5 4 3 2 1

To my father, Frank Richard Mascari,

Not a day goes by that I do not think about you and our many fun family times with Mom, Daniel, Barbara, Sandra, Frank, and Connie. At 38 years old, God took you from us way too young. I just wish you could have met my amazing and brilliant wife, Stacie, and our wonderful and loving children, Isabella and Michael. The kind, thoughtful wisdom you imparted to me at a very young age has stayed with me and made me a better man. I will always love you.

—Michael R. Devitt

To my wife, Alyson
—Lawrence A. Sannicandro

Contents

Foreword by Shannon P. Pratt xvii

Foreword by Jay E. Fishman xix

Preface xxi

CHAPTER 1
Tax Valuation and the Necessity for Expert Appraisals 1
 Summary 1
 The Need for Valuation Experts 1
  Valuation in Tax Reporting 2
  Valuation in Tax Litigation 3
  Valuation in Business and Familial Matters 4
 Valuation Calculation Standards 4
  Fair Market Value Defined 5
  Implied Assumptions 6
  Cash Value and Market Value 7
 Computing Fair Market Value 7
  Step 1: Calculating Net Asset Value 8
  Step 2: Applying Discounts and Premiums 9
 Common Tax Appraisal Reports 9
  Appraisal Reports to Support Tax Reporting Positions 9
  Appraisal Reports to Support Tax Litigation 10
 Proliferation of Litigation 10
 Conclusion 11

CHAPTER 2
Qualified Appraisal 12
 Summary 12
 Defining Qualified Appraisal 12
 Situations in Which a Qualified Appraisal May Be Required 13
 Qualified Appraisal Requirements for Charitable Contribution
   Deductions Context 14
  Requirements 15
  Legislative History 16
  Statutory Definition of a Qualified Appraisal 18
  Regulatory Definition of a Qualified Appraisal 18
   Requirement 1: The 60-Day Requirement: Treas. Reg.
    § 1.170A-13(c)(3)(i)(A) 19

Requirement 2: The Qualified Appraiser Requirement: Treas.
Reg. § 1.170A-13(c)(3)(i)(B)   19
Requirement 3: The Substantive Requirements: Treas.
Reg. § 1.170A-13(c)(3)(i)(C)   20
Requirement 3.1: Property Description: Treas.
Reg. § 1.170A-13(c)(3)(ii)(A)   20
Requirement 3.2: Tangible Property: Treas.
Reg. § 1.170A-13(c)(3)(ii)(B)   21
Requirement 3.3: Date of Contribution: Treas.
Reg. § 1.170A-13(c)(3)(ii)(C)   21
Requirement 3.4: Terms of Agreement: Treas.
Reg. § 1.170A-13(c)(3)(ii)(D)   22
Requirement 3.5: Identifying Information of the Qualified
Appraiser: Treas. Reg. § 1.170A-13(c)(3)(ii)(E)   23
Requirement 3.6: The Qualifications of the Qualified Appraiser:
Treas. Reg. § 1.170A-13(c)(3)(ii)(F)   24
Requirement 3.7: Statement of Preparation for Income Tax
Purposes: Treas. Reg. § 1.170A-13(c)(3)(ii)(G)   24
Requirement 3.8: Date(s) of Appraisal: Treas.
Reg. § 1.170A-13(c)(3)(ii)(H)   25
Requirement 3.9: Appraised Fair Market Value: Treas.
Reg. § 1.170A-13(c)(3)(ii)(I)   25
Requirements 3.10 and 3.11: Valuation and Basis Used to
Determine Fair Market Value: Treas.
Reg. §§ 1.170A-13(c)(3)(ii)(J) and (K)   26
Requirement 4: No Prohibited Fee Arrangement: Treas.
Reg. § 1.170A-13(c)(3)(i)(D)   27
The Qualified Appraisal Requirement and Pass-Through Entities   27
Interplay of the Qualified Appraisal and Appraisal Summary
Requirements   28
Litigation Concerning Qualified Appraisals   29
Conclusion   29

CHAPTER 3
Qualified Appraiser   **31**
Summary   31
Legislative History   31
Statutory Requirements   32
Statutory Requirement #1: Appraisal Designation or Certain
Minimum Education and Experience Requirements   33
Statutory Requirement #2: Regularly Performs Appraisals for
Compensation   34
Statutory Requirement #3: Verifiable Education and Experience   34
Statutory Requirement #4: Not Prohibited from Practice by
31 U.S.C. § 330(c)   34
Regulatory Requirements   35
Appraiser's Declaration   35
Regulatory Requirement #1: Declaration That Individual Is an
Appraiser: Treas. Reg. § 1.170A-13(c)(5)(i)(A)   36

Regulatory Requirement #2: Declaration That the
Appraiser Is Qualified to Value the Property: Treas.
Reg. § 1.170A-13(c)(5)(i)(B)   36
Regulatory Requirement #3: Declaration That the
Appraiser Is Not an Excluded Person: Treas.
Reg. § 1.170A-13(c)(5)(i)(C)   36
Regulatory Requirement #4: Declaration That the Appraiser
Understands Consequences of Fraudulent Valuation:
Treas. Reg. § 1.170A-13(c)(5)(i)(D)   38
Additional Declaration Requirements of Notice 2006-96   38
Denial of Appraiser Status   39
Appraisals by More than One Appraiser   40
Appraisal Fees   40
Judicial Interpretation of the Requirements   41
Sufficiency of Documentation   41
Scrutiny of Qualifications   42
Excluded Parties   42
Multiple Appraisers   42
Conclusion   42

CHAPTER 4

Substantial Compliance vs. Strict Compliance   43
Summary   43
Overview of the Strict and Substantial Compliance Doctrines   43
Applicability of the Substantial Compliance Doctrine   44
Judicial Approaches to the Substantial Compliance Doctrine   45
Survey of Cases Applying the Substantial Compliance
Doctrine   45
Bond v. Commissioner: The First Application of the Substantial
Compliance Doctrine in the Context of the Qualified
Appraisal Regulation   46
Post-Bond Decisions: Cases Finding Substantial Compliance   47
Supplemental Information from Form 8283   47
Sufficient Information for IRS to Evaluate Reported
Contributions as Intended by Congress   48
A New Trend?   48
Post-Bond Decisions: Cases Finding No Substantial
Compliance   49
Absence of Qualified Appraisal   49
Flawed Appraisal Reports   50
Post-Scheidelman Cases   53
Judicial Approaches to the Strict Compliance Doctrine   53
The Substantial Compliance Doctrine in the Appellate Courts   54
Reasonable Cause: Codification of the Substantial Compliance
Doctrine   55
Conclusion   56

CHAPTER 5

Government Expert Witnesses   **58**

Summary   58

The Government's Need for Expert Testimony   58

IRS Criteria for Expert Selection   59

Internal IRS Valuation Experts   60

    IRS Hiring, Training, and Evaluation of Internal Valuation Experts   62

        Hiring   62

        Training   62

        Performance Evaluation and Management Oversight   63

    IRS Use of Internal Valuation Expert Witnesses   63

        Advantages to Using an Internal Valuation Expert as an Expert
            Witness   63

        The Inherent Bias Problem   63

Court Reactions to Government Employee Expert Witnesses   64

Government's Decision to Not Present an Expert Witness   66

Conclusion   67

CHAPTER 6

The Practicalities of Selection and Preparation of Experts   **68**

Summary   68

Selecting an Appraiser   68

    Education, Training, Professional Experience, and Accrediting
        Organization Participation   69

    The American Society of Appraisers   69

    The Appraisal Institute   70

    The Institute of Business Appraisers   70

    The National Association of Valuers and Analysts   71

    The American Institute of Certified Public Accountants   71

Being a Good Communicator   71

Offering a Neutral, Detached Opinion of Value   71

    Avoiding the Bias Perception   71

    Selecting the Expert Who Prepared the Appraisal That Supports
        the Tax Reporting Position   72

Early and Significant Appraiser Involvement   72

Appraiser Scheduling and Availability   73

Correcting Errors in the Expert's Report   73

"Skeletons in the Closet"   73

Acquainting the Expert with the Cast of Characters and Venue   73

Attorney Comprehension of Expert Opinions   74

Planning the Testimony   74

Expert Testimony Preparation   74

Conclusion   75

CHAPTER 7

From *Daubert* to *Boltar*   **76**

Summary   76

Standard of Admissibility for Expert Witness Testimony—The
    Federal Rules of Evidence   76

Daubert and Its Progeny in Courts Other than the Tax Court 77
Boltar as the Modern Incarnation of *Daubert* in the Tax Court 81
Daubert Challenges Generally 82
  Illustrations of *Daubert* Factors in Practice 83
    Factor 1: Has the theory or technique been tested? 83
    Factor 2: Has the theory or technique been subjected to peer review and publication? 84
    Factor 3: Is there a known or potential rate of error or standards for the theory or technique applied? 86
    Factor 4: Has the theory or technique gained general acceptance? 88
    Factor 5: Is the expert testifying about matters growing naturally and directly out of research conducted independent of the litigation? 90
    Factor 6: Has the expert unjustifiably extrapolated from an accepted premise to an unfounded conclusion? 93
    Factor 7: Has the expert adequately accounted for obvious alternative explanations? 95
    Factor 8: Is the expert being as careful as he would be in his regular professional work? 96
    Factor 9: Is the field or expertise claimed by the expert known to reach reliable results for the type of opinion the expert would give? 97
    Factor 10: Has the theory or method offered by the expert been put to any non-judicial use? 97
    Factor 11: Whether the expert's opinion fails to square with a judge's opinion and common sense 97
  Conclusion 98

CHAPTER 8
Discovery of Expert Material **99**
  Summary 99
  Overview of Discovery 99
  Important Limitations on Discovery 100
    The Attorney–Client Privilege 100
    Work Product 101
    Unfairness Doctrine 102
  The IRS's Summons Authority 102
  Procedures with Respect to Expert Witnesses Prepared in Connection with Litigation 103
  Discovery in the Courts 103
    Tax Court 104
      General Provisions Regarding Discovery 105
      Interrogatories 107
      Production of Documents 108
      Depositions 110
      Admissions 112

U.S. District Courts 113
General Provisions Regarding Discovery 113
Interrogatories 117
Production of Documents, Electronically Stored Information,
and Other Similar Items 117
Depositions 118
Admissions 119
Court of Claims 119
Expert Should Be Present at Opposing Expert's Deposition 119
Conclusion 119

CHAPTER 9
Expert Appraisal Reports **120**
Summary 120
Valuation Standards 120
Revenue Ruling 59-60 121
USPAP Generally 122
Compliance with USPAP 122
Noncompliance with USPAP Does Not Render an Expert
Report Unreliable 122
Appraisal Reports Generally 122
Fair Market Value 123
Contents of the Appraisal Report 123
Table of Contents 123
Executive Summary or Cover Letter 123
Body of Report 124
Identifying the Retaining Party and Other Intended Users 124
Type of Appraisal 125
Standard of Value and Source 125
Effective Date of the Appraisal and the Date of the Report 126
Purpose of the Appraisal and Its Intended Use 128
Summary of the Scope of Work 128
Summary of Information Considered 129
Describing the Subject Property, the Type of Asset, the Interest
Valued, and Geographic Data 131
How Title Is Held 132
Restrictions, Hypotheticals, and Limiting Conditions 132
Highest and Best Use 132
Valuation of the Subject Property 132
Summary of Approaches Utilized 134
Reconciliation 135
Consider a Regression Analysis 135
Conclusion of Value 136
Appraiser's Signature 136
Signed Certification 136
Addenda 138
Work File as Support for an Appraisal Report 138
Contents of Work File 138
Retention Period 139
Conclusion 139

CHAPTER 10
  Assessing the Quality of the Appraisal Report **140**
    Summary 140
    Required Items Under the USPAP and Revenue Ruling 59-60 140
    Making the Report Understandable to the Audience 142
    Replicability 142
    Completeness 142
    Internal Consistency 142
    Reconciliation 143
    Regression Analysis 143
    Forecasting Future Results 144
    Economic and Industry Sections 144
    Supporting Exhibits 144
    Comply with Applicable Court Rules 145
      The Tax Court 145
      The District Courts 146
    Conclusion 146

CHAPTER 11
  Concurrent Evidence: A Novel Approach to Expert Testimony **147**
    Summary 147
    A New Approach to Expert Testimony 148
    Our Long and Deep Distrust of Partisan Experts 148
    Court-Appointed Experts 151
    Heating Up the Tub: The Concurrent Evidence Method 152
      Expert Bias 155
      Foreign Court Experiences 155
      American Experience with Concurrent Experts 157
    Suggested Four-Stage Hot Tub Approach for Tax Court Judges 159
      Stage One: Pretrial Expert Meeting and Joint Report 160
      Stage Two: The Expert Oath 161
      Stage Three: The Trial Hot Tub Conversation 161
      Stage Four: Cross-Examination and Rebuttal 163
    Common Misperceptions of the Concurrent Witness Model 164
      Myth 1: Concurrent Testimony Replaces the Traditional Model 164
      Myth 2: The Consent of Both Parties Is Needed 164
      Myth 3: More Work Is Created for the Trier of Fact 164
      Myth 4: Concurrent Evidence Is Received Off the Record 165
      Myth 5: The Concurrent Witness Model Is an Auction 165
      Myth 6: The Lawyers Lose All Control in the Courtroom 165
      Myth 7: Hot Tubbing Is Prevalent in Tax Cases 165
    Practical Benefits and Claimed Drawbacks 166
    Conclusion 169

CHAPTER 12
  Penalties Associated with Faulty Appraisals **170**
    Summary 170
    The Importance and Prevalence of Penalties in Modern-Day
      Appraisal Practice 170
    Framework for Examination 171

Accuracy-Related Penalties Possibly Applicable to Client–Taxpayers   171
    The Substantial Valuation Misstatement Penalty   172
        Imposition of the Penalty   172
        Substantial Valuation Misstatement Penalty Applies on a
            Property-by-Property Basis   172
        Dollar Limitation for Substantial Valuation Misstatements   173
        Substantial Valuation Misstatements and Pass-Through Entities   173
        Increase in Penalty Rate for Gross Valuation Misstatements   174
        Defenses   174
    The Gross Valuation Misstatement Penalty   176
        Gross Valuation Misstatement Applies on a
            Property-by-Property Basis   177
        Dollar Limitation for Gross Valuation Misstatements   177
        Gross Valuation Misstatements and Pass-Through Entities   177
        Elimination of Reasonable Cause Exception   178
        The Applicability of the Gross Valuation Misstatements to
            Transactions Determined to Lack Economic Substance   178
    Estate or Gift Tax Valuation Understatements   180
Civil Penalties Potentially Applicable to Appraisers   180
    The Section 6695A Accuracy-Related Penalty   180
        The Statute   181
        Statute of Limitations and Collection of Penalty   182
        Affirmative Defenses   182
        Referral for Professional Sanctions   182
    Paid Preparer Penalty—Section 6694   182
        The Statute   183
        Appraisers as Paid Return Preparers   185
        De Minimis Exception   185
        Affirmative Defenses   186
    Aiding and Abetting an Understatement of Tax—The Section
        6701 Penalty   186
        The Statute   187
        Coordination with Other Penalties   188
        Injunctions against Appraisers   188
        Effect of Imposition of the Section 6701 Penalty   188
Professional Sanctions   189
    Circular 230 Generally   189
    Disqualification of Appraisers under Circular 230   189
    Monetary Penalty   189
Conclusion   190

CHAPTER 13
Attorney Involvement   191
    Summary   191
    Framework for Examination   191
    Attorney Involvement in Selecting the Appraiser   192
        An Appraiser's Ability to Withstand a Daubert Challenge   193
        The Importance of Having the Attorney Engage the Appraiser   193

Attorney Involvement in the Appraisal Process   194
   The Fact-Gathering Process   194
   The Report Preparation Process   195
   The Review Process   196
   Sanctions for Improper Attorney Assistance   197
   The Tax Preparation Process   198
Coordinating the Attorney's and the Appraiser's Involvement in
   Negotiations with Tax Authorities   198
Attorney Involvement in Litigation Where Expert Reports Will Be
   Submitted   199
   Discovery and the Expert Appraiser   200
Submitting the Expert Appraisal Report to the Court   200
   Motions *in Limine*   201
   Rebuttal Reports   202
Qualifying the Appraiser as an Expert and Satisfying *Daubert*   203
Cross-Examination and Rehabilitation   203
   Cross-Examination   203
   Rehabilitating the Expert Witness   203
Conclusion   204

CHAPTER 14
Common Errors with Appraisal Reports and How to Avoid Them   **205**
Summary   205
Common Defects with Appraisals   205
   Defect 1: Untimely Appraisal Report   206
      Requirement and Error   206
      Remedy   206
   Defect 2: Inadequate Description of Property   207
      Requirement and Error   207
      Remedy   207
   Defect 3: Failing to Analyze Agreements and Restrictions with
      Respect to the Property   208
      Requirement and Error   208
      Remedy   208
   Defect 4: Qualifications Not Disclosed   209
      Requirement and Error   209
      Remedy   209
   Defect 5: No Statement That Appraisal Was Prepared for Federal
      Tax Purposes   210
      Requirement and Error   210
      Remedy   210
   Defect 6: Wrong Measure of Value   210
      Requirement and Error   210
      Remedy   212
   Defect 7: Lack of Reconciliation   213
      Requirement and Error   213
      Remedy   214

Defect 8: Consideration of Subsequent Events   215
    Requirement and Error   215
    Remedy   216
Defect 9: Tax-Affecting S Corporations   216
    Requirement and Opportunity for Error   216
    Remedy   217
Potential Defect 10: Failure to Include a Regression Analysis 217
Conclusion   218

Table of Cases   **219**

About the Authors   **223**

Index   **225**

Foreword

Valuators are often called upon to assist tax professionals in connection with the filing of tax returns and in tax litigation. And, while many valuators understand how to value property, few understand the specific technical requirements in tax that can affect the intended purpose of the valuation, whether that purpose be to secure an intended tax benefit in connection with filing a tax return or at trial.

The stakes in tax cases are high and mistakes are costly to everyone involved. Tax authorities frequently audit valuation-related tax issues to disallow tax benefits on hypertechnical grounds that can expose valuators and tax professionals, as well as clients, to significant civil penalties and professional sanctions. One such hyper-technical ground that has been at the forefront of tax litigation in recent years is the disallowance of tax benefits for failing to obtain a "qualified appraisal" prepared by a "qualified appraiser." What it means to be "qualified" in valuation and tax disciplines is the overarching focus of this book.

This book explains, in stunning detail, what it takes to have a "qualified appraisal" performed by a "qualified appraiser," requirements that are imposed in various sections of the Internal Revenue Code and related Treasury Regulations. Next, this book highlights the procedural rules and pragmatic considerations that bear on selecting an expert witness, ensuring the witness can testify at trial, and making sure expert witness reports are admitted at trial. Then, this book introduces readers to a relatively new technique some federal courts are using to receive expert testimony: concurrent witness testimony (or "hot tubbing" as it is known more informally). This book also covers a range of other topics, including the proper role of attorneys in the appraisal process; the penalties that can apply to valuators and tax return preparers; and practical strategies to overcome defects in appraisal reports when filing a tax return or during litigation.

The authors are uniquely qualified to educate the reader on the cross-disciplinarian areas of valuation and tax, with an emphasis on qualified appraisals and qualified appraisers. Professor Michael Devitt has more than 30 years' experience practicing complex civil litigation in various jurisdictions around the United States and teaching courtroom evidence and trial advocacy. Lawrence Sannicandro has a wealth of experience, including his former employment as counsel for the IRS and his service as a law clerk with the United States Tax Court. Together, these authors have created an invaluable resource for valuators and tax professionals working on assignments where valuation and tax overlap.

Shannon P. Pratt, CFA, FASA, MCBA, MCBC, CM & AA

Foreword

Who is a qualified appraiser and what constitutes a qualified appraisal? These are the questions that Professor Michael Devitt and Lawrence Sannicandro, Esq., answer in this volume. These authors provide a thoughtful, detailed practical approach for making such determinations, coupled with explanations designed to continue a necessary dialogue concerning these issues that all appraisal stakeholders should consider.

The authors are uniquely qualified to educate the reader on the issues and nuances of the subjects of qualified appraisers and appraisals. Professor Michael Devitt is both an accomplished lawyer and a highly respected *Professor of Law*, teaching in the areas of courtroom evidence and advocacy. Lawrence Sannicandro is an experienced tax practitioner. Together, these authors offer the readers vast experience and knowledge that will serve them in this dynamic field of valuation.

Billions of dollars are involved in the multitude of appraisals performed every year. The United States Tax Court is often the forum where many controversial valuation issues are litigated. These adjudications, while specifically pertaining to federal tax issues, have often found application in forums addressing non-tax issues. As such, this book can be seen as addressing the use of qualified appraisers performing qualified appraisals in a much broader context.

Everyone needing an appraisal wants both the appraisal and the appraiser to be qualified. This book addresses the multiple aspects of what it takes, in all appraisal disciplines, to be qualified. It covers topics ranging from the practicalities of expert selection, discovery, and preparation to the evolution of the Supreme Court decision in *Daubert* and its progeny mandating the trial judge to take a critical look at expert witness admissibility. At the same time, the book addresses a multitude of pragmatic topics such as expert reports and substantial compliance and offers fresh insight on very important valuation topics.

The novel and controversial topic of concurrent witness testimony, often called hot tubbing, is the subject of a very thoughtful chapter. Professor Devitt is a true expert on hot tubbing and a proponent for such methodology's utilization here in the United States. Indeed, Judge David Laro of the United States Tax Court has pioneered Professor Devitt's concepts by adopting the procedure of concurrent witness testimony in the courtroom.

With the proliferation of appraisal designations and the avalanche of written materials, webinars, and conferences available to appraisers and appraisal users, this volume comes at a very propitious time. We owe Professor Devitt and Lawrence Sannicandro a debt of gratitude for assembling a volume that provides clarity on these very important controversial issues.

Jay E. Fishman, FASA

Preface

Valuation events and issues permeate our very complex Internal Revenue Code. Billions of dollars are involved in the multitude of appraisals that are performed every year. To state the obvious, valuation is critical to our laws and our business transactions. It is the fabric of estate and gift planning as well as commercial activity.

Approximately 340 sections of the Internal Revenue Code require taxpayers to make fair market value determinations in order to accurately assess and report tax liabilities. Not surprisingly, the Internal Revenue Service (IRS), the IRS Office of Appeals, and the IRS Office of Chief Counsel have developed sophisticated techniques to challenge questionable valuations throughout the audit, litigation, and collection processes. These valuation-related issues are frequently litigated before the United States Tax Court (Tax Court). In 2016 alone, valuation was at issue in one form or another in upwards of 35 percent of all opinions released by the Tax Court where the taxpayer was represented by counsel.

As a result of the significant effect of abusive valuations on tax revenues, Congress, the United States Department of the Treasury, and the IRS have imposed specific technical requirements with which taxpayers must comply to receive many tax benefits. For example, tax law mandates that for charitable contribution deductions of more than $5,000, transfers to charitable remainder trusts and qualified settlement funds, and deductions for claims against an estate, taxpayers must obtain a "qualified appraisal" that is prepared by a "qualified appraiser."

Over the past ten-plus years, there have been a substantial number of tax controversies as to what constitutes a "qualified appraisal" and who is a "qualified appraiser." Armed with technical sections of the Internal Revenue Code and the Treasury Regulations, the IRS now vigorously and routinely challenges taxpayer appraisals intended to support and substantiate millions of dollars of tax deductions. Current Treasury Regulations establish multiple, specific requirements that must be met for the appraisal to be qualified and consequently useful to the taxpayer wanting to substantiate a deduction on her tax return. An appraisal that does not meet these mandated standards is likely to fail to achieve its purpose.

In a broader sense, everyone needing an appraisal wants the appraisal to be qualified and the person creating the appraisal analysis to be qualified regardless of whether a tax deduction is at issue. This book addresses the technical and commonsense standards that both the appraisal and appraiser must meet to be successful in the valuation world.

Chapter 1 of this book discusses basic concepts of tax valuation with which all competent valuators and tax professionals must be familiar. This chapter also documents the practical necessity for obtaining reliable expert appraisals in most valuation scenarios.

Chapters 2 through 4 of this book discuss what it takes to have a "qualified appraisal" performed by a "qualified appraiser," requirements that are imposed in various sections of the Internal Revenue Code and related Treasury Regulations. These chapters address the many technical hurdles necessary to meet and overcome IRS challenges to taxpayer appraisals and appraisers.

Given the omnipresent nature of valuations in the United States tax system, it is wise for valuators and tax professionals to develop wise and knowledgeable cross-disciplinary skills in valuation and tax. This is especially true since courts have adopted detailed rules concerning the qualification of valuators as expert witnesses, the admissibility of expert reports, and the discovery of expert material in connection with litigation. Thus, Chapters 5 through 10 inform readers of the procedural rules and practical considerations that bear on selecting an expert witness and making sure she can testify in a valuation case.

Chapter 11 discusses a relatively new technique some federal courts are using to receive expert testimony: concurrent witness testimony (known colloquially as "hot tubbing"). The authors have a special fondness for this unique chapter. It presents a new and exciting development in expert witness testimony. Attorneys and experts will want to get familiar with this new technique where the parties' experts have a joint discussion with the trial judge explaining their opinions and thoughts on the subject valuation.

Given the ubiquity of valuation in tax, numerous rules have been implemented to ensure that valuators satisfy a minimum duty of competence in tax and that tax practitioners satisfy a minimum duty of competence in valuation. Penalties abound for professionals who fail to exhibit this minimum duty of competence in valuation. Thus, Chapter 12 discusses penalties that can apply to preparers and valuators in connection with faulty appraisal reports.

Many attorneys struggle to understand their role in the appraisal process. Accordingly, Chapter 13 discusses attorney involvement in the appraisal report process during the tax reporting, administrative, and litigation stages of valuation cases.

Finally, Chapter 14 discusses common errors with appraisals and details the steps practitioners should take to remedy these problems in connection with filing a tax return or during litigation.

We would like to thank Judge David Laro for his many years of kind thoughtful mentorship to us both. Judge Laro stands as a shining example of selfless professionalism for us all. With his 25 years of service on the United States Tax Court and his commonsense deep critical thinking, Judge Laro has helped shape and define many areas of the law, including his thoughtful opinions in the area of qualified appraisals.

Many other people contributed to the ideas and concepts discussed in this book. We thank those who have made contributions to this book by way of research, writing, editing, or commenting. We especially thank Dr. Shannon Pratt, CEO, Shannon Pratt Valuations, Inc., Jay E. Fishman, FASA, Managing Director, Financial Research Associates, Jane Larrington, Head of Reference, University of San Diego School of Law, Helen Y. Trac, Esq., Hogan Lovells, and the many wonderfully hardworking and talented individuals from John Wiley & Sons, Inc., including Sheck Cho, Judy Howarth, Shelley Flannery, and Banurekha Venkatesan.

We hope you enjoy reading this book and wish you all the success in presenting your valuation cases and controversies.

Michael R. Devitt
Lawrence A. Sannicandro

Tax Valuation and the Necessity for Expert Appraisals

SUMMARY

The appraisal profession, which includes specialized valuation determinations of real estate, businesses, interests in businesses, intangible assets, machinery and equipment, and private personal property, has made great strides in the last decade. With these advancements, appraisals have become increasingly technical. Attorneys, return preparers, and appraisers are finding that courts and regulators are much more inclined to scrutinize all aspects of the valuation and appraisal processes. In response, tax professionals increasingly rely upon expert valuators to support tax reporting positions in civil and criminal tax controversies with the IRS, the Tax Division of the U.S. Department of Justice, and state and local tax authorities.

Tax professionals who rely upon valuators, and valuators who provide support to tax professionals, must develop cross-disciplinary skills in valuation and tax to better serve their clients. This chapter summarizes the necessity of involving well-qualified and knowledgeable experts in all aspects of the appraisal process, especially since appraisals often involve significant valuation technicalities and many deal with major sums of money for the participants.

THE NEED FOR VALUATION EXPERTS

Valuation is pervasive in our tax system; complex valuation disputes have filled court dockets for centuries. Approximately 340 sections of the Internal Revenue Code require determinations of fair market value in order to accurately assess and report tax liabilities.[1] Indeed, valuation litigation is so frequent that it accounts for between

---

[1] As of the time of this writing, the term *fair market value* appears in 344 different sections of the Internal Revenue Code. Roughly 290 of these sections concern the calculations of income, estate and gift, employment, and excises taxes. The other 54 sections deal with valuation in procedural and administrative areas of the tax law, mostly as it relates to third-party reporting on information returns. One section relates to Coal Industry Health Benefits.

20 and 35 percent of all Tax Court cases in which the taxpayers are represented by counsel.[2]

Valuation methodology has become highly sophisticated, and valuation-related tax issues often perplex even the most experienced tax professionals. It is against this backdrop that knowledgeable valuators have become indispensable to the tax reporting and tax litigation processes. Following are the areas where valuation and tax are likely to overlap.

Valuation in Tax Reporting

As applied to tax reporting, the federal tax law generally *requires* taxpayers to hire a *qualified appraiser* to prepare a *qualified appraisal* in connection with:

- Claiming a charitable contribution deduction of more than $5,000 where the donated property is not cash, publicly traded securities, a qualifying vehicle, or certain intellectual property;[3]
- Valuing assets of charitable remainder trusts;[4]
- Valuing claims and counterclaims against an estate;[5] and
- Transferring property to a qualified settlement fund.[6]

Moreover, obtaining a qualified appraisal prepared by a qualified appraiser may help a taxpayer avoid accuracy-related penalties under section 6662 of the Internal Revenue Code.[7] The terms *qualified appraisal* and *qualified appraiser* are technically and specifically defined in the Internal Revenue Code and the federal Treasury Regulations. Chapter 2, *Qualified Appraisal*, and Chapter 3, *Qualified Appraiser*, analyze and discuss each of these terms in detail.

As applied to tax reporting, practitioners may hire expert valuators to accurately compute and report tax liabilities. A nonexclusive list of the areas where such expertise is typically utilized is:

1. Charitable contribution deductions, including, but not limited to, donations to real property, personal property, grants of air rights, development rights, and conservation easements;
2. Business formations;
3. Inventory valuations;

---

[2]The Tax Court published 422 opinions in 2014. Of these 422 opinions, 148 involved taxpayers represented by counsel and 274 involved taxpayers appearing *pro se* (i.e., unrepresented by counsel). Questions of valuation were resolved, in one form or another, in roughly 52 of the 148 cases involving taxpayers represented by counsel, which means that valuation was at issue in approximately 35.1% of cases in represented taxpayer cases in 2014. Similarly, the Tax Court published 443 opinions in 2013. Of these 443 total opinions, 98 involved taxpayers represented by counsel and 345 involved taxpayers proceeding *pro se*. Valuation issues of some sort were resolved in 20 of the 98 cases involving taxpayers represented by counsel, which means that valuation was at issue in approximately 20.4% of cases in which practitioners had entered an appearance for taxpayers.

[3]*See* I.R.C. § 170(f)(11)(A), (C), (D).

[4]*See* Treas. Reg. § 1.664-1(a)(7).

[5]*See* Treas. Reg. § 20.2053-4(b).

[6]*See* Treas. Reg. § 1.468B-3(b).

[7]*See* Treas. Reg. § 1.6664-4(h).

    4. Corporate mergers, acquisitions, and spinoffs;

    5. Allocations of purchase price under section 1060 of the Internal Revenue Code;

    6. Business liquidations or reorganizations;

    7. Financings;

    8. Initial public offerings;

    9. Goodwill (both personal goodwill and business goodwill);

  10. Intangibles, including valuation of intangibles for transfer pricing purposes;

  11. Employee stock ownership plans;

  12. Retirement plan actions;

  13. Incentive stock options;

  14. Compensation received as property;

  15. Buy–sell agreements and related consequences;

  16. Stockholder disputes and related consequences;

  17. Mark-to-market valuations under section 475 of the Internal Revenue Code;

  18. Exchanges of property;

  19. Estate tax returns;

  20. Gift tax returns;

  21. Determinations of reasonable compensation;

  22. Foreign account reporting (e.g., in connection with reporting Form 8938, *Statement of Specified Financial Assets*);

  23. Collection cases, especially where an offer in compromise is requested (note, Form 433-A, *Collection Information Statement for Wage Earners and Self-Employed Individuals*, and Form 433-B, *Collection Information Statement for Businesses*, require valuation of real estate and businesses); and

  24. Marital dissolutions and related reporting.

Valuation in Tax Litigation

Valuation is often implicated in civil tax litigation, and occasionally arises in criminal tax matters. As applied to civil tax litigation where valuation is at issue, expert testimony is routinely sought and can be helpful to document and prove a client's tax reporting position. In addition to the areas identified earlier, which relate to substantive determinations of tax liability, valuation may be implicated in the following penalty-related areas:

    1. Substantial valuation misstatement penalty cases; and

    2. Gross valuation misstatement penalty cases.

Given the prevalence of valuation in tax, it is important to recognize when an expert valuator can assist in proving and documenting a client's position. It is generally appropriate, and often wise, to hire an expert in litigation whenever doing so will help the trier of fact (and/or the attorney) understand the evidence or decide a fact in issue. As discussed more fully in Chapter 7, *From Daubert to Boltar*, and Chapter 13, *Attorney Involvement*, Rule 702 of the Federal Rules of Evidence, provides:

> *A witness who is qualified as an expert by knowledge, skill, experience, training, or education may testify in the form of an opinion or otherwise if:*
>
> *(a) the expert's scientific, technical, or other specialized knowledge will help the trier of fact to understand the evidence or to determine a fact in issue;*

(b) the testimony is based on sufficient facts or data;

(c) the testimony is the product of reliable principles and methods; and

(d) the expert has reliably applied those principles and methods to the facts of the case.

As applied to tax litigation, it may also be helpful to hire an expert, either in connection with determining value or, as may be relevant in a criminal tax case, establishing tax loss. There are four areas in which an expert valuator may be utilized in such matters:

1. Determining the actual tax loss;
2. Assisting with the cross-examination of the government's expert or summary witness;
3. Challenging the reliability and credibility of the government's expert or summary witness; and
4. Explaining the correct treatment of the defendant's tax positions.

Valuation in Business and Familial Matters

Valuation disputes frequently arise, and the appraisal process is increasingly scrutinized, in business transactions and familial matters, including estate planning and divorces. The following highlights the importance of the appraisal process in these prevalent modern-day matters:

1. *For Gift, Estate, and Income Tax (including charitable contribution deductions)*—Appraisals will be reviewed by the IRS and are likely to be reviewed by appropriate state and local tax authorities;
2. *For Employee Stock Ownership Plans (ESOPs)*—Appraisals are subject to attack by plan participants, the Department of Labor, and the IRS;
3. *For Buying or Selling*—Appraisals are subject to negotiation by sellers/buyers, and the results of one or more appraisals may dictate the purchase price between the parties in the context of, for example, a buy–sell agreement;
4. *For Dissenting or Oppressed Stockholder Actions*—Appraisals are subject to review and critique by the opposing stockholder's expert;
5. *For Property Taxes*—Appraisals are reviewed and certified by the taxing authority;
6. *For Liability Cases (including insurance reimbursements)*—Appraisals are subject to review and critique by opposing experts; and
7. *For Marital Dissolution Matters*—Tax and valuation is routinely implicated in divorces, where appraisal reports are subject to review and critique by the opposing spouse's expert.

VALUATION CALCULATION STANDARDS

Almost all appraisals must be conducted under the rubric of some valuation standard, which is to say that the subject property's value must be measured. The appropriate measure of value depends upon the purpose for which the valuation is obtained.

There are numerous measures of value that may be encountered in connection with a tax matter, including:

1. *Fair market value*, which is the appropriate measure of value for the overwhelming majority of tax matters;
2. *Market value*, which may be utilized by valuators who prepare an appraisal report in accordance with the Uniform Standards of Professional Appraisal Practice (sometimes referred to herein as "USPAP");
3. *Fair value*, which may apply under state statutes governing dissenting stockholder and minority oppression actions, as well as under generally accepted accounting principles ("GAAP");
4. *Quick sale value*, which may apply in connection with IRS collection matters;
5. *Salvage value*, which may be used to compute allowable depreciation for tax purposes; and
6. *Investment value*, which connotes value to a particular investor or owner.

Most clients, and many tax practitioners for that matter, have never thought about the technical requirements with which an appraiser must comply when providing an appraisal under any given valuation standard. Choosing the proper valuation technique in a tax matter or an appraisal assignment is an important decision that should be thoughtfully undertaken by both the valuator and the tax practitioner.

Valuation standards for value determinations can be established by federal or state statute, case law, or agreement among the parties (e.g., buy–sell agreements). Although it is the tax practitioner's responsibility to identify the appropriate measure of value to be utilized in any given matter, it is also essential for the appraiser to assist the tax practitioner so as to create parity between the tax and valuation assignment. It is also imperative for the expert appraiser to be intimately familiar with the appropriate mechanism for determining value under the identified valuation standard.

By "standards" in this context, we mean definitions of value. These are not to be confused with rules for conducting and reporting appraisals, such as the USPAP, which are discussed in Chapter 9, *Expert Appraisal Reports*.

Set forth ahead in more detail are the most common measures of value applicable to appraisals. As will be seen, these valuation standards are often complex and can vary drastically, mandating the involvement of a qualified experienced professional appraiser. We emphasize fair market value over the other measures of value because fair market value is the measure of value generally required in federal tax matters.

Fair Market Value Defined

In the United States and Canada, the most commonly acknowledged standard of value is *fair market value*. It is this standard that applies to most U.S. federal and state tax issues relating to corporate, estate, gift, and individual income taxes, including, for example, valuation of property for estate and gift tax purposes and charitable contribution deductions. This is an important point to stress since some valuators fail to properly utilize a true fair market value as the appropriate measure of value in federal tax matters, even though they are required to do so.

The definition of *fair market value* is one of the most important definitions in tax. The U.S. Treasury Regulations define fair market value of property as "the price at which the property would change hands between a willing buyer and a willing seller, neither being under any compulsion to buy or sell and both having reasonable knowledge of relevant facts."[8] Included within this definition are a number of implied assumptions.

Implied Assumptions

Within the tax valuation industry, there is a general consensus that fair market value presumes that an arm's-length transaction exists where both the buyer and the seller have the ability and the willingness to effectuate a cash transaction. Within this definition, *market* refers to all potential buyers and sellers of assets in a situation where neither party is being forced to buy or sell.

When determining fair market value, an appraiser must identify the hypothetical willing buyer and hypothetical willing seller, making sure the two individuals are dealing with one another at arm's-length in the hypothetical sale. And an appraiser should not allow her fair market value determinations to be set by a price with parties driven by motivations not present in the typical hypothetical seller and buyer. In Canada, however, fair market value may include the value of synergies with a particular buyer.[9]

Consistent with this rationale, the Tax Court has mandated using the following six principles for fair market value determinations:

1. Fair market value is the price that a willing buyer would pay a willing seller, both persons having reasonable knowledge of all relevant facts and neither person being under any compulsion to buy or to sell.
2. The willing buyer and the willing seller are hypothetical persons, rather than specific individuals or entities, and the characteristics of these hypothetical persons are not necessarily the same as the personal characteristics of the actual seller or a particular buyer.
3. Fair market value is determined as of the valuation date, and no knowledge of unforeseeable future events which may have affected the value is given to the hypothetical persons.
4. Fair market value equals the highest and best use to which the property could be put on the valuation date, and fair market value takes into account special uses that are realistically available due to the property's adaptability to a particular business.
5. Fair market value is not affected by whether the owner has actually put the property to its highest and best use. The reasonable, realistic, and objective possible uses for the property in the near future control the valuation thereof.

---

[8] *See* Treas. Reg. §§ 1.170A-1(c)(2); 20.2031-3 (1992); *see also United States v. Cartwright*, 411 U.S. 546, 551 (1973); Rev. Rul. 59-60, 1959-1 C.B. 237.
[9] *See* Richard M. Wise, "The Effect of Special Interest Purchases on Fair Market Value in Canada," 22 *Bus. Valuation Rev.* 196, 196–203 (2003), for a thorough discussion of fair market value in Canada.

6. Elements affecting value that depend upon events or a combination of occurrences which, while within the realm of possibility, are not reasonably probable, are excluded from this consideration.[10]

It is important to remember that fair market value determinations are inherently factual in nature and that the trier of fact in any tax controversy "must weigh all relevant evidence of value and draw appropriate inferences."[11] Expert judgment is a critical part of this calculation. It is important that all evidence considered and all assumptions and inferences made be disclosed in the appraisal report.

Cash Value and Market Value

The terms *cash value* and *market value* are occasionally used interchangeably with *fair market value*. Indeed, real estate appraisers generally use the term *market value* in an attempt to denote the concepts of fair market value. An independent board of the Appraisal Foundation provides, through USPAP Advisory Opinion 22, the following definition of *market value*:

> [T]he most probable price which a property should bring in a competitive and open market under all conditions requisite to a fair sale, the buyer and seller each acting prudently and knowledgeably, and assuming the price is not affected by undue stimulus. Implicit in this definition are the consummation of a sale as of a specified date and the passing of title from seller to buyer under conditions whereby:
>
> 1. The buyer and the seller are typically motivated;
> 2. Both parties are well informed or well advised and acting in what they consider their best interests;
> 3. A reasonable time is allowed for exposure in the open market;
> 4. Payment is made in terms of cash in U.S. dollars or in terms of financial arrangements comparable thereto; and
> 5. The price represents the normal consideration for the property sold unaffected by special or creative financing or sales concessions granted by anyone associated with the sale.[12]

The Appraisal Foundation emphasizes that the definition of *market value* connotes an exchange that occurs for cash or cash equivalents.[13]

COMPUTING FAIR MARKET VALUE

A complete discussion of the various approaches to calculate fair market value is outside the scope of this book, but practitioners should understand the basic principles by which fair market value is computed.

---

[10]*Pabst Brewing Co. v. Comm'r*, T.C. Memo. 1996-506, 72 T.C.M. (CCH) 1236 (1996).
[11]*See Pabst Brewing Co. v. Comm'r*, T.C. Memo. 1996-506, 72 T.C.M. (CCH) 1236 (1996).
[12]USPAP Advisory Opinion 22 (2014–2015).
[13]USPAP U-3, 98-111 (2014).

The value of any property (real, tangible, intangible, and personal) can be calculated in a two-step process. Under step 1, valuators compute the subject property's net asset value. Under step 2, valuators apply appropriate valuation discounts and premiums to adjust the net asset value.

Step 1: Calculating Net Asset Value

This first step employs the three most common approaches to determine net asset value: the market approach, the income approach, and the asset-based approach.

The *market approach* assumes that the value of property can be determined by reference to the value of comparable properties for which values are known as a result of recent sales or quotes on a readily tradable market. Under the market approach, the valuator compares the subject property to similar comparable properties that were sold in an arm's-length transaction reasonably proximate to the valuation date. The value of the subject property is determined by taking into account the sales prices of comparable properties that were sold proximate to the valuation date and adjusting the value of each comparable property for features unique to the subject property, but not possessed by the comparable property. The market approach is most appropriately used when comparable properties have qualities substantially similar to those of the subject property.

The *income approach* assumes that the value of the subject property can be determined by computing the present value of the estimated future cash flows that may be realized with respect to that property. Within the income approach, there are at least two accepted methods: the *discounted cash flow method*, which typically uses a static growth rate assumption to estimate future cash flows; and the *income capitalization method*, which typically uses a variable growth rate assumption to estimate future cash flows.

The *asset-based approach* (also known as the *cost approach*) generally assumes that the value of property can be determined by calculating the cost to reproduce it, less any applicable depreciation or depletion. The approach is slightly more nuanced in business valuations. In that situation, valuators generally value the business or business interest by determining the cost to reproduce it and focusing on the company's net asset value (i.e., the fair market value of its total assets minus its total liabilities). In practice, the fair market value of assets (e.g., marketable securities or real estate valuation) is substituted for the respective book values on the balance sheet of the company being valued.

Valuators typically do not value property under just one approach. Rather, property is often valued under each of the above-referenced approaches, and the indicated value in each approach is weighted to derive a final opinion of value. In addition to containing the items discussed in Chapter 9, *Expert Appraisal Reports*, an appraisal report should:

1. Reconcile the different conclusions of value derived from the various approaches;
2. Explain the weighting of each valuation approach in determining a final opinion of value;
3. Disclose any assumptions that were made in valuing the property; and
4. Provide sufficient details and explanations about how the final opinion of value was derived so that another valuator can replicate this work after reviewing the report of related workpapers.

Step 2: Applying Discounts and Premiums

The second step in determining fair market value is to apply appropriate discounts and premiums. There are numerous types of valuation discounts and premiums, some of which are appropriate at the owner level, some of which are appropriate at the entity level, and some of which apply principally to property that can be jointly held (e.g., real estate, art, and collectibles). Among the types of valuation discounts and premiums are:

1. Discount for lack of marketability;
2. Blockage or market absorption discounts;
3. Lack of control discount;
4. Lack of voting rights discount;
5. Control premium/minority interest discount;
6. Discount for built-in capital gain;
7. Key person discount;
8. Discount for contingent liabilities;
9. Portfolio discount;
10. S corporation premiums; and
11. Fractional interest or partition discounts.

The fair market value of property can generally be computed by adding and subtracting appropriate premiums and discounts from the property's net asset value.

COMMON TAX APPRAISAL REPORTS

The valuation process, including any assumptions, is generally documented in a written report. The contents of the report will depend upon the purposes for which the report was procured.

Appraisal Reports to Support Tax Reporting Positions

An appraisal report is sometimes required to support a tax reporting position. For example, federal tax law generally *requires* taxpayers to hire a *qualified appraiser* to prepare a *qualified appraisal* in connection with:

- Claiming a charitable contribution deduction of more than $5,000 where the donated property is not cash, publicly traded securities, a qualifying vehicle, or certain intellectual property;
- Valuing assets of charitable remainder trusts;
- Valuing claims and counterclaims against an estate; and
- Transferring property to a qualified settlement fund.

The requirements of a qualified appraisal are discussed in Chapter 2, *Qualified Appraisal*, and the requirements of a qualified appraiser are discussed in Chapter 3, *Qualified Appraiser*.

In other cases, even though a qualified appraisal is not required, clients or practitioners may desire to obtain an appraisal report to support a tax reporting position.

We discuss best practices with respect to such appraisal reports in Chapter 9, *Expert Appraisal Reports*.

Appraisal Reports to Support Tax Litigation

Expert witness reports, which differ from appraisal reports used to support a tax reporting position, may be advisable where the question of value is to be litigated. The requirements for such reports are technically and specifically defined in applicable court rules. The requirements for appraisal reports to support litigation are discussed in Chapter 13, *Attorney Involvement*.

PROLIFERATION OF LITIGATION

In the past decade, courts have increasingly scrutinized appraisals and the underlying mechanics of such appraisals. Litigation is especially prominent in the area of qualified appraisals required to support a charitable contribution deduction. As a general matter, courts are becoming more sophisticated with respect to all types of appraisals. The degree of sophistication, however, varies among the courts and even among judges in the same court.

It is incumbent upon the lawyer and the valuation expert to explain to the court and the trier of fact, whether sophisticated or not, why the submitted appraisal best meets the applicable valuation methodology. An expert can be technically qualified and still not be a good expert in a litigation setting. Thus, unless the expert can adequately explain her appraisal methodology and how her appraisal fits into the particular valuation context at hand, the judge and/or finder of fact may very well find fault with the appraisal. In all situations, the appraiser must be a good communicator, with the ability to teach the judge and the trier of fact complex concepts of finance that may be outside their realm of knowledge; this is especially true in the areas of valuing businesses, business interests, and intangible assets.

Knowledgeable judges are not shy about criticizing unreliable work by appraisers. For example, one court excluded the report of the taxpayer's real estate appraiser as unreliable and inadmissible per rule 702 of the Federal Rules of Evidence, *Daubert v. Merrell Dow Pharmaceuticals, Inc.*,[14] and United States Tax Court Rule 143(g) because the expert made no effort to determine the highest and best use of property after the grant of a conservation easement.[15] Similarly, in *Kohler v. Commissioner*,[16] the Tax Court gave no weight to a stock valuation opinion of the IRS's expert where the expert spent little time with the company's management, invented his own expense structure for his income approach analysis, and decided not to use an unreliable dividend-based method despite the fact that the company had historically paid large dividends. In giving the expert's opinion no weight, the Court noted the lack of customary certification of the expert's report and that his report was not prepared in accordance with all USPAP standards. The Court also placed no weight on the expert's report in *Estate of Renier v. Commissioner*,[17] where the report contained

---

[14] *Daubert v. Merrell Dow Pharmaceuticals, Inc.*, 509 U.S. 597 (1993).
[15] *Boltar, L.L.C. v. Comm'r*, 136 T.C. 326 (2011).
[16] *Kohler v. Comm'r*, T.C. Memo. 2006-152, 92 T.C.M. (CCH) 48 (2006).
[17] *Estate of Renier v. Comm'r*, T.C. Memo. 2000-298, 80 T.C.M. (CCH) 401 (2000).

no explanation of, or analytical support for, the various rules of thumb employed in reaching several of his valuation estimates, thus making it almost impossible for the Court to assess the merits of his conclusions.

Therefore, regardless of whether a qualified appraisal prepared by a qualified appraiser is required in connection with a tax reporting position, it is beneficial to retain an appraiser who is not only "qualified," but also *well-qualified*. These court-driven criticisms of expert appraisers can be avoided by careful expert selection and thorough and thoughtful preparation. Selection and preparation of appraisers is the subject of Chapter 6, *The Practicalities of Selection and Preparation of Experts*.

CONCLUSION

Expert valuators and tax practitioners must develop cross-disciplinary skills in valuation and in tax. This cross-disciplinary approach first requires valuators and tax practitioners to recognize that fair market value is the proper standard of value for federal tax purposes, and then to understand how fair market value is computed. Within the cross-disciplinary approach, it is important for all professionals to appreciate: the gambit of appraisal reports that may be required; how valuators will prepare those reports; how practitioners will use those reports and what penalties may apply for faulty appraisals; and what judges look for in deciding a valuation case.

CHAPTER 2

Qualified Appraisal

SUMMARY

For federal tax purposes, and sometimes for non-tax reasons, one must often produce a qualified appraisal prepared by a qualified appraiser to meet statutory and regulatory requirements to support a fair market value determination. For example, in the federal income tax context, obtaining a qualified appraisal by a qualified appraiser is generally a condition precedent to the allowance of a charitable contribution deduction for noncash donations of property with a claimed value greater than $5,000.[1] For federal tax purposes, Treasury Regulations set forth numerous specific requirements for an appraisal report to be a qualified appraisal. This chapter details the statutory and regulatory requirements that must be met before an appraisal report will be recognized as a qualified appraisal.

DEFINING QUALIFIED APPRAISAL

The terms *qualified appraisal* and *qualified appraiser* are technically and specifically defined for federal tax purposes in section 170 of the Internal Revenue Code and, pursuant to a congressional delegation of authority, in section 1.170A-13(c)(3) and (5) of the Treasury Regulations, respectively. The terms refer to statutory and regulatory requirements with which taxpayers must comply to support a fair market value determination. The Treasury Regulations establish the minimum uniform standards

---

[1] *See, e.g., Gemperlee v. Comm'r*, T.C. Memo. 2016-1, 111 T.C.M. (CCH) 1001 (2016) (disallowing deduction for a donation of a conservation easement where the taxpayer did not obtain a qualified appraisal); *Isaacs v. Comm'r*, T.C. Memo. 2015-121, 109 T.C.M. (CCH) 1624 (2015) (disallowing deduction of fossils donated to the California Academy of Science where the taxpayer did not obtain a qualified appraisal by a qualified appraiser); *Costello v. Comm'r*, T.C. Memo. 2015-87, 109 T.C.M. (CCH) 1441 (2015) (declining to apply the substantial compliance doctrine and denying a $5,543,309 charitable contribution deduction because, in addition to other reasons, the taxpayers failed to obtain a qualified appraisal or include the required appraisal summary); *Alli v. Comm'r*, T.C. Memo. 2014-15, 107 T.C.M. (CCH) 1082 (2014) (denying charitable contribution deductions totaling roughly $1.5 million on the grounds that, in addition to other reasons, the taxpayers failed to obtain a qualified appraisal); *1982 East, LLC v. Comm'r*, T.C. Memo. 2011-84, 101 T.C.M. (CCH) 1380 (2011) (denying a $6.57 million deduction on ground that, in addition to other reasons, the partnership failed to obtain a qualified appraisal).

of what it means to be "qualified." The regulatory requirements are given deference by the courts and have the force of law.

In a broader sense, whether for tax or non-tax purposes, all appraisals and the appraisers who perform them need to be qualified to be credible. In this broader sense, *qualified* means that the appraiser and appraisal must be reliable, competent, and deserving of respect for the purpose of establishing value. In this more generic definition of *qualified*, all appraisals need to be founded in accurate data, as well as analyzed using transparent, replicable, and accurate methods and approaches, and interpreted and opined upon by educated, credentialed, and experienced practitioners. *Replicable* means that another appraisal professional reviewing and analyzing the submitted appraisal could find the sources used and apply them to arrive at the same result.

In this book the terms *qualified appraisal* and *qualified appraiser* are sometimes used interchangeably from the technical to the generic sense. These terms, however, have special application to the tax law, especially in the context of charitable contribution deductions.

SITUATIONS IN WHICH A QUALIFIED APPRAISAL MAY BE REQUIRED

The qualified appraisal requirement has, so far, been limited to a great extent to the federal tax arena.[2] Under existing law, a qualified appraisal may be required in connection with:

1. Claiming a charitable contribution deduction of more than $5,000 where the donated property is not cash, publicly traded securities, a qualifying vehicle, or certain intellectual property;[3]

---

[2]Congress has considered extending the qualified appraisal requirement to other areas of the law, but has not done so as of the time of this writing. For example, in 2007, the Mortgage Reform and Anti-Predatory Lending Act of 2007, H.R. 3915, 110th Cong. (2007), passed the House of Representatives and was referred to the Senate Committee on Banking, Housing, and Urban Affairs, where it died. The House Committee on Financial Services prepared a report on this bill, but the report did not discuss "qualified appraisers." H.R. Rep. No. 110-441 (2007). Title VII of the bill concerns appraisals and appraisers. H.R. 3915 tit. VII. Section 701 of the bill prohibits lenders from extending "high-cost mortgages" on property absent appraisals by "qualified appraisers." The bill defines a "qualified appraiser" as someone who (a) is licensed or certified by the States in which the property is located and (b) conducts each of his or her appraisals in conformity with the Uniform Standards of Professional Appraisal Practice and title XI of the Financial Institutions Reform, Recovery, and Enforcement Act of 1989, Pub. L. No. 101-73, 103 Stat. 183, and the regulations thereunder. H.R. 3915 § 701. The appraisal itself has to include a visit by the appraiser to the interior of property. H.R. 3915 § 701. The bill does not track the language of the Treasury Regulations on qualified appraisers, but it sets out proposals for professional standards in section 703. *Compare id.* § 703, *with* Treas. Reg. § 1.170A-13(c)(3).

[3]*See* I.R.C. § 170(f)(11)(A), (C), (D). A qualified appraisal is not required if the donated property is:

1. Publicly traded securities (i.e., securities for which, as of the contribution date, market quotations are readily available on an established securities market), *see* I.R.C. §§ 170(f)(11)(A)(ii)(I), 6050L(a)(2)(B);

2. Valuing assets of charitable remainder trusts;[4]
3. Valuing claims and counterclaims against an estate;[5] and
4. Transferring property to a qualified settlement fund.[6]

There has been an influx of litigation in recent years with respect to whether appraisal reports are *qualified appraisals*. The source of this litigation is largely attributable to the IRS's disallowance of otherwise legitimate charitable contribution deductions on the grounds that the taxpayer did not obtain a *qualified appraisal* prepared by a *qualified appraiser*. For this reason, this chapter discusses the qualified appraisal requirement in the context of charitable contribution deductions. However, any such discussion equally applies outside of the charitable contribution deduction context because the Treasury Regulations incorporate the same standard for what is a *qualified appraisal*; that standard is set forth in section 170(f)(11)(E) of the Internal Revenue Code and section 1.170A-13(c)(3) of the Treasury Regulations.[7]

QUALIFIED APPRAISAL REQUIREMENTS FOR CHARITABLE CONTRIBUTION DEDUCTIONS CONTEXT

Taxpayers who itemize deductions on a federal income tax return may be entitled to claim a deduction for a contribution to a qualifying charitable organization.[8] However, Congress imposes a number of substantiation and recordkeeping requirements in an effort to curtail abuses, such as taxpayers overvaluing donated property. The applicable substantiation requirements depend upon the type of property

---

2. Any patent, copyright (other than a copyright described in I.R.C. § 1221(a)(3) or 1231(b)(1)(C), trademark, trade name, trade secret, knowhow, software (other than software described in I.R.C. § 197(e)(3)(A)(i)), or similar property, or applications or registrations of such property, *see* I.R.C. § 170(f)(11)(A)(ii)(I), (e)(1)(B)(iii); or

3. Any vehicle which the qualifying organization sells without any significant intervening use or material improvement, so long as an acknowledgment is provided which states (i) a certification that the vehicle was sold in an arm's-length transaction between unrelated parties, (ii) the gross proceeds from the sale, and (iii) that the deductible amount may not exceed the amount of such gross proceeds, *see* I.R.C. § 170(f)(11)(A)(ii)(I), (12)(A)(ii), (12)(B)(iii).

[4]*See* Treas. Reg. § 1.664-1(a)(7).
[5]*See* Treas. Reg. § 20.2053-4(b).
[6]*See* Treas. Reg. § 1.468B-3(b). Additionally, obtaining a qualified appraisal may help a taxpayer avoid accuracy-related penalties under section 6662 of the Internal Revenue Code. *See* Treas. Reg. § 1.6664-4(h). Some commentators have urged the U.S. Department of the Treasury ("Treasury Department") and the Internal Revenue Service ("IRS") to adopt the qualified appraisal requirement in other areas, such as qualifying commercial loans, *see* Credit Risk Retention, 79 Fed. Reg. 77602-01 (proposed Dec. 24, 2014), but the Treasury Department and the IRS declined to act on these recommendations.
[7]*See, e.g.*, Treas. Reg. §§ 1.468B-3(b)1.664-1(a)(7); 20.2053-4(b) (all incorporating by reference the requirements of a qualified appraisal in the charitable contribution deduction context as set forth in Treas. Reg. § 1.170A-13(c)(3)).
[8]I.R.C. § 170(a).

contributed and the value of the deduction claimed.[9] As the amount of the reported deduction increases, the substantiation and recordkeeping requirements grow more detailed and onerous.

Requirements

One of the requirements to substantiate a charitable contribution deduction, promulgated by Congress and regulated by the Internal Revenue Service, is the qualified appraisal. The qualified appraisal rules achieve two tax policy objectives. First, the rules encourage taxpayers to use transparent, replicable, and accurate methods and approaches to value charitable contribution deductions for federal tax purposes. Second, the rules ensure that the IRS receives sufficient information to evaluate the propriety of the reported deduction so that, if the deduction is outside the range of normal, the deduction can be audited.[10]

The rules requiring a qualified appraisal are relatively straightforward. A donor who claims a charitable contribution deduction of more than $5,000 with respect to noncash property must obtain a qualified appraisal (i.e., she must procure a qualified appraisal before the tax return first reporting the deduction is filed, and if requested by the IRS under section 6001 of the Internal Revenue Code, produce that qualified appraisal). A donor who claims a charitable contribution deduction of more than $500,000 must attach a qualified appraisal to the tax return first claiming the deduction.

The rules related to the failure to obtain a qualified appraisal are equally straightforward. The failure to obtain (or attach) the qualified appraisal generally results in denial of a charitable contribution deduction, though the deduction will generally not be disallowed if the failure to obtain a qualified appraisal is due to reasonable cause and not due to willful neglect. Section 170(11) of the Internal Revenue Code,

---

[9]The charitable contribution deductions and the corresponding substantiation requirements are as follows:

Category	Substantiation Requirements
(1) Less than $250	Treas. Reg. § 1.170A-13(b)(1), (2)
(2) $250 to $500	26 U.S.C. § 170(f)(8); Treas. Reg. § 1.170A-13(f)
(3) $501 to $5,000	26 U.S.C. § 170(f)(11)(B)(i); Treas. Reg. § 1.170A-13(b)(3)
(4) $5,001 to $500,000	26 U.S.C. § 170(f)(11)(C); Treas. Reg. § 1.170A-13(c)
(5) More than $500,000	26 U.S.C. § 170(f)(11)(D)
(6) Quid pro quo payments of $75 or more	26 U.S.C. § 6115(a)
(7) Money (any amount)	26 U.S.C. § 170(f)(17)

The substantiation requirements for the varying levels of charitable contribution deductions to be cumulative. *See, e.g.*, IRS, Pub. 526, Charitable Contributions, 19-20 (rev. Jan. 15, 2016). That is, the substantiation for a deduction of more than $5,000 must contain the information required to substantiate a claimed deduction of $250 to $500 and less than $250.

[10]*Smith v. Comm'r*, T.C. Memo. 2007-368, 94 T.C.M. (CCH) 574, 586 (2007), *aff'd*, 364 Fed. Appx. 317 (9th Cir. 2009).

entitled "Qualified Appraisal and Other Documentation for Certain Contributions," provides as follows:

> **(A)** In general
>> (i) Denial of deduction
>>> In the case of an individual, partnership, or corporation, no deduction shall be allowed under subsection (a) for any contribution of property for which a deduction of more than $500 is claimed unless such person meets the requirements of subparagraphs (B), (C), and (D), as the case may be, with respect to such contribution.
>> (ii) Exceptions
>>> **(I)** Readily valued property
>>>> Subparagraphs (C) and (D) shall not apply to cash, property described in subsection (e)(1)(B)(iii) or section 1221(a)(1), publicly traded securities (as defined in section 6050L(a)(2)(B)), and any qualified vehicle described in paragraph (12)(A)(ii) for which an acknowledgment under paragraph (12)(B)(iii) is provided.
>>> **(II)** Reasonable cause
>>>> Clause (i) shall not apply if it is shown that the failure to meet such requirements is due to reasonable cause and not to willful neglect.
> **(B)** Property description for contributions of more than $500
>> In the case of contributions of property for which a deduction of more than $500 is claimed, the requirements of this subparagraph are met if the individual, partnership, or corporation includes with the return for the taxable year in which the contribution is made a description of such property and such other information as the Secretary may require. The requirements of this subparagraph shall not apply to a C corporation which is not a personal service corporation or a closely held C corporation.
> **(C)** Qualified appraisal for contributions of more than $5,000
>> In the case of contributions of property for which a deduction of more than $5,000 is claimed, the requirements of this subparagraph are met if the individual, partnership, or corporation obtains a qualified appraisal of such property and attaches to the return for the taxable year in which such contribution is made such information regarding such property and such appraisal as the Secretary may require.
> **(D)** Substantiation for contributions of more than $500,000
>> In the case of contributions of property for which a deduction of more than $500,000 is claimed, the requirements of this subparagraph are met if the individual, partnership, or corporation attaches to the return for the taxable year a qualified appraisal of such property.[11]

Legislative History

It may be helpful for readers to understand Congress's goal in requiring taxpayers to obtain a qualified appraisal. The first mention of the term *qualified appraisal* occurred

---

[11]I.R.C. § 170(f)(11).

in the Deficit Reduction Act of 1984 ("DEFRA").[12] Through DEFRA, Congress responded to the prevalence of overvaluations of charitable contribution deductions by creating a mechanism for the IRS to verify the fair market value of noncash property donations. Specifically, Congress directed the U.S. Department of the Treasury ("Treasury Department") to promulgate regulations requiring taxpayers to obtain a qualified appraisal prepared by a qualified appraiser whenever the taxpayer claimed a charitable contribution deduction where the amount of the claimed deduction is more than $5,000.[13] Congress provided that the term *qualified appraisal* means an appraisal report prepared by a qualified appraiser that includes the following six items:

1. A description of the property appraised;
2. The fair market value of such property on the date of contribution and the specific basis for the valuation;
3. A statement that such appraisal was prepared for income tax purposes;
4. The qualifications of the qualified appraiser;
5. The signature and taxpayer identification number of such appraiser; and
6. Such additional information as the Secretary of the Treasury Department prescribes in regulations.[14]

The Treasury Department responded to Congress's charge in DEFRA by promulgating the qualified appraisal rules found in section 1.170A-13(c) of the Treasury Regulations.[15]

The more recent legislative history surrounding the definition of a *qualified appraisal* has been marked not by substantive changes, but by the codification of regulatory requirements into statutory law. The American Jobs Creation Act of 2004 ("2004 AJCA"), similar to DEFRA, contained a statutory reference to the term *qualified appraiser*, but deferred the definition of the term to the Treasury Department by regulation.[16] Then, in the Pension Protection Act of 2006 ("2006 PPA"), Congress adopted a statutory definition of the terms *qualified appraisal* and *qualified appraiser*.[17] As provided in the 2006 PPA, for appraisals prepared with respect to returns filed after August 17, 2006, the term *qualified appraiser* means with respect to any property, an appraisal that:

- Is treated as a qualified appraisal under regulations or other guidance prescribed by the Secretary of the Treasury Department; and
- Is conducted by a qualified appraiser in accordance with generally accepted appraisal standards and any regulations or other guidance prescribed by the Secretary of the Treasury Department.[18]

---

[12] Deficit Reduction Act of 1984, Pub. L. No. 98-369, § 155, 98 Stat. 691.

[13] H.R. Rep. No. 98-861, at 996-999 (1984) (Conf. Rep.).

[14] Deficit Reduction Act of 1984, Pub. L. No. 98-369, § 155, 98 Stat. 691.

[15] *See* T.D. 8199, 1988-1 C.B. 99 (preamble).

[16] *See* American Jobs Creation Act of 2004, Pub. L. No. 108-357, § 883, 118 Stat. 1418 (2004). Congress specified in 2004 AJCA that "the term 'qualified appraisal' means, with respect to any property, an appraisal of such property which is treated for purposes of this paragraph as a qualified appraisal under regulations or other guidance prescribed by the Secretary." *Id.*

[17] Pension Protection Act of 2006, Pub. L. No. 109-280, § 1219, 120 Stat. 780, 1085 (2006).

[18] *Id.*

As detailed ahead, the definition Congress gave to the term *qualified appraisal* in 2006 PPA is the current statutory definition that exists today. Before we discuss that statute in greater detail, it is worth noting here that Congress's delegation of authority to the Treasury Department to define the terms *qualified appraisal* and *qualified appraiser* in DEFRA, the 2004 AJCA, and the 2006 PPA supports that section 1.170A-13(c) of the Treasury Regulations is entitled to considerable deference.

Statutory Definition of a Qualified Appraisal

Section 170(e)(i) of the Internal Revenue Code generally defines the term *qualified appraisal*, giving broad deference to the Treasury Regulations and "generally accepted appraisal standards." It provides as follows:

> (i) Qualified appraisal. The term "qualified appraisal" means, with respect to any property, an appraisal of such property which—
> (I) is treated for purposes of this paragraph as a qualified appraisal under regulations or other guidance prescribed by the Secretary, and
> (II) is conducted by a qualified appraiser in accordance with generally accepted appraisal standards, and any regulations or other guidance prescribed under subclause (I).[19]

Regulatory Definition of a Qualified Appraisal

As noted, section 170(e)(11) of the Internal Revenue Code delegates to the Treasury Department and the IRS the authority to more precisely define the term *qualified appraisal* by Treasury Regulations. Pursuant to that delegation of authority, Treasury Regulations define the term *qualified appraisal* to mean an appraisal document that:

(A) Relates to an appraisal that is made not earlier than 60 days prior to the date of contribution of the appraised property nor later than the [due date (including extensions) of the return on which the deduction is first claimed or reported or, if the deduction is first claimed or reported on an amended return, the date on which the return is filed];

(B) Is prepared, signed, and dated by a qualified appraiser (within the meaning of paragraph (c)(5) of this section);

(C) Includes the information required by [section 1.170A-13(c)(3)(ii) of the Treasury Regulations, which includes 11 additional items]; and

(D) Does not involve a prohibited appraisal fee prohibited by paragraph (c)(6) of this section.[20]

Subsections (A), (B), and (D) pertain to mechanical requirements of the appraisal, while subsection (C) pertains to the substantive requirements. Each requirement is discussed in the following.

---

[19]I.R.C. § 170(f)(11)(E)(i).
[20]Treas. Reg. §§ 1.170A-13(c)(3)(i)(A)-(D).

Requirement 1: The 60-Day Requirement: Treas. Reg. § 1.170A-13(c)(3)(i)(A)   To ensure accuracy, a qualified appraisal must generally be made no earlier than 60 days before the date of the charitable contribution and no later than the extended due date of the federal income tax return on which the charitable contribution is first claimed.[21] For a charitable contribution deduction first claimed on an amended tax return, the qualified appraisal must be secured no later than the date on which the amended return is filed.[22] The purpose of these temporal requirements is to ensure that the appraisal reflects the proper fair market value of the donated property as of the contribution date.[23] The Tax Court has ruled that a taxpayer can supplement his return with a qualified appraisal past the due date of the return as long as the original qualified appraisal was timely.[24]

Requirement 2: The Qualified Appraiser Requirement: Treas. Reg. § 1.170A-13(c)(3)(i)(B)   An appraisal must be performed by a qualified appraiser, as defined under applicable Treasury Regulations.[25] The specific requirements for a qualified appraiser under section 170(f)(11) of the Internal Revenue Code are detailed in Chapter 3, *Qualified Appraiser*. It is worth noting that the requirements for an individual to be recognized as a qualified appraiser under section 170(f)(11) of the Internal Revenue Code are more onerous than those under section 1.170A-13(c)(3)(i)(B) of the Treasury Regulations because the former incorporates the requirements of Notice 2006-96,[26] but the latter does not.

For purposes of section 1.170A-13(c)(3)(i)(B) of the Treasury Regulations, the term *qualified appraiser* means an individual who includes on the required appraisal summary (Form 8283, *Noncash Charitable Contributions*) a declaration affirming the following:

- The individual holds herself out to the public as an appraiser or performs appraisals on a regular basis;
- Because of the appraiser's qualifications as described in the appraisal, the appraiser is qualified to make appraisals of the type of property being valued;
- The appraiser is not: (1) the donor or taxpayer who claimed or reported the charitable contribution deduction; (2) a party to the transaction in which the donor acquired the property being appraised; (3) the donee of the property; (4) an employee or related party of the donor, the donee, or a party to the transaction in which the donor acquired the property being appraised; (5) an appraiser who is regularly used by the donor, the donee, or a party to the transaction in which the donor acquired the property being appraised, and who performs a majority of her appraisals made during the taxable year for other persons; and

---

[21] Treas. Reg. § 1.170A-13(c)(3)(i)(A), (iv)(B).
[22] Treas. Reg. § 1.170A-13(c)(3)(iv)(B).
[23] T.D. 8199, 53 Fed. Reg. 16076-01 (May 5, 1988). The Treasury Department and the IRS previously considered whether to extend the 60-day period, but decided not to. *See id.*
[24] *Bond v. Comm'r*, 100 T.C. 32 (1993).
[25] Treas. Reg. § 1.170A-13(c)(3)(i)(B).
[26] 2006-2 C.B. 902.

- The appraiser understands that (1) an intentionally false or fraudulent overstatement of the value of the property described in the qualified appraisal or appraisal summary may subject the appraiser to a civil penalty under section 6701 of the Internal Revenue Code for aiding and abetting an understatement of tax liability, and (2) the appraiser may have appraisals disregarded pursuant to 31 U.S.C. 330(c).[27]

Additionally, an individual is not a qualified appraiser for purposes of section 1.170A-13(c)(3)(i)(B) of the Treasury Regulations if the donor had knowledge of facts that would cause a reasonable person to expect the appraiser to falsely overstate the value of the donated property.[28] Chapter 3, *Qualified Appraiser*, discusses, in detail, the more nuanced requirements for an individual to be considered a qualified appraiser under section 170(f)(11) of the Internal Revenue Code.

Requirement 3: The Substantive Requirements: Treas. Reg. § 1.170A-13(c)(3)(i)(C)   An appraisal report that is intended to be a qualified appraisal must contain sufficient information to allow the IRS to evaluate both the fair market value of the donated property and the accuracy of the appraisal. The Treasury Regulations specify 11 items that must be included in the appraisal report for it to be considered a qualified appraisal. These items, which are discussed more fully ahead, are as follows:

(A) Description of the property;
(B) Physical condition of the property;
(C) Date of contribution;
(D) Terms of agreement;
(E) Identifying information of the qualified appraiser;
(F) The qualifications of the qualified appraiser;
(G) A statement that the appraisal was prepared for income tax purposes;
(H) The date(s) of the appraisal;
(I) The appraised fair market value;
(J) The method of valuation; and
(K) The specific basis for the valuation.[29]

A discussion of each sub-requirement is set forth in the following.

Requirement 3.1: Property Description: Treas. Reg. § 1.170A-13(c)(3)(ii)(A)
(A) A description of the property in sufficient detail for a person who is not generally familiar with the type of property to ascertain that the property that was appraised is the property that was (or will be) contributed

Recall that a significant purpose of the qualified appraisal requirement is to provide the IRS with adequate information to allow the IRS to evaluate the

---

[27]Treas. Reg. § 1.170A-13(c)(5)(i), (ii), (iv).
[28]Treas. Reg. § 1.170A-13(c)(5)(ii).
[29]Treas. Reg. §§ 1.170A-13(c)(3)(ii)(A)-(D); *see also Costello v. Comm'r*, T.C.M. (RIA) 2015-087 (2015).

reported donation. The requirement that a qualified appraisal describe the property in sufficient detail is important because it allows the IRS to identify the donated property and make appropriate inquiries. Treasury Regulations do not define what constitutes an adequate description of the property for these purposes, but it is advisable to err on the side of over-inclusion by (1) reciting the physical and legal attributes of the property in detail, and (2) attaching to the appraisal report any agreements related to the property.

Thus, where *real property* is contributed, an appraiser should usually provide the physical address of the property, the tax lot and parcel of the property, and a metes-and-bounds description of the property (as set forth on the deed of the property). Where *interests in real property* are donated, an appraiser should describe the right being valued (e.g., an easement or a lease) and a copy of any agreements related to the transferred interest. For all other types of property, including intangible and personal property, the appraiser should specifically describe the property being transferred and include copies of any agreement related to the property. The purpose of providing copies of any agreements affecting the donated property is simple: the information allows the IRS to understand the property rights being transferred and buttresses the physical description included in the appraisal report.

The failure to include an adequate description of the property can lead to a finding that an appraisal report is not qualified. For example, in *Costello v. Commissioner*, the Tax Court held that an appraisal report was not qualified because, in addition to other missing information, the report did not include an accurate description of the contributed property.[30]

Requirement 3.2: Tangible Property: Treas. Reg. § 1.170A-13(c)(3)(ii)(B)
(B) In the case of tangible property, the physical condition of the property

This requirement serves two purposes. First, listing the physical condition of the property allows the IRS to evaluate the reasonableness of the claimed value. Variations in physical condition can cause large discrepancies in value, and apprising the IRS of the physical condition of the donated is yet another tool by which the IRS can evaluate the reasonableness of the claimed value. Second, the physical condition of the property can also help to identify the property.

Requirement 3.3: Date of Contribution: Treas. Reg. § 1.170A-13(c)(3)(ii)(C)
(C) The date (or expected date) of contribution to the donee

Recall that a qualified appraisal must generally be procured no earlier than 60 days before the contribution date and no later than the extended due date of the federal income tax return on which the charitable contribution is first claimed. Treasury Regulations require a qualified appraisal to set forth the date (or expected date) of the donation. This mandate acknowledges the fact that the value of property can fluctuate between the appraisal date and the contribution date. It also provides the IRS with information to identify and account for

---

[30] *Costello v. Comm'r*, T.C. Memo. 2015-87, 109 T.C.M. (CCH) 1441 (2015).

fluctuations in the property's fair market value between the valuation date and the contribution date.[31]

Courts have been split on whether the failure to state the contribution date makes an appraisal report not qualified. For example, in *Costello v. Commissioner*, the Tax Court held that an appraisal report was not qualified because, in addition to other missing information, the report did not include the date of the contribution.[32] On the other hand, in *Dunlap v. Commissioner*, the Tax Court held that the failure to include the date of the contribution did not jeopardize the status of an appraisal report as a qualified appraisal because the information was set forth on IRS Form 8283, *Noncash Charitable Contributions*.[33] In view of this inconsistent approach, appraisers should unambiguously state the date or expected date of the contribution in the appraisal report.

Requirement 3.4: Terms of Agreement: Treas. Reg. § 1.170A-13(c)(3)(ii)(D)

(D) The terms of any agreement or understanding entered into (or expected to be entered into) by or on behalf of the donor or donee that relates to the use, sale, or other disposition of the property contributed, including, for example, the terms of any agreement or understanding that—

1. *Restricts temporarily or permanently a donee's right to use or dispose of the donated property,*
2. *Reserves to, or confers upon, anyone (other than a donee organization or an organization participating with a donee organization in cooperative fundraising) any right to the income from the contributed property or to the possession of the property, including the right to vote donated securities, to acquire the property by purchase or otherwise, or to designate the person having such income, possession, or right to acquire, or*
3. *Earmarks donated property for a particular use.*

The requirement to disclose the terms of any agreement or understanding entered into (or expected to be entered into) between the donor and the donee with respect to the property creates parity between the qualified appraisal regulations and the principles of the Uniform Standards of Professional Appraisal Practice ("USPAP"). The USPAP requires an appraisal report to take into account "any known easements, restrictions, encumbrances, leases, reservations, covenants, contracts, declarations, special assessments, ordinances, or other items of a similar nature."[34] More fundamentally, this requirement enables the IRS to evaluate whether the appraiser, in formulating an opinion of value, identified and analyzed any known restrictions,

---

[31] *Rothman v. Comm'r*, T.C. Memo. 2012-163, *vacated in part on other grounds*, T.C. Memo. 2012-218.

[32] *Costello v. Comm'r*, T.C. Memo. 2015-87, 109 T.C.M. (CCH) 1441 (2015).

[33] *Dunlap v. Comm'r*, 103 T.C.M. (CCH) 1689 (2012); *see also Simmons v. Comm'r*, T.C. Memo. 2009-208, 98 T.C.M. (CCH) 211 (2009).

[34] *See* USPAP, Standards Rules 1-2(e)(iv) and 1-3(a) (2014-2015); *see also* Internal Revenue Bulletin (Oct. 6, 2008), Notice of Proposed Rulemaking Substantiation and Reporting Requirements for Cash and Noncash Charitable Contributions, available at http://www.irs.gov/irb/2008-40_IRB/ar13.html#d0e6635.

ordinances, or similar items, as well as the likelihood of any modifications to those restrictions."[35]

There are three practice tips appraisers should follow with respect to disclosing and analyzing restrictions:

1. Identify and disclose any restrictions affecting the donated property.
2. Analyze these restrictions and include, as appendices, copies of any documents considered as actual or possible restrictions.
3. Determine the impact, if any, of those restrictions, agreements, and/or local ordinances on the use and value of the subject property. To the extent an agreement, restriction, or ordinance is deemed to be irrelevant to the question of value, the basis for that conclusion should also be stated.

The "terms of agreement" prong has proven to be controversial, especially in cases related to the donation of easements on historic buildings. To provide context, some taxpayers will contribute a "façade easement"—a property interest in a historic building co-owned by a preservation society or subject to special municipal laws. Such municipal laws may include a ban on demolition, additional construction, or any action that would change the building's outward appearance. Legal restrictions have an impact on a property's value, but are also difficult to quantify.

The Tax Court has found basic descriptions of the municipal laws to be adequate so long as they sufficiently and correctly identify an encumbrance on the property. In evaluating the valuation of easements, the Tax Court has rejected an approach that deducts a fixed percentage from the value of the property to account for the easement,[36] but has supported other approaches that examine the easement's terms and covenants to perform a "before-and-after" analysis of the property's value with regard to the easement.[37] The easements and covenants must also be analyzed both individually and collectively and compared to existing laws to estimate the extent to which the easement affects the property's value.

Requirement 3.5: Identifying Information of the Qualified Appraiser: Treas. Reg. § 1.170A-13(c) (3)(ii)(E)

(E) The name, address, and (if a taxpayer identification number is otherwise required by section 6109 and the regulations thereunder) the identifying number of the qualified appraiser; and, if the qualified appraiser is acting in his or her capacity as a partner in a partnership, an employee of any person (whether an individual, corporation, or partnerships [sic]), or an independent contractor engaged by a person other than the donor, the name, address, and taxpayer identification number (if a number is otherwise required by section 6109 and the regulations thereunder) of the partnership or the person who employs or engages the qualified appraiser

---

[35] *See* Internal Revenue Bulletin (Oct. 6, 2008), Notice of Proposed Rulemaking Substantiation and Reporting Requirements for Cash and Noncash Charitable Contributions, available at http://www.irs.gov/irb/2008-40_IRB/ar13.html#d0e6635.

[36] *See Scheidelman v. Comm'r*, 755 F.3d 148 (2d Cir. 2014); *Nicoladis v. Comm'r*, 55 T.C.M. (CCH) 624 (1988).

[37] *See Hilborn v. Comm'r*, 85 T.C. 677, 689 (1985).

The requirement that a qualified appraisal include the name, address, and tax-payer identification number of the putative qualified appraiser allows the IRS to ensure that appraisal reports prepared by the appraiser are not disregarded pursuant to 31 U.S.C. 330(c). This section authorizes the Secretary of the Treasury Department to suspend or disbar from practice before the agency any representative who, among other things, is incompetent, disreputable, or who violates applicable Treasury Regulations.[38] The appraiser is also required to include this information on IRS Form 8283.

Requirement 3.6: The Qualifications of the Qualified Appraiser: Treas. Reg. § 1.170A-13(c) (3)(ii)(F)

(F) The qualifications of the qualified appraiser who signs the appraisal, including the appraiser's background, experience, education, and membership, if any, in professional appraisal associations

The purpose of including the appraiser's qualifications is to allow a revenue agent who examines the appraisal report to evaluate whether the appraiser is qualified to prepare appraisals of the type of property valued. If an appraiser's qualifications do not suggest reliability, the IRS may audit the return to determine the correctness of the value of the contributed property. Chapter 3, *Qualified Appraiser*, discusses in detail who is a qualified appraiser.

Requirement 3.7: Statement of Preparation for Income Tax Purposes: Treas. Reg. § 1.170A-13(c)(3)(ii)(G)

(G) A statement that the appraisal was prepared for income tax purposes

The requirement that a qualified appraisal include a statement that the appraisal was prepared for income tax purposes is not insignificant. The Tax Court stated in *Rothman v. Commissioner* that "such a statement serves as notice to the appraiser that he or she may be subject to a civil penalty under section 6701 for aiding and abetting an understatement of tax liability, and as a result, that appraisals he or she prepared may be disregarded pursuant to 31 U.S.C. [§] 330(c)."[39] The failure to include a statement that an appraisal was prepared for income tax purposes has not historically resulted in disallowance of the deduction. For example, the Tax Court held that a qualified appraisal stating that it was intended for IRS use, but did not contain an explicit statement that it was prepared for income tax purposes, met this requirement.[40] Still, appraisers should strive for literal compliance with this relatively straightforward requirement.

---

[38] 31 U.S.C. § 330(c). Technically, 31 U.S.C. § 330(d) is the section pursuant to which appraisals may be disregarded. However, 31 U.S.C. § 330(c) specifies the types of misconduct giving rise to this sanction.

[39] *Rothman v. Comm'r*, T.C. Memo. 2012-163, *vacated in part on other grounds*, T.C. Memo. 2012-218; cf. Treas. Reg. § 1.170A-13(c)(5)(i) (requiring a qualified appraiser to declare on the appraisal summary that he or she understands that intentionally false or fraudulent overstatements of the property valued may result in civil penalties and disciplinary action).

[40] *Dunlap*, 103 T.C.M. (CCH) 1689.

Requirement 3.8: Date(s) of Appraisal: Treas. Reg. § 1.170A-13(c)(3)(ii)(H)

(H) The date (or dates) on which the property was appraised

The requirement that a qualified appraisal include the date on which the property was appraised enables the IRS to evaluate whether the report was prepared sufficiently close to the contribution date such that the reported value is current. To the extent the date of the appraisal and the date of the contribution are not close, then the IRS may seek to examine the tax return to determine if the facts on the valuation date were the same as on the appraisal date.

Requirement 3.9: Appraised Fair Market Value: Treas. Reg. § 1.170A-13(c)(3)(ii)(I)

(I) The appraised fair market value (within the meaning of [Treas. Reg.] § 1.170A-1 (c)(2)) of the property on the date (or expected date) of contribution

The requirement that a qualified appraisal use *fair market value* as the appropriate measure of value is important. The standard of value for federal tax purposes, and the one that section 1.170A-13(c)(3)(ii) of the Treasury Regulations requires appraisers to use, is fair market value. As explained in Chapter 1, *Tax Valuation and the Necessity for Expert Appraisals*, fair market value is "the price at which the property would change hands between a willing buyer and a willing seller, neither being under any compulsion to buy or sell and both having reasonable knowledge of relevant facts."[41]

Appraisers, who generally speak in terms of the USPAP, often use market value as the appropriate measure of value in appraisal reports. USPAP Advisory Opinion 22 defines *market value* as:

> *the most probable price which a property should bring in a competitive and open market under all conditions requisite to a fair sale, the buyer and seller each acting prudently and knowledgeably, and assuming the price is not affected by undue stimulus. Implicit in this definition are the consummation of a sale as of a specified date and the passing of title from seller to buyer under conditions whereby:*
>
> 1. *Buyer and seller are typically motivated;*
> 2. *Both parties are well informed or well advised and acting in what they consider their best interests;*
> 3. *A reasonable time is allowed for exposure in the open market;*
> 4. *Payment is made in terms of cash in U.S. dollars or in terms of financial arrangements comparable thereto; and*
> 5. *The price represents the normal consideration for the property sold unaffected by special or creative financing or sales concessions granted by anyone associated with the sale.*

The Tax Court has repeatedly observed that "market value" is "an approximate value for fair market value" and the "two terms are not necessarily synonymous

---

[41] *United States v. Cartwright*, 411 U.S. 546, 551 (1973); *see also* Rev. Rul. 59-60, 1959-1 C.B. 237; Treas. Reg. § 1.170A-1(c)(2).

depending on how they are defined."[42] A complete discussion of the ways in which market value and fair market value differ is outside the scope of this book, but the following points help to explain the key differences between the terms:

- Fair market value contemplates a transaction between a hypothetical willing buyer and a hypothetical willing seller; market value contemplates a transaction between an actual buyer and an actual seller;
- Fair market value assumes a hypothetical transfer of title; market value assumes an actual transfer of title;
- Fair market value requires the buyer and the seller to have "reasonable knowledge of relevant facts"; market value requires only that the buyer and seller are well informed and well advised; and
- Fair market value does not require an actual date on which the title changes hands; market value requires an actual transfer of title on a certain date.[43]

The fair market value acknowledgment required by the Treasury Regulations serves as a reminder to appraisers that the appropriate measure of value for federal income tax purposes is *fair market value*, not *market value* under the USPAP.

Requirements 3.10 and 3.11: Valuation and Basis Used to Determine Fair Market Value: Treas. Reg. §§ 1.170A-13(c)(3)(ii)(J) and (K)

(J) The method of valuation used to determine the fair market value, such as the income approach, the market-data approach, and the replacement-cost-less-depreciation approach

(K) The specific basis for the valuation, such as specific comparable sales transactions or statistical sampling, including a justification for using sampling and an explanation of the sampling procedure employed

Courts have historically evaluated these requirements concurrently, and for that reason, this book considers both requirements in the same subsection. The first requirement, that the appraiser include a method of valuation, ensures that the appraisal is the product of reliable principles and methods. The second requirement, that the appraiser state the specific basis for the valuation, ensures that the appraiser includes the specific facts and data in support of her opinion of value. Together, these requirements allow the IRS to evaluate the soundness of the appraiser's methods

---

[42] *See, e.g., Crimi v. Comm'r*, T.C. Memo. 2013-51, 105 T.C.M. (CCH) 1330 (2013); *Alli v. Comm'r*, T.C. Memo. 2014-15 n.17, 107 T.C.M. (CCH) 1082 (2014); *Rothman v. Comm'r*, T.C. Memo. 2012-163, 103 T.C.M. (CCH) 1864 (2012) (comparing Treas. Reg. § 1.170A-1(a) and (c)(1) (defining fair market value) with USPAP, Advisory Opinion 22 (2008) (defining market value)), *vacated in part on reconsideration on other grounds*, T.C. Memo. 2012-218, 104 T.C.M. (CCH) 126 (2012); *DiDonato v. Comm'r*, T.C. Memo. 2011-153 n.8, 101 T.C.M. (CCH) 1739 (2011).

[43] For a comprehensive discussion of the differences between market value and fair market value, *see Alli v. Comm'r*, T.C. Memo. 2014-15 n.17, 107 T.C.M. (CCH) 1082 (2014); David Maloney, *Market Value vs. Fair Market Value: What's the Difference?*, available at http://www.appraisalcourseassociates.com/2012/10/01/1265/ (as excerpted from David J. Maloney, *Appraising Personal Property: Principles & Methodology* (5th ed. 2012).

and analysis. To the extent the IRS considers the principles, methods, or analysis deficient, an examination may be appropriate.

In *Scheidelman v. Commissioner*,[44] Court of Appeals for the Second Circuit held that sections 1.170A-13(c)(3)(ii)(J) and (K) of the Treasury Regulations do not require an appraisal report to include a "reasoned analysis" to support the proffered value. Rather, the Second Circuit stated that the purpose of the method of value and specific basis requirements is for the appraiser to provide the information and analysis informing the opinion of value, not necessarily that the method of value or the specific basis be persuasive. It is now well settled that an appraisal report's failure to apply the method of value and specific facts in a reasoned analysis does not necessarily mean that the report is not a qualified appraisal.[45]

Requirement 4: No Prohibited Fee Arrangement: Treas. Reg. § 1.170A-13(c)(3)(i)(D)   To prevent bias in the appraisal process, an appraisal report is a qualified appraisal only if it does not involve a fee prohibited by applicable Treasury Regulations.[46] Those Treasury Regulations provide that the fee arrangement for a qualified appraisal cannot be based in whole or in part on a percentage of the appraised value of the property.[47] Fee arrangements based in whole or in part on the value of the deduction tied to the appraised property are also prohibited.[48] If the fee structure of an appraisal is prohibited, then the appraisal is not a qualified appraisal.[49] However, there is an exception for any "fee paid to a generally recognized association that regulates appraisers," provided that the organization is not-for-profit; the appraiser receives no compensation from the organization; and the fee arrangement is not based on the value of the property.[50]

The Qualified Appraisal Requirement and Pass-Through Entities

The qualified appraisal rules can be confusing when it comes to pass-through entities, such as small business corporations (i.e., S corporation), partnerships, and certain trusts. By way of background, S corporations, partnerships, and some trusts do not deduct charitable contribution when computing taxable income. Rather, the pass-through entity notifies shareholders, partners, or beneficiaries of their pro-rata share of the charitable contribution. Those individuals may then deduct their proportionate share of the deduction subject to the limitations of section 170(b)(1) of the Internal Revenue Code. The qualified appraisal rules apply to any charitable

---

[44]*Scheidelman v. Comm'r*, 682 F.3d 189, 195-199 (2d Cir. 2012), *rev'g*, T.C. Memo. 2010-151, 100 T.C.M. (CCH) 24 (2010).

[45]*Accord Rothman v. Comm'r*, T.C. Memo. 2012-218, 104 T.C.M. (CCH) 126 (2012) (concluding that an appraisal report which was in all material respects identical to the one at issue in *Scheidelman* would not be disregarded as a qualified appraisal because the appraisal report lacked a method of value or a specific basis for the valuation), *vacating in part on reconsideration on these grounds*, T.C. Memo. 2012-163, 103 T.C.M. (CCH) 1864 (2012).

[46]Treas. Reg. § 1.170A-13(c)(3)(D).

[47]Treas. Reg. § 1.170A-13(c)(6)(i).

[48]*Id.*

[49]Treas. Reg. § 1.170A-13(c)(3)(i)(D).

[50]Treas. Reg. § 1.170A-13(c)(6)(ii).

contribution made after December 31, 1984 (other than for money and publicly traded securities), by an individual, closely held corporation, personal service corporation, partnership, or S corporation.[51] To determine the existence of a qualified appraisal prepared by a qualified appraiser for a given year, the compliance is tested at the entity level.[52]

Interplay of the Qualified Appraisal and Appraisal Summary Requirements

As mentioned, some courts have refused to disqualify an appraisal report where the taxpayer included the missing information on an IRS Form 8283 (an appraisal summary). For this reason, readers should understand the appraisal summary, when it is required, and what information is required to be included on that form. Notwithstanding some courts' willingness to allow information on the IRS Form 8283 to supplement information omitted from the qualified appraisal, it is advisable to ensure that all information required for a qualified appraisal is included in the appraisal report.

By way of background, a donor who contributes property and claims a deduction exceeding $5,000 must, in addition to obtaining a qualified appraisal, attach an appraisal summary to the income tax return on which the deduction is claimed.[53] A separate appraisal summary is generally required for each item of property contributed.[54] An appraisal summary is a summary of a qualified appraisal that:

(A) Is made on the form prescribed by the IRS (IRS Form 8283);
(B) Is generally signed and dated by the donee;[55]
(C) Is signed and dated by the qualified appraiser who prepared the qualified appraisal; and
(D) Includes the following information:
  (i) The name and tax identification of the donor;
  (ii) A description of the property in sufficient detail so that a person who is not generally familiar with the type of property contributed could ascertain whether the property appraised was the contributed property;
  (iii) If tangible personal property is contributed, a brief summary of the overall physical condition of the property at the time of the contribution;
  (iv) The manner and date of acquisition of the property by the donor or, if the property was created or produced by the donor, a statement to that effect and the approximate date on which the property was substantially completed;
  (v) The adjusted basis of the property;

---

[51]Treas. Reg. § 1.170A-13(c)(1)(i).

[52]*See* I.R.C. § 170(f)(11)(G); *see also* Treas. Reg. § 1.170A-13(c)(2)(i)(B).

[53]Treas. Reg. § 1.170A-13(c)(2)(i)(B).

[54]Treas. Reg. § 1.170A-13(c)(4)(iv)(B).

[55]If a donor is unable to obtain a donee's signature on the appraisal summary, the deduction under I.R.C. § 170 will not be disallowed if the donor attaches to the appraisal summary a detailed explanation of why it was not possible to obtain the signature. Treas. Reg. § 1.170A-13(c)(4)(iv)(C)(2).

(vi) The name, address, and taxpayer identification number of the donee;

(vii) The date on which the donee received the property;

(viii) A statement explaining whether or not the charitable contribution was made by means of a bargain sale and the amount of any consideration received from the donee for the contribution;

(ix) The name, address, and taxpayer identification number of the qualified appraiser who signed the appraisal summary, and, if the qualified appraiser is a partner in a partnership, an employee of any person, or an independent contractor engaged by any person other than the donor, the name, address, and taxpayer identification number of the partnership or person who employs or engages the qualified appraiser;

(x) The appraised fair market value of the property on the date of contribution;

(xi) The required declaration by the appraiser described in section 1.170A-13(c)(5)(i) of the Treasury Regulations;

(xii) A declaration by the appraiser that the fee arrangement was not a prohibited fee arrangement and that the appraisals prepared by the appraiser are not being disregarded pursuant to section 330(c) of Title 31 of the United States Code on the date the appraisal summary is being signed; and

(xiii) Any other information required to be furnished by Form 8283 or its instructions.

This information may seem duplicative of the information already required to be included in the qualified appraisal, but Treasury Regulations require the information to be provided in this summary format. Some courts have been willing to allow information on the IRS Form 8283 to supplement information omitted from the qualified appraisal. However, it is advisable to ensure that all information required for a qualified appraisal is included in the appraisal report and not rely on IRS Form 8283 to meet the regulatory requirements for a qualified appraisal. This rationale for this conclusion is explained more fully in Chapter 4, *Substantial Compliance vs. Strict Compliance.*

LITIGATION CONCERNING QUALIFIED APPRAISALS

There has been considerable litigation in the Tax Court concerning whether a taxpayer complied with the qualified appraisal requirements. If a taxpayer fails to comply with the requirements for a qualified appraisal as discussed in this chapter, she will face an uphill battle in litigation, but is not necessarily without recourse. Chapter 14, *Common Errors with Appraisal Reports and How to Avoid Them*, discusses how to address errors with qualified appraisals in connection with litigation.

CONCLUSION

Initially issued to complement the existing substantiation requirements, the qualified appraisal requirements add another significant regulatory layer with the primary tax policy goal of stopping abuse from inflated charitable contribution deductions. Unfortunately, this additional requirement has made the navigation of the regulations even more confusing, leaving taxpayers, the IRS, and courts struggling to determine what information is required. While the Tax Court resolves litigation concerning qualified appraisals on a case-by-case basis with a strong view of the circumstances, a few essential guidelines for taxpayers have emerged:

- In preparing qualified appraisals, practitioners and taxpayers should pay close attention to the quantitative aspects, such as the timing of the appraisal, the methodology, and the basis for the fair market value;
- Qualitative provisions, such as description of the property or its condition, should be provided in one or more of the required filings to the extent that it affects the fair market value; and
- Practitioners and taxpayers should strive for literal compliance with all requirements for a qualified appraisal, including those that are seemingly technical or procedural in nature.

CHAPTER 3

Qualified Appraiser

SUMMARY

A crucial aspect of the rules for obtaining a qualified appraisal is that the appraisal be prepared, signed, and dated by a qualified appraiser. A donor who fails to use a qualified appraiser to prepare a qualified appraisal may not be entitled to a deduction for a charitable contribution of property valued in excess of $5,000.[1] From a macro-perspective, the term *qualified appraiser* is defined by statute to include individuals who meet certain minimum professional and educational standards.[2] Treasury Regulations further refine the statutory definition to impose additional requirements to ensure that the individual possesses qualities allowing her to render a detached and neutral opinion of value. This chapter examines the statutory and regulatory requirements that must be met before an individual may be considered a qualified appraiser.

LEGISLATIVE HISTORY

The legislative history of the qualified appraiser requirement essentially mirrors that of the qualified appraisal requirement discussed more fully in Chapter 2, *Qualified Appraisal*. The first reference to the term *qualified appraiser* occurred in the Deficit Reduction Act of 1984 ("DEFRA").[3] Through DEFRA, Congress sought to constrain taxpayer overvaluations of charitable contribution deductions. It did so by designing a mechanism for the Internal Revenue Service to authenticate the fair market value of taxpayer noncash property donations. Specifically, Congress directed the U.S. Department of the Treasury ("Treasury Department") to promulgate regulations requiring that taxpayers obtain a qualified appraisal by a qualified appraiser for charitable contributions where the amount of the claimed deduction is greater than $5,000.[4] And as noted earlier, the Treasury Department responded to Congress's charge in DEFRA by promulgating the qualified appraisal and qualified appraiser regulations found in section 1.170A-13(c) of the Treasury Regulations.[5]

---

[1]*See, e.g.*, I.R.C. § 170(f)(11)(A)(i); T.D. 8199, 1988-1 C.B. 99 (preamble).
[2]I.R.C. § 170(f)(11)(E)(ii).
[3]Deficit Reduction Act of 1984, Pub. L. No. 98-369, § 155, 98 Stat. 691.
[4]H.R. REP. NO. 98-861, at 996-999 (1984) (Conf. Rep.).
[5]*See* T.D. 8199, 1988-1 C.B. 99 (preamble).

In the Pension Protection Act of 2006 ("2006 PPA"), Congress adopted a statutory definition of the terms *qualified appraisal* and *qualified appraiser*.[6] The 2006 PPA, dictates that, for appraisals prepared with respect to returns filed after August 17, 2006, the term *qualified appraiser* means an individual who:

1. Has earned an appraisal designation from a recognized professional appraiser organization or has otherwise met minimum education and experience requirements as may be defined by regulation;
2. Regularly performs appraisals for compensation; and
3. Meets such other requirements as may be prescribed by the Secretary of the Treasury in regulations or other guidance.[7]

It is clear from the express terms of the statute that the 2006 PPA delegated considerable authority to the Treasury Department to clarify the meaning of the term *qualified appraiser*.[8] Moreover, as discussed more fully in Chapter 12, *Penalties Associated with Faulty Appraisals*, the 2006 PPA also enacted section 6695A of the Internal Revenue Code, which authorized the imposition of accuracy-related penalties for valuation misstatements attributable to defective appraisals.[9]

The dual statutory and regulatory approach to the qualified appraiser requirements necessitates several clarifications born of administrative law. First, the regulations apply insofar as they do not contradict the statute.[10] The United States Tax Court has consistently upheld the validity of the qualified appraisal and qualified appraiser regulations as consistent with Congress's grant of authority.[11] Second, the IRS issued Notice 2006-96 to provide guidance with respect to some of the perceived ambiguities in the then-new qualified appraiser and qualified appraisal statute. Notice 2006-96 advises taxpayers how the IRS will interpret section 170(f)(11) of the Internal Revenue Code for purposes of determining an individual's status as a qualified appraiser.[12] Notice 2006-96 is discussed in more detail later in this chapter.

STATUTORY REQUIREMENTS

Section 170(f)(11)(E)(ii) of the Internal Revenue Code defines the term *qualified appraiser* to mean an individual who:

(I) Has earned an appraisal designation from a recognized professional appraiser organization or has otherwise met minimum education and experience requirements as may be defined by regulation;

---

[6]Pension Protection Act of 2006, Pub. L. No. 109-280, § 1219, 120 Stat. 780 (2006).
[7]I.R.C. § 170(f)(11)(E)(ii).
[8]I.R.C. § 170(f)(11)(E)(ii)(III).
[9]I.R.C. § 6695A.
[10]Barbara L. Kirschten and Carla Neeley Freitag, "Charitable Contributions: Income Tax Aspects," *Tax Management 2010*, at 168 (BNA Tax Management Portfolios, 3d ed.).
[11]*See, e.g., Costello v. Comm'r*, T.C. Memo. 2015-87, 109 T.C.M. (CCH) 1441 (2015); *Rothman v. Comm'r*, T.C. Memo. 2012-218, 104 T.C.M. (CCH) 126 (2012); *Mohamed v. Comm'r*, T.C. Memo. 2012-152, 103 T.C.M. (CCH) 1814 (2012).
[12]I.R.S. Notice 2006-96, 2006-2 C.B. 902.

(II) Regularly performs appraisals for compensation;

(III) Meets such other requirements as may be prescribed by the Secretary of the Treasury in regulations or other guidance; and

(IV) Demonstrates verifiable education and experience in valuing the type of property subject to the appraisal, and has not been prohibited from practice before the IRS under section 330(c) of Title 31 of the United States Code at any time during the three-year period ending on the date of the appraisal.[13]

Each of the foregoing statutory requirements is discussed in what follows.

Statutory Requirement #1: Appraisal Designation or Certain Minimum Education and Experience Requirements

An individual may become a qualified appraiser by earning an appraisal designation from a recognized professional appraisal organization or by meeting certain minimum education and experience requirements as specified by the regulations.[14] The class of "recognized professional appraiser organizations" from which an appraisal designation satisfies the qualified appraiser requirement is not defined in the statute or regulations. Notice 2006-96 explains that an appraiser will be treated as having earned an appraisal designation from a recognized professional appraiser organization if the appraisal designation is awarded on the basis of demonstrated competency in valuing the type of property for which the appraisal is performed.[15] Qualifying organizations may include general appraisal organizations, such as the American Society of Appraisers, the National Association of Certified Valuators and Analysts, or the Institute of Business Appraisers. CPAs who have undertaken further training beyond the basic CPA certification to become qualified in business valuation appraisals may earn the designation "ABV," which stands for "Accredited in Business Valuation," and may satisfy the required appraisal designation.

More generally, it is arguable that a recognized appraisal organization is an organization that follows generally accepted appraisal standards. The IRS has interpreted the phrase "generally accepted appraisal standards" to mean the substance and principles of the Uniform Standards of Professional Appraisal Practice, which were developed by the Appraisal Foundation and are discussed in more detail in Chapter 9, *Expert Appraisal Reports*.[16]

The minimum requisite education and experience necessary to satisfy the qualified appraiser requirement are likewise neither statutorily defined nor defined in regulations. Notice 2006-96 provides that a declaration, made on the appraisal, that the appraiser is qualified to make appraisals of the type of property being valued because of her background, experience, education, and membership in professional associations, is sufficient to meet the education and experience requirements.[17]

---

[13]I.R.C. § 170(f)(11)(E)(ii), (iii).
[14]I.R.C. § 170(f)(11)(E)(ii)(I).
[15]I.R.S. Notice 2006-96, § 3.03, 2006-2 C.B. 902.
[16]Notice 2006-96.
[17]Notice 2006-96, § 3.03, 2006-2 C.B. 902.

Notice 2006-96 also details the minimum education and experience requirements by reference to the type of property to be valued.

With respect to real property, an appraiser meets the minimum education and experience requirements if she is licensed or certified for the type of property being appraised in the state in which the real property is located.[18] With respect to property other than real property, an appraiser meets the minimum education and experience requirements if she:

1. Successfully completed college or professional-level coursework that is relevant to the property being valued;
2. Obtained at least two years of experience in the trade or business of buying, selling, or valuing the type of property being valued; and
3. Fully describes in the appraisal her education and experience qualifying her to value the type of property being valued.[19]

Statutory Requirement #2: Regularly Performs Appraisals for Compensation

A qualified appraiser must regularly perform appraisals for compensation.[20] Section 170(f)(11)(E) of the Internal Revenue Code codifies Congress's preference for professional appraisers rather than hired-gun experts or self-designated appraisers because, it is generally understood in the tax community, professional appraisers are more likely to provide an accurate and neutral appraisal.

Statutory Requirement #3: Verifiable Education and Experience

A qualified appraiser must demonstrate verifiable education and experience in valuing the type of property subject to the appraisal.[21] The verification requirement allows the IRS and others to check the appraiser's educational qualifications; of course, this requirement provides deterrence for a valuation appraiser's exaggeration or misstatement of her credentials. The specific property requirement ensures that the qualified appraiser understands the qualities and market of the property being valued. This is particularly important since the value of a specific type of property reflects specialized standards and is often based on comparable transactions.

Statutory Requirement #4: Not Prohibited from Practice by 31 U.S.C. § 330(c)

A qualified appraiser must not have been prohibited from practicing before the IRS under section 330(c) of Title 31 of the United States Code. If the IRS prohibited an

---

[18] *Id.*
[19] *Id.*
[20] I.R.C. § 170(f)(11)(E)(ii)(II).
[21] I.R.C. § 170(f)(11)(E)(iii)(I).

individual from practicing within three years before the date of the appraisal, then the individual is not a qualified appraiser.[22]

REGULATORY REQUIREMENTS

The regulations outline both what constitutes a qualified appraiser and the steps a qualified appraiser must take in order to prepare a qualified appraisal. Many of the requirements detailed in Chapter 2, *Qualified Appraisal*, govern the qualification and practice of a qualified appraiser. For example, when a qualified appraisal is required, it must be prepared, signed, and dated by a qualified appraiser.[23] The qualified appraiser must perform the appraisal within 60 days of the contribution and provide the appraisal to the donor before the due date of the donor's tax return.[24] The regulations also impose a basic mechanical requirement for a qualified appraiser to attach a declaration to the appraisal summary identifying the appraiser as a qualified appraiser and providing basic information substantiating the appraiser's credentials.[25]

Appraiser's Declaration

Section 1.170A-13(c)(5)(i) of the Treasury Regulations requires that, in order to be a *qualified appraiser*, this person must declare that:

(A) The individual either holds himself or herself out to the public as an appraiser or performs appraisals on a regular basis;
(B) Because of the appraiser's qualifications as described in the appraisal * * *, the appraiser is qualified to make appraisals of the type of property being valued;
(C) The appraiser is not [an excluded person]; and
(D) The appraiser understands that an intentionally false or fraudulent overstatement of the value of the property described in the qualified appraisal or appraisal summary may subject the appraiser to a civil penalty under section 6701 for aiding and abetting an understatement of tax liability, and, moreover, the appraiser may have appraisals disregarded pursuant to 31 U.S.C. 330(c).

Additionally, Notice 2006-96 provides that the declaration must also include a statement that the appraiser understands that a substantial or gross valuation misstatement resulting from an appraisal that the appraiser knows or should have known would be used in connection with a return or a claim for refund may subject the appraiser to a civil penalty under section 6695A of the Internal Revenue Code. The requirements must not only be affirmatively met, but also must be attested to in a declaration attached to the appraisal summary. The appraisal summary requirements are discussed more fully in Chapter 2, *Qualified Appraisal*.

---

[22]I.R.C. § 330(c).
[23]I.R.C. § 170(f)(11)(C).
[24]Treas. Reg. § 1.170A-13(c)(3)(i)(A).
[25]Treas. Reg. § 1.170A-13(c)(5)(i).

Regulatory Requirement #1: Declaration That Individual Is an Appraiser: Treas. Reg. § 1.170A-13(c)(5)(i)(A)

(A) The individual either holds himself or herself out to the public as an appraiser or performs appraisals on a regular basis

A person who regularly performs appraisals, or who identifies herself to the public as an appraiser, is more likely to be a professional appraiser and have the requisite skills, knowledge, and expertise to appraise the subject property. Due to standards issued by professional appraisal organizations and possible consequences to the appraiser's professional reputation, a professional appraiser is more likely to offer an objective and accurate opinion. Additionally, since the appraisal of noncash property often requires technical expertise, understanding of market dynamics, and knowledge of comparable properties and transactions, an appraiser must be consistently engaged in the field for such factors to be accurately reflected in the valuation.

Regulatory Requirement #2: Declaration That the Appraiser Is Qualified to Value the Property: Treas. Reg. § 1.170A-13(c)(5)(i)(B)

*(B) Because of the appraiser's qualifications as described in the appraisal * * *, the appraiser is qualified to make appraisals of the type of property being valued*

This condition complements the requirement discussed earlier that a qualified appraisal must set forth the qualifications of the qualified appraiser who signs the appraisal, including the appraiser's background, experience, education, and any memberships in professional appraisal associations.[26] The appraisal report may also include any other facts bearing upon the appraiser's ability to value the subject property. The qualifications listed by the appraiser are necessary to enable the IRS to determine the appraiser's ability to value the subject property and the appraiser's knowledge in a specific field. The appraiser's education, any specialized study of the type of property being appraised, and other activities, such as publications, representative engagements, and general research all impact a determination of whether the appraiser is qualified to make appraisals of the type of property being valued. These various items collectively indicate the appraiser's ability to perform the qualified appraisal based on the totality of the appraiser's experience and knowledge.

Regulatory Requirement #3: Declaration That the Appraiser Is Not an Excluded Person: Treas. Reg. § 1.170A-13(c)(5)(i)(C)

(C) The appraiser is not [an excluded person]

To qualify as a qualified appraiser, the appraiser may not be an excluded person. Among the persons who cannot be a qualified appraiser with respect to a particular piece of property are the following individuals:

- The donor or the taxpayer who claims or reports a deduction under section 170 of the Internal Revenue Code for the contribution of the property that is being appraised;

---

[26]Treas. Reg. § 1.170A-13(c)(3)(ii)(F).

- A party to the transaction in which the donor acquired the property being appraised (i.e., the person who sold, exchanged, or gave the property to the donor, or any person who acted as an agent for the transferor or for the donor with respect to such sale, exchange, or gift), unless the property is donated within two months of the date of acquisition and its appraised value does not exceed its acquisition price;
- The donee of the property;
- Any person employed by any of the foregoing persons (e.g., if the donor acquired a painting from an art dealer, neither the art dealer nor persons employed by the dealer can be qualified appraisers with respect to the painting);
- Any person related to the foregoing persons under section 267(b) of the Internal Revenue Code or, with respect to appraisals made after June 6, 1988, married to a person who is in a relationship described in section 267(b) with any of the foregoing persons; or
- An appraiser who is regularly used by the donor, the donee, or a party to the transaction and who does not perform a majority of his or her appraisals made during his or her taxable year for other persons.[27]

For purposes of section 1.170A-13(c)(5)(i)(C), the appraiser may not be the donor of the property, the donee of the property, or any of the following:

1. Members of a family (i.e., his or her spouse, siblings, ancestors, and lineal descendants);
2. An individual and corporation more than 50% in value of the outstanding stock of which is directly or indirectly owned by or for such individual;
3. Two corporations which are members of the same controlled group;
4. A grantor and a fiduciary of a trust;
5. A fiduciary of a trust and a fiduciary of another trust where the same person is a grantor of both trusts;
6. A fiduciary and beneficiary of the same trust;
7. A fiduciary of a trust and a beneficiary of another trust where the same person is a grantor of both trusts;
8. A fiduciary of a trust and a corporation more than 50% in value of the outstanding stock of which is directly or indirectly owned by or for the trust or by or for a person who is a grantor of the trust;
9. A person and an organization to which section 501 of the Internal Revenue Code (relating to certain educational and charitable organizations which are exempt from tax) applies and which is controlled directly or indirectly by such person or by members of the family of such individual;
10. A corporation and a partnership if the same persons own (i) more than 50% in value of the outstanding stock of the corporation, and (ii) more than 50% in value of the capital or profits interest in the partnership;
11. An S corporation and another S corporation if the same person owns more than 50% in value of the outstanding stock of each corporation;

---

[27]Treas. Reg. § 1.170A-13(c)(5)(iv).

12. An S corporation and a C corporation if the same person owns more than 50% in value of the outstanding stock of each corporation; or
13. An executor of an estate and a beneficiary of such estate (except in the case of a sale or exchange in satisfaction of a pecuniary bequest).[28]

The regulations seek an objective appraisal and one procured in an arm's-length transaction with respect to the property, as evidenced by the foregoing requirements. Individuals or firms with an economic interest or motivation to inaccurately report the value of the property for tax purposes are precluded from being a qualified appraiser. Such could be third-party property sellers who factor favorable appraisal services into the price; donating parties seeking to maximize their deduction through a high appraisal value; or corporate entities looking to maximize their deduction by valuing a subsidiary's charitable contribution.

Regulatory Requirement #4: Declaration That the Appraiser Understands Consequences of Fraudulent Valuation: Treas. Reg. § 1.170A-13(c)(5)(i)(D)

(D) The appraiser understands that an intentionally false or fraudulent overstatement of the value of the property described in the qualified appraisal or appraisal summary may subject the appraiser to a civil penalty under Section 6701 for aiding and abetting an understatement of tax liability, and, moreover, the appraiser may have appraisals disregarded pursuant to 31 U.S.C. 330(c)

This requirement references a statutory enforcement mechanism that allows the IRS to levy civil penalties on the appraiser in the case of a false or fraudulent overstatement in the qualified appraisal. As discussed in detail in Chapter 12, *Penalties Associated with Faulty Appraisals*, section 6701 of the Internal Revenue Code authorizes the imposition of a $1,000 penalty on any individual who aids or assists, procures, or advises with respect to the preparation or presentation of any portion of a return, affidavit, claim, or other document submitted to the IRS. Additionally, after imposing the section 6701 penalty upon any appraiser, the IRS may bar the appraiser from presenting evidence or testimony in any proceeding before the IRS or the Treasury Department and may provide that the appraisal has no probative effect in any such proceeding.

Additional Declaration Requirements of Notice 2006-96

Notice 2006-96 requires, for returns filed after February 16, 2007, that the appraiser's declaration must also include a statement that the appraiser understands that a substantial or gross valuation misstatement resulting from an appraisal that the appraiser knows or should have known would be used in connection with a return or a claim for refund may subject the appraiser to a civil penalty under section 6695A of the Internal Revenue Code.[29] The section 6695A penalty is discussed more fully in Chapter 12, *Penalties Associated with Faulty Appraisals*.

---

[28]I.R.C. § 267(b).
[29]Notice 2006-96.

Denial of Appraiser Status

Several provisions allow the IRS to deny qualified appraiser status even though the taxpayer may correctly file the above-described appraiser's declaration. These provisions exist to minimize the influence of outside factors that may inhibit the appraisal's accuracy and objectivity by subjecting the qualified appraiser to an additional round of administrative and judicial review. The provisions are set forth in section 1.170A-13(c)(5)(ii) of the Treasury Regulations as follows:

> *An individual is not a qualified appraiser with respect to a particular donation, even if the declaration specified in paragraph (c)(5)(i) … is provided in the appraisal summary, if the donor had knowledge of facts that would cause a reasonable person to expect the appraiser falsely to overstate the value of the donated property (e.g., the donor and the appraiser make an agreement concerning the amount at which the property will be valued and the donor knows that such amount exceeds the fair market value of the property).*[30]

Complementing the earlier sections requiring objectivity, this provision allows the IRS to exclude a person from qualified appraiser status even if the appraiser is not an excluded party under section 1.170A-13(c)(5)(iv) of the Treasury Regulation, but may still be prone to bias. Here, the analysis is undertaken from the point of view of the donor and a determination is made based on information pertaining to the appraiser's objectivity available to the donor.

Courts have generally used a two-step inquiry to decide whether the donor knew or had reason to know that the appraisal unreasonably overstated the fair market value of the donated property. In the first step, courts have examined whether the donor knew or should have known that the appraiser might overstate the value of the property in the appraisal. For example, in *Dunlap v. Commissioner*,[31] the Tax Court decided whether an individual should not be deemed a qualified appraiser because the appraiser was referred to the taxpayer-donor by an interested entity associated with easements on historic properties. The Court concluded that the taxpayer was not charged with actual or constructive knowledge of this referral, and as such, that the appraiser was not disqualified for this reason alone. As to the second step, if the donor actually knows the information relating to potential appraiser bias, then courts decide whether a reasonable person standing in the shoes of the taxpayer-donor would have expected the appraiser to falsely overstate the value of the property. In *Dunlap*, the Court concluded that even if the donor-taxpayer knew that the qualified appraiser was referred by an interested entity, an expectation of overvaluation is unreasonable because it is common practice for historical preservation trusts to recommend qualified appraisers to property donors.

---

[30] Treas. Reg. § 1.170A-13(c)(5)(ii).
[31] *Dunlap v. Comm'r*, T.C. Memo. 2012-126, 2012 WL1524660 (2012).

Appraisals by More than One Appraiser

The regulations also contain rules with respect to appraisals prepared by more than one appraiser. Section 1.170A-13(c)(5)(iii) of the Treasury Regulations provides:

> *More than one appraiser may appraise the donated property. If more than one appraiser appraises the property, the donor does not have to use each appraiser's appraisal for purposes of substantiating the charitable contribution deduction.... If the donor uses the appraisal of more than one appraiser, or if two or more appraisers contribute to a single appraisal, each appraiser shall comply with the ... regulatory requirements, including signing the qualified appraisal and appraisal summary.*[32]

Treasury Regulations provide the donor-taxpayer with the flexibility to use more than one appraiser to value the property, or to use multiple qualified appraisal reports. A donor-taxpayer may want to use multiple appraisers to strengthen the tax reporting position by offering multiple qualified appraisals or combine the expertise of two experts in different fields for a single qualified appraisal. However, any appraiser involved in the preparation of a qualified appraisal, either as the main author or as a contributing author, must meet the qualification requirements. In practice, courts have also ruled that in situations where it is not clear which appraisal contributed to various portions of the appraisal report, any appraiser who materially contributed to an appraisal report must be available to testify.

Appraisal Fees

Another factor that may infringe on the objectivity of the appraisal is the fee paid to the qualified appraiser. The regulations aim to balance the economic reality of a professional appraiser charging for services with the possibility of bias emanating from a fee arrangement.

Appraisal fees based on a percentage of the appraised value of the property or the amount of the deduction are strictly prohibited, except in limited circumstances discussed more fully in what follows.[33] Even if a part of the overall appraisal fee is based on the valuation, then the whole appraisal is disqualified.[34] The purpose of this regulatory requirement is to remove economic incentives that the appraiser might have to overvalue the property.

The regulations provide an exception to the general rule with respect to fees paid to certain appraisal associations. An appraisal fee based on percentage or set of percentages of the appraised value of the property is allowed if each of the following requirements is met:

(A) The association is not organized for profit and no part of the net earnings of the association inures to the benefit of any private shareholder or individual;

---

[32]Treas. Reg. § 1.170A-13(c)(5)(iii).
[33]Treas. Reg. § 1.170A-13(c)(6)(i).
[34]*Id.*

(B) The appraiser does not receive any compensation from the association or any other persons for making the appraisal; and

(C) The fee arrangement is not based in whole or in part on the amount of the appraised value of the donated property, if any, that is allowed as a deduction under section 170 after Internal Revenue Service examination or otherwise.[35]

Thus, the organization must be a generally recognized appraisal association and meet the basic requirements for a nonprofit entity under section 501(c) of the Internal Revenue Code, which mandates that a nonprofit organization cannot be organized for profit or for the benefit of any private shareholder or individual. Additionally, the individual appraiser actually performing the appraisal cannot receive any compensation either from the appraisal association or anyone else. This exception assumes that a nonprofit appraisal organization will act neutrally, and should be fairly compensated to recover its costs associated with larger appraisals.

JUDICIAL INTERPRETATION OF THE REQUIREMENTS

Litigation surrounding whether an appraiser is "qualified" as required by section 170(f)(11) of the Internal Revenue Code typically arises with respect to four issues: sufficiency of documentation; scrutiny of qualifications; excluded parties; and multiple appraisers.

Sufficiency of Documentation

First, courts are sometimes called upon to decide whether the appraiser included with the appraisal proof of her credentials sufficient to meet the requirements of the regulations. Although an appraiser may not strictly comply with the requirements establishing that she is a qualified appraiser, courts have at times relied upon the substantial compliance doctrine to nonetheless treat the regulatory requirements as having been met. The substantial compliance doctrine is discussed more fully in Chapter 12, *Penalties Associated with Faulty Appraisals*.

In *Brusewicz v. United States,* the U.S. District Court for the Northern District of Illinois held that the qualified appraiser requirements were not met where the appraisal specified the appraiser's license number, but not the appraiser's background, experience, education, and membership in professional appraisal associations.[36] The Court stated that the appraiser must include those details, holding that these requirements were neither confusing nor inoperable, and that Congress would not have included them if reporting a license number would have been sufficient to establish the appraiser's qualification. These qualitative credentials are the key to assessing the appraiser's credentials. Attaching the appraiser's qualifications during litigation, but well after the date of the contribution and the return, does not warrant the application of the substantial compliance doctrine because the appraiser might not have been qualified when he performed the appraisal.[37]

---

[35]Treas. Reg. § 1.170A-13(c)(6)(ii).

[36]*See Brusewicz v. United States*, 604 F. Supp. 2d 1197 (N.D. Ill. 2009).

[37]*Hendrix v. United States*, 2010 WL 2900391 (S.D. Oh. 2010).

Scrutiny of Qualifications

Second, once an appraiser's credentials are correctly reported, the courts may then scrutinize the appraiser's summary and qualifications to see if the standard for a qualified appraiser is met. Generally, the courts look at the totality of the appraiser's background, experience, education, and membership in professional organizations to make this determination. For example, a certified public accountant with no previous appraisal experience was held to not be a qualified appraiser.[38] Similarly, a school principal who valued property was not found to be a qualified appraiser with respect to the value of donated art supplies.[39]

Excluded Parties

Third, the courts are also sometimes faced with the question of whether the appraiser is an excluded party under the regulations. In *Mohamed v. Commissioner*, the Tax Court ruled that a donor, despite years of experience in real estate brokerage and an appraisal certification, cannot act as a qualified appraiser, even if the appraisal is seemingly accurate.[40] Even though the donor may have undervalued the property, the Court held that "the problems of misvalued property are so great that Congress was quite specific about what the charitably inclined have to do to defend their deductions" and denied the deduction due to the donor failing to obtain a qualified appraisal.[41] Furthermore, taxpayers without appraisal qualifications, who value their own property, are not qualified appraisers, either.[42]

Multiple Appraisers

Fourth, courts have sometimes been asked to decide whether the qualified appraiser requirements extend to all authors of a report or only the primary author. For example, in *Zarlengo v. Commissioner*,[43] the Tax Court was asked to decide whether a valuator who performed the site inspection, but did not principally author the report, was a qualified appraiser. The Tax Court concluded that the qualified appraiser requirement applied to the principal author of the appraisal report, but not to valuators who assisted in the preparation of the report by, for example, performing a site inspection.

CONCLUSION

The law with respect to the elements of a qualified appraisal is relatively straightforward and unambiguous. The failure to secure an appraisal prepared, signed, and dated by a qualified appraiser can be fatal to the allowance of a federal income tax deduction and may subject the taxpayer and appraiser to disallowed deductions, penalties, and/or professional sanctions.

---

[38] *Smith v. Comm'r*, T.C. Memo. 2007-368, 94 T.C.M. (CCH) 574 (2007).

[39] *D'Arcangelo v. Comm'r*, T.C. Memo. 1994-572, 68 T.C.M. (CCH) 1223 (1994).

[40] *Mohamed v. Comm'r*, T.C. Memo. 2012-152, 103 T.C.M. (CCH) 1814 (2012).

[41] *Mohamed v. Comm'r*, T.C. Memo. 2012-152, 103 T.C.M. 1814 (2012).

[42] *Riether v. United States*, 2012 WL 6934116 (N.M. 2012).

[43] *Zarlengo v. Comm'r*, T.C. Memo. 2014-161, 108 T.C.M. (CCH) 155 (2014).

CHAPTER 4

Substantial Compliance vs. Strict Compliance

SUMMARY

Noncompliance with the substantiation and recordkeeping requirements related to a qualified appraisal generally results in the disallowance of certain tax benefits claimed in connection with the appraisal.[1] Courts have applied two doctrines to evaluate whether a taxpayer has complied with the qualified appraisal requirements: the strict compliance doctrine and the substantial compliance doctrine. Although taxpayers and professionals should strive for literal compliance with the substantiation and recordkeeping requirements related to a qualified appraisal, the substantial compliance doctrine may, in limited circumstances, prevent a defective appraisal report from disqualifying a taxpayer's entitlement to certain tax benefits. This chapter discusses the current state of the substantial compliance and strict compliance doctrines and their relevance to modern appraisal practice.

OVERVIEW OF THE STRICT AND SUBSTANTIAL COMPLIANCE DOCTRINES

The strict and substantial compliance doctrines are particularly germane when the law imposes upon the taxpayer certain substantiation and recordkeeping requirements. These doctrines have recently been at the forefront of litigation concerning whether the taxpayer has secured a qualified appraisal in connection with claiming certain charitable contribution deductions.[2] Each doctrine is discussed in the following.

To determine whether a taxpayer has obtained a qualified appraisal for purposes of a charitable contribution deduction, the *strict compliance doctrine* provides that a deduction will be allowed only if the taxpayer literally and unequivocally complies with the substantiation and recordkeeping requirements discussed in Chapter 2, *Qualified Appraisal*. Thus, the strict compliance doctrine imposes a standard of

---

[1]*See, e.g.*, I.R.C. § 170(f)(11)(A)(i) (disallowing certain charitable contribution deductions to a taxpayer who fails to obtain a qualified appraisal).
[2]*See, e.g., Rothman v. Comm'r*, T.C. Memo. 2012-163, *vacated in part by Rothman v. Comm'r*, T.C. Memo. 2012-218, 104 T.C.M. (CCH) 126 (2012).

absolute conformity to the substantiation and recordkeeping requirements before certain tax benefits are allowed. Strict compliance mandates that the form and content of the documents used to substantiate a taxpayer's deduction (e.g., a qualified appraisal, a contemporaneous written acknowledgment, and an appraisal summary [e.g., Internal Revenue Service ("IRS") Form 8283, *Noncash Charitable Contributions*]) exactly follow the statutory and regulatory requirements. If the taxpayer fails to literally comply with those requirements, then the strict compliance doctrine precludes the taxpayer's claim to a tax benefit. The effect of the strict compliance doctrine may be harsh, particularly as applied to the complex substantiation requirements for qualified appraisals.

Alternatively, the *substantial compliance doctrine* provides that a tax benefit may be allowed where the taxpayer has done all that can be reasonably expected of him, but is still noncompliant with the substantiation and recordkeeping requirements of a particular Treasury Regulation. The doctrine of substantial compliance is designed to mitigate the harsh effect of failing to strictly comply with certain substantiation and recordkeeping requirements (e.g., disallowance of the deduction).[3] Significantly, the substantial compliance doctrine does not apply where the doctrine's invocation would defeat the policies underlying the particular substantiation and recordkeeping requirements.[4] As discussed ahead, the doctrine of substantial compliance has been argued with varying levels of success, though the current trend in courts is to insist on strict compliance with the statutory and regulatory requirements.

APPLICABILITY OF THE SUBSTANTIAL COMPLIANCE DOCTRINE

The substantial compliance doctrine has been used to excuse taxpayers from strict compliance with procedural regulatory requirements so long as the taxpayers substantially complied with the requirement by fulfilling the essential statutory purpose.[5] Whether the substantial compliance doctrine applies in a case is a factually intensive determination in which courts typically examine the surrounding facts and circumstances in light of the following five factors:

1. Whether the taxpayer's imperfect compliance defeats the purpose of the statute;
2. Whether the taxpayer attempts to benefit from hindsight by adopting a position inconsistent with his or her original action or omission;
3. Whether the government is prejudiced;
4. Whether the sanction imposed on the taxpayer for the failure is excessive and out of proportion to the default; and
5. Whether the regulation provided with detailed specificity the manner in which the law was to be complied.[6]

---

[3] *See generally Estate of Chamberlain v. Comm'r*, T.C. Memo. 1999-181, 77 T.C.M. (CCH) 2080 (1999), *aff'd*, 9 Fed. Appx. 713 (9th Cir. 2001).
[4] *Id.*; *see also Alli v. Comm'r*, T.C. Memo. 2014-15, 107 T.C.M. (CCH) 1082 (2014).
[5] For example, *Estate of Chamberlain*, T.C. Memo. 1999-181, 77 T.C.M. (CCH) 2080.
[6] *See Am. Air Filter Co. v. Comm'r*, 81 T.C. 709, 719 (1983).

As applied to substantiation cases involving charitable contribution deductions, the critical factor to be examined is whether the taxpayer has provided the government with sufficient information to evaluate the reported contribution in the manner intended by Congress.[7]

JUDICIAL APPROACHES TO THE SUBSTANTIAL COMPLIANCE DOCTRINE

As is evident from the cases discussed ahead, the continued selective application of the strict and substantial compliance doctrines ensures that both approaches remain relevant today. Regrettably, the sustained relevance of these conflicting doctrines makes the litigation of substantiation issues highly unpredictable for taxpayers. The U.S. Court of Appeals for the Seventh Circuit, in *Prussner v. United States,* remarked:

> *Reading the Tax Court's decisions on the subject of substantial compliance is enough to make one's head swim. Tax lawyers can have no confidence concerning the circumstances in which noncompliance with regulations governing the election of favorable tax treatment will or will not work a forfeiture. The result has been a surge of unnecessary litigation well illustrated by the present suit. We think the doctrine should be interpreted narrowly.... The common law doctrine of substantial compliance should not be allowed to spread beyond cases in which the taxpayer had good excuse (though not a legal justification) for failing to comply with either an unimportant requirement or one unclearly or confusingly stated in the regulations or the statute.[8]*

At a minimum, in the context of the failure to obtain a qualified appraisal in connection with certain charitable contribution deductions, Congress created a statutory reasonable cause exception that functions much like the substantial compliance doctrine.[9] Under the reasonable cause exception of section 170(f)(11)(A)(ii)(II) of the Internal Revenue Code, if the taxpayer proves that the noncompliance was due to reasonable cause and not due to willful neglect, then a charitable contribution deduction that should have been substantiated with a qualified appraisal, but was not, will not be disallowed. Similar to the substantial compliance doctrine, the existence of reasonable cause is a highly factual determination requiring the courts to examine the taxpayer's noncompliance in light of all surrounding facts and circumstances.

SURVEY OF CASES APPLYING THE SUBSTANTIAL COMPLIANCE DOCTRINE

It is worth noting that the applicability of the substantial compliance doctrine is not confined to the qualified appraisal context. Indeed, courts have considered invocation of the substantial compliance doctrine in connection with the requirements

---

[7]*See, e.g., Costello v. Comm'r,* T.C. Memo. 2015-87, 109 T.C.M. (CCH) 1441 (2015); *Smith v. Comm'r,* T.C. Memo. 2007-368, 94 T.C.M. (CCH) 574, 586 (2007), *aff'd,* 364 F. Appx. 317 (9th Cir. 2009).
[8]*Prussner v. United States,* 896 F.2d 218, 224 (7th Cir. 1990).
[9]I.R.C. § 170(f)(11)(A)(ii)(II).

for executing a Last Will and Testament, making appropriate tax elections, and filing necessary forms to support a dependency exemption deduction for a child.[10] However, because this book focuses on qualified appraisals and qualified appraisers, we limit our survey of cases to those addressing the substantial compliance doctrine in the context most directly related to qualified appraisals: the charitable contribution substantiation requirements.

The Internal Revenue Code adopts numerous statutory provisions that condition the allowance of certain charitable contribution deductions on compliance with substantiation and recordkeeping requirements, which vary with the amount and type of property donated.[11] As discussed more fully in Chapter 3, *Qualified Appraiser*, Treasury Regulations promulgated in response to Congress's express delegation of authority further add to this complexity. Section 170(a) of the Internal Revenue Code provides that a charitable contribution shall be allowed as a deduction only if "verified under regulations prescribed by the Secretary" of the Treasury.[12] Recall also that the regulations set out an elaborate definition of no less than 15 requirements before an appraisal is considered qualified.[13] Recall further that section 170(f)(11) of the Internal Revenue Code requires taxpayers to obtain a qualified appraisal for charitable contribution deductions exceeding $5,000, and to attach a copy of a qualified appraisal to any return claiming a charitable contribution deduction of more than $500,000.[14] It is against the backdrop of these various substantiation requirements that courts have been asked to decide whether the substantial compliance doctrine excuses a taxpayer's noncompliance with certain provisions of the law under varying fact patterns. We turn to examine some of the more recent decisions of the courts to understand the application of the substantial compliance doctrine.

Bond v. Commissioner: The First Application of the Substantial Compliance Doctrine in the Context of the Qualified Appraisal Regulation

The substantial compliance doctrine was first applied in the context of section 1.170A-13(c)(3) of the Treasury Regulations (the qualified appraisal regulation) in *Bond v. Commissioner*.[15] The issue in *Bond* was whether the taxpayers were entitled to a charitable contribution deduction for the donation of two blimps to a charitable organization. The *Bond* parties agreed upon the value of the contributed property, that a qualified appraiser completed the appraisal, and that the donee organization was qualified to receive the contribution. However, the government

---

[10]*See, e.g., Kohli v. Comm'r*, T.C. Memo. 2009-287, 98 T.C.M. (CCH) 572 (2009) (stating that the substantial compliance doctrine "has no place in determining whether a timely election has been made"); *see also Armstrong v. Comm'r*, 139 T.C. 468 (2012) (declining to invoke the substantial compliance doctrine in the context of a dependency exemption deduction).

[11]For a detailed account of the history and substance of these substantiation rules, *see* Ellen Aprill, "Reforming the Charitable Contribution Substantiation Rules," 14 *Fla. Tax Rev.* 275 (2013).

[12]I.R.C. § 170(a)(1).

[13]Treas. Reg. § 1.170A-13(c)(3).

[14]I.R.C. § 170(f)(11)(C), (D).

[15]*Bond v. Comm'r*, 100 T.C. 32 (1993).

asserted that the taxpayers were not entitled to the claimed deduction because they failed to obtain and attach to their return a separate written appraisal including the reporting information specified in section 1.170A-13 of the Treasury Regulations. In concluding that the requirements of section 1.170A-13 of the Treasury Regulations were directory as opposed to mandatory, the United States Tax Court ("Tax Court") explained:

> [I]t is apparent that the essence of section 170 is to allow certain taxpayers a charitable deduction for contributions made to certain organizations. It is equally apparent that the reporting requirements of section 1.170A-13, Income Tax Regs., are helpful to [the IRS] in the processing and auditing of returns on which charitable deductions are claimed. However, the reporting requirements do not relate to the substance or essence of whether or not a charitable contribution was actually made. We conclude, therefore, that the reporting requirements are directory and not mandatory.

The Tax Court held that the taxpayers had substantially complied with a charitable contribution substantiation requirement, noting that information missing from the taxpayers' return was promptly furnished to the government at or near the beginning of the audit. In resolving this issue, the Tax Court drew upon the substantial compliance test as articulated in *Taylor v. Commissioner*.[16] The *Taylor* test required two discrete inquiries:

1. Determine if the procedural requirements relate to "the substance or essence of the statute." If they do, then strict adherence to the statute is required; and
2. Determine if the requirements are only for convenience or administrative purposes, rather than carrying out the purpose of the statute. If so, then substantial compliance may apply.

The Tax Court in *Bond* then analyzed the substantiation requirements with respect to the statutory purpose of section 170 of the Internal Revenue Code. The Tax Court reasoned that the goal of section 170 of the Internal Revenue Code was to allow certain taxpayers a charitable deduction for contributions made to certain organizations. The reporting requirements, although helpful for administrative purposes, were found to be unrelated to the substance or essence of whether a charitable contribution was actually made. The Tax Court also declined to apply a literal reading to section 170(a) of the Internal Revenue Code, which provides that "a charitable contribution shall be allowed as a deduction only if verified under regulations prescribed by the Secretary."[17] The Tax Court noted that the existence of a condition on the deduction did not necessitate a literal reading of the statute, and allowed space for substantial compliance.

Post-*Bond* Decisions: Cases Finding Substantial Compliance

Supplemental Information from Form 8283   The substantial compliance standard was next applied in the tax context in *Simmons v. Commissioner*.[18] The issue was whether a

---

[16] *Taylor v. Comm'r*, 67 T.C. 1071, 1077-1078 (1977).
[17] *Bond*, 100 T.C. at 41; *see also* I.R.C. § 170(a).
[18] *Simmons v. Comm'r*, T.C. Memo. 2009-208, 98 T.C.M. (CCH) 211 (2009).

taxpayer obtained a qualified appraisal for the contribution of a historic easement. The appraisal report did not contain the date of the contribution or an explicit statement by the appraiser that the appraisal was prepared for income tax purposes. The Tax Court determined that the taxpayer substantially complied with the qualified appraisal regulation. In so ruling, the Tax Court noted that the appraisal contained a statement that the taxpayer was contemplating a donation and discussed the IRS's policy regarding charitable contributions. From this information, the Tax Court deduced that the appraiser was aware that the appraisal was being prepared for income tax purposes and that the existence of the appraisal was sufficient to place the IRS on notice of the donation. Additionally, the dates of the contribution were supplied to the IRS through the taxpayer's appraisal summary (Form 8283) and an acknowledgment from the donee organization. Thus, the *Simmons* court concluded that the IRS had access to all the information necessary to evaluate the appraisal and that the statutory purpose of the substantiation requirements were met.

Sufficient Information for IRS to Evaluate Reported Contributions as Intended by Congress   In *Consolidated Investors Group v. Commissioner,*[19] the Tax Court invoked the substantial compliance doctrine to hold that a partnership that failed to strictly comply with the substantiation requirements for charitable contribution deductions was nonetheless entitled to a tax deduction for a bargain sale of real property to the Ohio Turnpike Commission. The Tax Court held that the taxpayer was entitled to a charitable contribution despite its failure to fully comply with the requirements of the qualified appraisal regulation. In particular, the Court was not persuaded that the deduction should be disallowed even though (i) the appraisal was not performed within 60 days of the contribution, (ii) the appraisal did not state the date on which the contribution was made, (iii) the appraisal did not state that the report was prepared for income tax purposes, and (iv) the appraisal did not state the fair market value of the property as of the date of the contribution.

The Tax Court noted that the taxpayer "timely provided [the IRS] with nearly all of the information required in the regulations," had acquired an appraisal report before filing its tax return, and that the "premature nature, by approximately 3 months, of the [taxpayer's] appraisal report was insubstantial."[20] The Court concluded:

> [T]he information provided to [the IRS] was sufficient to permit respondent to evaluate the partnership's reported contribution and monitor and address concerns about overvaluation and other aspects of the reported charitable contribution. Accordingly, the partnership has substantially complied with the regulations.[21]

A New Trend?   It remains to be seen whether the Tax Court is reversing course with respect to the import of the strict compliance doctrine in the qualified appraisal context. In its most recent decision to address the role of the strict compliance

---

[19] *Consol. Investors Group v. Comm'r*, T.C. Memo. 2009-290, 98 T.C.M. (CCH) 601 (2009).
[20] *Id.* at 614.
[21] *Id.*

doctrine, *Cave Buttes, L.L.C. v. Commissioner*,[22] the Tax Court relied upon the substantial compliance doctrine to allow a $2.167 million charitable contribution deduction even though the donor-entity submitted with its tax return an appraisal report that (among other defects asserted by the IRS):

- Was not prepared by a qualified appraiser and did not include the qualification of the appraiser who prepared the report;
- Did not include a statement that the appraisal was prepared for income-tax purposes;
- Failed to value the property as of the contribution date; and
- Used a standard of value that was not the same as the definition of fair market value section 1.170A-1(c)(2) of the Treasury Regulations.

The Tax Court held that the donor-entity substantially complied with each of the above defects. The *Cave Buttes* opinion was published as a "Tax Court opinion" (also known as a division opinion) as opposed to a memorandum opinion. Division opinions are judicial reports "in which a legal issue of first impression is decided, a legal principle is applied or extended to a recurring factual pattern, a significant exception to a previously announced general rule is created, or there are similarly significant and precedentially valuable cases."[23] Significantly, division opinions are binding precedent in the Tax Court. By contrast, memorandum opinions are not regarded as binding precedent.[24]

Cave Buttes may be the beginning of a trend by the Tax Court to apply the substantial compliance doctrine in cases challenging the status of an appraisal report as a qualified appraisal or whether *Cave Buttes* will be narrowly construed to its facts. *Cave Buttes* will likely invite additional litigation on this point.

Post-*Bond* Decisions: Cases Finding No Substantial Compliance

Notwithstanding the aforementioned cases in which the substantial compliance doctrine was applied, the substantial compliance doctrine does not grant the taxpayer a free pass to disregard the regulatory requirements. On many more occasions, and certainly in most current cases, the Tax Court has ruled that the substantial compliance doctrine applies, but that the taxpayer did not substantially comply with the specific substantiation requirements.

Absence of Qualified Appraisal   In *Jorgenson v. Commissioner*,[25] the Tax Court disallowed a charitable contribution deduction because the taxpayers did not obtain qualified appraisals for the donated property, but instead provided draft appraisal reports conducted after the donation and during the audit.

---

[22]*Cave Buttes, L.L.C. v. Commissioner*, 147 T.C. ___, ___, 2016 WL 5107038 (2016).

[23]*See* Hon. Mary Ann Cohen, "How to Read Tax Court Opinions," address at the Corporation & Taxation Law Soc'y at the Univ. of Houston Law Ctr. (Nov. 11, 1999), available at http://www.hbtlj.org/v01/v01_cohen.pdf.

[24]*Huffman v. Comm'r*, 126 T.C. 322, 350 (2006) (citing *Dunaway v. Comm'r*, 124 T.C. 80, 87 (2005).

[25]*Jorgenson v. Comm'r*, T.C. Memo. 2000-38, 79 T.C.M. (CCH) 1444 (2000).

In *D'Arcangelo v. Commissioner*,[26] the Tax Court held that a letter from a high school principal valuing donated art supplies did not substantially comply with the qualified appraisal requirements. The Court noted that the principal did not: (1) identify himself as a qualified appraiser or as a non-prohibited party in his letter, (2) provide in the appraisal report a valuation method, or (3) complete an appraisal summary (the required IRS Form 8283). The Tax Court further held that expert testimony provided at the trial did not, as the taxpayer argued, constitute a qualified appraisal, because the expert had no experience valuing the type of art supplies donated and did not value them at the time of the donation.

In *Hewitt v. Commissioner*,[27] the Tax Court decided whether taxpayers were entitled to charitable contribution deductions for shares of non-publicly traded stock contributed to qualifying charitable organizations. The taxpayers in *Hewitt* failed to obtain a qualified appraisal before filing their returns for the years at issue, and instead determined the amounts of the charitable contribution deductions from the average per-share price of the stock traded in arm's-length transactions at approximately the same time as the contributions. The Tax Court held the taxpayers were not entitled to deductions greater than those allowed by the government because, the Court reasoned, to hold otherwise would have created an exemption from the clear statutory and regulatory requirements that Congress did not intend. In refusing to invoke the substantial compliance doctrine, the *Hewitt* court noted that the "appraisal requirements may not be entirely procedural so as to justify the application of the substantial compliance rules under any and all circumstances."

Flawed Appraisal Reports   In *Smith v. Commissioner*,[28] the Tax Court sought to clarify the applicability of the substantial compliance doctrine in charitable contribution deduction cases. There, the taxpayers obtained two separate appraisal reports for a donation, but the reports did not constitute qualified appraisals because they were neither timely procured nor created by a qualified appraiser. The taxpayers conceded that they failed to fully comply with the Treasury Regulations, but argued that they provided enough information to implicate the substantial compliance doctrine. The Tax Court, in response, refined the substantial compliance doctrine as follows:

> *Under these circumstances we consider whether petitioners' compliance was substantial or whether they failed to meet the statutorily mandated regulatory requirements.* Bond v. Commissioner, 100 T.C. 32 (1993), *and* Hewitt v. Commissioner, 109 T.C. 258 (1997), *considered together, provide a standard by which we can consider whether petitioners provided sufficient information to permit respondent to evaluate their reported contributions, as intended by Congress. If they provided sufficient information, their "substantial compliance" would adequately serve the purposes intended by Congress.*[29]

---

[26] *D'Arcangelo v. Comm'r*, T.C. Memo. 1994-572, 68 T.C.M. (CCH) 1223 (1994).
[27] *Hewitt v. Comm'r*, 109 T.C. 258 (1997).
[28] *Smith v. Comm'r*, T.C. Memo. 2007-368, 94 T.C.M. (CCH) 574 (2007).
[29] *Id.* at 586.

The *Smith* court then applied this formulation of the substantial compliance doctrine and denied the claimed charitable contribution deduction. The Tax Court concluded that the taxpayers did not provide timely appraisals, and for certain years even failed to provide documents establishing value. The Court concluded that as a result, important information that would have enabled the IRS to understand and monitor the claimed contribution deductions was not supplied, and thus, the taxpayers were not in substantial compliance with the substantiation requirements.

In *Scheidelman v. Commissioner* ("*Scheidelman I*"),[30] the Tax Court concluded that an appraisal report was not qualified because it failed to include a valuation method and specific basis for the valuation as required by sections 1.170A-13(c)(3)(ii)(J) and (K) of the Treasury Regulations. The donated property in *Scheidelman I* was a façade easement, the preferred valuation of which, as set forth in the Treasury Regulations, is the before-and-after methodology.[31] The before-and-after method approximates the easement's fair market value by measuring the difference between the fair market value of the underlying property without regard to the easement (the before value) and the fair market value of the underlying property encumbered by the easement (the after value). To calculate the after value, the appraiser in *Scheidelman I* simply multiplied the before value times a percentage reduction factor. The government argued that the appraisal was not qualified because, among other deficiencies, it lacked a valuation method and specific basis for the valuation. The taxpayers argued that the percentage reduction factor was in line with estimates in prior cases the IRS handled and that the appraisal was substantially compliant with the qualified appraisal regulation.

The Tax Court in *Scheidelman I* concluded that the appraisal at issue was not qualified and that the taxpayers were not entitled to a deduction for the fair market value of the donated easement. In so ruling, the Court found that the appraisal lacked a valuation methodology and a specific basis for the valuation. The Tax Court termed these requirements "essential" because, the Court asserted, "'[w]ithout any reasoned analysis, [the appraiser's] report is useless.'"[32] In rejecting the taxpayers' plea for substantial compliance, the Tax Court stated as follows:

> *Petitioners claim they substantially complied with the substantiation requirements of section 170 because, as in* Bond *and* Simmons, *the documents that they submitted included the information required for a qualified appraisal and appraisal summary. We disagree. In this case the lack of a recognized methodology or specific basis for the calculated after-donation value is too significant for us to ignore under the guise of substantial compliance.*[33]

The taxpayers in *Scheidelman I* subsequently appealed to the U.S. Court of Appeals for the Second Circuit, the results of which are discussed ahead.

---

[30] *Scheidelman v. Comm'r*, T.C. Memo. 2010-151, 100 T.C.M. (CCH) 24 (2010), *vacated and remanded by* 682 F.3d 189 (2d Cir. 2012).
[31] Treas. Reg. § 1.170A-14(h)(3).
[32] *Scheidelman*, T.C. Memo. 2010-151, 100 T.C.M. (CCH) at 29.
[33] *Id.* at 30.

During the pendency of the appeal of *Scheidelman I*, the Tax Court filed its opinion in *Rothman v. Commissioner*.[34]

At issue in *Rothman* was whether an appraisal materially identical to the appraisal in *Scheidelman I* was qualified for purposes of substantiating a charitable contribution of a façade easement. The primary argument advanced by the taxpayers in *Rothman* was that their appraisal strictly complied with the qualified appraisal requirements. The taxpayers' alternative argument was that their appraisal substantially complied with those requirements. In deciding whether the strict or substantial compliance doctrines controlled the outcome of the case, the Tax Court confirmed that the substantial compliance doctrine has "continuing but limited application in a post-section 170(f)(11) world." In this regard, the Tax Court stated that "the prevailing view is that where the appraisal contained sufficient information to allow the Commissioner to evaluate the contribution and unconditionally included the valuation method and specific basis for the valuation the taxpayer's substantial compliance will adequately serve the purpose Congress intended."

Setting forth this general rule, the *Rothman* court then examined whether the appraisal at issue complied with two sets of requirements. As to the first set, the valuation method and the specific basis for the valuation, the *Rothman* court, relying on *Scheidelman I*, concluded that the substantial compliance doctrine did not apply because the appraisal failed to include a valuation method or specific basis for the underlying value. As to the second set, the balance of the qualified appraisal requirements, the *Rothman* court noted that even if the substantial compliance doctrine could be invoked with respect to the method and specific basis of the valuation, it did not apply because the taxpayers failed to substantially comply with the remaining regulatory requirements. The Court examined in detail numerous appraisal defects that were not presented, or not emphasized in, *Scheidelman I*. The Court ruled that the collective weight of these failures precluded the application of the substantial compliance doctrine.

The *Rothman* opinion was filed just four days before the Second Circuit filed its opinion on *Scheidelman I*. In *Scheidelman v. Commissioner* ("*Scheidelman II*"),[35] the U.S. Court of Appeals for the Second Circuit vacated and remanded *Scheidelman I* on the grounds that the appraisal sufficiently detailed the method and basis for valuation as contemplated by the qualified appraisal regulation. The Second Circuit, departing from the Tax Court, concluded that the appraisal provided sufficient justification for the methodology to be considered as satisfying the qualified appraisal requirements. With respect to the applicability of the substantial compliance doctrine, the Second Circuit explicitly stated that the substantial compliance doctrine may be used to excuse "the most technical of deficiencies."

On remand, in *Scheidelman v. Commissioner* ("*Scheidelman III*"),[36] the Tax Court remained entrenched in its position that no deduction should be allowed, but abandoned its earlier conclusion that the taxpayers failed to obtain a qualified appraisal. Instead, the Tax Court ruled that the taxpayers' experts' methodology for

---

[34]*Rothman v. Comm'r*, T.C. Memo. 2012-163, 103 T.C.M. (CCH) 1864 (2012), *vacated in part on reconsideration*, T.C. Memo. 2012-218, 104 T.C.M. (CCH) 126 (2012).
[35]*Scheidelman v. Comm'r*, 682 F.3d 189, 192 (2d Cir. 2012).
[36]*Scheidelman v. Comm'r*, T.C. Memo. 2013-18, 105 T.C.M. (CCH) 1117 (2013).

determining the value reduction was faulty because it relied on valuation discounts that had been allowed in prior dissimilar cases, without justification or independent calculation. The Tax Court further rejected the taxpayers' experts' opinions on similar technical grounds. Thus, because the taxpayers' expert report and testimony were found to be unpersuasive, no deduction was allowed. The taxpayers appealed the Tax Court's decision in *Scheidelman III* to the Second Circuit, but the Second Circuit affirmed the Tax Court's decision.[37]

Post-*Scheidelman* Cases   In the cases that followed *Scheidelman*, taxpayers continued to claim that the substantial compliance doctrine excused their noncompliance with the qualified appraisal requirements, but the Tax Court was uniformly unwilling to apply the doctrine. For example, in *Alli v. Commissioner*, the Tax Court ruled that the substantial compliance doctrine did not apply because the taxpayers did not submit an appraisal report that satisfied the qualified appraisal requirements, and because the taxpayers did not provide an IRS Form 8283 that included the missing information.[38] As support for its ruling, the Tax Court stated that "the substantial compliance doctrine should not be liberally applied."

Similarly, in a 2015 case, *Costello v. Commissioner*, the Tax Court declined to apply the substantial compliance doctrine where the "taxpayer's reporting fail[ed] to meet substantive requirements set forth in the regulations or omit[ted] entire categories of required information."[39] The taxpayer's appraisal did not value the correct asset, and omitted the date of the contribution and salient terms of the agreements of the parties.

Thus, until the Tax Court's 2016 decision in *Cave Buttes v. Commissioner*, it was relatively clear that the substantial compliance doctrine had continuing but limited applicability to the requirement that taxpayers must obtain a qualified appraisal. The *Cave Buttes* opinion breathes new life into the substantial compliance doctrine in the context of qualified appraisals.

JUDICIAL APPROACHES TO THE STRICT COMPLIANCE DOCTRINE

The strict compliance doctrine requires absolute conformity with procedural requirements before a tax benefit will be allowed. In addition to those cases previously identified in which the Tax Court declined to apply the substantial compliance doctrine, taxpayers in several cases have been denied deductions based on their failure to strictly comply with the qualified appraisal requirement. A survey of these cases is provided in the following.

---

[37] *Scheidelman v. Comm'r*, 755 F.3d 148 (2d Cir. 2014).

[38] *Alli v. Comm'r*, T.C. Memo. 2014-15, 107 T.C.M. (CCH) 1082 (2014); *see also RERI Holdings I, LLC v. Comm'r*, 149 T.C. ___, ___, 2017 WL 2839773 (2017) (holding that a partnerships failure to disclose its cost or other basis in the donated property on a Form 8283 precluded the application of the substantial compliance doctrine); *Izen v. Comm'r*, 148 T.C. ___, ___, 2017 WL 809946 (2017) (holding the doctrine of substantial compliance does not excuse a taxpayer's failure to obtain a contemporaneous written acknowledgment).

[39] *Costello v. Comm'r*, T.C. Memo. 2015-87, 109 T.C.M. (CCH) 1441 (2015).

In *Hill v. Commissioner*,[40] no deduction was allowed for a donation when the taxpayers failed to timely provide a contemporaneous written acknowledgment as required by section 170(f)(8) of the Internal Revenue Code (for charitable contribution deductions of $250 or more). Similarly, in *Whitehurst v. Commissioner*,[41] the Tax Court denied a charitable contribution deduction when a contribution was substantiated only by the taxpayer's inconsistent testimony at trial and no other documentary evidence was produced. In both *Hill* and *Whitehurst*, the Court held that the Treasury Regulations at issue propagated unbendable requirements.

The Tax Court may also apply the strict compliance doctrine where a donor substantiates the contribution with an erroneous or incomplete statement. For example, in *Addis v. Commissioner*,[42] the taxpayers made contributions to a charity that in turn used the funds to pay the premiums on life insurance policies of the taxpayers and their family members. The Tax Court denied the deduction because section 170(f)(8) of the Internal Revenue Code requires taxpayers to obtain from the donee a contemporaneous written acknowledgment that states whether the donor-taxpayer received a benefit from the contribution. In *Addis*, the taxpayers' written acknowledgment failed to disclose the payment of the life insurance premiums. The Tax Court ruled, on the basis of the legislative history to section 170(f)(8) of the Internal Revenue Code, that only strict compliance with the statute would accomplish Congress's original goal of disallowing deductions in cases of *quid pro quo* donations. The Tax Court's ruling was upheld on appeal to the U.S. Court of Appeals for the Ninth Circuit, which reasoned that no deduction should be allowed because the taxpayers' acknowledgment did not meet the literal requirements of section 170(f)(8) of the Internal Revenue Code.[43]

THE SUBSTANTIAL COMPLIANCE DOCTRINE IN THE APPELLATE COURTS

The appellate courts have generally endorsed the view taken by the *Rothman* court with respect to when the substantial compliance doctrine applies. That is, where the appraisal contained all required information to allow the Commissioner to evaluate the contribution, the appraisal adequately served the purpose Congress intended, and the tax benefit should be allowed. For example, the U.S. Court of Appeals for the First Circuit adheres to the view that the substantial compliance doctrine may be used

---

[40] *Hill v. Comm'r*, T.C. Memo. 2004-156, 87 T.C.M. (CCH) 156 (2004). Similarly, in *Embroidery Express, LLC v. Comm'r*, T.C. Memo. 2016-136, 112 T.C.M. (CCH) 76 (2016), and *French v. Comm'r*, T.C. Memo. 2016-53, 111 T.C.M. (CCH) 1241 (2016), the Tax Court declined to apply the substantial compliance doctrine to excuse noncompliance with section 170(f)(8) of the Internal Revenue Code, which generally requires taxpayers to obtain a contemporaneous written acknowledgment for a charitable contribution deduction in which the amount of the deduction is $250 or more.

[41] *Whitehurst v. Comm'r*, T.C. Summ. Op. 2003-7 (2003).

[42] *Addis v. Comm'r*, 118 T.C. 528 (2002), *aff'd*, 374 F.3d 881 (9th Cir. 2004).

[43] *Addis v. Comm'r*, 374 F.3d 881 (9th Cir. 2004).

to forgive "minor discrepancies" relating to the qualified appraisal requirements.[44] In *Kaufman v. Shulman*, the First Circuit stated:

> *The procedural regulations requiring an appraisal report and summary are designed to provide information "sufficient to permit [the IRS] to evaluate the [taxpayer]'s reported contribution and monitor and address concerns about overvaluation." But whether the valuation was overstated, grossly or otherwise, is a factual question different from whether the formal procedural requirements were met, either strictly or under the "substantial compliance" doctrine which may forgive minor discrepancies.[45]*

As discussed earlier, the U.S. Court of Appeals for the Second Circuit has also implied that the substantial compliance doctrine may be used to excuse "the most technical of deficiencies."[46] Finally, in *Prussner v. United States*, the U.S. Court of Appeals for the Seventh Circuit advised that the substantial compliance doctrine should be invoked narrowly and only in those cases in which "the taxpayer had good excuse (though not a legal justification) for failing to comply with either an unimportant requirement or one clearly or confusingly stated in the regulations or the statute."[47]

REASONABLE CAUSE: CODIFICATION OF THE SUBSTANTIAL COMPLIANCE DOCTRINE

Section 170(f)(11) of the Internal Revenue Code adopts a statutory reasonable cause exception to the otherwise strict requirement that a taxpayer obtain a qualified appraisal for charitable contribution deductions of more than $5,000. Under the reasonable cause exception, a charitable contribution deduction will not be disallowed for failing to obtain a qualified appraisal if the taxpayer shows that the failure to obtain a qualified appraisal is due to reasonable cause and not to willful neglect.[48] Neither the Internal Revenue Code nor the Treasury Regulations define reasonable cause in the context of the qualified appraisal requirement. However, the Tax Court has ruled that the same standard that applies to reasonable cause in other areas of the Code, such as accuracy-related penalties, also applies to the qualified appraisal requirement.[49] The Tax Court articulated that test in *Crimi v. Commissioner*:

> *Reasonable cause requires that the taxpayer have exercised ordinary business care and prudence as to the challenged item . . . . Thus, the inquiry is inherently a fact-intensive one, and the facts and circumstances must be judged*

---

[44]*Kaufman v. Schulman*, 687 F.3d 21 (1st Cir. 2012), *aff'g in part, vacating in part, and remanding in part*, 134 T.C. 182 (2010).

[45]*Id.* (internal citations omitted).

[46]*Scheidelman v. Comm'r*, 682 F.3d 189 (2d Cir. 2012).

[47]*Prussner v. United States*, 896 F.2d 218, 224 (7th Cir. 1990).

[48]I.R.C. § 170(f)(11)(A)(ii)(II).

[49]*Crimi v. Comm'r*, T.C. Memo. 2013-51, 105 T.C.M. (CCH) 1330 (2013).

on a case-by-case basis.... A taxpayer's reliance on the advice of a profes-
sional, such as a certified public accountant, would constitute reasonable
cause and good faith if the taxpayer could prove by a preponderance of
the evidence that: (1) the taxpayer reasonably believed that the professional
was a competent tax adviser with sufficient expertise to justify reliance; (2)
the taxpayer provided necessary and accurate information to the advising
professional; and (3) the taxpayer actually relied in good faith on the pro-
fessional's advice.[50]

The reasonable cause exception of section 170(f)(11) of the Internal Revenue
Code functions much like a codification of the substantial compliance doctrine by
allowing a charitable contribution deduction if sufficient grounds exist for allowing
the deduction. The courts who have been asked to decide this issue have generally
found reasonable cause to exist.

For example, in *Crimi*, the Tax Court found that a taxpayer demonstrated
reasonable cause for failing to obtain a qualified appraisal when the taxpayer relied
on an appraisal prepared for him and reviewed by his CPA of more than 20 years.
The Court noted that the taxpayer's accountant routinely prepared tax returns
with claimed charitable contribution deductions without any legal mishaps, was
intimately familiar with the taxpayer's financial situation, and had access to all
relevant documents in preparing the appraisal. As such, the Tax Court ruled that
the taxpayer had "no reason to know or suspect" that the appraisal he obtained did
not meet the literal qualified appraisal requirements when the taxpayer's accountant
did not raise any questions regarding the appraisal.

On the other hand, where taxpayers do not disclose material information relative
to the donation, the courts have been unwilling to find the existence of reasonable
cause. For example, in *Costello v. Commissioner*, the Tax Court ruled that reasonable cause did not exist to excuse the failure to obtain a qualified appraisal because
the taxpayers omitted numerous categories of important information, such as, among
other items, an accurate description of the donated property, the terms of the parties'
agreement, and an explanation of the parties' *quid pro quo* arrangement.[51]

CONCLUSION

Adherence to the strict compliance doctrine by courts establishes a bright-line rule
for taxpayers to follow with respect to the qualified appraisal requirement, but may
result in the denial of otherwise allowable deductions due to the smallest procedural
deficiency. By contrast, the substantial compliance doctrine gives courts flexibility
in assessing whether a taxpayer has sufficiently complied with the substantiation
and recordkeeping requirements to support a deduction. This flexibility in turn
injects considerable uncertainty into the issues of whether and when a court will
invoke the substantial compliance doctrine. Recent jurisprudence has advanced
both doctrines, applying strict compliance when the taxpayer fails to include any
information and applying substantial compliance when the taxpayer provides the

---

[50] *Id.* at 1353 (internal citations omitted).
[51] *Costello v. Comm'r*, T.C. Memo. 2015-87, 109 T.C.M. (CCH) 1441 (2015).

required information, but not in the form prescribed by the internal revenue laws. The reasonable cause exception indicates a legislative preference for substantial compliance and taxpayer flexibility, but is limited in its application to qualified appraisals. Until the courts begin to clearly favor one doctrine over another or the reasonable cause exception encompasses the entirety of substantiation requirements, taxpayers are advised to be diligent. All returns and appraisals should include not only all information required by the internal revenue regulations, but also all other information relevant to the deduction and, in the case of a charitable contribution deduction, all information relevant to the charitable contribution.

CHAPTER 5

Government Expert Witnesses

SUMMARY

Similar to the taxpayer who may need an expert witness to prove her valuation in court, the government may also need to establish its valuation by way of expert witness testimony. The government often engages third-party experts to testify on its behalf, and occasionally the government will use its own employees, trained in valuation, to provide expert opinion testimony. Naturally, when the government uses its own employees, the issues of witness bias and lack of independence should be and often are of concern to the trier of fact. Courts are sensitive to witness bias and cases may be lost if the court determines that the bias affects the reasonableness or the reliability of the expert witness's opinion.

THE GOVERNMENT'S NEED FOR EXPERT TESTIMONY

The expert witness's ability to testify based on ordinarily inadmissible evidence makes expert witness testimony a powerful tool that, regrettably, creates opportunities for abuse. As detailed in Chapter 7, *From* Daubert *to* Boltar, the United States Supreme Court, in *Daubert v. Merrell Dow Pharmaceuticals, Inc.*[1] and its progeny, has set forth a number of factors for courts to consider in determining whether an expert's testimony meets the minimum standards of reliability to be admissible. It is against this backdrop that we discuss the use of expert witnesses by the government.

In most federal tax cases where valuation is at issue, the taxpayer has the burden of proving by a preponderance of the evidence that her valuation is correct.[2] Once the taxpayer satisfies her burden of proof, the government must rebut the taxpayer's valuation or else risk losing the case.

To challenge a taxpayer-asserted valuation, the government could simply elect to discredit the taxpayer's expert and forgo having its own expert testify. In this situation, if the taxpayer's valuation expert is discredited, the taxpayer might not be able to successfully carry her burden of proof. Courts have been critical of such practice, and the Internal Revenue Manual ("I.R.M."), a compendium of guidelines for IRS personnel, specifically counsels against it. As to the courts' criticisms, the U.S. Court of Appeals for the Fifth Circuit was highly critical of the government for

---

[1] *Daubert v. Merrell Dow Pharmaceuticals, Inc.*, 509 U.S. 579, 580 (1993).
[2] *Welch v. Helvering*, 290 U.S. 111, 115 (1933). The burden of proof as to factual matters may shift to the government in certain limited circumstances. I.R.C. § 7491(a).

utilizing this tactic and chastised the government for using "guerilla warfare" in an effort to win.[3] The I.R.M. instructs as follows:

> *In many cases, it is not enough for [the IRS] to present expert witness evidence as part of [the IRS's] case-in-chief and then cross-examine [the taxpayer's] expert(s). Instead, [the IRS] must also present rebuttal evidence by way of an expert witness. Whether such rebuttal evidence may be presented through [the IRS's] case-in-chief expert(s), or must be presented through an additional one or more expert witnesses, depends on the circumstances of the individual case, on the qualifications of the case-in-chief expert(s) and, to some extent, on the strategy adopted by [the taxpayer in the taxpayer's] use of an expert witness. An informed decision in this regard cannot be made without information concerning the identity, qualifications, and expected testimony of [the taxpayer's] expert(s). Such information should be sought from [the taxpayer] on a continuing basis.[4]*

Although the government is always free to attack the reliability of the taxpayer's expert, a prudent approach for the government is to introduce testimony by its own valuation expert. Additionally, the highly factual, and often complex, nature of valuation gives rise to the court's need for expert opinion.

IRS CRITERIA FOR EXPERT SELECTION

The resources available to government attorneys in selecting an expert witness are numerous and are set forth in part 35.4.4.8.1 of the I.R.M. Indeed, the IRS's Office of Chief Counsel maintains extensive library material detailing expert witness biographies and other information for experts who the IRS have used in prior cases. And of course, the IRS has access to a database of expert witnesses throughout the country. This information is available to certain IRS employees to assist in expert retention and trial preparation.

Primary considerations in the selection of an expert witness should be the degree to which the expert will be helpful to the court in understanding and determining ultimate issues of fact, the expert's ability to express facts and opinions orally and in writing, and the cost associated with hiring the expert.[5] Secondary considerations include the expert's overall qualifications, her demeanor and professional appearance, her experience as an expert witness, her experience with the specific matters at issue, books and articles she has written, the degree to which the report writing and background work will be performed personally by her as opposed to her staff, and her vulnerability to cross-examination.[6]

Competitive bidding may be required to hire a government expert witness. Moreover, even where competitive bidding is forgone due to "unusual time constraints" or the "unique abilities" of the individual, the I.R.M. requires attorneys representing

---

[3] *See Dunn v. Comm'r*, 301 F.3d 339, 349 (5th Cir. 2002).
[4] I.R.M., pt. 35.4.4.8.1 (Aug. 11, 2004).
[5] *Id.*
[6] *Id.*

the United States to consider three or more qualified experts before making a final retention determination.[7]

In some cases, IRS specialists may serve as expert witnesses. In those instances, the government attorney "must be satisfied that he/she can minimize allegations of bias against the Service specialist."[8] The I.R.M. further counsels that it may be appropriate to hire a third-party expert witness rather than a specialist of the IRS where theoretical or particularly complex matters are involved.[9] Finally, employees of the IRS's Office of Appeals ("Appeals") may be used as expert witnesses only when no other qualified IRS employee is available.[10]

INTERNAL IRS VALUATION EXPERTS

The IRS employs specialists who sometimes serve as government expert witnesses as well. Generally these governmental experts work in one of three programs: the IRS Engineering Program; the Economist Program; or the Art Appraisal Service.

The IRS Engineering Program provides support for complex engineering and valuation issues to all IRS governmental organizations that examine tax returns, as well as non-examination governmental organizations.[11] For example, these government engineers provide assistance to non-examination organizations such as Appeals, the Office of Chief Counsel, the IRS's Criminal Investigations division, and the U.S. Department of Justice by providing expert advice, expert reports, and expert testimony as required.[12] Such assistance includes valuation of business interests, valuation of intangibles, and appraisals of tangible property. Organizationally, the Engineering Program consists of a national program manager, territory managers, and teams. As of 2006, there were approximately 300 IRS Engineers allocated among 30 teams located across the United States.[13]

---

[7]*Id.*
[8]*Id.*
[9]*Id.*
[10]*Id.* pt. 8.1.1.5.3 (Feb. 10, 2012).
[11]*Id.*, pt. 4.48.1.1 (May 1, 2006). In audits involving corporate valuation issues, the I.R.M. instructs that an examiner should, at a minimum, consult with an engineer "to determine if the underlying asset valuations and discounts applied are reasonable...." *Id.*, pt. 4.25.12.1.4 (Jan. 6, 2014). In addition, examiners are encouraged to refer cases to the Engineering Program where real property assets are valued at over $500,000. *Id.*
[12]*Id.*, pt. 4.48.1 (May 1, 2006).
[13]Previously available information indicated that IRS Engineers were assigned to the following locations:

Territory			
Plantation, FL	**Pittsburgh, PA**	**San Francisco, CA**	**Bloomington, MN**
Jacksonville, FL	New York, NY	Los Angeles, CA	Houston, TX
Atlanta, GA	Mountainside, NJ	Laguna Niguel, CA	Wichita, KS
Plantation, FL	King of Prussia, NJ	Seattle, WA	Farmers Branch, TX
Nashville, TN	Stoneham, MA	Denver, CO	Birmingham, AL
Baltimore, MD	New Haven, CT	San Francisco, CA	Brooklyn Center, MN
Chicago, IL	Pittsburgh, PA	Phoenix, AZ	Waukesha, WI

The Economist Program provides assistance to IRS personnel in addressing the economics underlying various tax issues, particularly those involving international cases.[14] Such economic issues involve the value of closely held stock and closely held businesses, arm's-length pricing of goods and services, valuation of intangible assets, value of partnership interests, and value and validity of certain types of financial and legal arrangements, among other issues. As with engineers, expert economists are assigned to teams located nationwide. As noted, these governmental economists may also serve as expert witnesses.[15]

The Art Appraisal Service ("AAS") provides advice and assistance to the IRS on valuation questions regarding works of art. The AAS also manages the Commissioner's Art Advisory Panel.[16] The details of the AAS's duties are set forth in part 4.48.2.1 of the I.R.M., but some background may be useful. The Art Advisory Panel is a group of "nationally prominent art museum directors, curators, scholars, art dealers, auction representatives, and appraisers" who aid the IRS in its review of cases involving the valuation of art objects.[17] The Art Advisory Panel members initially make recommendations regarding the acceptability of reported values on the basis of taxpayer-provided documentation. If the claimed values are deemed unacceptable to the IRS, panelists may make alternative value recommendations. While these recommendations are merely advisory, once reviewed by the AAS, they become the IRS's position.[18] IRS employees are required to refer cases that involve art appraisals of $50,000 or more to AAS.[19] AAS appraisers may also provide assistance with the valuation of artwork valued at under $50,000, as well as artwork not referred to the Art Advisory Panel.[20] Upon request, AAS appraisers may provide further assistance by preparing an expert report and testifying as an expert witness.[21]

Under IRS policy, "examiners should refer relevant cases with appraisals above certain thresholds to Engineering and AAS appraisers for assistance."[22] For example, examiners must refer "corporate returns with assets worth $10 million or more, and partnership returns with 11 or more partners and gross deductions greater than $1 million to Engineering."[23] In addition, "examiners should refer income tax returns with a valuation issue of $500,000 or more, and estate and gift tax returns with assets valued at $500,000 or more, or with a total tax of $1 million or more, to Engineering."[24] At a minimum, gift and estate tax examiners must "consult with Engineering for assistance in determining the accuracy of appraised values" for examinations focusing on appraisal issues.[25] Also, examiners must

---

[14] *Id.* 4.49.1.1 (Nov. 3, 2006).

[15] *Id.* pt. 4.49.1.4 (Nov. 3, 2006).

[16] *Id.* pt. 4.48.2.1 (Oct. 1, 2012). The Office of Art Appraisal Services is located in the Appeals Headquarters Office in Washington, D.C. *See id.* pt. 4.25.12 (Jan. 6, 2014).

[17] *Id.* pt. 4.48.2.1.1 (Oct. 1, 2012).

[18] *Id.*

[19] *Id.* pt. 4.48.2.2 (Oct. 1, 2012).

[20] *Id.*

[21] *Id.* pt. 4.48.2.1.1 (Oct. 1, 2012).

[22] U.S. Gov't Accountability Office, GAO-12-608, *Appraised Values on Tax Returns: Burdens on Taxpayers Could Be Reduced and Selected Practices Improved* 15 (2012).

[23] *Id.* at 15, n.27.

[24] *Id.*

[25] *Id.* at 15.

"refer all cases selected for examination with art valued at $50,000 or more to AAS for review."[26] Finally, examiners are encouraged to request assistance from Engineering and AAS for cases that do not require mandatory referral, if valuation assistance may be appropriate.[27]

IRS Hiring, Training, and Evaluation of Internal Valuation Experts

To ensure the quality of its valuation programs and of its valuation experts, the IRS has implemented certain requirements for its hiring, training, and evaluation and oversight.[28]

Hiring   When the IRS Engineering Program hires appraisers, the qualifications listed in the job description specifically require applicants to have appraisal and valuation skills.[29] As an example, the job description may require applicants to have a "mastery of appraisal principles and concepts needed to serve as a technical authority." The hiring process is comprised of a combination of personal review and automated scoring. Initially, the automated Career Connector scoring system assesses the applicants' qualifications. The IRS then hires its appraisers from among the pool of qualified applicants. The appraiser hiring process and required qualifications are similar for Engineering and AAS.

Training   In its review of the IRS Engineering and AAS training procedures, the Government Accountability Office (GAO) found that:

> [The] IRS maintains a formal training program for its Engineering appraisers that starts with new hires and continues with advanced, specialized training, including training on appraisal skills.... The IRM specifies two appraisal organizations—the American Society of Appraisers and the Appraisal Institute—that may offer acceptable continuing education. LB&I [the Large Business and International Division] has brought in trainers for some courses and maintains a budget for engineers to seek outside training....[30]

The Office of Appeals requires its employees, including AAS staff, to complete 24 to 40 hours of continuing education every year.[31] However, appraisal skills are not explicitly identified as a training subject and the "training guidance does not mention any relevant skills that appraisers must maintain, leaving the possibility that appraisers are not keeping up their skills...."[32]

---

[26] *Id.* at 15, n.27.
[27] *Id.* at 15.
[28] *See id.* at 16–20.
[29] *Id.* at 17.
[30] *Id.*
[31] *Id.*
[32] *Id.*

Performance Evaluation and Management Oversight   "LB&I uses an audit quality assurance system as part of its LB&I Quality Measurement System."[33] The quality assurance system evaluates engineers on four technical standards: (1) planning; (2) "inspecting and fact finding;" (3) "development, proposal, and resolution of issues"; and (4) workpapers and reports.[34] To conduct its quality assurance reviews:

> *LB&I randomly selects coordinated industry cases (CIC) and industry cases (IC). The results are reported in quarterly reports.... On a more routine basis, team managers are required to review case performance, including [the] technical aspects of an engineer's work....*
>
> *Appeals operates a case-review program called the Appeals Quality Measurement System (AQMS); however, most of the cases [on which] AAS works are not Appeals cases, and are [thus] not covered by this system.... Aside from AQMS, IRS guidance encourages examination offices to provide feedback on AAS's performance that "would be beneficial to the viability of this program." The AAS manager also reviews all cases that AAS completes before they are issued.*[35]

However, at the present time, the AAS review results are neither compiled nor tracked.[36]

IRS Use of Internal Valuation Expert Witnesses

Advantages to Using an Internal Valuation Expert as an Expert Witness   There are a number of potential advantages for the government to utilize an internal valuation expert as opposed to an outside expert. First, utilizing an internal valuation expert allows the IRS to avoid cumbersome competitive bidding procedures potentially required to retain an outside expert. Second, use of an internal expert may be significantly more cost-effective. Third, a valuation expert who has routinely been involved in the examination process may have more familiarity with the case and process and thus lead to better, more efficient thoughtful work product and trial preparation. In addition, these internal experts will likely have already prepared a report of findings and recommendations during the examination process, which can serve as the basis for an expert report.

The Inherent Bias Problem   Potential downsides also exist to using an employee valuation expert. Chief among them is the perceived lack of independence and objectivity of the witness. While the IRS's policy states that "[i]t is never appropriate to dictate to a proposed expert the opinion the expert is expected to render," the IRS may select or reject an expert based on the approach and the types of evidence the expert intends to use.[37] Moreover, a valuation expert's involvement in the examination process could further undermine her perceived objectivity.

---

[33] *Id.* at 18.
[34] *Id.*
[35] *Id.* at 18–19 (footnotes omitted).
[36] *Id.*
[37] I.R.M., pt. 35.4.4.8.1 (Aug. 11, 2014).

COURT REACTIONS TO GOVERNMENT EMPLOYEE EXPERT WITNESSES

A survey of federal tax cases shows that court reaction to government employee valuation experts varies widely. On one end of the spectrum, one court expressed dissatisfaction that the government did not utilize an IRS specialist as an expert witness in a reasonable compensation case, stating:

> *[W]hile there are highly competent experts and other qualified employees in the Internal Revenue Service, for some reason none of them was called as a witness.... [I]t seems to this court that, once the taxpayer has produced substantial evidence in favor of such reasonableness, especially in a case involving so difficult and technical a question as this one, some qualified member of the Internal Revenue Staff should be called as a witness to inform the court fully as to the actual reasons which in fact impelled to government to make its findings....*[38]

On the other end of the spectrum, some courts have questioned the impartiality of valuation experts who are employees of the IRS. For example, in a case involving the valuation of corporate stock, one court expressed concern that the Commissioner's expert "might be biased because he was a full-time employee of the Commissioner."[39] Another court, in a case involving the valuation of tangible property, concluded that the Commissioner's expert "may not have been altogether disinterested."[40] The majority of courts, however, show little interest in whether the government's expert witness is an employee of the IRS. These courts credit both parties' expert witnesses based on the quality of the testimony, the correctness of the valuation approach, the reasonableness of the data relied upon, the thoroughness of the expert's analysis, and the expert's credentials and experience.

The quality of expert testimony varies drastically among IRS internal specialists and non-internal IRS experts. Many courts have been openly critical of certain government employee expert witnesses; for example, one court went as far as to call the government's witness a "so-called expert."[41] In that case, the government's expert determined the fair rental value of a property based solely on a purchase price and fair market value given to him; indeed this expert never even visited the property and had no experience with the area in which the property was located. In another case, where the value of a reversionary interest in a trust depended on the life expectancy of both the settlor decedent and the trust beneficiary, the court rejected the valuation approach utilized by the government expert, which determined life expectancy based solely on a United States Life Table, and further credited the approach utilized by the taxpayer's expert who took into account an abundance of medical testimony.[42] Finally, in a case involving the valuation of donated gravesites, the court rejected the

---

[38] *Capitol Market, Ltd. v. United States*, 207 F. Supp. 376, 382 (D. Haw. 1962).

[39] *Kaufman v. Comm'r*, 77 T.C.M. (CCH) 1779, 1785 (1999), *rev'd on other grounds sub. nom. Morrissey v. Comm'r*, 243 F.3d 1145 (9th Cir. 2001).

[40] *Black Indus., Inc. v. Comm'r*, 38 T.C.M. (CCH) 242, 255 (1979).

[41] *Sherman Concrete Pipe, Co. v. United States*, No. 3542, 1978 WL 4511, at *2 (M.D. Tenn. 1978).

[42] *Hall v. United States*, 353 F.2d 500 (7th Cir. 1965).

resale-based valuation method utilized by the government's expert because the actual market involved sales to individuals purchasing for their personal use.[43]

In contrast, where the IRS employee is well-qualified and produces credible, reliable opinions based upon a sound methodology, courts often adopt the expert's valuation without modification. For example, in a case involving a casualty loss determination, the Tax Court accepted, in its totality, the loss amount set forth by the Commissioner's expert because his analysis of comparable sales controlled for the size of the damaged areas and his opinion "was based on more data and more thoroughly explained."[44]

In another case, the Tax Court accepted the Commissioner's expert's valuation of fruit inventories without modification where the court was favorably impressed with the "witness's expertise and the logic of his testimony," the expert's approach was reasonable, and the expert's opinion was "arrived at through a well-thought-out and sensible process of appraisal."[45] And in a case where neither expert was particularly persuasive, the Tax Court, nonetheless, adopted the valuation of the Commissioner's expert witness even though he was "unable to provide a satisfactory explanation" for the treatment of certain items and the court "fail[ed] to follow the reasoning and logic of [his] method."[46] Compare these results, however, to a stock valuation case in which the Tax Court adopted the valuation methodology of the Commissioner's expert but adopted the discount for lack of marketability and control of the taxpayer's expert.[47]

Courts seem more resistant to adopting taxpayer valuations in their entirety, even where they find the taxpayer's expert to be credible. For example, in a case involving the valuation of corporate shares, the Tax Court found the capitalization of earnings method of valuation used by the taxpayer's expert to be more appropriate than the underlying assets method of valuation used by the government's expert, because the company was "clearly an operating company."[48] However, despite speaking favorably of the taxpayer's expert's methodology, the court found the value of the stock to be $300 per share, which was greater than the taxpayer's valuation of $216 per share.

In another case involving a dispute over which portion of a hotel's value was allocable to land as opposed to the hotel building, the Tax Court faulted the Commissioner's expert for not making a physical examination of the property and credited the taxpayer's expert for making a "careful survey of all the property and a visual appraisal of each class of assets."[49] Nonetheless, the court found the value of the land to be $1,505,900, closer to the government's expert's appraisal of $1,642,800 than the taxpayer's expert's appraisal at $608,777. Compare this result, however, to a case involving the valuation of gas wells, where the court adopted the appraisal of the taxpayer's expert in totality because of his "wealth of experience in the oil and gas industry" and because the approach utilized by the Commissioner's expert did

---

[43] *Weiss v. Comm'r*, 65 T.C.M. (CCH) 2768 (1993).

[44] *Goodfriend v. Comm'r*, 52 T.C.M. (CCH) 845, 850 (1986).

[45] *Zeropack Co. v. Comm'r*, 47 T.C.M. (CCH) 181, 189 (1983).

[46] *Oughton v. Comm'r*, 67 T.C.M. (CCH) 2271, 2276-77 (1994).

[47] *Gow v. Comm'r*, 79 T.C.M. (CCH) 1680 (2000).

[48] *Estate of Kirkpatrick v. Comm'r*, 34 T.C.M. (CCH) 1490, 1499-1500 (1975).

[49] *Raleigh Props., Inc. v. Comm'r*, 21 T.C.M. (CCH) 812, 818 (1962).

"not compare, from the standpoint of accuracy, with the ... approach employed by [the taxpayer's] witness."[50]

GOVERNMENT'S DECISION TO NOT PRESENT AN EXPERT WITNESS

The Commissioner is not obligated to produce an expert witness to offer an independent valuation of the property in question. Instead, as noted earlier, the Commissioner may choose to produce no expert or to produce an expert witness only to discredit the valuation methods employed by the taxpayer's expert. Some courts have not received this tactic favorably.

In *Dunn v. Commissioner*,[51] the primary issue was valuation of stock in a closely held corporation. At trial, the taxpayer produced an expert witness who prepared a report estimating the fair market value of the stock. The Commissioner's witness did not offer her own valuation of the stock. Instead, she criticized the techniques employed by the taxpayer's expert. The Tax Court agreed with the Commissioner that the valuation method used by the taxpayer's expert was improper and arrived at its own valuation using the method it found to be most appropriate. The taxpayer appealed the case. On appeal, the Court of Appeals for the Fifth Circuit held that the Tax Court "erred as a matter of law" with respect to its valuation of the property and that the Commissioner engaged in "guerilla warfare, presenting only an *accounting* expert to snipe at the methodology of the Estate's *valuation* expert."[52] The Fifth Circuit stressed that the Commissioner had the burden of proof for his proposed higher valuation and "his posture at trial is seen to be so extreme and so far removed from reality as to be totally lacking in probative value." The Court of Appeals then remanded the case back to the Tax Court and instructed the Tax Court to entertain any possible claims by the taxpayer for litigation costs.

In another case, *Estate of Elkins v. Commissioner*,[53] the Commissioner challenged the taxpayer's valuation of undivided, fractional interests in various pieces of art. At trial, the taxpayer produced three expert witnesses who proposed values for the fractional interest. The Commissioner's experts did not propose their own independent values for the assets. The Tax Court held that the analysis employed by both sets of experts was lacking and arrived at its own valuation figure. The taxpayer appealed the case to the Fifth Circuit. Although the Fifth Circuit Court of Appeals agreed with a portion of the Tax Court's determination, it found that the Tax Court erred in not shifting the burden of proof from the taxpayer to the Commissioner where the taxpayer produced "a plethora of credible and highly probative evidence" concerning various valuation discounts and the Commissioner "chose not to adduce any evidence ... whatsoever."[54] The Fifth Circuit concluded that the Tax

---

[50]*McAlpin v. United States*, No. EC81-156-LS-P, 1982 WL 1714, at *2-3 (N.D. Miss. Aug. 27, 1982).
[51]*Dunn v. Comm'r*, T.C. Memo. 2000-12, 79 T.C.M. (CCH) 1337 (2000), *rev'd and remanded*, *Dunn v. Comm'r*, 301 F.3d 339 (5th Cir. 2002).
[52]*Dunn v. Comm'r*, 301 F.3d 339, 342, 349 (5th Cir. 2002) (emphasis in original).
[53]*Estate of Elkins v. Comm'r*, 140 T.C. 86 (2013), *rev'd in part*, 767 F.3d 443 (5th Cir. 2014).
[54]*Estate of Elkins v. Comm'r*, 767 F.3d 443, 449-450 (5th Cir. 2014), *rev'g in part*, 140 T.C. 86 (2013).

Court should have accepted the taxpayer's valuation discounts as a result of the Commissioner's failure to contest them.

CONCLUSION

IRS employee-specialists have long been utilized as government expert witnesses and will likely continue to be utilized for the foreseeable future. Although a few courts have questioned the impartiality of these experts, most courts have been receptive to their role as expert witnesses. As the cases reviewed illustrate, the quality of IRS valuation specialists varies greatly. However, these cases also demonstrate that IRS valuation specialists can greatly increase their credibility and usefulness to the court by using reliable data, utilizing the most accurate valuation approach available, and being detailed and thorough in their analysis. Due to concerns of bias by virtue of their being employed by the government, the specialists' credibility needs to be well-established. Whether for a government expert or a taxpayer expert, the next chapter details the practicalities involved in expert selection and preparation.

CHAPTER 6

The Practicalities of Selection and Preparation of Experts

SUMMARY

In valuation controversies, credible, relevant, and reliable expert testimony is often the cornerstone of a successful outcome. Not surprisingly, retaining an unprepared and unqualified expert can be disastrous. As a result, clients and their counsel must seek out and retain highly capable experts who will bring persuasive, thoughtful believability to the litigation process. Lawyers hiring and preparing experts should be especially vigilant since attorneys have been found liable for malpractice in retaining an expert witness who was found not qualified to offer the necessary opinions for a client.[1]

This chapter provides a practical approach to retaining, preparing, and presenting expert witnesses at depositions, hearings, and trials. Following this approach can assist in avoiding the presentation of unsuccessful weak testimony and the prevention of the devastating consequence of having one's expert excluded from testifying at trial.

SELECTING AN APPRAISER

One of the most critical decisions a client and lawyer make in a valuation case is the selection of an expert appraiser. This expert, if properly trained and prepared, can provide the necessary critical persuasive testimony that can dramatically assist in a decision favorable to the client. When hiring a qualified expert appraiser, the following ten simple truths should always be followed:

1. Start early and allow sufficient time to select the appropriate needed experts;
2. Refrain from hiring experts based solely upon referrals, telephone conversations, or email communications; instead endeavor to meet each expert in person before deciding to hire and disclose this expert;

---

[1] *See, e.g., Quad City Bank & Trust v. Elderkin & Pirnie, P.L.C.*, 863 N.W.2d 35 (Iowa Ct. Appeals 2015) (upholding a jury's verdict that a law firm committed malpractice when, in addition to other errors, the law firm retained a witness who "was not qualified to offer the necessary opinions in the [] lawsuit").

3. Refrain from convincing the hired expert to render opinions outside of her expertise;
4. The expert must be competent by skill, education, and/or training to render the requested value analysis;
5. The expert must conduct a thorough review of the relevant literature, documentation, testimony, and other information to properly formulate her opinions;
6. The expert's analysis and preparation must be thoroughly thought out and complete;
7. The expert must provide opinions that are helpful to the trier of fact in comprehending the submitted evidence or determining a fact in issue;
8. The expert must offer only relevant and reliable analysis and opinions consistent with Rule 702 of the Federal Rules of Evidence and *Daubert v. Merrell Dow Pharmaceuticals, Inc.*[2] (explained in detail in Chapter 7, *From* Daubert *to* Boltar);
9. The expert appraiser must avoid being an overzealous advocate and instead present herself as a believable nonpartisan person presenting thoughtful, independent expertise to the court and the trier of fact; and
10. The expert appraiser must be a good communicator both in writing and orally.

Education, Training, Professional Experience, and Accrediting Organization Participation

It is imperative to hire experts that have the necessary education, knowledge, training, experience, and other skills in the valuation industry. The expert's skills should fit the particular issues in the case. The selected expert should have detailed knowledge and skills commensurate with the actual valuation task at hand, not simply general valuation industry knowledge. Her detailed knowledge must include a thorough understanding of the valuation model to be utilized, as well as knowledge of all other relevant factors such as industry environment and pertinent economic data.

The expert's education, training, and credentials are also important. In other words, ask whether the potential expert has the necessary background to perform a reliable appraisal. Greater technical involvement in the profession, such as writing books and articles, teaching, speaking at professional meetings, and providing testimony, may enhance an expert's credentials and reliability. If the appraiser has any honors and awards bestowed by colleagues, these are additional positive expert attributes.

Whether the potential expert is a member of, or accredited by, one or more recognized appraisal organizations are additional factors to consider. There are a variety of organizations that offer accreditations in valuation in the United States. It is desirable to select an appraiser with an accreditation from one or more of these organizations, especially if the assignment may involve litigation.

The American Society of Appraisers   The American Society of Appraisers ("ASA") is an interdisciplinary organization, offering designations in appraisal of businesses,

---

[2]*Daubert v. Merrell Dow Pharmaceuticals, Inc.*, 509 U.S. 597 (1993).

real estate, machinery and equipment, personal property, and gems and jewelry. The ASA's designations are:

- A.M., Accredited Member, which requires two years' experience;
- A.S.A., Accredited Senior Member, which requires five years' experience; and
- FASA, Member of the College of Fellows, the highest designation, awarded to only a little over 50 members among all disciplines.

The Appraisal Institute   The Appraisal Institute (sometimes, "AI") is a global professional association of real estate appraisers that promotes the highest standards of practice through its designation programs, peer review process, education, and research and publishing endeavors. The AI's designations are:

- MAI, Member of the Appraisal Institute, which is awarded to appraisers with experience in the valuation of commercial, industrial, agricultural, residential, and vacant land properties, as well as to valuators who advise clients on real estate investment decisions;
- SRPA, Senior Real Property Appraiser, which is awarded to appraisers with experience in the valuation of commercial, industrial, agricultural, residential, and vacant land properties;
- SRA, Senior Residential Appraiser, which is awarded to appraisers with experience in the valuation of single family homes, townhouses, and residential income properties of up to four units;
- AI-GRS, Appraisal Institute, General Review Specialist, which is awarded to appraisers who can review appraisals of commercial, industrial, agricultural, residential, and vacant land properties;
- AI-RRS, Appraisal Institute, Residential Review Specialist, which is awarded to appraisers who can review appraisals of residential properties;
- SREA, Senior Real Estate Analyst, which is held by appraisers who are experienced in real estate appraisals, real estate analysis, and advising clients on real estate investment decisions; and
- RM, Residential Member, which is held by appraisers who are experienced in the valuation of single- and multifamily properties.

Each designation requires the valuator to possess varying types of specialized experience, to hold certain education requirements, and to pass a variety of examinations.

The Institute of Business Appraisers   The Institute of Business Appraisers ("IBA") is the oldest professional society devoted solely to the appraisal of closely held businesses. The IBA's designations are:

- CBA, Certified Business Appraiser, which requires that the appraiser have at least five years' experience, at least 90 hours of appraisal education, pass an examination, and submit two appraisal reports for peer review; and
- MCBA, Master Certified Business Appraiser, which is a designation conferred on recommendation by peers and based on achievements.

The National Association of Valuers and Analysts   The National Association of Valuers and Analysts ("NACVA") is a business appraisal training and accrediting organization. NACVA's primary designations are:

- CVA, Certified Valuation Analyst, the organization's primary designation; and
- ABAR, Accredited in Business Appraisal Review.

NACVA also owns the IBA, listed previously.

The American Institute of Certified Public Accountants   The American Institute of Certified Public Accountants ("AICPA") offers the designation of CPA, which is an accounting credential, the curriculum and exams for which contain *nothing* regarding appraisals of *anything*. The organization offers training in business valuation, and a small percentage of CPAs have successfully completed this training and earned the designation "Accredited in Business Valuation" CPA/ABV, which is awarded to certain certified public accountants who specialize in business valuation.

It is also important to determine the expert's hands-on experience, both in the particular valuation methodology to be used, as well as in the valuation industry in general.

Being a Good Communicator

One of the most important characteristics of a good appraiser is that she be an excellent communicator, both in writing and orally. Lawyers and clients should therefore be diligent in selecting an expert who can effectively communicate complex issues in a simple, straightforward, persuasive manner that can be readily understood by the trier of fact. Finding well-seasoned experts who have already gone through the rigorous trial and pretrial process is also a positive.

Most appraisal companies are willing to provide redacted report and testimony examples so attorneys can assess the potential expert's written and oral skills. Likewise, appraisers and their companies usually have a list of references for cases in which they have either testified or played a major role in settling, for assessment of their skills.

Offering a Neutral, Detached Opinion of Value

Recall from Chapter 3, *Qualified Appraiser*, that an appraisal report will not be considered prepared by a "qualified appraiser" if the report is authored by a valuator who is interested in the valuation (e.g., the donor or donee of the property or any person employed by the donor or the donee). The same is true for expert reports procured in connection with litigation. Thus, practitioners should select as an expert a person who is neutrally detached from the property and transaction at issue so as to offer an unbiased opinion of value.

Avoiding the Bias Perception   In any case, if possible, an appraiser who has "walked both sides of the street" should be retained. For example, in an estate or gift tax case, it is best to select an appraiser who has been retained both by the IRS and by taxpayers. In a dissenting stockholder case, it is best to select an appraiser who has been retained both by dissenters and by companies defending against such dissent lawsuits. In marital dissolution matters, it is desirable to select an appraiser who has been retained both by the spouse operating the business as well as by the non-operating spouse. Hiring this type of expert enhances her credibility since it can be shown that both sides have trusted this person to come up with a proper valuation in the past.

The reverse is also true. Experts who are perceived to be aligned with one side of a dispute in all matters can detract from this person's credibility. The following quote from a recent case illustrates this point:

> *The court accepted Hanlon as an expert appraiser of partial interests in property but evaluated his testimony with some skepticism given his "closeness to [the Trust] and the singularity of his experience in valuing façade easements for clients and for a patron all interested in establishing high values for the easements." ... The court ultimately rejected Hanlon's methodology and assumptions as unsupported and unreliable.[3]*

Selecting the Expert Who Prepared the Appraisal That Supports the Tax Reporting Position

Practitioners may want to select as the party's expert at trial (or one of a few trial experts) the valuator who prepared the appraisal report to support a tax reporting position, such as the author of a qualified appraisal. This practice may benefit the client's litigation position to the extent the valuator's opinions at trial are consistent with her opinions in the report used to support the tax reporting position. However, to the extent there are variations between the appraisal used to support the tax reporting position and the appraisal used in litigation, this inconsistency will be ripe for cross-examination and may impugn the expert's credibility.

Early and Significant Appraiser Involvement

A best practice is to hire the necessary experts as early in the client interaction as possible. As the case progresses and the issues become more focused, the relative roles of each expert will become clearer. For example, perhaps one expert may testify on industry conditions and unique factors in the industry that bears on valuation; another may present the valuation. Having experts involved early in the process gives the flexibility to develop a case that will persuade the court and trier of fact. If the attorney provides the expert appraiser time to develop a thorough command of the relevant documentation, data, and other information, she may be able to advance the case in a variety of ways through the lifecycle of a case:

- Assist the lawyer in reviewing the relevant valuation documents and literature;
- Participate in the pretrial stages of litigation, including the deposition and document discovery planning;
- Assist the attorney with preparation for the deposition of the opposing party's expert;

---

[3] *Kaufman v. Comm'r*, 784 F.3d 56, 63-64 (1st Cir. 2015). [Internal citations omitted].

- Attend the deposition of the opposing party's expert and assist when needed;
- Work closely with counsel to prepare for any *Daubert* challenges (as more fully discussed in Chapter 7, *From* Daubert *to* Boltar); and
- Work closely with counsel to create an effective trial testimony presentation, including thoughtful, informative visual aids.

Appraiser Scheduling and Availability

The expert appraiser should coordinate scheduling with the attorney for all document reviews, depositions, hearings, and trial attendance. The appraiser should also communicate to the lawyer any dates that she may be unavailable, preferably in writing, and should promptly inform counsel of any changes in availability. This may seem obvious but it is important to stress because a lack of communication can lead to major problems in the case—such as the expert not being available when needed.

Correcting Errors in the Expert's Report

Sometimes expert appraisers make errors, both major and minor ones. It is important to avoid these errors as much as possible. Giving the expert ample time to do her analysis and construct her report will minimize these errors. However, if an error has been identified in the expert's report prior to trial, it should be corrected and pointed out to opposing counsel and the court (if already filed) as soon as practicable, before trial or even during trial if it is already underway when the error is found.

"Skeletons in the Closet"

Experts with significant problems in their background should be avoided. Attorneys should perform due diligence to discover any skeletons in the closet. Problematic items in a prospective expert appraiser's history include, but are not necessarily limited to:

- Prior court criticism of her valuation methodology;
- Previous exclusions of her valuation testimony from trial;
- Professional discipline;
- Involvement in wrongful conduct; and
- Any past testimony or written material that may conflict with her anticipated testimony in the present case.

Acquainting the Expert with the Cast of Characters and Venue

The expert should be informed about both the judge and the opposing attorney, including their style and skills and, with regard to the opposing attorney, preferred tactics. The expert witness may be told the kinds of questions to expect from the opposing attorney. Counsel is responsible for apprising the expert of the rules of the particular court or venue. This includes any restrictions on the expert's communications with attorneys or others.

Attorney Comprehension of Expert Opinions

The expert should help the attorney to understand her opinions and the rationale for them almost as well as the expert. This is to facilitate the attorney's ability to do the most effective direct examination, and to be able to identify important redirect questioning. This will also assist the attorney in cross-examining the other party's expert.

Planning the Testimony

The expert appraiser should go over, in detail, the opposing expert's report with the attorney and identify the dollar value of the most important differences between the parties' positions and the reasons for the differences. The differences may be attributable to either legal issues (e.g., interpretation of the meaning of an applicable statute) or valuation issues. To the extent that the differences are clearly attributable to legal issues, it is perfectly appropriate for the expert to say "I handled it this way on the advice of counsel." To the extent that the differences are valuation issues, it is incumbent on the expert to build the strongest possible case in defense of her position and in opposition to the opponent's position.

An expert must remember at all times that she is an advocate for her position, not an advocate for the client. The expert's responsibility is to educate the court and to convince the court of the merits of her position without regard to advocacy for the client. However, beware the opposing attorney's tendency to paint the expert with the taint of advocacy.

Sometimes there is a blur between whether the disagreement is a legal issue or a valuation issue. In these cases the expert and the attorney should discuss the best way to handle the issue. If the expert has opinions, he or she should express them, but the attorney should make the final decision.

In general, most of the expert's time should be spent on the largest dollar issues. Sometimes, however, additional time must be allocated to issues that are more controversial, regardless of dollar value. Also, some issues may be more complicated than others, and enough time needs to be spent to ensure that the judge understands the complicated issues. Remember, the judge is not necessarily a valuation expert.

Often it is possible to anticipate one or more of the opposition's major positions. In these cases, an effective technique may be to build the rebuttal to these positions into the direct testimony.

It is important that the expert be both convincing and likable. To this end, the witness must not allow the opposing attorney to bait her into an argument.

EXPERT TESTIMONY PREPARATION

The attorney and the expert should rehearse the entire direct examination and expected cross-examination at least once, and ideally, multiples times. During trial is not the time for surprises. Even the best expert can be thrown off-guard by an unexpected question or by a question he or she does not understand. The attorney should coach the witness ahead of time on style and warn the witness about traps the opposing attorney might set.

CONCLUSION

Deciding which expert appraiser to retain is one of the most important choices a client and her attorney can make in a valuation case or controversy. This testifying expert should be able to, in writing and orally, present to the court and the trier of fact a straightforward, non-argumentative, and persuasive explanation of the client's proposed valuation determination. A poorly trained or unprepared expert can and often does have disastrous consequences.

CHAPTER 7

From *Daubert* to *Boltar*

SUMMARY

Modern tax cases, particularly those in which valuation is at issue, are frequently decided on the basis of expert witness testimony. Valuation experts are generally aware that their testimony is subject to challenge by the opposing party under the United States Supreme Court's decision in *Daubert v. Merrell Dow Pharmaceuticals, Inc.*[1] However, many valuation experts are unaware of the detailed legal and practical mandates of *Daubert* and its progeny, and how such requirements affect the admissibility of the expert's written report and direct testimony in federal courts, specifically in the Tax Court. This chapter addresses these key questions and provides readers with a framework for analyzing, developing, and defending against *Daubert* challenges on numerous grounds.

This chapter begins with an overview of the standards of admissibility for expert witness testimony in federal courts as required by the Federal Rules of Evidence. Next, this chapter highlights the factors identified by *Daubert* and its progeny that impact the admissibility of expert witness testimony, providing a historical sample of cases in which *Daubert* challenges were made and decided. Last, this chapter examines the Tax Court's decision in *Boltar, L.L.C. v. Commissioner*,[2] which evidences the Tax Court's critical thinking and criteria used to exclude unreasonable and/or unreliable expert witness testimony from evidence.

STANDARD OF ADMISSIBILITY FOR EXPERT WITNESS TESTIMONY—THE FEDERAL RULES OF EVIDENCE

Tax litigation in the United States features three types of witnesses: lay witnesses, summary witnesses, and expert witnesses. Lay witnesses, or fact witnesses as they are sometimes called, testify on matters about which they have direct personal knowledge. Summary witnesses are fact witnesses whose testimonies are used to efficiently and effectively present voluminous and complex data. A lay witness may only give opinion testimony that is rationally based on her perception.[3] In contrast, expert witnesses may testify without personal knowledge and may give opinions on matters

---

[1] *Daubert v. Merrell Dow Pharm., Inc.*, 509 U.S. 579 (1993).
[2] *Boltar, L.L.C. v. Comm'r*, 136 T.C. 326 (2011).
[3] *Fed. R. Evid.* 701.

in which they possess scientific, technical, or other specialized knowledge. Moreover, an expert's testimony can be based on inadmissible evidence as long as such evidence is the kind an expert in the particular field would reasonably rely upon.[4]

Rule 702 of the Federal Rules of Evidence provides the standards for the admissibility of expert testimony at trial, including Tax Court trials. In 2011, Rule 702 was amended in response to *Daubert* and the many cases then applying *Daubert*'s rationale. As such, Rule 702 now prescribes the following specific set of rules as to when an expert witness may testify:

> *A witness who is qualified as an expert by knowledge, skill, experience, training, or education may testify in the form of an opinion or otherwise if:*
>
> *(a) the expert's scientific, technical, or other specialized knowledge will help the trier of fact to understand the evidence or to determine a fact in issue;*
> *(b) the testimony is based on sufficient facts or data;*
> *(c) the testimony is the product of reliable principles and methods; and*
> *(d) the expert has reliably applied the principles and methods to the facts of the case.[5]*

Thus, Rule 702 recognizes the reality that modern cases are often problematic without the submission of specialized knowledge testimony given by expert witnesses.[6] Fundamental to the courts' determination of whether expert testimony should be permitted in any particular case is evaluating whether the proposed expert testimony will aid the trier of fact in comprehending the trial evidence or deciding a fact in issue.[7] Put simply, even the highest paid, most qualified expert will have her testimony excluded from trial if it is not helpful to the factfinder.

However, as a result of the court's decision in *Daubert*, Rule 702 of the Federal Rules of Evidence now recognizes that helpfulness and qualification by experience, skill, training, or education is by itself no longer sufficient. The testimony must also satisfy the mandates of Rule 702(b), (c), and (d).

DAUBERT AND ITS PROGENY IN COURTS OTHER THAN THE TAX COURT

Prior to the turn of the twentieth century, courts routinely required that admissible trial testimony be based upon firsthand knowledge and direct observation.[8] However, as litigation grew increasingly complex, industrious lawyers began convincing courts to allow for expert witness opinion testimony to supplement lay testimony.

With the advent of expert witness opinion testimony came new substantial trial risks; qualified experts were allowed to testify on the basis of circumstantial

---

[4]*Fed. R. Evid.* 703.
[5]*Fed. R. Evid.* 702.
[6]*Id.* advisory committee's note.
[7]*Id.*
[8]Frank A. Wisehart, *Why* Daubert *Matters When Giving Expert Testimony*, 16 *Valuation Strategies* 40 (2013).

evidence, third-party information, and the scientific methods the experts applied. Additionally, expert witnesses enjoyed a heightened level of perceived reliability that transcended that of lay witnesses in many material respects. Not surprisingly, as courts and juries increasingly relied upon expert opinions, experts often abandoned their duty of candor to the court in favor of advancing their respective client's litigation position.

Many trial courts were at an impasse as to how to determine which expert witnesses could and could not present evidence at trial. Indeed, evidentiary rulings varied substantially between jurisdictions, courts, and even judges. Against this backdrop, the District of Columbia Court of Appeals in 1923 decided *Frye v. United States.*[9] In *Frye*, the court analyzed whether expert evidence derived from a systolic blood pressure deception test, a crude precursor to the polygraph machine, should be admissible. In rejecting this testimony, the D.C. Circuit Court laid out a rather uncomplicated analysis. As long as the proposed expert testimony is "sufficiently established to have gained general acceptance in the particular field in which it belongs," then such testimony is admissible. Thus, with little fanfare, the general acceptance test for expert testimony admissibility was born and, as such, the federal common law abdicated the most crucial aspect of responsibility for expert admissibility determinations to the scientific community. This general acceptance test gained overwhelming approval in federal courts and some states that lasted for 70 years until 1993 when the Supreme Court rendered its landmark opinion in *Daubert v. Merrell Dow Pharmaceuticals, Inc.*[10]

Daubert, the seminal case on the admissibility of expert witness testimony, broadly affects the admissibility of all expert testimony in the federal court system. Under *Daubert*, the matter is no longer effectively punted to the scientific community under a general acceptance test, but instead the trial judge is now assigned an important and oftentimes difficult role as the gatekeeper for the admissibility of expert testimony.

We briefly recount the facts that informed the Supreme Court's decision in *Daubert*. From 1956 until 1983, the defendant, Merrell Dow Pharmaceuticals, Inc., manufactured Bendectin, a popular anti-nausea drug marketed and prescribed to pregnant women to combat morning sickness during pregnancy. Prenatal ingestion of Bendectin was suspected of causing human birth defects. The plaintiffs were two children who were born with serious birth defects allegedly caused by their respective mothers' ingestion of Bendectin during pregnancy. The children's parents joined them as plaintiffs. The plaintiffs offered the opinion testimony of eight expert witnesses, each of whom concluded that Bendectin could cause birth defects in humans. Significantly, these experts prepared and submitted scientific studies that were neither published nor subject to peer review. The defendant-pharmaceutical company offered expert testimony to refute the plaintiffs' claims; specifically, the defendant claimed that there had been no published reports linking Bendectin to human birth defects. The defendant moved for summary judgment on the basis of its experts' reports and argued that the plaintiffs' experts' reports were inadmissible as unreliable and generally not accepted by the scientific community.

---

[9]*Frye v. United States*, 54 App. D.C. 46 (D.C. Cir. 1923).
[10]*Daubert v. Merrell Dow Pharmaceuticals, Inc.*, 509 U.S. 579 (1993).

The trial court granted the defendant's motion for summary judgment and the U.S. Court of Appeals for the Ninth Circuit affirmed. The United States Supreme Court vacated and remanded the decision, holding that nothing in the then–newly enacted Federal Rules of Evidence mandated general acceptance in the scientific community as an absolute predicate for expert opinion testimony admissibility. With that, the Supreme Court did away with the *Frye* general acceptance test that had become entrenched in the federal common law for seven decades. In its decision, the Supreme Court relegated general acceptance to be considered only as one of many other factors the trial judge should consider when determining expert testimony admissibility.

The Supreme Court described the trial judge as a gatekeeper who must "ensure that any and all scientific testimony or evidence admitted is not only relevant, but reliable." In emphasizing the trial judge's important gatekeeping role, the Court noted that the trial judge must make a preliminary assessment as to whether the reasoning or methodology underlying the testimony is scientifically valid and whether the reasoning or methodology can be applied to the facts at issue. Although directing significant additional responsibilities to our trial judges, the Supreme Court left them with a nice pat on the back: "We are confident that federal judges possess the capacity to undertake this review." This confidence, however, was replaced a few years later by Justice Breyer's stern warning in his concurring opinion in *General Electric Co. v. Joiner*:

> "*Of course, neither the difficulty of the task nor any comparative lack of expertise can excuse the judge from exercising the "gatekeeper" duties that the Federal Rules [of Evidence] impose—determining, for example, whether particular expert testimony is reliable and "will assist the trier of fact.*"[11]

Daubert and its progeny establish the admissibility criteria for all expert testimony in federal courts. Restated in a more relevant way and consistent with Rule 702 of the Federal Rules of Evidence, a judge, when presented with a proffer of expert valuation testimony, should only allow such testimony based upon a finding that all five of the following requirements are satisfied:

- Such proposed expert testimony will assist the court to understand the evidence or to determine a fact in issue;
- Such proposed expert is qualified as an expert by knowledge, skill, experience, training, or education;
- Such proposed expert testimony is based upon sufficient facts or data;
- Such proposed expert testimony is the product of reliable principles and methods; and
- Such proposed expert has applied the principles and methods reliably to the facts of the case.

Much discretion is vested in our trial judges' *Daubert* determinations. In fact, the "path charting the judiciary's standards for admitting or excluding expert

---

[11] *Gen. Elec. Co. v. Joiner*, 522 U.S. 136, 148 (1997) (Breyer, J., concurring).

testimony—from the early *Frye* standard to *Kumho's* clarification of *Daubert*—has been a movement toward granting district judges greater discretion in making expert testimony determinations."[12] It is the trial judge's role to "determine whether expert testimony is essentially 'junk science' rather than testimony falling within the 'range where experts might reasonably differ.'"[13] Accordingly, lawyers, experts, and clients should understand that the real battleground for any litigant will (or at least should) take place at the *Daubert* pretrial hearing before the trial judge.

Of course, many factors will bear upon this trial judge's determination and the Supreme Court does not attempt to set out a definitive checklist of all factors to be considered by a trial judge when making her determination.[14] The *Daubert* Court does, however, articulate the following four pertinent factors to consider:

Factor 1: Whether the proposed theory or technique can and has been tested;

Factor 2: Whether the theory or technique "has been subjected to peer review and publication";

Factor 3: Whether there exists a known or potential rate of error for the theory or technique applied; and

Factor 4: Whether the theory or technique has gained general acceptance in the particular field in which it belongs.[15]

Approximately six years later, in *Kumho Tire Co. v. Carmichael*,[16] the Supreme Court extended *Daubert's* holding to apply not only to scientific testimony, but to all expert testimony that is based upon technical and other specialized knowledge. Thus, the reasoning in *Daubert* applies to all expert testimony based on "scientific, technical, or other specialized knowledge,"[17] which is offered to assist the trier of fact in understanding the evidence or determining a fact in issue. This would, of course, include expert valuation testimony.

In the years following *Daubert* and *Kumho Tire*, courts adopted a number of other factors that trial courts should consider in deciding whether to admit expert witness testimony. These additional factors are:

Factor 5: "[W]hether the experts are proposing to testify about matters growing naturally and directly out of research they have conducted independent of the litigation, or whether they have developed their opinions expressly for purposes of testifying;"[18]

Factor 6: Whether the expert has unjustifiably extrapolated from an accepted premise to an unfounded conclusion;[19]

---

[12]*Tamraz v. Lincoln Elec. Co.*, 620 F.3d 665, 681 (6th Cir. 2010).
[13]*Id.* at 681-82.
[14]*Daubert*, 509 U.S. at 593.
[15]*Id.* at 593–594.
[16]*Kumho Tire Co. v. Carmichael*, 526 U.S. 137 (1999).
[17]*Fed. R. Evid.* 702.
[18]*Daubert v. Merrell Dow Pharm., Inc.*, 43 F.3d 1311, 1317 (9th Cir. 1995).
[19]*See Gen. Elec. Co. v. Joiner*, 522 U.S. 136, 146 (1997).

Factor 7: Whether the expert has adequately accounted for obvious alternative explanations;[20]

Factor 8: Whether "the expert is being as careful as he would be in his regular professional work outside his paid litigation consulting";[21]

Factor 9: Whether the field of expertise claimed by the expert is known to reach reliable results for the type of opinion the expert would give;[22]

Factor 10: Whether the theory or method offered by the expert has been put to any non-judicial use;[23] and

Factor 11: Whether the expert's opinion fails to square with a judge's opinion and common sense.[24]

The *Daubert* analysis applies to both jury and non-jury trials in federal courts, including non-jury trials held before the Tax Court. No single factor is intended to be dispositive as to whether the expert testimony is admissible. Rather, the trial judge should evaluate each expert's opinion "practically and flexibly without bright-line exclusionary (or inclusionary) rules."[25] The "overarching subject" of any *Daubert* analysis is the validity of the expert's testimony and "thus the evidentiary relevance and reliability."[26] Therefore, the focus is upon the expert's "principles and methodology, not on the conclusions that they generate."[27] This chapter will examine each of the foregoing factors more fully, but before it does so, it first discusses the application of the *Daubert* factors in the Tax Court.

BOLTAR AS THE MODERN INCARNATION OF *DAUBERT* IN THE TAX COURT

Trials before the Tax Court are non-jury trials conducted in accordance with the Federal Rules of Evidence.[28] Tax Court judges, by virtue of the fact that they often hear cases involving complicated valuation, accounting, and finance issues, are especially likely to hear and rely upon an expert's specialized knowledge, experience, and training when deciding a case. However, litigants in tax controversy cases are not given the unfettered right to submit trial expert testimony. Indeed, as the Tax Court confirmed in *Boltar, L.L.C. v. Commissioner*,[29] denying experts the right to testify if they do not satisfy *Daubert* is both appropriate and necessary in Tax Court litigation.

At issue in *Boltar* was the valuation of a conservation easement restricting the use of roughly eight acres of land, of which approximately 2.82 acres were

---

[20] *See Claar v. Burlington N. R.R. Co.*, 29 F.3d 499, 502 (9th Cir. 1994).

[21] *Sheehan v. Daily Racing Form, Inc.*, 104 F.3d 940, 942 (7th Cir. 1997).

[22] *See Kumho Tire Co. v. Carmichael*, 526 U.S. 137, 151 (1999).

[23] *See Cabrera v. Cordis Corp.*, 134 F.3d 1418, 1420-21 (9th Cir. 1998).

[24] *Cowan v. Treetop Enters., Inc.*, 120 F. Supp. 2d 672, 683 (M.D. Tenn. 1999).

[25] *Heller v. Shaw Indus., Inc.*, 167 F.3d 146, 155 (3rd Cir. 1999).

[26] *Daubert v. Merrell Dow Pharm., Inc.*, 509 U.S. 579, 594-95 (1993).

[27] *Id.*

[28] *See* I.R.C. § 7453; *Tax Ct. R.* 143(a).

[29] *Boltar, L.L.C. v. Comm'r*, 136 T.C. 326 (2011).

designated forested wetlands that fell within the jurisdiction of the U.S. Army
Corps of Engineers. The taxpayer secured an appraisal that erroneously valued
the property as if it was under the jurisdiction of the municipality and as zoned
for a planned unit development. The IRS filed a pretrial motion with the Tax
Court to exclude the taxpayer's appraisal as unreliable and irrelevant. The Tax
Court initially deferred ruling on the motion "because of the importance of the
issues raised and the substantial effect on the case of eliminating [the taxpayer's]
primary evidence," and instead first focused upon whether *Daubert* would apply in
Tax Court trials.

The taxpayer asserted that *Daubert* mandates do not apply to Tax Court proceedings because there is no jury in such matters. The Tax Court disagreed, noting
that the gatekeeper function in bench trials "serves to increase the efficiency of trials" and preserve the objectivity of the Court's decisions. As such, the Tax Court
concluded that the principles expressed in *Daubert* controlled the admissibility of the
taxpayer's appraisal, and thereby, the outcome of the case. Moreover, the Tax Court
concluded that it "may fairly reject the burden on the parties and on the Court created
by unreasonable, unreliable, and irrelevant expert testimony" to, among other reasons, dissuade the "cottage industry of experts who function primarily in the market
for tax benefits."[30]

As *Boltar* makes clear, lawyers are well advised to challenge the opposing party's
expert witnesses under *Daubert*, and to prepare their own expert witnesses for a
vigorous *voir dire* under the standards as set forth in *Daubert*.[31] With the appropriateness of *Daubert* in all federal courts, including the Tax Court, firmly established,
this chapter next examines empirical evidence as to the prevalence of *Daubert* challenges. It then examines the various factors enumerated by the *Daubert* court and
the cases that followed.

DAUBERT CHALLENGES GENERALLY

Attorneys may move a court *in limine* to request a pretrial ruling as to the admissibility of any evidence, including an expert witness's written report in a Tax Court
matter. In addition, attorneys may *voir dire* a purported expert witness to probe
weaknesses in that witness' qualifications, possibly for the purpose of having the
expert disqualified from testifying before the court as an expert witness. Whether
taken individually or in the aggregate, these tactics are considered *Daubert* challenges
to the admissibility of the expert witness's testimony.

A trial court's discretion to accept or reject an expert's analysis in whole or in
part is broad, and as such, the battle for the admission or exclusion of expert witness
opinion testimony will be won or loss before the gatekeeper—the trial judge. The following section provides example cases in which *Daubert* challenges were made and
decided along with cites to empirical data referencing the likelihood of succeeding
on such challenges.

---

[30] *Id.* at 335–336.
[31] A *voir dire* is a preliminary examination of a prospective expert by a Judge or a lawyer to
decide whether the prospect is qualified and suitable to be recognized as an expert. *Black's
Law Dictionary* 1569 (7th ed. 1999).

Illustrations of *Daubert* Factors in Practice

In its ongoing study of *Daubert*, PricewaterhouseCoopers ("PwC") identified 12,533 *Daubert* expert witness challenges for the years 2000 through 2016.[32] Of these challenges, 2,200 were directed at excluding the trial testimony of financial experts, including attacks on the reliability of opinions rendered by financial analysts, business professors, accountants, appraisers, economists, and business consultants.[33] Also significant is that PwC documents that the number of *Daubert* challenges has significantly decreased from 2015 to 2016 and that over 50% of the financial expert witness *Daubert* challenges have resulted in complete or partial testimonial exclusion.[34]

The remainder of this chapter examines the factors that a trial judge may consider in a *Daubert* challenge in the context of a survey of reported cases. These factors may very well serve as the basis for a challenge to the admissibility of the expert witness's testimony under one or more of the factors enumerated in *Daubert* or its progeny. The reasoning behind the Court's decision with respect to each factor is included under the appropriate factor heading, and, in some instances, arises under multiple factors.

Factor 1: Has the theory or technique been tested?   The first factor the *Daubert* court enumerated was whether the theory or technique in question can be and in fact has been tested. This section summarizes example cases in which expert witness testimony was excluded from and admitted in evidence under this first factor.

Expert Testimony Excluded   In *Champagne Metals v. Ken-Mac Metals, Inc.*,[35] the Court excluded the plaintiff's expert's lost profit analysis in part because the technique had not been tested by others and there was no way the expert's method or technique could be tested. The expert's analysis was "based on his consideration of multiple factors, weighed and evaluated by him as a matter of professional judgment, but not otherwise disclosed." The expert acknowledged that there was no "formula or particular principle … which guided [the] analysis, though he did test his [damage estimates] in various ways." *This case was also decided on factor 4, 5, and 6 grounds and is included under each of those sections.*

In *James River Insurance Co. v. Rapid Funding, LLC*,[36] the Court found that the defendant's method could not be tested for accuracy or reliability. The expert's

---

[32]Doug Branch, Charles Reddin, and Saleema Damji, PwC, "Daubert Challenges to Financial Experts: A Yearly Study of Trends and Outcomes 2000–2016" (2017) [hereinafter "PwC Study"]. Several points should be noted regarding the PwC Study: first, the study does not address those cases where experts were used at trial and not challenged. Nor does the study state how many cases during the relevant period used financial experts. Second, the challenges studied were found in written opinions, and did not include challenges made by motions not reported in a published decision.

[33]*Id.*

[34]*Id.*

[35]*Champagne Metals v. Ken-Mac Metals, Inc.*, No. CIV-02-0528-HE, 2008 WL 5205204, at *11 (W.D. Okla. Dec. 11, 2008).

[36]*James River Ins. Co. v. Rapid Funding, LLC*, No. 07CV01146CMABNB, 2009 WL 481688, at *10 (D. Colo. Feb. 24, 2009).

pre-fire rehabilitation cost valuation was based on the expert's general feeling. That feeling was the only evidence in the record in support of the expert's cost calculation. *This case was also decided on factor 2, 4, and 6 grounds and is included under each of those sections.*

In *Kaufman v. Motorola, Inc.,*[37] the plaintiff brought a securities fraud class action against Motorola, Inc. The plaintiff's expert applied a "proportional trading model" to determine aggregate damages. Utilizing the proportional trading model, the expert multiplied the "alleged per share price differential by the aggregate number of shares that were 'damaged' by the alleged fraud." Both parties agreed that the appropriate test of reliability for an economic theory is to compare the test to reality. The expert acknowledged that the proportional trading model had never been tested against reality. In determining that the expert's testimony should be excluded from evidence, the Court found that not only did his method not meet the test of factor 1, but also that it did not meet "any of the *Daubert* standards." *This case was also decided on factor 4 grounds and is included under that section.*

In *Multimatic, Inc. v. Faurecia Interior Systems USA, Inc.,*[38] the Court excluded expert testimony in part for lack of testing. The plaintiff's expert made a ten-year lost-profit projection without providing historical data to support the projection. Moreover, the plaintiff's expert "made no effort" to test the model against historical data to assess the model's predictive power. The trial court excluded the evidence in part because the method had not been scientifically tested. The U.S. Court of Appeals for the Sixth Circuit affirmed the trial court's decision to exclude on those grounds. *This case was also decided on factor 4 and 6 grounds and is included under each of those sections.*

Factor 2: Has the theory or technique been subjected to peer review and publication?   The second factor the *Daubert* court listed was whether the theory or technique has been subjected to peer review and publication. The *Daubert* court stated that whether a theory or technique has been subjected to peer review and publication "is a pertinent consideration, but not an indispensable condition of admissibility" because the factor does not "necessarily correlate with reliability."[39] Indeed, there will be some cases where the utilized technique is too new, too particular, too innovative, or too specialized to have been published. However, peer review for most techniques will be an important component of a reliable methodology because peer publication "increases the likelihood that substantive flaws in methodology will be detected."[40] Thus, publication or lack thereof in a peer-reviewed journal will be relevant, but not dispositive, when assessing the validity of a particular technique or methodology. This section now summarizes example cases in which expert witness testimony was excluded from and admitted in evidence under this second factor.

---

[37] *Kaufman v. Motorola, Inc.,* No. 95 C 1069, 2000 WL 1506892, at *1 (N.D. Ill. Sept. 21, 2000).
[38] *Multimatic, Inc. v. Faurecia Interior Sys. USA, Inc.,* 358 Fed. Appx. 643, 654 (6th Cir. 2009).
[39] *Daubert v. Merrell Dow Pharm., Inc.,* 509 U.S. 579, 593 (1993).
[40] *Id.*

Expert Testimony Admissible   In *Ambrosini v. Labarraque*,[41] a birth defect case, the appellate court overruled the trial court's decision to exclude the plaintiff's expert on the grounds that the expert's findings had not been peer reviewed. The appellate court stressed that "publication in a peer-reviewed journal is not dispositive in evaluating whether an opinion is based on scientific knowledge." *This case was also decided on factors 7 and 10 grounds and is included under each of those sections.*

In *Gross v. Commissioner*,[42] the petitioner-taxpayers moved to exclude the testimony of the government's expert in part on the grounds that the expert's underlying data and empirical analysis had not been published "or otherwise submitted for peer review by the appraisal profession." The Court declined to exclude the expert's evidence reasoning that the expert used a discounted cash-flow analysis to determine the present value of future cash flows. The Court found that the difference between the opinions of each party's experts was due to a difference in variables and noted that a discounted cash-flow analysis is "a reliable tool for financial analysis." *This case was also decided on factor 4 grounds and is included under that section.*

Expert Testimony Excluded   In *In re Nellson Nutraceutical, Inc.*,[43] the Court found the unprecedented use by a debtor's expert of earnings before interest, taxation, depreciation, and amortization (EBITDA) minus capital expenditures to determine the debtor's terminal value in a discounted cash-flow analysis to be inadmissible. The Court stated that the methodology was "unprecedented in both the legal context and in the relevant scientific community" and pointed to, among other issues, the expert's inability to identify any treatises, publications, or articles that validated the methodology. *This case was also decided on factor 4 grounds and is included under that section.*

In *In re Med Diversified, Inc.*,[44] the defendant's expert determined the value of an asset using a guideline company multiple approach and a guideline transaction multiple approach, notwithstanding the fact that leading authorities on business valuation "recognize that the most reliable method for determining the value of a business" is the discounted cash-flow method. The Court found that the expert's failure to use the discounted cash-flow method amounted to "a material flaw in his methodology sufficient to bar his testimony as an expert witness" because his conclusions lack sufficient grounds on which to place reliance. The Court concluded that it could not accept the testimony of an alleged expert in business valuations when the purported expert "failed to employ the necessary peer-reviewed methods of business valuation." *This case was also decided on factor 3 and 6 grounds and is included under each of those sections.*

In *James River Insurance Co. v. Rapid Funding, LLC* (previously discussed under factor 1),[45] the Court declined to accept articles written by the defendant's expert

---

[41] *Ambrosini v. Labarraque*, 101 F.3d 129, 136 (D.C. Cir. 1996).

[42] *Gross v. Comm'r*, 78 T.C.M. (CCH) 201 (1999).

[43] *In re Nellson Nutraceutical, Inc.*, 356 B.R. 364, 374 (Bankr. D. Del. 2006).

[44] *Chartwell Litig. Trust v. Addus Healthcare, Inc. (In re Med Diversified, Inc.)*, 334 B.R. 89, 98 (Bankr. E.D.N.Y. 2005).

[45] *James River Ins. Co. v. Rapid Funding, LLC*, No. 07CV01146CMABNB, 2009 WL 481688, at *11 (D. Colo. Feb. 24, 2009).

on property valuation as satisfying the peer review factor. The defendant had no evidence that the expert's methodology had been "reviewed, critiqued, or analyzed by other experts in the property appraisal or valuation industries." Moreover, the expert's articles on property valuation did not indicate "any measure of peer review" of the specifics of the expert's methodology. The Court noted that the fact that an expert has been published is not particularly relevant because the Court was concerned with whether the methodology employed by the expert has been peer reviewed. *This case was also decided on factor 4 and 6 grounds and is included under each of those sections.*

In *United States of America, ex rel. Loughren v. UnumProvident Corp.*,[46] in a *qui tam* suit[47] brought under the False Claims Act, the plaintiff alleged that the defendant, a group health insurer, had caused its insureds to file a large number of false Social Security disability insurance claims. The plaintiff proposed to submit expert testimony with respect to statistical techniques used to "extrapolate from the number of false claims within a sample of claims to an estimation of the total number of false claims filed." The defendant-insurer moved to exclude the plaintiff's purported expert testimony. The trial court held that the plaintiff's expert's methodology, which utilized sampling from overlapping cohorts and weighted averages, was to be excluded as insufficiently reliable. The Court further found that the expert "failed to cite any peer-reviewed literature to support his novel approach to overlapping cohorts." The Court found the lack of review particularly troublesome given the defendant's expert's criticism of the plaintiff's expert's method. *This case was also decided on factor 4 grounds and is included under that section.*

Factor 3: Is there a known or potential rate of error or standards for the theory or technique applied?　The third factor the *Daubert* court delineated was whether there is a known or potential rate of error or standards for the theory or technique applied. This factor becomes relevant if the trial judge considers the validity of a particular scientific technique. A court should consider a technique's known or potential rate of error and the "existence and maintenance of standards controlling the technique's operation."[48] This section now summarizes example cases in which expert witness testimony has been admitted in and excluded from evidence under this third factor.

Expert Testimony Admissible　In *Trout Ranch, LLC v. Commissioner*,[49] the Tax Court allowed the government's expert testimony over objections from the taxpayer-petitioner that the government's experts failed to follow the method prescribed in the Treasury Regulations for such appraisals. In so ruling, the Tax Court noted that the government's experts utilized a before-and-after method and constructed a discounted cash flow model to determine the present value of the property at issue. The Tax Court determined that this was a reliable method and that the taxpayer's

---

[46] *U.S. ex rel. Loughren v. UnumProvident Corp.*, 604 F. Supp. 2d 259 (D. Mass. 2009).

[47] In a *qui tam* action, a private party called a relator brings an action on behalf of the government. The government, not the relator, is considered the real plaintiff. If the government succeeds, the relator receives a share of the award.

[48] *Daubert v. Merrell Dow Pharm., Inc.*, 509 U.S. 579, 594-95 (1993).

[49] *Trout Ranch, LLC v. Comm'r*, 100 T.C.M. (CCH) 581 (2010), *aff'd* 493 Fed. Appx. 944, 949-50 (10th Cir. 2012).

objections were based upon the expert's failure to explain their reasons for not using the comparable sales method in their report. The U.S. Court of Appeals for the Tenth Circuit found the Tax Court properly admitted the government's expert witness report.

In *Whitehouse Hotel Ltd. Partnership v. Commissioner*,[50] the taxpayer-petitioner failed in its *Daubert*-challenge of the government's expert witness. The taxpayer challenged government's expert report on the grounds that it was not compliant with the Uniform Standards of Professional Appraisal Practice (USPAP). The Court determined that this was an issue of credibility, not admissibility, stating that the taxpayer "has not cited any authority, nor do we know of any, for the proposition that an appraiser's compliance with USPAP is the sole determining factor as to whether an appraiser's valuation report is reliable."

In *Crimi v. Commissioner*,[51] a valuation case involving a part-sale, part-gift of land that had a highest and best use of residential subdevelopment, the Tax Court admitted both parties' expert witness reports over cross-objections that the other party's expert's report failed *Daubert*. The Court admitted the government's expert's report even though the Court found that the government's expert's report incorrectly applied the subdivision development approach. The Court also found that the tax-payers' expert witness's report was empirically sound insofar as it used, for purposes of determining the per-lot value, a "polynomial regression to correlate a relation-ship between the number of lots into which an undeveloped parcel of land may be subdivided and the sale price per lot."

Expert Testimony Excluded In *Ralston v. Mortgage Investors Group, Inc.*,[52] a class action involving alleged violations of the Truth in Lending Act,[53] as well as state law, the Court excluded the plaintiff's expert testimony on damage calculations. The plaintiff's expert used the "benefit-of-the-bargain" method to calculate dam-ages. This method calculates the difference between a borrower's current principal balance based on how the loan actually played out, and the principal balance that would exist had the loan behaved as the defendant represented it would. According to California law, the appropriate methodology for determining damages in a suit under the Truth in Lending Act is the "out-of-pocket" loss rule.[54] The Court deter-mined the expert's testimony was not the product of reliable principles and methods as it was precluded by law. Thus, the plaintiff's expert's testimony was not admissible.

As discussed earlier, in *Boltar, L.L.C. v. Commissioner*,[55] the petitioner-taxpayer's expert valued a conservation easement based on the "highest and best" use of the property, rather than the "before-and-after" valuation method. The Tax Court ruled to exclude the evidence, noting as follows: "[W]e conclude that the [expert's] report is not admissible under Rule 702 of the Federal Rules of Evidence,

---

[50] *Whitehouse Hotel Ltd. P'ship v. Comm'r*, 131 T.C. 112, 127 (2008), vacated and remanded on other grounds, 615 F.3d 321 (5th Cir. 2010).
[51] *Crimi v. Comm'r*, 105 T.C.M. (CCH) 1330 (2013).
[52] *Ralston v. Mortg. Inv'rs Grp., Inc.*, No. 08–536–JF (PSG), 2011 WL 6002640, at *1 (N.D. Cal. Nov. 30, 2011).
[53] Truth in Lending Act, Pub. L. No. 90-321, 2 Stat. 146 (1968).
[54] *Ralston*, 2011 WL 6002640, at *7.
[55] *Boltar, L.L.C. v. Comm'r*, 136 T.C. 326, 334 (2011).

because it is not the product of reliable methods and the authors have not applied reliable principles and methods reliably to the facts of the case."

In *In re Med Diversified* (also discussed under factor 2),[56] the Court noted that the Black-Scholes method is "customarily applied" when "valuing an option for a minority of *publicly traded* shares" as was required in that case. The Court did not allow the Black-Scholes method to be applied in this case, finding the Black-Scholes method had "not been shown to provide a reliable measure of the value of an option to purchase 100% of controlled shares in a privately held company...." *This case was also decided on factor 6 grounds and is included that section.*

Factor 4: Has the theory or technique gained general acceptance? The fourth factor the *Daubert* court listed was whether the theory or technique has gained general acceptance. This factor incorporates the pre-*Daubert* test for admissibility of evidence in federal courts into the relevant inquiry to be made for the admissibility of a theory or technique into evidence. "Widespread acceptance can be an important factor in ruling [that] particular evidence [is] admissible, and 'a known technique which has been able to attract only minimal support within the community,' may properly be viewed with skepticism."[57] We now summarize example cases in which expert witness testimony has been admitted in and excluded from evidence under this fourth factor.

Expert Testimony Admissible In *Esgar Corp. v. Commissioner*,[58] the Tax Court admitted the petitioner's expert's report into evidence despite evidentiary objections from the IRS. The Court found that the taxpayer's expert used a "generally accepted methodology, and applied it in a ... straightforward manner." The IRS argued that the taxpayer's expert's report was essentially "based on the opinions and analysis of [petitioner's other experts], not on independent data and information." The IRS further argued that the petitioner's expert performed no independent analysis and that such expert's report was "not based on a reliable foundation." Those arguments ultimately failed, and the Court did not exclude the taxpayer's report or preclude the witness's testimony.

At issue in *Okerlund v. United States*[59] was the valuation of stock for purposes of determining the taxpayer's alleged gift tax liability. Each party's expert employed a valuation method that was generally accepted within the valuation community for appraising the value of closely held stock. Although the two experts disagreed on the pricing multiples and claimed discount for lack of marketability, the Court found that these discrepancies related to the credibility of each report and not their admissibility. Consequently, the Court admitted both parties' reports into evidence. *This case was also decided on factor 5 grounds and is included under that section.*

In *Hutchison v. Parent*,[60] the Court declined to exclude the plaintiff's expert's testimony over the defendant's objections that the expert's capitalization rate analysis was based on insufficient data and utilized an alternative methodology

---

[56] *In re Med Diversified*, 334 B.R. 89, 102-103 (Bankr. E.D.N.Y. 2005).
[57] *Daubert v. Merrell Dow Pharm., Inc.*, 509 U.S. 579, 594 (1993) (internal citation omitted).
[58] *Esgar Corp. v. Comm'r*, T.C. Memo. 2012-35, 103 T.C.M. (CCH) 1185 (2012).
[59] *Okerlund v. United States*, 53 Fed. Cl. 341 (2002).
[60] *Hutchison v. Parent*, No. 3:12 cv 320, 2015 WL 1914794, at *2 (N.D. Ohio Apr. 27, 2015).

for differing years. Plaintiff's expert cited to the American Institute of Certified Public Accountants ("AICPA") Standards for Valuation Services to support his use of an alternative methodology of valuation. These guidelines allow for the use of alternative methods of valuation when it is "not practical or not reasonable to obtain or use relevant information and because of the unreliability of the financial data you can't apply the standard appraisal methods." The Court determined that, granted the absence of complete and reliable financial data, and due to the difficulties of getting "current and accurate information in a timely fashion," the plaintiff's use of an alternative methodology of valuation was permitted by the AICPA.

Expert Testimony Excluded In *Multimatic, Inc. v. Faurecia Interior Systems USA, Inc.*[61] (previously discussed under factor 1), the Court excluded the plaintiff's expert testimony because it was not "generally accepted in the economic community." As discussed under the first factor, the plaintiff's expert made a ten-year lost-profit projection without providing historical data to support the projection, and "made no effort to test his model against historical data to confirm its predictive power." The Court stated that the plaintiff had introduced no evidence that this method "would be well-received by professional economists." *This case was also decided on factor 6 grounds and is included under that section.*

In *Frymire-Brinati v. KPMG Peat Marwick,*[62] the U.S. Court of Appeals for the Seventh Circuit determined that the trial court erred by admitting the plaintiff's expert's testimony in evidence. The plaintiff's expert used a discounted cash-flow analysis to value a partnership's projects at ten times the annual cash flow. "Many of these projects had low or negative net cash flows," which the plaintiff's expert assigned a value of zero. Thus, the plaintiff's expert's methodology used historical rather than potential cash flows in his analysis. The plaintiff's expert's methodology further implied that raw land and an office building that was in the final stages of construction had no value, a clearly suspect claim. The Court stated that the proper way to determine market value using a discounted cash-flow analysis was to consider potential cash flows and "not simply historical cash flows." The appellate court found that the trial court erred by admitting the plaintiff's expert's report in evidence because such expert conceded that "he did not employ the methodology that experts in valuation find essential."

In *Lippe v. Bairnco Corp.,*[63] the Court excluded plaintiff's expert's testimony for failing to use the discounted cash-flow method and using only the comparable companies method. The Court found that by failing to use the discounted cash-flow method and solely relying on the comparable companies method, the expert was unable to check (i.e., reconcile) his determinations of value. The Court noted that many authorities recognize that the "most reliable method for determining the value of a business" is the discounted cash-flow method. *This case was also decided on factor 5 grounds and is included under that section.*

In *In re Nellson Nutraceutical, Inc.* (previously discussed under factor 2),[64] the Court took issue under the fourth factor with the debtor's expert's use of EBITDA

[61] *Multimatic, Inc. v. Faurecia Interior Sys. USA, Inc.,* 358 Fed. Appx. 643 (6th Cir. 2009).

[62] *Frymire-Brinati v. KPMG Peat Marwick,* 2 F.3d 183 (7th Cir. 1993).

[63] *Lippe v. Bairnco Corp.,* 288 B.R. 678 (S.D.N.Y. 2003).

[64] *In re Nellson Nutraceutical, Inc.,* 356 B.R. 364, 374 (Bankr. D. Del. 2006).

minus capital expenditures to determine the debtor's terminal value in a discounted cash-flow analysis. The Court stated that the evidence indicated the expert "simply invented the methodology of using EBITDA minus [capital expenditures] to determine a company's terminal value under a [discounted cash-flow] analysis." Notwithstanding the expert's failure to satisfy the second *Daubert* factor, the Court found that "[r]eliance on an invented methodology that has not been generally accepted by experts in the field" was sufficient to exclude the expert's opinion.

In *Champagne Metals v. Ken-Mac Metals, Inc.*[65] (previously discussed under factor 1), the Court rejected the plaintiff's argument that its expert's analysis had been generally accepted in the scientific community. The expert never identified his technique "beyond saying he exercised professional judgment," which, the Court ruled, falls far short of meeting the *Daubert* standard. *This case was also decided on factor 5 and 6 grounds and is included under those sections.*

In *James River Insurance Co. v. Rapid Funding, LLC* (previously discussed under factors 1 and 2),[66] both parties indicated that the "broad evidence rule" should apply. "This rule mandates that an appraiser ... should base his property valuation on 'every fact and circumstance that would logically bear on determining the value of the property,'" and then offers 21 separate factors to consider. The defendant's expert did not identify any facts or circumstances that went into his valuation although the rule required that he do so. Thus, the Court determined that the expert had not presented any evidence that his method had been generally accepted in the property valuation community. This case was also decided on factor 6 grounds and is included under that section.

In *U.S. ex rel. Loughren v. UnumProvident Corp.* (previously discussed under factor 2),[67] the insurer moved to exclude the proposed expert testimony of the plaintiff's statistician on the number of false claims. The trial court held that the expert's statistical methodology, which utilized sampling from overlapping cohorts and weighted averages, was excludible because it was not sufficiently reliable. The Court found that the method had not been generally accepted in the relevant field.

Factor 5: Is the expert testifying about matters growing naturally and directly out of research conducted independent of the litigation?   Following remand of the *Daubert* case from the Supreme Court to the U.S. Court of Appeals for the Ninth Circuit, the latter court identified the following additional factor when deciding whether expert witness testimony is admissible: whether the expert is testifying "about matters growing naturally and directly out of research that they have conducted independent of the litigation."[68] The Ninth Circuit stated that the fact an expert is paid to testify does not in and of itself cast doubt on the reliability of her testimony as most expert witnesses are paid. However, the Court went on to note that an expert who testifies on the basis of research independent of litigation "provides important, objective proof that

[65] *Champagne Metals v. Ken-Mac Metals, Inc.*, No. CIV-02-0528-HE, 2008 WL 5205204, at *11 (W.D. Okla. Dec. 11, 2008).
[66] *James River Ins.. Co. v. Rapid Funding*, LLC, No. 07CV01146CMABNB, 2009 WL 481688, at *11 (D. Colo. Feb. 24, 2009).
[67] *U.S. ex rel. Loughren v. UnumProvident Corp.*, 604 F. Supp. 2d 259 (D. Mass. 2009).
[68] *Daubert v. Merrell Dow Pharm., Inc.*, 43 F.3d 1311, 1317 (9th Cir. 1995).

the research comports with the dictates of good science."[69] This fifth factor serves the following three purposes:

1. "[E]xperts whose findings flow from existing research are less likely to [be] biased toward a particular conclusion by the promise" of money. When reports and findings are prepared "before [the expert is] hired as a witness, that record will limit" the expert's ability to tailor her testimony to serve a party's interests;
2. Independent research carries its own mark of reliability as it is conducted "in the usual course of business" and must satisfy a number of standards "to attract funding and institutional support;" and
3. Generally, there are a "limited number of scientists actively conducting research" on the subject that is the topic of a particular case, providing a "natural constraint on [the] parties' ability to shop for experts" who will testify to their desired conclusion.[70]

We now summarize example cases in which expert witness testimony has been admitted in and excluded from evidence under this fifth factor.

Expert Testimony Admissible In *Champagne Metals v. Ken-Mac Metals Inc.* (previously discussed under factors 1 and 4),[71] the Court declined to exclude the plaintiff's expert's testimony given that it was unclear to the Court whether some of the statements in the expert's report came from facts supplied by the client, which the expert assumed to be true, or if the expert confirmed the facts on the basis of his own investigation. The Court stated that those deficiencies were in and of themselves not sufficient to warrant the exclusion of the expert's testimony. *This case was also decided on factor 6 grounds and is included under that section.*

In *Okerlund v. United States* (discussed *supra* under factor 4),[72] the U.S. Court of Federal Claims declined to exclude the defendant's expert on the grounds that the expert billed a small number of hours relative to the number of hours billed by the expert's assistants. The Court determined that it was "well-settled that an expert may render an opinion on hypothetical questions and may testify not only from facts or data perceived by him but also from what is made known during or before a hearing. In other words, an expert's testimony need not be based on personal knowledge." On direct examination, the expert testified that he supervised "all of the firm's work, directed the staff in conducting valuation research, and was familiar with the conclusion and methodologies" in the report. The Court found that the expert was "sufficiently involved in the production" of the report and "knowledgeable about its methods and conclusions to provide relevant and reliable testimony."

In *Clear-View Technologies, Inc. v. Rasnick,*[73] the Court declined to exclude the plaintiff's expert testimony. Defendants claimed that the plaintiff's expert did

---

[69] *Id.*

[70] *Id.*

[71] *Champagne Metals v. Ken-Mac Metals, Inc.,* No. CIV-02-0528-HE, 2008 WL 5205204, at *9 (W.D. Okla. Dec. 11, 2008).

[72] *Okerlund v. United States,* 53 Fed. Cl. 341 (2002).

[73] *Clear-View Techs., Inc. v. Rasnick,* No. 13-cv-02744-BLF, 2015 WL 3505003, at *3 (N.D. Cal. July 2, 2015).

not independently verify the financial statements and projections provided to him, and that "an economic expert can only rely on data provided by the client when the expert engages in such independent verification." The Court concluded that although the defendants were correct that "an expert may not rely merely on the self-serving projections of his client," his valuation was consistent with his obligations under *Daubert* because the plaintiff's expert also considered third-party analyses in reaching his valuation, and did not premise his valuation on plaintiff's mere "say-so." *This case was also decided on factor 6 grounds and is included under that section.*

Expert Testimony Excluded In *Lippe v. Bairnco Corp.* (previously discussed under factor 4),[74] one of the plaintiff's experts was excluded from testifying because the expert was also the plaintiff's counsel. The Court stated as follows:

> *[The plaintiff's expert] carried on the traditional functions of a lawyer-advocate—developing arguments and theories, anticipating and preparing responses to defendant's defenses and preparing lines of cross examination. [The expert] saw himself as "counsel" to plaintiff's lawyers and he acted in a completely partisan manner. It would be most inappropriate to permit him now to testify as an expert witness about the very matters he helped develop as a lawyer-advocate.*[75]

In *MDG International, Inc. v. Australian Gold, Inc.,*[76] the plaintiff's expert submitted a lost-profit report in a contract dispute action based upon facts predominantly provided by plaintiff's counsel. Furthermore, the expert failed to consider that the defendant "would and could terminate [the plaintiff's] rights in any territory." The Court stated that this omission made any opinion the expert offered on value and lost profits "inherently incomplete and thus unreliable to a trier of fact." The expert also made several faulty assumptions and failed to verify information provided to him regarding markups and sales growth rate. Because of the expert's mistaken assumptions and failure to verify facts, the Court found his lost-profit calculation report to be inadmissible.

In *Auto Industries Supplier Employee Stock Ownership Plan v. Ford Motor Co.,*[77] the U.S. Court of Appeals for the Sixth Circuit upheld the district court's decision to exclude the plaintiff's expert testimony. The plaintiff's expert used information provided by the plaintiff to calculate damages, and the expert did not undertake any independent verification or due diligence to verify such information on his own. Rather, the expert accepted facts and figures at face value from the plaintiff on more than one occasion and the expert was unaware of who at plaintiff's organization had prepared the data the expert was using.

---

[74] *Lippe v. Bairnco Corp.*, 288 B.R. 678, 687-88 (S.D.N.Y. 2003).
[75] *Id.* at 688.
[76] *MDG Int'l, Inc. v. Austl. Gold, Inc.*, No. 1:07–cv–1096–SEB–TAB, 2009 WL 1916728, at *4 (S.D. Ind. June 29, 2009).
[77] *Auto Indus. Supplier Emp. Stock Ownership Plan v. Ford Motor Co.*, 435 Fed. Appx. 430, 456 (6th Cir. 2011).

Experts Who Offer Legal Opinions Anecdotally, parties increasingly attempt to have expert witness reports admitted with respect to opinions that are, by most accounts, legal in nature. Recall from the discussion in Chapter 2, *Qualified Appraisal*, that an appraisal report is a "qualified appraisal" only if it is conducted by a "qualified appraiser in accordance with generally accepted appraisal standards."[78] Recall also from Chapter 2, *Qualified Appraisal*, that one method of showing that an appraisal is made in accordance with generally accepted appraisal standards is that the report complies with the Uniform Standards of Professional Appraisal Practice ("USPAP"). As a relatively recent practice, the government often seeks to offer in evidence expert reports that the taxpayer's appraisal report does not comply with the USPAP (and is therefore not a qualified appraisal). Arguably, these reports are offered not for the discrete premise of showing that the report did not satisfy the USPAP, but for the broader proposition that the report is not a qualified appraisal because it was not made in accordance with generally accepted appraisal standards. Indeed, these "expert reports" often discuss not only whether the taxpayer's report is USPAP-compliant (which is only relevant if the government asserts that the report was not based on generally accepted appraisal standards), but also whether that claimed noncompliance renders the report not a qualified appraisal under section 170(f)(11) of the Internal Revenue Code.

Factor 6: Has the expert unjustifiably extrapolated from an accepted premise to an unfounded conclusion?

The sixth factor identified by courts regarding the admissibility of expert witness testimony is whether the expert has unjustifiably extrapolated from an accepted premise to an unfounded conclusion. In *General Electric v. Joiner*,[79] the Court stated that "nothing in either *Daubert* or the Federal Rules of Evidence requires a district court to admit opinion evidence that is connected to existing data only by the *ipse dixit* of the expert." *Ipse dixit* is translated from Latin to mean "he himself said it," or more figuratively, something that is asserted but not proven.[80] Thus, *Joiner* stands for the proposition that experts must integrate their opinions and analyses into a coherent analysis in which the conclusion flows from the expert's analysis of relevant facts and data. We now summarize example cases in which expert witness testimony has been admitted in and excluded from evidence under this sixth factor.

Expert Testimony Admissible In *Clear-View Technologies, Inc. v. Rasnick* (previously discussed under factor 5), the Court declined to exclude the plaintiff's expert's reports and testimony given that the expert's assumptions related to sales projections were based on "clear indicia of demand for the product."[81] The Court determined that because plaintiff's expert used actual expressions of interest from potential purchasers as his baseline for sales projections, rather than "mere expressions of corporate hope," the expert's foundation "is not so unreliable as to be inadmissible." The Court stated that the defendants could cross-examine plaintiff's expert "as to his

---

[78] I.R.C. § 170(f)(11)(E)(i).

[79] *Gen. Elec. v. Joiner*, 522 U.S. 136 (1997).

[80] *Ipse dixit*, *Black's Law Dictionary* (9th ed. 2009).

[81] *Clear-View Techs., Inc. v. Rasnick*, No. 13-cv-02744-BLF, 2015 WL 3505003, at *2 (N.D. Cal. July 2, 2015).

presumption that all of [the] non-binding orders would manifest into sales," however, they could not exclude his report as unreliable.

Expert Testimony Excluded In *In re Med Diversified, Inc.* (previously discussed under factors 2 and 3),[82] the Court found that the defendant's expert's "opinion and testimony were loaded with multiple *ipse dixits*" (i.e., something asserted but not proven), and for that reason the opinion should be excluded. Examples of these unproven assertions from the expert's testimony abound throughout the Court's opinion. For example, the expert applied a marketability discount equal to 25 percent even though the expert's approach was to use "data from actual transactions of privately held companies" in which illiquidity was, at least to some degree, already built into the results.

In *James River Insurance Co. v. Rapid Funding, LLC* (as previously discussed under factors 1, 2, and 4),[83] the defendant's expert submitted a valuation of a building's pre-damage and post-damage fire values on the basis of two figures both of which lacked evidence to support the cost estimates. When the expert was asked how he arrived at his pre-fire rehabilitation estimate, he stated that he had "a feeling about how much it would cost." The Court found that because the expert's testimony was "riddled by an impermissible lack of facts or data, his opinion must be excluded in this case as unreliable."

In *Harris v. United States*,[84] the Court precluded the plaintiff's expert from testifying about hedonic damages (i.e., loss of enjoyment of life damages) using a hypothetical benchmark of $550,000. The expert's discussion of the proposed benchmark figure was "intermingled with the discussion of the statistical life" studies despite having what the Court determined to be a lack of connection. In addition, the expert's report contained no obvious discussion as to how the expert "generated the proposed benchmark figure or any citation to credible sources that support[ed] such a figure." In sum, the Court found the basis of the expert's benchmark figure to be largely arbitrary.

In *Weiner v. Snapple Beverage Corp.*,[85] a class-action breach of warranty case, the plaintiff's expert attempted to quantify a price-premium paid for Snapple's "All Natural" claim on its packaging. The Court determined that the plaintiff's report was lacking on several fronts. First, the report was based on a "cursory review of the underlying record" in that the expert "reviewed the complaints, but no other pleadings or testimony." Second, the expert did not perform any empirical analysis or identify any relevant data, and he conceded that he did not yet know whether his proposed methodology would be workable in the case. On the basis of the foregoing facts, the Court determined the expert's opinion was speculative and therefore inadmissible.

---

[82] *Chartwell Litig. Trust v. Addus Healthcare, Inc.* (*In re Med Diversified, Inc.*), 334 B.R. 89, 102-103 (Bankr. E.D.N.Y. 2005).

[83] *James River Ins. Co. v. Rapid Funding, LLC*, No. 07CV01146CMABNB, 2009 WL 481688, at *8 (D. Colo. Feb. 24, 2009).

[84] *Harris v. United States*, No. 06–0412 JP/KBM., 2008 WL 5600225, at *2 (D.N.M. July 31, 2008).

[85] *Weiner v. Snapple Beverage Corp.*, No. 07 Civ. 8742(DLC), 2010 WL 3119452, at *6 (S.D.N.Y. Aug. 5, 2010).

In *Technology Licensing Corp. v. Gennum Corp.*,[86] a patent infringement case, the plaintiff's expert utilized a method to calculate damages based on a reasonable royalty rate to which he applied a multiplier. The expert conceded in a deposition that many of the factors used in his calculation were "purely judgmental," including the number of the defendant's customers that the plaintiff would have been able to license. The expert admitted that he had created a novel method where he "simply 'used his judgment' to arrive at figures he determined were 'reasonable' and 'conservative.'" The Court found that the methodology failed to comport with applicable law which did not sanction the use of a multiplier. The Court ruled that such an enhancement to the reasonable royalty calculation was simply unsupportable in law or fact, and consequently excluded the report of the plaintiff's expert.

Factor 7: Has the expert adequately accounted for obvious alternative explanations?   The seventh factor identified by courts in post-*Daubert* jurisprudence is whether the expert considered other *obvious* causes for the opinion she is advocating. An expert's report that does not consider any other relevant explanations may likely be excluded from evidence. However, as the cases ahead illustrate, an expert need not consider every single possible reason so long as the most obvious alternative explanations have been addressed.

Expert Testimony Admissible   In *Ambrosini v. Labarraque* (previously discussed under factor 2),[87] a birth defect case involving the plaintiff's mother's use of Depo-Provera during pregnancy, the plaintiff's expert explained that he considered other possible causes for the plaintiff's condition, "including chromosomal abnormalities, genetic defects, and viruses...." The expert further explained that after reviewing the plaintiff's and the plaintiff's mother's medical records, he ruled out those alternative explanations. The defendant sought to discredit the expert's methodology by directing the Court to the limits of the expert's research, specifically, that the expert had not performed a critical family history and did not order a state-of-the-art chromosomal study. In concluding that the defendant's argument went to the weight of the testimony and not its admissibility, the Court stated as follows:

> *The fact that several possible causes might remain "uneliminated," ... only goes to the accuracy of the conclusion, not the soundness of the methodology. [The expert's] review of the various literatures as well as the relevant medical records and studies of [the plaintiff] and her mother constituted a sufficient foundation for the admissibility of [the expert's] testimony on specific causation.*[88]

This case was also decided on factor 10 grounds and is included under that section.

---

[86] *Tech. Licensing Corp. v. Gennum Corp.*, No. 3:01–cv–4204–RS, 2004 WL 1274391, at *4-5 (N.D. Cal. Mar. 26, 2004).
[87] *Ambrosini v. Labarraque*, 101 F.3d 129 (D.C. Cir. 1996).
[88] *Id.* (internal citations omitted).

Expert Testimony Excluded In *Claar v. Burlington Northern Railroad*,[89] testimony was excluded where the experts failed to consider other obvious causes for the plaintiffs' conditions. For example, one of the experts diagnosed a plaintiff as having dyscalculia (poor arithmetic ability) and dyspraxia (poor spelling ability), without first reviewing the plaintiff's school records, which indicated that the plaintiff had suffered from the conditions since childhood. Because the expert failed to review these records, the Court concluded that the expert could testify reliably only that the plaintiff's "spelling and arithmetic abilities [were] below average." The expert "offered no scientific basis for concluding that chemical exposure played any part at all" in the plaintiff's condition.

In *Equal Employment Opportunity Commission v. Bloomberg L.P.*,[90] one of the plaintiffs' economic experts used a regression model to determine whether maternity leave played a role in the defendant's pay decisions. However, the expert failed to consider other employees who had taken a substantial amount of leave, albeit not maternity leave. The Court found that because the expert did not compare class members to other similarly situated employees (leave takers), the expert's report could not assist the trier of fact and was therefore inadmissible.

Factor 8: Is the expert being as careful as he would be in his regular professional work? The U.S. Court of Appeals for the Seventh Circuit expressed an additional factor for consideration in *Sheehan v. Daily Racing Form, Inc.*[91] Specifically, the Court added to the list of *Daubert* factors whether the "expert is being as careful as he would be in his regular professional work outside his paid litigation consulting."[92] We now summarize example cases in which expert witness testimony has been excluded from evidence under this eighth factor.

Expert Testimony Excluded In *Sheehan* the expert excluded from his statistical analysis two people from the sample test, which the Court characterized as "arbitrary." The expert also declined to indicate the sensitivity of his analysis and failed to correct for other explanatory variables. These shortcomings indicated to the Court that the expert was not exercising the same degree of care in this litigation as he would use in his normal scientific work. The Court speculated that the expert may have had financial incentive to apply looser standards and ultimately found that the study would not be admissible at trial.

In *Bone Care International LLC v. Pentech Pharmaceuticals, Inc.*,[93] the Court excluded the plaintiff's expert's testimony on the grounds that the expert's analysis was incomplete and thus did not "adhere to the same standards of intellectual rigor that are demanded in [his] professional work." The expert, a biostatistician, submitted a report comparing two clinical studies. The expert admitted the report was incomplete and identified additional work that should be done. Even though the

---

[89] *Claar v. Burlington N. R.R.*, 29 F.3d 499, 502 (9th Cir. 1994).

[90] *E.E.O.C. v. Bloomberg L.P.*, No. 07 Civ. 8383 (LAP), 2010 WL 3466370, at *11-12 (S.D.N.Y. Aug. 31, 2010).

[91] *Sheehan v. Daily Racing Form, Inc.*, 104 F.3d 940, 942 (7th Cir. 1997).

[92] *Id.*

[93] *Bone Care Intern. LLC v. Pentech Pharm., Inc.*, No. 08–cv–1083, 2010 WL 3928598, at *6 (N.D. Ill. Oct. 1, 2010).

information needed to complete the report was unavailable to the expert through no fault of his own when the report was due, the Court did not allow the report to be entered into evidence.

Factor 9: Is the field or expertise claimed by the expert known to reach reliable results for the type of opinion the expert would give?   In *Kumho Tire Co. v. Carmichael*,[94] the Supreme Court articulated an additional factor for consideration: specifically, whether the field of expertise claimed by the expert is known to reach reliable results for the type of opinion the expert would give. In particular, the Court noted that a method could be generally accepted in its field and still lack reliability when the entire discipline is found to be unreliable. Such disciplines where testimony would not be admissible in any event include, for example, astrology and necromancy (communicating with the dead).[95]

Factor 10: Has the theory or method offered by the expert been put to any non-judicial use?
   Courts may also look to whether the method employed by the expert has been used in other contexts. This tenth factor seeks to find methods that have been used in a nonjudicial context and support the method's scientific validity and thus its admissibility. We now summarize an example case in which expert witness testimony has been excluded from evidence under this tenth factor.

Expert Testimony Admissible   In *Ambrosini v. Labarraque* (discussed under factors 2 and 7),[96] the Court stated:

> That [the expert] testified to his opinion of general causation in a public hearing, without any connection to the [instant] litigation, reduces concerns that [the expert] is simply "a gun for hire." That he was called upon by the F.D.A. to testify on causation of birth defects suggests that he is recognized in his field and that he employs scientifically valid methodologies.

Factor 11: Whether the expert's opinion fails to square with a judge's opinion and common sense
The Court in *Hein v. Merck & Co.* articulated an eleventh factor: whether the expert's opinion squares with a "judge's experience and common sense."[97] This example case in which expert witness testimony has been excluded from evidence under this eleventh factor is set forth below.

Expert Testimony Excluded   In *Hein*, the plaintiff's expert utilized the survey model, a method in which individuals are asked to state what they are willing to pay to reduce their chance of dying by a specified percentage, to calculate hedonic damages. The Court was persuaded by criticism that most people fail to perceive their risks accurately due to a "that won't happen to me" mentality. In concluding that the survey model failed the commonsense test, the authoring judge noted as follows:

---

[94]*Kumho Tire Co. v. Carmichael*, 526 U.S. 137 (1999).
[95]*Id.* at 151.
[96]*Ambrosini v. Labarraque*, 101 F.3d 129, 139-140 (D.C. Cir. 1996).
[97]*Hein v. Merck & Co.*, 868 F. Supp. 230, 231 (M.D. Tenn. 1994).

"Even at my somewhat advanced age, I'm not ready or willing to put a price on my continued existence. Honest answers to hypothetical questions of this kind are not possible."

CONCLUSION

Valuation experts should be intimately familiar with the idea that their testimony is subject to challenge by the opposing party under the Supreme Court's decision in *Daubert v. Merrell Dow Pharmaceuticals, Inc.*[98] These challenges are appropriate in all federal courts, including the Tax Court. Additionally, attorneys should make appropriate *Daubert* challenges to exclude unreliable and/or unreasonable expert witness testimony and experts should be prepared to defend their methodologies and analyses against rigorous challenges from the opposing party's counsel and the presiding judge.

---

[98]Daubert v. Merrell Dow Pharm., Inc., 509 U.S. 579 (1993).

CHAPTER 8

Discovery of Expert Material

SUMMARY

Tax cases, especially those in which valuation is at issue, are often decided on the basis of expert witness testimony. Not surprisingly, litigants find it important to discover, and perhaps use at trial, documents, information, opinions, and conclusions of an opposing party's expert witness. The Tax Court Rules of Practice and Procedure (which govern the practice and procedure in all cases and proceedings before the Tax Court) and the Federal Rules of Civil Procedure (which govern the procedure in all civil actions and proceedings before the U.S. district courts) provide detailed rules for the exchange of information during the pretrial phase of litigation. This chapter provides an overview of discovery devices available in the Tax Court and the U.S. district courts, with a particular focus on discovery as it relates to expert witnesses.

OVERVIEW OF DISCOVERY

Discovery is the pretrial phase of litigation during which a party can obtain evidence from an opposing party by using various procedural devices. Discovery serves a number of important objectives: it encourages cases to settle; it prevents false claims from going to trial; it helps to develop and narrow the issues to be tried; it prevents the concealment of evidence relevant to the case; it eliminates surprise; and it allows attorneys to prepare for effective direct, cross, and rebuttal examinations. Among the discovery devices generally available in courts are requests for answers to interrogatories, requests for production of documents, requests for admissions, and depositions.

Federal and state courts have all adopted rules of practice and procedure with respect to the timing, availability, and mechanics of conducting discovery. The mechanics of discovery practice varies between courts, though certain common discovery devices emerge with great regularity.

Court rules regarding discovery are broadly construed to allow parties to obtain documents and other information with respect to any non-privileged matter that is relevant to any party's claim or defense and is proportional to the needs of the given case.[1] It is important to note that relevant discoverable information need not

---

[1]*See Fed. R. Civ. P.* 26(b)(1) ("Parties may obtain discovery regarding any nonprivileged matter that is relevant to any party's claim or defense and proportional to the needs of the case...."); *Tax Ct. R.* 70(b) ("The information or response sought through discovery may concern any matter not privileged and which is relevant to the subject matter involved in the pending case.").

necessarily be admissible at trial. Rather, proper discovery includes information that is merely reasonably calculated to lead to admissible evidence.[2]

IMPORTANT LIMITATIONS ON DISCOVERY

Numerous limitations may apply to discovery. First, the information sought to be discovered must be relevant to the discovering party's claim or defense.[3] Information is relevant if (i) it has any tendency to make a fact more or less probable than the fact would be without the information, and (ii) the information is of consequence in determining a party's claim or defense.[4]

Second, the information sought to be discovered must not be privileged.[5] Privileged information is generally seen in the following forms: attorney–client privileged information; work product protected information; and public policy protected information.

Third, in relation to expert witnesses, both the Tax Court Rules of Practice and Procedure and the Federal Rules of Civil Procedure impose varying limitations upon pretrial discovery of facts known and opinions held by expert witnesses.[6]

Fourth, the Federal Rules of Civil Procedure have recently been amended to add proportionality limitations. As such, the scope of discovery is restricted to that which is "proportional to the needs of the case, considering the importance of the issues at stake in the action, the amount in controversy, the parties' relative access to relevant information, the parties' resources, the importance of the discovery in resolving the issues, and whether the burden or expense of the proposed discovery outweighs its likely benefit."[7] It is important to note that in order to be discoverable, the information need not necessarily be admissible.[8] Concepts of discovery proportionality are also embedded in Tax Court Rule 70(c), which discussed in more detail later in this chapter.

The Attorney–Client Privilege

The attorney–client privilege may protect confidential communications between an attorney and the attorney's client from discovery. The attorney–client privilege generally applies to "communications made in confidence by a client to an attorney for the purpose of obtaining legal advice, and also to confidential communications made by the attorney to the client if such communications contain legal advice or reveal confidential information on which the client seeks advice."[9] The attorney–client privilege

---

[2] *See, e.g., Tax Ct. R.* 70(b).
[3] *See, e.g., id.*
[4] *Fed. R. Evid.* 401 (setting forth the test for the admissibility of relevant evidence).
[5] *See, e.g., Tax Ct. R.* 70(b).
[6] *See Tax Ct. R.* 70(c)(4); *Fed. R. Civ. P.* 26(b)(4).
[7] *See Fed. R. Civ. P.* 26(b)(1).
[8] *See Fed. R. Civ. P.* 26(b)(1).
[9] *Upjohn Co. v. United States,* 449 U.S. 383, 389 (1981).

serves the public policy goal of encouraging a client to provide her attorney with all facts relevant to a case, regardless of whether those facts are favorable or unfavorable to the client's position.

Significantly, the attorney–client privilege does not create a blanket exemption from discovery of all communications between an attorney and an expert witness even though the communications may concern the client.[10]

Rule 70(c)(4) of the Tax Court Rules of Practice and Procedure provides that communications between a party's counsel and any witness required to provide a report under Rule 143(g) are immune from discovery, except to the extent the communication (i) relates to compensation for the expert's study or testimony, (ii) identifies facts or data that the party's counsel provided and that the expert considered in forming the opinions to be expressed, or (iii) identifies assumptions that the party's counsel provided and that the expert relied on in forming the opinions to be expressed.[11] Importantly, the *Kovel* doctrine may extend the attorney–client privilege to communications between an expert and an attorney when the attorney retains an expert to assist her in understanding complex issues for the purpose of providing legal advice to the client.[12]

Work Product

The work product doctrine may also protect certain documentary items, including expert witness reports prepared in anticipation of litigation from discovery. The work product doctrine generally protects documents, interviews, statements, memoranda, correspondence, briefs, mental impressions, and tangible things prepared by an attorney in anticipation of litigation or trial.[13] The scope of protections afforded by the work product doctrine is generally broader than those offered by the attorney–client privilege. Thus, the work product doctrine, unlike the attorney–client privilege, may prevent discovery of an expert's report when the expert has been hired by the attorney as her agent to assist in the preparation of anticipated litigation.[14]

The Tax Court expressly adopted the work product doctrine in its Rule 70, which provides that "[a] party generally may not discover documents and tangible things

---

[10]*See, e.g., United States v. McKay*, 372 F.2d 174, 176-77 (5th Cir. 1967); *Colton v. United States*, 306 F.2d 633, 639-40 (2d Cir. 1962), *cert. denied*, 371 U.S. 951 (1963).

[11]*Tax Ct. R.* 70(c)(4).

[12]The *Kovel* doctrine, which was first articulated in *United States v. Kovel*, 296 F.2d 918 (2d Cir. 1961), extends the attorney–client privilege to third-party requests made at the attorney's or client's request where the report's purpose is to distill complicated information into a form that the attorney can use in connection with the representation of her client. This was a significant departure from then-existing law because the attorney–client privilege is usually waived if an attorney–client communication is disclosed to a third party. *Kovel* arrangements should not be entered into lightly. As a best practice, the attorney should directly engage the expert before services are performed to make it clear that the expert is providing services to assist the attorney in providing legal services to the client, rather than that the client is engaging the expert to provide non-legal services to the client.

[13]*Hickman v. Taylor*, 329 U.S. 495, 510-511 (1947).

[14]*See, e.g., Alltmont v. United States*, 177 F.2d 971, 976 (3d Cir. 1949), *cert. denied*, 339 U.S. 967 (1950).

that are prepared in anticipation of litigation or for trial by or for another party or its representative."[15]

Unfairness Doctrine

A third limitation upon discovery is a judicial limitation known as the doctrine of unfairness. The unfairness doctrine is premised upon fundamental notions of fairness that the party seeking discovery should not be able to obtain from an adverse party's expert information that is readily available for independent evaluation.[16] There are at least two rationalizations for the unfairness doctrine. First, courts should not permit discovery to be used to allow a party to obtain an adverse party's trial preparation materials. Second, courts should not permit a party to obtain the results of work done by an adverse party's expert because to do so would be tantamount to giving property without providing adequate compensation. At the same time, if the party seeking discovery can establish good cause for discovery by demonstrating that the expert's report is essential to the discovering party's case and otherwise unavailable to that party, the unfairness doctrine may not preclude discovery.[17]

THE IRS'S SUMMONS AUTHORITY

Section 7602(a) of the Internal Revenue Code empowers the Internal Revenue Service ("IRS") "to examine any books, papers, records, or other data that may be relevant or material" in ascertaining the correctness of any tax return. The breadth of section 7602 of the Internal Revenue Code is broadly drafted to enable the IRS to have access to most, if not all, documents and testimony in the possession of a taxpayer. Notably, section 7602 of the Internal Revenue Code empowers the IRS to enforce any summons and represent the government's interests before the Tax Court.

The IRS has argued that neither the attorney–client privilege nor the work product doctrine apply to summonses issued in connection with the IRS's investigations.[18] However, courts have been unwilling to adopt this absolutist approach.[19] Practitioners should keep in mind that because documents used to support a federal tax reporting position are typically not prepared in advance of litigation, such documents are by definition outside the scope of the work product doctrine, and therefore within the types of documents able to be summonsed under section 7602 of the Internal Revenue Code.

---

[15] *Tax Ct. R.* 70(c)(3)(A); *see also Tax Ct. R.* 70(c)(4)(C) (extending the same standard to interrogatories or depositions).
[16] *See, e.g., United States v. 23.76 Acres of Land*, 32 F.R.D. 593, 597 (D. Md. 1963); 4 *Moore's Federal Practice* § 26.23 (2d ed. 1966).
[17] *See, e.g., Walsh v. Reynolds Metals Co.*, 15 F.R.D. 376, 378 (D.N.J. 1954).
[18] *Colton v. United States*, 306 F.2d 633, 640 (2d Cir. 1962); *United States v. Summe*, 208 F. Supp. 925, 926 (E.D. Ky. 1962).
[19] *See, e.g., In re Kearney*, 227 F. Supp. 174, 177-78 (S.D.N.Y. 1964); *Summe*, 208 F. Supp. at 926.

PROCEDURES WITH RESPECT TO EXPERT WITNESSES PREPARED IN CONNECTION WITH LITIGATION

Discovery procedures concerning expert witnesses may vary depending upon the court and the presiding judge. The rules that apply to discovery and the manner in which those rules apply necessarily depend upon whether the information sought to be discovered, typically an expert's report (or draft thereof), was prepared in anticipation of litigation or to support a tax reporting position. For expert reports prepared in anticipation of litigation and intended to be used at trial, court rules provide detailed content and procedural requirements that must be satisfied before the report will be admissible.

As discussed more fully in Chapter 13, *Attorney Involvement*, the Tax Court Rules of Practice and Procedure require an expert witness to prepare and submit a written report to the Court and to the opposing party no later than 30 days before trial.[20] Rule 143(g)(1) requires the report to set forth:

1. A complete statement of all opinions the witness expresses and the basis and reasons for them;
2. The facts or data considered by the witness in forming them;
3. Any exhibits used to summarize or support them;
4. The witness's qualifications, including a list of all publications authored in the previous ten years;
5. A list of all other cases in which, during the previous four years, the witness testified as an expert at trial or by deposition; and
6. A statement of the compensation to be paid for the study and testimony in the case.

The presiding judge usually reviews the parties' expert witness reports before trial. At trial, assuming that the Court qualifies her as an expert, the report is marked as an exhibit, identified by the expert witness and received in evidence as the expert witness's direct testimony. Additional direct testimony may be allowed to clarify or emphasize matters with respect to that expert's report. Following any additional direct testimony, the witness is tendered for cross-examination by the opposing party.

DISCOVERY IN THE COURTS

Discovery in the Tax Court tends to be much more limited than might be available to litigants in the U.S. district courts. Three practical reasons necessitate the distinction. First, more than 70 percent of petitions filed in the Tax Court are filed by *pro se*

---

[20]*See Tax Ct. R.* 143(g). On July 6, 2012, the Tax Court amended *Tax Ct. R.* 143(g) to require that an expert witness report contain the same information required under *Fed. R. Civ. P.* 26(a)(2)(B). Press Release dated July 6, 2012, pp. 9–10. Prior to the amendment, *Tax Ct. R.* 143(g) required that an expert report contain: (1) the expert witness's qualifications; (2) the expert witness's opinion and the facts or data on which that opinion is based; and (3) in detail the reasons for the expert witness's conclusion.

(i.e., unrepresented) litigants[21] who are not well-versed in the objects of discovery.[22] Second, the IRS is expected to have developed the facts supporting its position before the issuance of the notice of deficiency.[23] Third, insofar as section 7602 of the Internal Revenue Code empowers the IRS to obtain books, papers, records, testimony, or other data that may be relevant or material in ascertaining the correctness of any tax return, the need for depositions in the Tax Court is significantly more limited than in the U.S. district courts where depositions are routine.[24]

Notwithstanding the foregoing differences, litigants in the Tax Court and the U.S. district courts may obtain discovery by the following methods: written interrogatories; production of documents, electronically stored information, or other similar items; depositions; and admissions by the opposing party.

Tax Court

The Tax Court Rules of Practice and Procedure parallel the Federal Rules of Civil Procedure in many respects, including those with respect to formal discovery. It is important to note at the outset that the Tax Court expects its litigants to "attain the objectives of discovery through informal consultation or communication" before using the formal discovery procedure provided in its Rules of Practice and Procedure.[25] The Tax Court's reliance on informal discovery is a significant departure from the more formal discovery process favored by the Federal Rules of Civil Procedure. Nevertheless, once informal discovery has run its course in a proceeding before the Tax Court, the parties may obtain discovery by any one or more of the following formal discovery procedures:

- Written interrogatories;[26]
- Production of documents, electronically stored information, and other similar items;[27]
- Deposition upon consent of the parties;[28]
- Deposition without consent of the parties;[29] and
- Admissions from the opposing party.[30]

Again, unlike other federal courts where depositions are common, the Tax Court deems depositions an extraordinary method of discovery that should be used sparingly.

---

[21] A *pro se* litigant is one who represents herself before a court.

[22] T. Keith Fogg, "An Access to Justice Milestone," *A.B.A. Sec. of Tax'n News Quarterly* 10 (Jan. 2013), http://works.bepress.com/cgi/viewcontent.cgi?article=1032&context=t_keith_fogg.

[23] Alex E. Sadler and Daniel G. Kim, "Scope of Pretrial Discovery: A Key Difference in Litigating Tax Cases in the Tax Court and Refund Tribunals," 11 *J. Tax Prac. & Proc.* 39, 53 (2009).

[24] *Id. See also* I.R.C. § 7602(a).

[25] *Tax Ct. R.* 70(a)(1).

[26] *Tax Ct. R.* 71.

[27] *Tax Ct. R.* 72–73.

[28] *Tax Ct. R.* 74(b).

[29] *Tax Ct. R.* 74(c).

[30] *Tax Ct. R.* 90.

General Provisions Regarding Discovery

Time for Discovery Discovery may not generally be initiated in the Tax Court "before the expiration of 30 days after joinder of issue" (i.e., 30 days after the answer or, if required, the reply, is filed).[31] Discovery must typically be completed, and any motion to compel discovery must be filed no later than 45 days prior to the trial date.[32] Tax Court judges have broad discretion to modify the discovery timeline depending upon the issues presented, the diligence of the parties in obtaining discovery, and the availability and location of the evidence to be discovered. As valuation issues routinely present complex issues, it is common for judges to modify these general discovery deadlines vis-à-vis a pretrial discovery Order.

Scope of Discovery The scope of discovery is broad. The information or responses sought through discovery may concern any matter not privileged and which is relevant to the subject matter involved in the pending case.[33] A party may not object to a discovery request on grounds that the information sought will not be admissible at trial so long as that information or response "appears reasonably calculated to lead to discovery of admissible evidence."[34]

Limitations on Discovery Generally Pursuant to Rule 70(c)(1) of the Tax Court Rules of Practice and Procedure, the Court may limit the frequency or extent of use of the discovery methods allowed if the Court determines that:

(A) The discovery sought is unreasonably cumulative or duplicative, or is obtainable from some other source that is more convenient, less burdensome, or less expensive;

(B) The party seeking discovery has had ample opportunity by discovery in the action to obtain the information sought; or

(C) The discovery is unduly burdensome or expensive, taking into account the needs of the case, the amount in controversy, limitations on the parties' resources, and the importance of the issues at stake in the litigation.

Discovery of Experts The Tax Court has adopted specific rulings concerning discovery from expert witnesses, which are generally set forth in Rule 70(c)(4) of the Tax Court's Rules of Practice and Procedure.[35] That Rule, which is set forth in Rule 70(c)(4), provides as follows:

(A) Rule 70(c)(3) protects drafts of any expert witness report required under Rule 143(g), regardless of the form in which the draft is recorded.

---

[31] *Tax Ct. R.* 70(a)(2). A party may request leave of Court for a modified discovery schedule, though such requests are usually made to back-load rather than accelerate discovery.
[32] *Id.*
[33] *Tax Ct. R.* 70(b).
[34] *Id.*
[35] *Tax Ct. R.* 70(c)(4).

(B) Rule 70(c)(3) protects communications between a party's counsel and any witness required to provide a report under Rule 143(g), regardless of the form of
the communications, except to the extent the communications:
  (i) relate to compensation for the expert's study or testimony;
  (ii) identify facts or data that the party's counsel provided and that the expert
       considered in forming the opinions to be expressed; or
  (iii) identify assumptions that the party's counsel provided and that the expert
        relied on in forming the opinions to be expressed.
(C) A party generally may not, by interrogatories or depositions, discover facts
known or opinions held by an expert who has been retained or specially
employed by another party in anticipation of litigation or to prepare for trial
and who is not expected to be called as a witness at trial, except on a showing
of exceptional circumstances under which it is impracticable for the party to
obtain facts or opinions on the same subject by other means.

Limitations on Discovery Related to Experts
I. Work Product As noted, the Tax Court's Rules of Practice and Procedure incorporate the work product doctrine. Thus, draft expert witness reports that are procured
in connection with ongoing litigation generally are not discoverable.[36] Rule 70(c)(3)
of the Tax Court Rules of Practice and Procedure provides that "[a] party generally
may not discover documents and tangible things that are prepared in anticipation of
litigation or for trial by or for another party or its representative."[37]
    As an exception to the general rule, documents and tangible things that are
prepared in advance of litigation may nonetheless be discoverable if (i) they concern any unprivileged matter that is relevant to the subject matter of the pending
case, *and* (ii) the party seeking discovery establishes that it has "substantial need
for the materials to prepare its case and cannot, without undue hardship, obtain
their substantial equivalent by other means."[38] The Tax Court will, however, take
protective measures to ensure that "mental impressions, conclusions, opinions, or
legal theories of a party's counsel or other representatives concerning the litigation" are not subject to discovery.[39] Such protective measures may, upon motion
of the potentially aggrieved party, include the Court's issuance of a protective order
to protect a party or other person from disclosing "mental impressions, conclusions, opinions, or legal theories of a party's counsel or other representatives concerning the litigation."[40] A motion for a protective order against certain discovery
must attach as an exhibit a copy of any discovery request with respect to which the
motion is filed.[41]

II. Attorney–Client Privilege May Extend to Experts The Tax Court has also incorporated the attorney–client privilege into its Rules of Practice and Procedure, and
it has included specific provisions as to communications between a party's lawyer

---

[36] *See id.*
[37] *Tax Ct. R.* 70(c)(3)(A).
[38] *Id.*
[39] *Tax Ct. R.* 70(c)(3)(B).
[40] *Id.*
[41] *Tax Ct. R.* 103.

and a party's expert witness. Communications between a party's counsel and any expert witness who submits an expert witness report under Rule 143(g) are generally protected except to the extent the communications:

- Relate to compensation for the expert's study or testimony;
- Identify facts or data that the party's counsel provided and that the expert considered in forming the opinions to be expressed; or
- Identify assumptions that the party's counsel provided and that the expert relied upon in forming the opinions to be expressed.[42]

Interrogatories

Interrogatories Served Upon a Party The use of interrogatories as a discovery device is covered by Rule 71 of the Tax Court Rules of Practice and Procedure, which provides that a party may serve on any other party "no more than 25 interrogatories, including all discrete subparts" other than those related to expert witnesses, to be answered by the party served.[43] Tax Court judges have broad discretion to grant leave to a party to serve additional interrogatories so long as such request is consistent with the general objectives of discovery (i.e., the additional interrogatories seek information that is not unreasonably cumulative or duplicative or that is not obtainable from other sources that are "more convenient, less burdensome, or less expensive").[44]

Interrogatories must be answered within 30 days of service unless the Court allows otherwise.[45] Each interrogatory must be answered in good faith and the answers must be as complete as the answering party's information permits.[46] Interrogatories must "be answered separately and fully under oath," unless an interrogatory is objected to, in which case "the reason for the objection shall be stated in lieu of the answer."[47] The interrogatories and responses need not be filed with the Court absent a motion with respect to an "objection or other failure to answer an interrogatory."[48] A special set of rules apply with respect to interrogatories related to an expert witness.

Interrogatories Concerning Expert Witnesses A party may use interrogatories to obtain limited information with respect to the other party's expert witness. Specifically, with respect to expert witnesses, a party may require another party to respond to the following requests for information:

- Identify each person whom the other party expects to call as an expert witness at the trial of the case, giving the witnesses' names, addresses, vocations or occupations, and a statement of the witnesses' qualifications; and

---

[42] *Tax Ct. R.* 70(c)(4)(B).
[43] *Tax Ct. R.* 71(a).
[44] *Tax Ct. R.* 71(a); *see also Tax Ct. R.* 70(c).
[45] *Tax Ct. R.* 71(c).
[46] *Tax Ct. R.* 71(b).
[47] *Tax Ct. R.* 71(c).
[48] *Id.*

- State the subject matter and the substance of the facts and opinions to which the expert is expected to testify, and give a summary of the grounds for each such opinion, or, in lieu of such statement, to furnish a copy of the report of such expert presenting the foregoing information as is otherwise required by Rule 143(g).[49]

There are limitations on the ability of the parties to obtain information from expert witnesses through interrogatories. A party may *not* use interrogatories to

> *discover facts known or opinions held by an expert who has been retained or specifically employed by another party in anticipation of litigation or to prepare for trial and who is not expected to be called as a witness at trial, except [upon] a showing of exceptional circumstances under which it is impracticable for [the] party to obtain facts or opinions on the same subject by other means.*[50]

Production of Documents

Production of Materials   Requests for production of documents are another discovery device available in the Tax Court that is covered by Rule 72 of the Tax Court Rules of Practice and Procedure. That Rule provides that a party may, without leave of Court, serve on another a party a request to:

- Produce and permit the party making the request, or someone acting on such party's behalf, to inspect and copy, test, or sample any designated documents or electronically stored information (including writings, drawings, graphs, charts, photographs, sound recordings, images, and other data compilations stored in any medium from which information can be obtained, either directly or translated, if necessary, by the responding party into a reasonably usable form), or to inspect and copy, test, or sample any tangible thing, to the extent that any of the foregoing items are in the possession, custody, or control of the party on whom the request is served; or
- Permit entry upon designated land or other property in the possession or control of the party upon whom the request is served for the purpose of inspection and measuring, surveying, photographing, testing, or sampling the property or any designated object or operation thereon.[51]

Requests for production of documents, electronically stored information, and other items must set forth the items to be inspected, either by individual item or category, describe each item and category with reasonable particularity, and may specify the form or forms in which electronically stored information is to be produced.[52] In addition, the request must specify a reasonable time, place, and manner of making the inspection and performing the related acts.[53]

---

[49] *Tax Ct. R.* 71(d).
[50] *Tax Ct. R.* 70(c)(4)(C).
[51] *Tax Ct. R.* 72(a).
[52] *Tax Ct. R.* 72(b).
[53] *Id.*

A party generally must respond to a request for production of documents, electronically stored information, and other items within 30 days of the service of request unless the Court allows an alternative timeline.[54] "The response shall state, [as] to each item or category, that inspection and related activities will be permitted as requested, unless the request is objected to, ... in which [case] the reasons for objection shall be stated."[55] Neither the request nor the response need to be filed with the Court absent a motion to compel production of the document, electronically stored information, or other item.[56]

Production of Documents Relating to Expert Witnesses There is a subtle but important difference between appraisal reports secured in advance of litigation and appraisal reports procured to support a tax reporting position. Under Rule 70 of the Tax Court Rules of Practice and Procedure, draft expert reports prepared in advance of litigation are not discoverable. However, appraisal reports to support a tax reporting position, including a qualified appraisal obtained with respect to a charitable contribution deduction of more than $5,000, but not required to be attached to the taxpayer's return because the value of the deduction claimed is $500,000 or less, may be subject to discovery.[57]

I. Using Draft Appraisals and Work Files Pretrial Appraisers typically send a draft appraisal report to the client or the client's attorneys and/or accountants for review or comment before finalizing the report. This review process can, and often does, result in changes to the assumptions underlying the appraisal report, the subset of comparable sales reviewed (for real property appraisals), and/or the appraiser's opinion of value.

As discussed in Chapter 9, *Expert Appraisal Reports*, the Uniform Standards of Professional Appraisal Practice ("USPAP") require an appraiser to keep a work file for each appraisal report for a period of at least five years after the appraisal report is prepared, or at least two years after the final disposition of any judicial proceeding in which the appraiser provides testimony with respect to the appraisal report, whichever is later. The work file must contain the name of the client, "true copies of any written reports, documented on any type of media, summaries of any oral reports or testimony, or a transcript of testimony, ... [and] all other data, information, and documentation necessary to support the appraiser's opinions and conclusions ...."[58]

Requesting and reviewing the changes between drafts and documents within the work file may reveal strengths or weaknesses with respect to an opposing party's tax reporting position and ultimate opinion of value. Therefore, attorneys routinely seek to discover such draft reports.

---

[54] *Id.*
[55] *Id.*
[56] *Id.*
[57] *Tax Ct. R.* 72(a)(1); *see also Tax Ct. R.* 70(b), (c).
[58] *Uniform Standards of Professional Appraisal Practice U-10* (Appraisal Standards Bd., The Appraisal Found., 2014–2015).

II. Using Draft Appraisals and Work Files at Trial Draft appraisal reports and work files, especially to the extent they are inconsistent with the report tendered at trial, may prove a useful tool on cross-examination to call into question the veracity of an expert's conclusions and to discredit her testimony. Rule 613(b) of the Federal Rules of Evidence allows a party to impeach the credibility of the opposing party's witness through the use of prior inconsistent statements. A party may, after laying a proper foundation, establish that the opposing party's witness has made oral or written statements on another occasion which are inconsistent with the witness's testimony. The purpose of emphasizing these prior inconsistent statements is generally to impeach the credibility of the witness and discredit her testimony. Prior draft appraisal reports, to the extent they are inconsistent with the witness's testimony, may be used on cross-examination to impeach the credibility of an appraiser's testimony.

III. Using the Absence of Draft Appraisal Reports and Work Files for Impeachment Purposes Retaining the work files required by USPAP is a mandatory part of USPAP's ethics rules. Where an appraiser fails to maintain a complete work file as required by USPAP, a lawyer can impugn the appraiser's credibility by showing that the appraiser has violated the appraiser's ethics rules. Thus, an attorney may use the absence of work files as impeachment through the absence of records.

Depositions Depositions are considered an "extraordinary method of discovery" and are generally not available to litigants except to the limited extend provided in Rule 74 of the Tax Court Rules of Practice and Procedure.[59] Rule 74 of the Tax Court Rules of Practice and Procedure bifurcates depositions into those occurring with the consent of the parties and those occurring without the consent of the parties. Special rules discussed ahead apply with respect to depositions of expert witnesses.

Depositions with the Consent of the Parties A deposition of a party, a nonparty witness, or an expert witness may be taken with the consent of all parties in a proceeding before the Tax Court.[60] Discovery by deposition may not commence until a notice of trial is issued or the case has been assigned to a judge for disposition.[61] A notice of deposition must be served upon a nonparty witness or an expert witness for whom the deposition is sought.[62] Pursuant to Rule 74(b)(2) of the Tax Court's Rules of Practice and Procedure, the notice must state:

1. That the deposition is to be taken under Rule 74(c)(2) of the Tax Court Rules of Practice and Procedure;
2. The name of the party or parties seeking the deposition;
3. The name and address of the person to be deposed;

---

[59] *Tax Ct. R.* 74(c)(1)(B).
[60] *Tax Ct. R.* 74(b)(1).
[61] *Tax Ct. R.* 70(a)(2).
[62] *Tax Ct. R.* 74(b)(2).

4. The time and place proposed for the deposition;
5. The name of the officer before whom the deposition is to be taken;
6. A statement describing any books, papers, documents, electronically stored information, or tangible things to be produced at the deposition; and
7. A statement of the reasons for deposing the witness and the issues in controversy to which the expected testimony of the witness or the document, electronically stored information, or thing relates.

A nonparty witness or expert who objects to the deposition must serve on the party seeking the deposition any objections thereto.[63]

Depositions without Consent of the Parties   A deposition of a party, a nonparty witness, or an expert witness may also be taken without the consent of the parties.[64] Discovery by deposition without the consent of the parties, like a deposition with the consent of the parties, may not be commenced until a notice of trial is issued or the case has been assigned to a judge for trial or disposition.[65] The Tax Court Rules of Practice and Procedure provide that the deposition of a party, nonparty witness, or an expert witness may be used only where (1) the person sought to be deposed can give testimony or possesses documents, electronically stored information, or other discoverable things, *and* (2) where such testimony, documents, electronically stored information, or things practicably cannot be obtained through informal consultation, interrogatories, or a request for production of documents, electronically stored information, or things.[66] The procedure for deposing a party or a nonparty witness without the consent of the parties is set forth in Rule 74(c) of the Tax Court Rules of Practice and Procedure. This section discusses the procedure for taking the deposition of an expert witness without the consent of the parties.

I. Scope of Discovery by Deposition without Consent   As noted, the Tax Court Rules of Practice and Procedure allow for the taking of a deposition of an expert witness. The deposition of an expert witness is limited to:

1. The knowledge, skill, experience, training, or education that qualifies the witness to testify as an expert in respect of the issue or issues in dispute;
2. The opinion of the witness in respect of which the witness's expert testimony is relevant to the issue or issues in dispute;
3. The facts or data that underlie that opinion; and
4. The witness's analysis, showing how the witness proceeded from the facts or data to draw the conclusion that represents the opinion of the witness.[67]

---

[63]*Id.*
[64]*Tax Ct. R.* 74(c).
[65]*Tax Ct. R.* 74(c)(1)(A).
[66]*Tax Ct. R.* 74(c)(1)(B).
[67]*Tax Ct. R.* 74(c)(4)(A).

Significantly, a party generally may not, by deposition, "discover facts known or opinions held by an expert who has been retained or specifically employed by another party in anticipation of litigation or to prepare for trial and who is not expected to be called as a witness at trial," except upon "showing exceptional circumstances under which it is impracticable for the party to obtain facts or opinions on the same subject by other means."[68] This rule, of course, ensures that the work product doctrine applies to all phases of litigation.

II. Procedure for Obtaining Permission to Depose Expert Witness without the Consent of the Parties A party seeking to depose an expert witness without the consent of all parties must file a written motion setting forth:

1. The name and address of the witness to be examined;
2. A statement describing any books, papers, documents, electronically stored information, or tangible things to be produced at the deposition of the witness to be examined;
3. A statement of issues in controversy to which the expected testimony of the expert witness, or the document, electronically stored information, or thing relates, and the reasons for deposing the witness;
4. The time and place proposed for the deposition;
5. The officer before whom the deposition is to be taken;
6. Any provisions desired with respect to the payment of the costs, expenses, fees, and charges relating to the deposition; and
7. If the movant proposes to video record the deposition, then a statement to that effect, as well as the name and address of the video recorder operator and the video record operator's employer.[69]

The Tax Court's Rules also provide: "[t]he movant shall also [(i)] show that prior notice of the motion has been given to the expert witness whose deposition is sought and to each other party, or counsel for each other party, and [(ii)] shall state the position of each of these persons" (as is otherwise required by Rule 50(a) of the Tax Court Rules of Practice and Procedure).[70] "Any objection or other response to the motion for order to depose an expert witness [without the consent of the parties] shall be filed with the Court within 15 days after service of the motion."[71] Following the filing of such a motion, the Court will then issue an order with respect to the deposition request.[72]

Admissions Although not technically a formal discovery device, admissions are another tool the parties may use during the pretrial phase of litigation to obtain

---

[68] *Tax Ct. R.* 70(c)(4)(C).
[69] *Tax Ct. R.* 74(c)(4)(B). The party taking the deposition shall pay, among other costs, expenses, and fees, a reasonable fee for the expert witness for time spent attending and preparing for the deposition. *Tax Ct. R.* 74(c)(4)(D).
[70] *Tax Ct. R.* 74(c)(4)(B).
[71] *Tax Ct. R.* 74(c)(4)(B).
[72] *Id.*

information and otherwise limit the scope of triable issues. The Tax Court's Rules of Practice and Procedure provide that

> *[a] party may serve [on] another party a written request for the admission, for purposes of the pending action only, of the truth of any matters which are not privileged and [which] are relevant to the subject matter involved in the pending action, but only if such matters are set forth in the request and relate to statements or opinions of fact or of the application of law to fact.[73]*

A party generally may not make a request for admissions until 30 days after the joinder of issues (i.e., after the answer and reply have been filed).[74] A party has 30 days to respond to the request for admissions or each matter is deemed admitted, and requests for admissions must be completed no later than 45 days before trial.[75]

U.S. District Courts

Discovery with respect to civil tax cases in the U.S. district courts is governed by the Federal Rules of Civil Procedure, which require extensive pretrial discovery. As a preliminary matter, Rule 26 of the Federal Rules of Civil Procedure requires the parties to confer as soon as possible after a cause of action is filed to develop a joint discovery plan to be submitted to the court, and without any formal discovery request, to make a series of initial disclosures.[76] After the initial disclosures are made, litigants are generally given broad latitude to issue formal discovery requests, which typically includes:

- Written interrogatories;[77]
- Production of documents, electronically stored information, and other similar items;[78]
- Oral deposition;[79] or
- Admissions from the opposing party.[80]

Before discussing each discovery device in detail, this section first summarizes the general provisions relating to discovery and those related to expert witnesses.

General Provisions Regarding Discovery

Rule 26 Conference and Plan Rule 26(f) of the Federal Rules of Civil Procedure requires the parties to confer to develop a joint schedule to be submitted to the court with respect to the discovery requests.[81] In conferring, the parties must:

---

[73] *Tax Ct. R.* 90(a).
[74] *Id.*
[75] *Tax Ct. R.* 90(a), (c).
[76] *Fed. R. Civ. P.* 26.
[77] *Fed. R. Civ. P.* 33.
[78] *Fed. R. Civ. P.* 34.
[79] *Fed. R. Civ. P.* 30.
[80] *Fed. R. Civ. P.* 36.
[81] *Fed. R. Civ. P.* 26(f)(1).

(i) consider the nature and basis of their claims and defenses and the possibilities for promptly settling or resolving the case; (ii) make or arrange for the initial disclosures; (iii) discuss any issues about preserving discoverable information; and (iv) develop a proposed discovery plan.[82] The Rule 26 plan will in most material respects set the schedule and scope of discovery to be pursued by the parties.

Initial Disclosures

I. Initial Disclosure for All Cases Rule 26 of the Federal Rules of Civil Procedure requires a party, without awaiting a discovery request, to provide the following information to the other parties:

- The name, address, and telephone number of each individual likely to have discoverable information, along with the subject of that information, that the disclosing party may use to support its claims or defenses;
- A copy, or a description by category and location, of all documents, electronically stored information, and tangible things that the disclosing party has in its possession, custody, or control, and may use to support its claims or defenses;
- A computation of each category of damages claimed by the disclosing party, who must also make available for inspection and copying, all unprivileged and unprotected documents or other evidentiary material on which each computation is based; and
- For inspection and copying, any insurance agreement under which an insurance business may be liable to satisfy all or part of a possible judgment in the action or to indemnify or reimburse for payments made to satisfy the judgment.[83]

The foregoing items (referred to as the initial disclosures) must be made within 14 days of the parties' Rule 26 conference unless the parties agree to a different schedule by stipulation or pursuant to court order.[84]

II. Initial Disclosure of Expert Testimony In addition to the initial disclosure items summarized earlier, "a party must disclose to the other parties the identity of any witness" the party may use at trial as an expert witness.[85] Unless otherwise stipulated to by the parties or ordered by the court, the expert witness disclosure must be accompanied by a written report that is prepared and signed by the expert witness.[86] The report must contain the following information:

- A complete statement of all opinions the witness will express and the basis and reasons for them;
- The facts or data considered by the witness in forming them;
- Any exhibits that will be used to summarize or support them;
- The witness's qualifications, including a list of all publications authored in the previous ten years;

---

[82] *Fed. R. Civ. P.* 26(f)(2).
[83] *Fed. R. Civ. P.* 26(a)(1)(A).
[84] *Fed. R. Civ. P.* 26(a)(1)(C).
[85] *Fed. R. Civ. P.* 26(a)(2)(A).
[86] *Fed. R. Civ. P.* 26(a)(2)(B).

- A list of all other cases in which, during the previous four years, the witness testified as an expert at trial or by deposition; and
- A statement of the compensation to be paid for the study and the testimony in the case.[87]

As a practical matter, most taxpayers who bring a refund case in a U.S. district court or the U.S. Court of Federal Claims ("Court of Claims") in connection with a valuation issue will have already provided their expert's report to the government before the complaint is ever filed. Some background may be helpful.

A condition, precedent to a judicial action for a refund of tax, is that the taxpayer timely file a claim for refund with the IRS.[88] Refund courts, unlike the Tax Court, prohibit reliance on legal theories and factual bases that vary from those set forth in the administrative refund claim.[89] This principle is generally known as the "doctrine of variance." Thus, as a practical matter, the doctrine of variance generally requires that the taxpayer provide a copy of the appraisal report she intends to use in the refund action before the complaint is ever filed. For most practical purposes, the government is in possession of the expert's report well before Rule 26 disclosures are made. However, to the extent a taxpayer intends to deviate from the appraisal report presented in the administrative claim for refund, she should turn that report over to the government as soon as possible because, if the government does not object to its use on the grounds of the doctrine of variance, that report may still be admissible.

III. Disclosure within 30 Days of Trial Notwithstanding the doctrine of variance, the parties must disclose to the adverse party the following items within 30 days before trial:

- The name, address, and telephone number of each witness, separately identifying those the party expects to present and those it may call if the need arises;
- The designation of those witnesses whose testimony the party expects to present by deposition and, if not taken via stenography, a transcript of the pertinent parts of the deposition; and
- An identification of each document or other exhibit, including summaries of other evidence, separately identifying those items the party expects to offer and those it may offer if the need arises.[90]

Timing of Discovery Discovery generally may not be commenced in U.S. district courts until after the Rule 26 conference described above.[91] Unlike the Tax Court, no preference is given as to the method of discovery or when it is to be used in the discovery process (e.g., depositions may be used before interrogatories). Indeed, depositions tend to be the preferred discovery device for many U.S. Department of Justice attorneys.

---

[87] *Id.*
[88] *See* I.R.C. § 7422.
[89] *See, e.g., Lockheed Martin Corp. v. United States*, 210 F.3d 1366 (Fed. Cir. 2000).
[90] *Fed. R. Civ. P.* 26(a)(3).
[91] *Fed. R. Civ. P.* 26(d).

Scope of Discovery Parties before the U.S. district courts "may obtain discovery regarding any nonprivileged matter that is relevant to any party's claim or defense and proportional to the needs of the case."[92] District courts, like the Tax Court, retain broad discretion to order discovery of any matter relevant to the subject matter involved in the action. Moreover, relevant information need not be admissible at the trial to be discoverable.[93]

General Limitations on Discovery The frequency or extent of use of the discovery methods allowed by the U.S. district courts may be limited in the same manner as before the Tax Court. The court may limit discovery if the court determines that: (A) the discovery sought is unreasonably cumulative or duplicative, or can be obtained from some other source that is more convenient, less burdensome, or less expensive; (B) the party seeking discovery has had ample opportunity by discovery in the action to obtain the information sought; or (C) the discovery is unduly burdensome or expensive, taking into account the needs of the case, the amount in controversy, limitations on the parties' resources, and the importance of the issues at stake in the litigation.[94]

Discovery of Experts Discovery concerning expert witnesses in the U.S. district courts is generally set forth in Rule 26(b)(4) of the Federal Rules of Civil Procedure, which provides:

> (A) *Deposition of an Expert Who May Testify.* A party may depose any person who has been identified as an expert whose opinions may be presented at trial. If Rule 26(a)(2)(B) requires a report from the expert, the deposition may be conducted only after the report is provided.
>
> (B) *Trial-Preparation Protection for Draft Reports or Disclosures.* Rules 26(b)(3)(A) and (B) protect drafts of any report or disclosure required under Rule 26(a)(2), regardless of the form in which the draft is recorded.
>
> (C) *Trial-Preparation Protection for Communications Between a Party's Attorney and Expert Witnesses.* Rules 26(b)(3)(A) and (B) protect communications between the party's attorney and any witness required to provide a report under Rule 26(a)(2)(B), regardless of the form of the communications, except to the extent that the communications:
>
> > (i) relate to compensation for the expert's study or testimony;
> >
> > (ii) identify facts or data that the party's attorney provided and that the expert considered in forming the opinions to be expressed; or
> >
> > (iii) identify assumptions that the party's attorney provided and that the expert relied on in forming the opinions to be expressed.
>
> (D) *Expert Employed Only for Trial Preparation.* Ordinarily, a party may not, by interrogatories or deposition, discover facts known or opinions held by an expert who has been retained or specially employed by another party in anticipation of litigation or to prepare for trial and

---

[92] *Fed. R. Civ. P.* 26(b).
[93] *Id.*
[94] *Fed. R. Civ. P.* 26(b)(2)(C).

who is not expected to be called as a witness at trial. But a party may do so only:

(i) as provided in Rule 35(b); or

(ii) on showing exceptional circumstances under which it is impracticable for the party to obtain facts or opinions on the same subject by other means.

(E) *Payment.* Unless manifest injustice would result, the court must require that the party seeking discovery:

(i) pay the expert a reasonable fee for time spent in responding to discovery under Rule 26(b)(4)(A) or (D); and

(ii) for discovery under (D), also pay the other party a fair portion of the fees and expenses it reasonably incurred in obtaining the expert's facts and opinions.

Limitations on Discovery Related to Experts Limitations with respect to expert witnesses, namely those for attorney–client privileged information and under the work product doctrine, apply in the same manner as in proceedings before the Tax Court, which were discussed earlier.

Interrogatories The use of interrogatories as a discovery device in the U.S. district courts is governed by Rule 33 of the Federal Rules of Civil Procedure. The Federal Rules of Civil Procedure parallel the Tax Court Rules of Practice and Procedure with respect to the use of interrogatories, except that the Federal Rules of Civil Procedure does not include special rules for interrogatories served upon expert witnesses. Thus, a party may serve on any other party no more than 25 written interrogatories, including all discrete subparts, to be answered by the party served.[95] The U.S. district courts, like the Tax Court, have broad discretion to grant leave to a party to serve additional interrogatories so long as such request is consistent with the general objectives of discovery (i.e., the additional interrogatories seek information that is not unreasonably cumulative or duplicative or that is not obtainable from other sources that are more convenient, less burdensome, or less expensive).[96]

Interrogatories must be answered by the party to whom they are directed within 30 days after being served, unless otherwise stipulated to by the parties or ordered by the court.[97] Each interrogatory must be answered separately and fully under oath, unless an interrogatory is objected to, in which case the reason for the objection shall be stated with specificity in lieu of the answer.[98]

Production of Documents, Electronically Stored Information, and Other Similar Items
Production Pursuant to a Request Requests served upon parties for production of documents, electronically stored information, and tangible things are governed by Rule 34 of the Federal Rules of Civil Procedure. The Federal Rules of Civil Procedure again parallel the rules with respect to requests for production of documents, electronically stored information, and other similar items. Thus, pursuant to Rule 34(a)

---

[95] *Fed. R. Civ. P.* 33(a)(1).
[96] *Id.*
[97] *Fed. R. Civ. P.* 33(b)(1), (2).
[98] *See Fed. R. Civ. P.* 33(b)(3), (4).

of the Federal Rules of Civil Procedure, a party may serve on another a party a request to:

> *Produce and permit the requesting party, or its representative, to inspect, copy, test, or sample ... any designated documents or electronically stored information—including writings, drawings, graphs, charts, photographs, sound recordings, images, and other data or data compilations stored in any medium from which information can be obtained either directly or, if necessary, after translation by the responding party into a reasonably usable form; or*

> *Permit entry upon designated land or other property possessed or controlled by the responding party so that the requesting party may inspect, measure, survey, photograph, test, or sample the property or any designated objects or operation on it.*

The request for production of documents, electronically stored information, and other items must set forth with reasonable particularity each item or category of items to be inspected, must specify a reasonable time, place, and manner for the inspection and for performing the related acts, and may specify the form or forms in which electronically stored information is to be produced.[99]

The party to whom the request is directed generally must respond to a request for production of documents, electronically stored information, and things within 30 days of the service of request unless an alternative timeline is stipulated to by the parties or ordered by the court.[100] The response shall state, as to each item or category, that "inspection and related activities will be permitted as requested or state an objection to the request" together with the reasons for the objection.[101]

Production Pursuant to a Subpoena   The Federal Rules of Civil Procedure states that "a nonparty may be compelled to produce documents and tangible things or to permit an inspection" as provided in Rule 45, relating to subpoenas.[102]

Depositions   Discovery by deposition is addressed in Rules 30 and 31 of the Federal Rules of Civil Procedure, with the former covering the more prevalent depositions by oral examination and the latter rule covering the less widely used deposition by written questions. Depositions of fact and expert witnesses are allowed, and as a practical matter, seem to be the favored discovery device of many attorneys appearing in federal courts other than the Tax Court.[103] A party appearing in a U.S. district court may generally depose up to ten individuals, including an opposing party, without leave of court.[104] A party seeking to depose more than ten individuals must

---

[99] *Fed. R. Civ. P.* 34(b)(1).

[100] *Fed. R. Civ. P.* 34(b)(2)(A).

[101] *Fed. R. Civ. P.* 34(b)(2)(B).

[102] *Fed. R. Civ. P.* 34(c); *see also Fed. R. Civ. P.* 45(a)(1)(C) ("A command to produce documents, electronically stored information, or tangible things or to permit the inspection of premises may be included in a subpoena commanding attendance at a deposition, hearing, or trial, or may be set out in a separate subpoena.").

[103] *Fed. R. Civ. P.* 30(a).

[104] *Fed. R. Civ. P.* 30(a)(1), (2).

obtain leave of court to do so.[105] The length of a deposition is generally limited to one day or seven hours, unless otherwise stipulated to by the parties or ordered by the court.[106]

Admissions   The Federal Rules of Civil procedure likewise allows for admissions to expedite the trial process. Rule 36 permits a party to serve on any other party a written request for the admission, for purposes of the pending action only, of the truth of any matters which are not privileged and that are relevant to the subject matter involved in the pending action, but only if such matters are set forth in the request and relate to statements or opinions of fact or of the application of law to fact.[107] As in the Tax Court, a matter is deemed admitted unless, "within 30 days after being served, the party to whom the request is directed serve[d] on the requesting party a written answer or objection addressed to the matter and signed by the party or [the party's] attorney."[108]

Court of Claims

The Rules of the Court of Claims are substantially similar to the Federal Rules of Civil Procedure. Thus, our discussion with respect to the Federal Rules of Civil Procedure generally applies to cases before the Court of Claims.

EXPERT SHOULD BE PRESENT AT OPPOSING EXPERT'S DEPOSITION

Preliminarily, at least in relation to disputed business valuations, depositions are generally far more productive than interrogatories. This results from the attorney's ability to ask a series of follow-up questions during a deposition.

CONCLUSION

The prevalence of expert witness testimony in civil tax cases has increased markedly in recent years. Given the important role experts play in tax litigation, litigants find it imperative to discover, and perhaps to use at trial, information, opinions, and conclusions of an opposing party's expert witness. There are many substantive and procedural differences between the Tax Court and the U.S. district courts and the Court of Claims as to the type of information that may be discoverable. Attorneys and their clients should know the discovery rules discussed in this chapter so as to obtain discoverable information and to protect undiscoverable information.

---

[105] *Fed. R. Civ. P.* 30(a)(2).
[106] *Fed. R. Civ. P.* 30(d).
[107] *Fed. R. Civ. P.* 36(a)(1).
[108] Fed. R. Civ. P. 36(a)(3).

CHAPTER 9

Expert Appraisal Reports

SUMMARY

Modern appraisal practice requires that appraisers develop and clearly communicate their analyses, opinions, assumptions, and conclusions to clients and intended users in a way that is meaningful, candid, and unbiased. The characteristics of any given appraised property may vary widely, but nearly any property can be valued by adopting and applying a systematic valuation process. There are many valuation standards available to appraisers that can be used to value property. The Uniform Standards of Professional Appraisal Practice ("USPAP") is one such valuation standard that is often used to assist appraisers in developing the valuation process by setting forth generally accepted standards for professional appraisal preparation, appraisal review, and appraisal consulting in North America.[1] This chapter focuses primarily on proper appraisal preparation under USPAP and Revenue Ruling 59-60,[2] and more specifically, those items that can be expected to be found in appraisal reports. In addition, this chapter highlights practical deficiencies commonly observed in connection with appraisals to support tax reporting positions.

VALUATION STANDARDS

Appraisers have a broad range of valuation standards at their disposal to help guide them when drafting an appraisal report. Revenue Ruling 59-60, widely considered the seminal authority on the valuation of closely held business ownership interests for U.S. tax purposes, has impacted the development of comprehensive business valuation standards now prevalent in modern appraisal practice.[3] Among the valuation standards available to appraisers are USPAP (issued by the Appraisal Foundation) and the standards from various professional associations such as the American Society of Appraisers ("ASA"), the Institute of Business

---

[1] *Uniform Standards of Professional Appraisal Practice* (Appraisal Standards Bd., The Appraisal Found., 2014-2015) [hereinafter "USPAP"].

[2] Rev. Rul. 59-60, 1959-1 C.B. 237.

[3] *See* Martin J. Lieberman and David Anderson, "Will the Real Business Valuation Standards Please Stand Up? The AICPA's SSVS Compared to USPAP and Other Business Valuation Standards," *CPA J.* (Jan. 2008), at 22 (discussing various valuation standards).

Appraisers ("IBA"), the National Association of Certified Valuation Analysts ("NACVA"), and the American Institute of Certified Public Accountants ("AICPA"). This chapter begins by discussing Revenue Ruling 59-60, upon which a number of business valuation standards depend. The chapter then focuses primarily on the contents of an appraisal report required by USPAP, which is the valuation standard most generally applicable to the valuation of closely held businesses, real property, and intangibles. Additionally, USPAP has received recognition from Congress as the valuation standard for valuing, among other property, certain federally funded real estate projects and intangibles.[4] Nevertheless, appraisal reports, especially those valuing ownership interests in closely held businesses, should consider the appropriateness of one or more of these other valuation standards.

Revenue Ruling 59-60

Revenue Ruling 59-60 outlines the general approach, methods, and criteria to be considered when determining the fair market value of a closely held business.[5] The ruling lists eight factors to consider when valuing a closely held business. These factors are:

1. The nature of the business and the history of the enterprise from its inception;
2. The economic outlook in general and the condition and outlook of the specific industry in particular;
3. The book value of the stock and the financial condition of the business;
4. The earning capacity of the company;
5. The dividend-paying capacity;
6. Whether the enterprise has goodwill or other intangible value;
7. Sales of the stock and the size of the block of stock to be valued; and
8. The market price of stocks of corporations engaged in the same or a similar line of business having their stocks actively traded in a free and open market, either on an exchange or over-the-counter.[6]

The foregoing eight factors are incorporated in one form or another into USPAP and the standards established by the ASA, the IBA, and the NACVA. The AICPA's Statement on Standards for Valuation Services 1, *Valuation of a Business, Business Ownership Interest, Security, or Intangible Assets (SSVS)*, similarly incorporates these standards with a greater emphasis on the effect of intangible assets on the value of a company.[7] In business valuations, one of the most important factors to consider is the earning capacity of the company. For the reasons discussed earlier, the balance of this chapter focuses on the contents of appraisal reports as required by USPAP.

---

[4]*See id.* (discussing the reasons why USPAP has emerged as the preferred valuation standard).
[5]Rev. Rul. 59-60, *supra* note 2.
[6]*Id.* § 4.01.
[7]See *Statements on Standards for Valuation Services: Valuation of a Business, Business Ownership Interest, Security, or Intangible Asset*, Valuation Section (Am. Inst. Certified Pub. Accountants, 2007) [hereinafter "SSVS"].

USPAP Generally

The Appraisal Standards Board of the Appraisal Foundation developed USPAP to prescribe generally accepted standards for professional appraisal practice in North America. USPAP specifies the procedures to follow in developing and communicating an appraisal, as well as the ethical rules for professional appraisal practice. The purpose of USPAP, as stated in its preamble, "is to promote and maintain a high level of public trust in appraisal practice by establishing requirements for appraisers."[8]

Compliance with USPAP   Compliance with USPAP is necessary when required by law, regulation, or agreement with the client or intended users.[9] Compliance with USPAP is recommended whenever an individual holds herself out to the public as an appraiser.[10] Finally, even in situations where compliance with USPAP is not expressly mandated, appraisers may, and indeed should, to the extent practicable, comply with USPAP.[11]

Noncompliance with USPAP Does Not Render an Expert Report Unreliable   USPAP is only one set of standards that may apply to a given appraisal assignment. As the Tax Court observed in *Whitehouse Hotel Ltd. P'ship v. Commissioner*,[12] adherence to USPAP is evidence that the valuator is applying methods that are generally accepted within the appraisal profession. However, failure to comply with USPAP in an appraisal assignment does not necessarily mean that the report is unreliable. The Tax Court in *Whitehouse* declined "to adopt USPAP as the sole standard for reliability of an expert appraiser under Rule 702 of the Federal Rules of Evidence."[13] Thus, noncompliance with USPAP does not mean that the report is *per se* unreliable.

APPRAISAL REPORTS GENERALLY

Appraisal reports generally include "any communication, written or oral, of an appraisal or appraisal review that is transmitted to the client upon completion of an assignment."[14] A discussion of oral appraisals is outside the scope of this chapter. The type, format, and contents of a written appraisal report may vary widely depending upon the client's requirements and the intended use of the appraisal. In all written appraisals, however, the report should enable the reader to follow the appraiser's rationale in a logical and reasonable manner.[15] Thus, whenever possible, an appraisal report of any type should endeavor to include the information discussed in this chapter.

---

[8]USPAP, *supra* note 1, pmbl.
[9]*Id.*
[10]*Id.*
[11]*See id.*
[12]131 T.C. 112, 126-127 (2008), *vacated on other grounds*, 615 F.3d 321 (5th Cir. 2010).
[13]*Id.*
[14]USPAP, *supra* note 1, U-4.
[15]*Id.* at U-23, Standard 2-2(a)(viii), cmt, and U-56, Standard 8-2, cmt.

Fair Market Value

Appraisal reports used for federal tax purposes must be made in accordance with the applicable provisions of the Internal Revenue Code, including adopting fair market value as the measure of value. Fair market value is the "price at which the property would change hands between a willing buyer and a willing seller," neither being under a compulsion to buy or to sell, and each party having "reasonable knowledge of [all] relevant facts."[16] "A determination of fair market value, being a question of fact, will depend upon the [facts and] circumstances in each case."[17] Appraisers may express varying differences of opinion as to the fair market value of a particular piece of property. Thus, a sound appraisal report will be based upon (and disclose) all relevant facts as well as "the elements of common sense, informed judgment," and reasoning that an appraiser uses to reach his or her ultimate opinion of value.[18]

CONTENTS OF THE APPRAISAL REPORT

Table of Contents

Appraisal reports should include a table of contents with at least first-level headings and sometimes second-level headings. In especially long reports, there could even be chapter headings and first- and second-level headings within chapters. The table of contents will not only be helpful to the reader, but also help the writer to produce a well-organized report.

Executive Summary or Cover Letter

Every appraisal report should include an executive summary or cover letter that sets forth the material terms and assumptions associated with the valuation. Among the items that should be detailed in the executive summary, each of which is discussed more fully in this chapter, are the following:

- The retaining party and other intended users;
- The name, address, and (as applicable) identifying number of the appraiser;
- The type of appraisal (e.g., appraisal report or restricted appraisal report);
- The standard of value, its definition, and its source;
- The effective date of the appraisal *and* the date of the report;
- The purpose of the appraisal and its intended use;
- A statement as to the reason for which the appraisal was prepared (e.g., whether the appraisal was prepared for income, estate, or gift tax purposes, condemnation proceedings, or bank financing);
- A summary of the scope of work;
- A summary of the information considered;
- A brief description of the subject property and the specific interest valued;

---

[16]Rev. Rul. 59-60, *supra* note 2, § 2.
[17]*Id.* § 3.
[18]*Id.*

- A summary of how title to the property is held (e.g., in fee simple, as joint tenants, or as tenants-in-common);
- A summary of the terms of any agreement that affects the beneficial ownership of the property (e.g., a reserved life estate in the property, restrictions on use of the property, etc.);
- A summary of the methodologies used to value the property;
- A summary of any caveats, hypotheticals, or limiting conditions adopted;
- A summary of the owner's control over the subject property;
- A summary of any liquidity constraints affecting the subject property;
- A summary of any premiums attributable to the subject property;
- The conclusion of value; and
- The appraiser's signature.

Body of Report

As previously mentioned, this chapter principally focuses on the information to be included in an appraisal report (as compared with a restricted appraisal report).[19] The requirements for a "qualified appraisal" as set forth in Chapter 3 and the general appraisal report requirements discussed in this chapter are sufficiently similar such that an appraiser can easily adopt a methodology that satisfies both standards.[20]

Before we discuss the items to be included in the body of an appraisal report, the following caution is appropriate: appraisal reports can, and indeed should, vary widely depending upon the purpose and intended use of the appraisal. The discussion that follows is intended to provide readers with an overview of the key elements they should expect to find and include in any given appraisal report.

Identifying the Retaining Party and Other Intended Users   An appraisal must identify the client and intended users of the report. The term *client* is defined in USPAP to mean "the party or parties who engage, by employment or contract, an appraiser in a specific assignment."[21] The term *intended user* is defined in USPAP to mean the client as well as any other party identified by the appraiser as a user of the report at the time of the appraisal assignment.[22] In identifying the potential intended users, it is of critical import that the appraiser *intend* for the party named to use the report. Unintended users need not be named in the report. Intended users include the client, and may, depending upon the circumstances for which the appraisal is obtained, include third parties such as a court, the IRS, a state tax authority, a municipality, one or more attorneys, one or more accountants, or a lender. It is also advisable for the report to include, most likely on the cover page or in the executive summary, the name, address, and identifying number of the appraiser.

---

[19]It is important to note that there were formerly three types of written reports for real and personal property appraisal reports: self-contained appraisal reports; summary appraisal reports; and restricted appraisal reports. Effective as of January 1, 2014, USPAP eliminated the self-contained appraisal report and now recognizes only two types of written reports, namely, Appraisal Reports and Restricted Appraisal Reports.

[20]*See* Treas. Reg. § 1.170A-13(c)(3).

[21]USPAP, *supra* note 1, at U-2.

[22]*Id.* at U-3.

Identifying the foregoing parties achieves three objectives. First, identifying the client and the intended users ensures that the appraiser is able to identify the problem to be solved and understand her development and reporting responsibilities in the appraisal preparation process. Second, identifying the client and intended users ensures that the appraiser understands the parties to whom she is responsible and the parties to whom the confidentiality rule under USPAP applies. Third, as discussed in Chapter 3, *Qualified Appraiser*, supplying the appraiser's name, address, and (as applicable) identifying number moves an appraiser one step closer to securing a "qualified appraisal" (as may be required for federal tax purposes).

Type of Appraisal USPAP Standard Rules 2-2 and 8-2 allow an appraiser to communicate the results of the appraisal in one of the following two formats: (i) an appraisal report, or (ii) a restricted appraisal report. An *appraisal report* provides a summary of the appraiser's research and the information being analyzed as well as the reasoning behind her analysis. In comparison, a *restricted appraisal report* simply states the conclusions of the appraisal. Additionally, the only permitted intended user of a restricted appraisal report is the client.[23] Both of these appraisal types have reporting rules that serve as a content outline and are specified in USPAP.[24] USPAP Advisory Opinion 11 includes a chart that specifies the essential differences among the two options.

Standard of Value and Source An appraisal report must identify the standard of value the appraiser uses in her report.[25] The standards of value are numerous and may include fair market value, fair value, market value, investment value, intrinsic value, book value, going-concern value, and liquidation value. The specific standard of value to be applied depends upon the scope of work and the legal and regulatory requirements.

Incompatibility of "Market Value" for Federal Tax Valuations The Tax Court has expressed dissatisfaction with appraisers who adopted market value,[26] as opposed to fair market value, as the standard of value in their appraisals to support a federal tax reporting position.[27] Treasury Regulations are clear that fair market value is the standard of value to be used for federal tax purposes. The Tax Court recognized in *Rothman v. Commissioner* that "although market value adopts selective elements of fair market value, the two are not identical."[28]

[23]*Id.* at A-22, Advisory Opinion 11.
[24]*See, e.g., id.* at U-21, Standard 2, and U-53, Standard 8.
[25]*See, e.g., id.*
[26]*See id.* at U-3.
[27]*See, e.g., Rothman v. Comm'r*, 104 T.C.M. (CCH) 126 (2012).
[28]*Rothman v. Comm'r*, 103 T.C.M. (CCH) 1864, 1873 (2012) (comparing Treas. Reg. § 1.170A-1(c)(2) (defining fair market value) and Advisory Opinion 22 in the 2008 version of USPAP (defining market value)), *vacated in part on reconsideration on other grounds*, 104 T.C.M. (CCH) 126 (2012); *see also DiDonato v. Comm'r*, 101 T.C.M. (CCH) 1739, 1741 n.8 (2011).

The Jurisdictional Exception Rule as a Panacea for Aligning USPAP with Federal Tax Law How an appraiser is to reconcile the apparent incongruity between that which is required by federal tax law (fair market value) and that which is seemingly favored by USPAP (market value) is contained in the USPAP jurisdictional exception rule. Under USPAP's jurisdictional exception rule, "[i]f any applicable law or regulation precludes compliance with any part of USPAP, [then] only that portion of USPAP becomes void" for purposes of the assignment, and the law or regulation controls.[29] The appraiser is, however, placed under an affirmative duty to note the variance between that which is required by USPAP (market value) and that which is required by the federal tax law (fair market value). Thus, where an appraiser adopts fair market value rather than market value as her standard of value, the appraiser should:

1. Identify the law or regulation that precludes compliance with USPAP;
2. Comply with that law or regulation;
3. Clearly and conspicuously disclose in the report the part of USPAP that is voided by that law or regulation; and
4. Cite in the report the law or regulation requiring this exception to USPAP compliance.[30]

USPAP is also equally clear that "[w]hen an appraiser properly follows [the jurisdictional exception rule] in disregarding a part of USPAP, there is no violation of USPAP."[31] Thus, when an appraiser prepares a report for federal tax purposes, the jurisdictional exception rule should be invoked to adopt fair market value as the standard of value.

Effective Date of the Appraisal and the Date of the Report USPAP requires that an appraisal set forth the effective date of the appraisal as well as the date of the report.[32] The *effective date* of the appraisal is the date as of which the appraiser expresses her opinions and conclusions of value. The effective date is important because that date "establishes the context" for the opinion of value.[33] The *date of the report* indicates to a reader whether the appraiser's perspective of the property was prospective, current, or retrospective.

Current Appraisals A current appraisal is made when "the effective date of the appraisal is contemporaneous with the date of the report."[34] Current appraisals are commonly secured in connection with bank financings and valuations of personal property.

---

[29] *See* USPAP, *supra* note 1, at U-15.
[30] *Id.*
[31] *Id.*
[32] *Id.* at U-22, Standard 2, U-53, Standard 8, and U-74, Statement 3.
[33] *Id.* at U-74, Statement 3.
[34] *Id.*

Retrospective Appraisals A retrospective appraisal is made when the effective date of the appraisal is prior to the date of the report. Retrospective appraisals are common in estate, gift, and income tax matters, property tax matters, suits to recover damages, and condemnation proceedings.[35] The question often arises with respect to retrospective appraisals as to what extent, if any, an appraiser may rely upon events occurring after the valuation date to determine fair market value.

In *Ithaca Trust Co. v. United States*,[36] the Supreme Court sets forth the general rule that subsequent events should generally not be considered in determining the fair market value of property on the valuation date. A number of exceptions to the general rule have developed over the years, although these exceptions are generally outside the scope of this book.[37] It is worth noting, however, that subsequent events may be considered when determining fair market value to the extent the events were reasonably foreseeable on the valuation date.[38] Thus, in a majority of the federal circuit courts,[39] a retrospective appraisal may consider relevant subsequent events to the extent those events are reasonably foreseeable because the events would likewise be foreseeable by a willing buyer and a willing seller. By contrast, in some federal circuit courts, valuators may take into account post-valuation date events.[40] Thus, valuators must be mindful of governing case law in deciding whether to consider events arising after the valuation date.

Prospective Appraisals Prospective appraisals occur when the effective date of the appraisal is subsequent to the date of the report. Prospective appraisals are most common when valuing business interests.

---

[35]*Id.*

[36]*Ithaca Trust Co. v. United States*, 279 U.S. 151, 155 (1929).

[37]For a more complete discussion of subsequent events, *see* David Laro and Shannon P. Pratt, *Business Valuation and Federal Taxes: Procedure, Law, and Perspective*, chapter 2 (2d ed. 2011).

[38]*Estate of Gilford v. Comm'r*, 88 T.C. 38, 52 (1987).

[39]In *Propstra v. United States*, 680 F.2d 1248, 1253-1256 (9th Cir. 1982), the U.S. Court of Appeals for the Ninth Circuit held that post-death events are not relevant in computing a permissible deduction where the claims are for sums certain and are legally enforceable as of the date of death. The U.S. Courts of Appeals for the Fifth agreed with the Ninth Circuit in *Estate of Smith v. Comm'r*, 198 F.3d 515, 517 (5th Cir. 1999), *rev'g*, 108 T.C. 412 (1997), in which the Fifth Circuit held that claims against an estate must be valued as of the decedent's date of death and therefore must be appraised on information known or available up to (but not after) that date.

[40]In *Estate of Sachs v. Comm'r*, 856 F.2d 1158, 1160 (8th Cir. 1988), *rev'g*, 88 T.C. 769 (1987), the U.S. Court of Appeals for the Eighth Circuit held that events occurring after the date of death may be considered in determining whether the estate is entitled to a deduction for a claim against the estate. Similarly, the U.S. Court of Appeals for the Second Circuit endorses the view of the Eighth Circuit, though it measures the relevant date for testing the foreseeability of the subsequent events as the date the estate tax return is filed, not the date of death. *See Comm'r v. Estate of Shively*, 276 F.2d 372, 375 (2d Cir. 1959) ("We hold that where, prior to the date on which the estate tax return is filed, the total amount of a claim against the estate is clearly established under state law, the estate may obtain under … no greater deduction than the established sum, irrespective of whether this amount is established through events occurring before or after the decedent's death.").

Purpose of the Appraisal and Its Intended Use   The appraisal must state the purpose for which the report was prepared and its intended use.[41] The purpose of the appraisal should be straightforward, unambiguous, and conspicuously noted. Potential purposes for which an appraisal might be obtained include, but are not limited to, the following: (i) income tax purposes, including to substantiate a charitable contribution deduction or a claimed loss; (ii) estate and/or gift tax purposes; (iii) condemnation proceedings; (iv) financing purposes; (v) the basis for a collateral loan decision; (vi) insurance purposes; (vii) equitable distribution purposes; (viii) the basis for distribution decisions; (ix) establishing liquidation value; and (x) determining net worth.

The appraisal should also state the intended use of the report. The term *intended use* means "the use or uses of an appraiser's reported ... opinions and conclusions, as identified by the appraiser based on communication with the client at the time of the assignment."[42] For example, an appraiser might state: "The intended use of the appraisal is for submission to the Internal Revenue Service as required by I.R.C. § 170(f)(11)." In accordance with USPAP, "An appraiser identifies the intended use by communicating with the client before accepting [the assignment]" and conveys the intended use to the client and other intended users with clear and unambiguous language.[43]

Summary of the Scope of Work   An appraisal report must include a summary of the scope of work, including the type and extent of research and analysis in any given assignment.[44] The scope of work serves the practical purpose of ensuring that the intended users are informed and not misled about the scope of the work performed. USPAP requires that, for each appraisal, an appraiser must:

1. Identify the problem to be solved;
2. Determine and perform the scope of work necessary to develop credible assignment results, and
3. Disclose the scope of work in the report.[45]

Appraisers are granted broad flexibility to determine the appropriate scope of work for each appraisal. The scope of work may include, but is not limited to, the following items:

- The extent to which the property is identified;
- The extent to which tangible property is inspected;
- The type and extent of data researched; and
- The type and extent of analyses applied to arrive at opinions or conclusions.[46]

Many appraisals involve the participation of more than one appraiser. All appraisers who participate in the preparation of an appraisal should sign

---

[41]USPAP, *supra* note 1, at U-22, Standard 2, U-53, Standard 8, U-83, Statement 9.
[42]*Id.* at U-3.
[43]*Id.* at U-84, Statement 9.
[44]*Id.* at U-13.
[45]*Id.*
[46]*Id.*

the report.[47] Moreover, all authoring appraisers should be available to testify at trial. Indeed, some Tax Court judges and the IRS take the position that an individual may not testify in a proceeding with respect to portions of an appraisal that he did not prepare.[48] Among the situations where joint appraisals are produced, the most commonly scenarios include:

- Two appraisers who work on an assignment as equals;
- A staff or junior appraiser whose work is subject to review or direction by a senior appraiser;
- A trainee appraiser who requires supervision by a fully qualified or credentialed appraiser;
- An independent contractor who works for an appraisal firm; and
- Collaborations between appraisers specializing in different appraisal practice disciplines.[49]

To the extent any portion of the appraisal work performed involves significant appraisal assistance, the appraiser must describe the scope of that assistance, provide the name or names of the assistant, and include a certification by the assistant.[50]

Summary of Information Considered   Before drafting the appraisal report, the appraiser must first gather general and historical data with respect to the subject property, comparable properties, and the market to which the valuation applies. The appraisal report must summarize the data collected, the information analyzed, the appraisal methods and techniques employed, and the reasoning in support of the analyses, opinions, and conclusions reached in the report.[51] Although the amount of detail required will undeniably vary between assignments, an appraiser must provide "sufficient information to enable the client and intended users to understand the rationale for the opinions and conclusions, including reconciliation of the data and approaches."[52] Additionally, the appraiser should disclose the specific comparable properties analyzed and discuss how (if at all) the subject property differs from the comparables. Such an analysis allows the reader to more easily determine whether the purported comparables are true comparables. Enabling this understanding

---

[47]*See Tax Ct. R.* 143(g)(1) (requiring that an expert report be "prepared and signed by the [expert] witness"), (g)(3) ("The Court ordinarily will not grant a request to permit an expert witness to testify without a written report where the expert witness's testimony is based on third-party contacts, comparable sales, statistical data, or other detailed, technical information.").

[48]*See Estate of Noble v. Comm'r*, T.C. Memo. 2005-2, 89 T.C.M. (CCH) 649 (2005) (excluding an expert report that was authored by three individuals, where only one of those individuals was available to testify at trial); *see also* I.R.S. Chief. Couns. Notice CC-2004-023 (June 4, 2004).

[49]USPAP, *supra* note 1, at A-107, Advisory Opinion 31. Alternatively, the author of the appraisal report can disclose in the Extraordinary Assumption section the fact that one or more appraisers from different disciplines provides assistance.

[50]*Id.*

[51]*See id.* at U-22, Standard 2, U-53, Standard 8.

[52]*Id.*

requires not only that the report be clear about its conclusions, but also that the information relied upon to reach the conclusion be adequately disclosed.

Transactional Documents—Business Valuations As discussed ahead, the appraisal report should reflect and disclose those restrictions that are imposed upon the property as a result of the contractual claims of all potential users of the property.[53] An understanding of the imposed restrictions is necessarily derived by reviewing certain underlying transactional documents. Among the documents that should be examined in evaluating said contractual rights, preferences, and privileges of interest are the following:

- Articles of incorporation;
- Corporate bylaws;
- Operating agreement;
- Rights of first refusal;
- Buy–sell agreements; and
- Leases, including any options associated therewith.

A best practice is to include copies of these various transactional documents as addenda to the appraisal report.

Transactional Documents—Real Property Valuations The appraisal should reflect and disclose those transactional documents reviewed to determine the title and legal description of the property valued.[54] Among the documents that should be examined and attached to the appraisal as addenda are, in addition to other relevant documents, any deeds of real property, any deeds of easement, and a legal description of the property to be valued. In addition, it is advisable for appraisers to include said documents as part of the appendices to the report.

Prior Transactions—Real Property Valuations As applied to real property valuations, an appraiser should seek to discover, and an appraisal should disclose, all relevant information about current and recent market activity involving the property being valued.[55] This requirement necessarily imposes upon the appraiser a duty of inquiry to conduct due diligence with respect to the property being valued. Indeed, appraisers are under an affirmative duty to analyze certain information about the subject property that is "available to the appraiser in the normal course of business."[56] This standard is undeniably subjective. Thus, an appraiser must identify the types of documents and other information that is generally available to and sought out by appraisers who have a similar competency and area of expertise, clients who function in the market for the subject property, and intended users of the appraisal report. Significant events that should be disclosed in the appraisal report include, but are not limited to, offers of sale, sale listings, rights of first refusal, options, the

---

[53] *See id.* at U-60, Standard 9, U-64, Standard 10.
[54] *See id.* at U-16, Standard 1, U-21, Standard 2.
[55] *See id.* at A-73, Advisory Opinion 22.
[56] *Id.* at A-84, Advisory Opinion 24.

creation or existence of easements or encumbrances on the subject property, and other significant transactions in the subject property's market. Finally, prior sales should be closely scrutinized to ensure that they are representative of arm's-length transactions, because forced or isolated sales are not necessarily determinative of fair market value.[57]

Describing the Subject Property, the Type of Asset, the Interest Valued, and Geographic Data

Separate and distinct from any regulatory requirement imposed upon an appraiser who intends to author a "qualified appraisal" (as discussed in Chapter 3, *Qualified Appraiser*), the report must include a description of the property, a statement of the condition of the property, the terms of agreement relating to the property, and an analysis of the general data and trends indicated in the relevant geographic region.[58] Among the geographic data that may be included in the appraisal report are the following:

- Overall data with respect to the economy;
- Market specific data;
- Industry specific data; and
- Summary and conclusions.

The appraisal report should not merely summarize this data, but should also analyze and explain how the data collected impacts the valuation of the subject property.

Description of Property The appraisal report should describe the subject property in sufficient detail to enable a person who is generally not familiar with the type of property being appraised to understand the property in question.[59] The appraiser should include information sufficient to identify the property appraised, including but not limited to the physical, legal, and/or economic property characteristics relevant to the assignment. Also, the appraiser should provide substantiation of the property to be appraised, including but not limited to copies or summaries of title descriptions or other documents that set forth any known encumbrances.

Condition of Property The appraisal report should provide a description of the physical condition of the property valued.[60]

Terms of Agreement Relating to Property The appraisal report should disclose "any agreement or understanding entered into (or expected to be entered into)" with respect to the property valued.[61] Such terms of agreement would necessarily disclose any agreement or understanding that (i) restricts a person's right to use or dispose of the property, or (ii) "[r]eserves to, or confers upon, anyone" other than the property owner the right to possess the property or use any income which may be derived from the property.[62]

---

[57]*See, e.g.,* Rev. Rul. 59-60, *supra* note 2, § 4.02(g) (discussing prior transactions in the context of a closely held business).
[58]*See* Treas. Reg. § 1.170A-13(c)(3).
[59]*Id.*
[60]Treas. Reg. § 1.170A-13(c)(3)(ii)(B).
[61]Treas. Reg. § 1.170A-13(c)(3)(ii)(D).
[62]*Id.*

Geographic Data and Trends An appraiser must gather, and an appraisal report must disclose, general data with respect to the market to which the valuation applies. The specific data and trends to be examined will no doubt vary between appraisal assignments. Supply and demand data should be analyzed to understand the competitive position of the subject property in the relevant market.

How Title Is Held The appraisal should clearly and unambiguously state how the title to the property being valued is held, including, but not limited to, whether the property is held as joint owners, tenants in the entirety, or tenants-in-common. Specifying how property is titled is imperative because the titling of the property may affect the economic rights associated with an ownership interest in the property and may implicate a fractional interest discount.

Restrictions, Hypotheticals, and Limiting Conditions An appraisal report must "clearly and accurately disclose all assumptions, extraordinary assumptions, hypothetical conditions, and limiting conditions used" in the appraisal process.[63] The purpose of stating these restrictions, hypotheticals, and limiting conditions is so that an intended user of the report can comprehend their significance. An *assumption* is defined in USPAP as "that which is taken to be true."[64] A *hypothetical condition* is defined in USPAP as "a condition, directly related to a specific assignment, which is contrary to what is known by the appraiser to exist on the effective date of the assignment results, but is used for the purpose of analysis."[65] A *limiting condition* is defined as "a special condition that limits the use of an appraisal," primarily "by specifying the intended use and intended user of the appraisal report."[66]

Highest and Best Use Highest and best use is a critical determination in the valuation process. The term *highest and best use* refers to "the reasonably probable and legal use of property [which] is physically possible, appropriately supported, financially feasible, and that results in the highest value."[67] The appraisal report should clearly state the highest and best use of the subject property, as well as the specific basis therefore (e.g., the most profitable use of the subject property in view of existing land use laws).

Valuation of the Subject Property Each appraisal report must be specifically tailored to the assignment and balance the relevant factors discussed throughout this chapter. A discussion of all the factors that must be included in an appraisal report is outside the scope of this chapter; however, this section discusses several factors that routinely arise in the appraisal process along with best practices for drafting the appraisal report.

---

[63]USPAP, *supra* note 1, at U-21, Standard 2-1, U-53, Standard 8-1.
[64]*Id.* at U-2.
[65]*Id.* at U-3.
[66]*The Dictionary of Real Estate Appraisal* 166, 4th ed. (Appraisal Inst., 2002).
[67]*The Dictionary of Real Estate Appraisal* 135, 4th ed. (Appraisal Inst., 2002).

Nature and History of the Property Being Valued As previously mentioned, an appraisal report must disclose the transactional documents underlying an ownership interest in property. The appraisal report should not only summarize the information considered, but also provide a brief history of the property being valued. Among the more salient information to include is how the property was acquired, whether the current owner disposed of any interest in the property, and any changes affecting the value or development of the property. For example, "The history of a corporate enterprise will show its past stability or instability, its growth or lack of growth, the diversity or lack of diversity of its operations, and other facts needed to form an opinion [as to] the degree of risk involved in the business."[68]

Economic Conditions An appraisal report should consider "current and prospective economic conditions as of the date of the appraisal, both in the national economy and in the industry or industries" to which the property relates.[69] For example, when valuing a closely held business, such information will inform the reader as to the subject company's success as compared to that of its competitors, and whether the subject company maintains a stable position relative to its competitors.[70]

Description of all Interests in the Property The appraisal should include a clear and complete description of all interests being valued and, for business appraisals, a summary of all interests that may have a say in the affairs of the company.

Financial Analysis When valuing a business using key financial and/or accounting ratios, the appraisal report should disclose the methodology for calculating the ratios and explain how the ratios impact the valuation, if at all.

The appraiser should obtain balance sheets, "preferably in the form of comparative annual statements for two or more years immediately preceding" the valuation date, as well as an end-of-month balance sheet for the month preceding the valuation date.[71] In addition, the appraiser should obtain and examine detailed profit-and-loss statements for a representative period that immediately precedes the valuation date.[72] "Any balance sheet descriptions that are not self-explanatory, and balance sheet items comprehending diverse assets or liabilities, should be clarified in essential detail [with] supporting supplemental schedules."[73] These statements will allow the appraiser to determine the following: "(1) liquid position (ratio of current assets to current liabilities); (2) gross and net book value of principal classes of fixed assets; (3) working capital; (4) long-term indebtedness; (5) capital structure; and (6) net worth."

The appraiser should also give consideration to "any assets not essential to the operation of the business" (e.g., investments in securities and real estate) and the effect, if any, of such non-operating assets on the valuation of the company.[74]

---

[68]Rev. Rul. 59-60, *supra* note 2, § 4.02(a).

[69]*Id.* § 402(b).

[70]*Id.*

[71]*Id.* § 4.02(c).

[72]*Id.* § 4.02(d).

[73]*Id.* § 4.02(c).

[74]*Id.*

As required by Revenue Ruling 59-60, the appraiser should give primary consideration to the closely held business's earning capacity and capacity to pay dividends.[75] Finally, the appraisal report should include as addenda any financial statements reviewed (e.g., income statement and balance sheet) and a computation showing the calculation of ratios determined.

Specific Rights, Preferences, and Privileges of Interest The appraisal should reflect those restrictions that are imposed upon the property as a result of federal, state, and local law. Moreover, the appraisal should reflect those restrictions that are imposed upon the property as a result of the contractual claims of all potential users of the property. The contractual rights, preferences, and privileges of interest can be determined from evaluating the transactional documents noted earlier. For example, in valuing a closely held corporation, if the subject corporation has more than one outstanding class of stock, the appraiser should examine the certificate of incorporation to determine the rights and privileges of each class of stock, including voting power, liquidation preferences, and preference as to dividends.[76]

Economic Rights, Preferences, and Privileges of Interest The appraisal should reflect those economic considerations related to the property. Among the economic rights, preferences, and privileges that should be considered are:

- Lack of marketability discount;
- Lack of control discount;
- Fractional interest or partition discount;
- Key person discount;
- Blockage and/or market absorption;
- Subchapter S tax benefit; and
- Influence.

Summary of Approaches Utilized An appraisal report must introduce and apply methodologies used to determine value on the basis of the facts and circumstances of a given case.[77] Three approaches are generally utilized in modern appraisal practice to determine value: (i) the market approach; (ii) the income approach; and (iii) the asset-based approach. A complete discussion of these methodologies is outside the scope of this book, but appraisers should understand (and include in their appraisal report) certain basic concepts with respect to each. As applied to business valuations, the *market approach* requires a comparison of the subject interest with similar interests or the market price of publicly traded companies in the same or similar lines of business. As applied to real property valuations, the market approach requires a comparison of the subject property with similar property sold in an arm's-length transaction in the same time frame. The market approach values the subject property by taking into account the sales price of comparable interests or properties and adjusting the comparable interests or properties to reflect the features of the

---

[75] *Id.* § 4.02(e).
[76] *Id.* § 4.02(c).
[77] *Id.* § 3.

subject interest or property. The *income approach* requires a valuation of the subject property by computing the present value of estimated future cash flows with respect to that property. The estimated value of the subject property equals the sum of the present value of the available cash flow plus the present value of the residual value. The *asset-based approach* generally values property by determining the cost to reproduce that property.

Reconciliation   An appraisal report should reconcile different conclusions of value derived using the various methodologies employed.[78] Reconciliation allows the appraiser to evaluate alternative conclusions of value and select a final opinion of value from among two or more indicated values. Reconciliation also provides the appraiser with an opportunity to address shortcomings in her report, to determine which indication of value is most reliable, and to resolve any differences between the values indicated by her various approaches. Finally, reconciliation allows the reader of the appraisal report to understand the basis for the final opinion of value.

During the reconciliation process, the appraiser should review all evidence contained in the appraisal to weigh the relative significance, reliability, and defensibility of each valuation methodology. As a means of deriving the final opinion of value, the appraiser should analyze, and the appraisal report should disclose, the following four considerations:

1. Address conflicting indications of value derived using the various methodologies;
2. Explain which methodology provides the best indication of value;
3. Consider the quality and quantity of the data examined and how those factors might impact the quality of the opinion of value; and
4. Discuss any reasons why the opinion of value may "not be sustainable into the foreseeable future."[79]

Consider a Regression Analysis   An item that is technically not required to be included in an appraisal report, but that may be helpful nonetheless, is a regression analysis. A regression analysis is a statistical technique that can be used to determine the effect that one or more explanatory independent variables (e.g., the respective price paid to purchase the company with those earnings or revenues) has on a single dependent variable (e.g., the earnings or revenues of recently acquired companies). The regression analysis allows valuators to test the causal relationship, if any, between the independent and dependent variables.

In a typical linear regression analysis, the dependent and independent variables are plotted on a graph on which the y-axis is the dependent variable (e.g., the earnings of a company or the size of a parcel of property) and the x-axis is the independent variable (e.g., the price paid). Through a process known as *interpolation*, the regression analysis fits a line through the scatter of plotted data that minimizes the distance between the regression line and all of the plotted data. The slope of the regression line, statistically known as a *correlation coefficient* or *coefficient of determination*, reflects

---

[78] USPAP, *supra* note 1, at U-20, Standard 1-6, U-52, Standard 7-6.
[79] *See* Appraisal Inst., Guide Note 12, "Analyzing Market Trends," 6, available at http://www.appraisalinstitute.org/assets/1/7/guide-note-12.pdf.

the unit change in the dependent variable for every unit change in the independent variable. The correlation coefficient will fall in the range of –1 to 1. The closer a correlation coefficient is to 1, or –1 as the case may be, the better a fit the model is (i.e., the more the dependent variable helps explain the independent variable). The closer a correlation coefficient is to zero, the worse a fit the model is (i.e., the less the dependent variable helps explain the independent variable). Then, using the regression analysis, the known dependent variable in the valuation assignment (e.g., the subject company's revenues or earnings) can be fitted to extrapolate the independent variable (e.g., the subject company's indicated value).

Where valuators have used a wide range of data in their regression analysis, courts have cited such regression analyses favorably. For example, in *Crimi v. Commissioner*, the Tax Court relied upon a regression analysis that used polynomial curve fitting to derive an indicated per-lot value for developable land.[80] In so ruling, the Court observed that "[t]he benefit of a regression analysis is its ability to draw a wider range of data to produce a better approximation of the dependent variable … as a function of the independent variable." By contrast, where valuators have based their regression analyses on a small sample, courts have been skeptical. For example, in *Estate of Giovacchini v. Commissioner* and *Karlin v. Commissioner*,[81] the Tax Court faulted a taxpayer for limiting his regression analysis to "an extremely small sample." Similarly, where valuators did not effectively communicate the basis for the regression analysis, courts have rejected it.[82]

Regression analysis can be a useful tool in appropriate appraisal assignments, and should be considered.

Conclusion of Value   The appraisal report should state in clear and unequivocal terms the appraiser's conclusion of value.

Appraiser's Signature   An appraisal report must be signed by all appraisers who participated in the preparation of the report.[83] This signature requirement achieves two objectives. First, the signature is "personalized evidence indicating authentication of the work performed by the appraiser."[84] Second, the signature connotes "acceptance of the responsibility for content, analyses, and the conclusions in the report."[85]

Signed Certification

A signed certification is a necessary and significant element of any appraisal report. By signing the certification, the appraiser accepts "full responsibility for all elements of the certification, for the assignment results, and for the contents of the

---

[80] *Crimi v. Comm'r*, T.C. Memo. 2013-51, 105 T.C.M. (CCH) 1330 (2013).
[81] *Estate of Giovacchini v. Comm'r*, T.C. Memo. 2013-27, 105 T.C.M. (CCH) 1179 (2013); *Karin v. Comm'r*, T.C. Memo. 1987-552, 54 T.C.M. (CCH) 909 (1987).
[82] *See, e.g.*, *Vitamin Village, Inc. v. Comm'r*, T.C. Memo. 2007-272, 94 T.C.M. (CCH) 278 (2007).
[83] *See supra* notes 44–47.
[84] USPAP, *supra* note 1, at U-4.
[85] *Id.*

appraisal report."[86] The certification should follow the format specified in USPAP. The following certification is intended to provide readers with a sample certification under USPAP:

> *I certify that, to the best of my knowledge and belief:*
>
>> *The statements of facts contained in this report are true and correct.*
>>
>> *The reported analyses, opinions, and conclusions are limited only by the reported assumptions and limiting conditions and are my personal, impartial, and unbiased professional analyses, opinions, and conclusions.*
>>
>> *I have no (or the specified) present or prospective interest in the property that is the subject of this report and no (or the specified) personal interest with respect to the parties involved.*
>>
>> *I have performed no (or the specified) services, as an appraiser or in any other capacity, regarding the property that is the subject of this report within the three-year period immediately preceding acceptance of this assignment.*
>>
>> *I have no bias with respect to the property that is the subject of this report or to the parties involved with this assignment.*
>>
>> *My engagement in this assignment was not contingent upon developing or reporting predetermined results.*
>>
>> *My compensation for completing this assignment is not contingent upon the development or reporting of a predetermined value or direction in value that favors the cause of the client, the amount of the value opinion, the attainment of a stipulated result, or the occurrence of a subsequent event directly related to the intended use of this appraisal.*
>>
>> *My analyses, opinions, and conclusions were developed, and this report has been prepared, in conformity with the* Uniform Standards of Professional Appraisal Practice.
>>
>> *I have (or have not) made a personal inspection of the property that is the subject of this report. (If more than one person signs this certification, the certification must clearly specify which individuals did and which individuals did not make a personal inspection of the appraised property. [Note: For a business or intangible asset appraisal assignment, the inspection portion of this certification is not applicable.])*
>>
>> *No one provided significant real property appraisal assistance to the person signing this certification. (If there are exceptions, the name of the individuals providing appraisal assistance must be stated.)*[87]

---

[86] *Id.* at U-25, Standard 2-3, cmt., U-57, Standard 8-3, cmt.
[87] *Id.* (internal footnotes omitted).

Although the foregoing certification does not have to be exactly the same as that specified in USPAP, it has to be similar in content. An appraiser who signs any part of the appraisal report, including the transmittal letter, must also sign the certification. Further, the names of individuals providing significant appraisal assistance who do not sign the certification must nevertheless be identified in the certification and the scope of their assistance disclosed to the reader.[88] Finally, if the signing appraiser has relied upon the work done by an appraiser who does not sign the certification, the signing appraiser accepts responsibility for her decision to rely on the reliability of another individual's work.[89]

Addenda

Appraisal reports should include as addenda or exhibits the following five items:

1. The appraiser's curriculum vitae or statement of qualifications;[90]
2. Any company financials reviewed in connection with the valuation of a business;
3. Any financial ratio comparisons (and the related computations) created in connection with the valuation of a business;
4. Any legal documents related to the ownership of the property (e.g., deeds, mortgages, easements and encumbrances, a legal description of the property (by metes and bounds or otherwise));
5. Any legal documents related to the contractual rights, preferences, and privileges of an interest in the property (e.g., formation documents, buy–sell agreements, and leases).

WORK FILE AS SUPPORT FOR AN APPRAISAL REPORT

Contents of Work File

USPAP requires appraisers to prepare a work file for each appraisal or appraisal review assignment.[91] "An appraiser who willfully or knowingly fails to comply" with the recordkeeping requirements of USPAP is in violation of USPAP ethics rules.[92] A work file and supporting workpapers must include the following five items of information:

1. The name of the client and the identity, by name or type, of any other intended users;
2. True copies of any written reports, documented on any type of media. (A true copy is a replica of the report transmitted to the client. A photocopy or an electronic copy of the entire report transmitted to the client satisfies the requirement of a true copy.);

---

[88] *Id.* at A-107, Advisory Opinion 31.
[89] *Id.* at U-27, Standard 2-3, cmt., U-58, Standard 8-3, cmt.
[90] *See* Treas. Reg. § 1.170A-13(c)(3).
[91] USPAP, *supra* note 1, at U-10.
[92] *Id.*

3. Summaries of all oral reports or testimony, or a transcript of testimony, including the appraiser's signed and dated certification;
4. All other data, information, and documentation necessary to support the appraiser's opinions and conclusions as well as to show compliance with USPAP, or references to the location(s) of such documentation; and
5. A work file in support of a Restricted Appraisal Report must be sufficient for the appraiser to produce an Appraisal Report.[93]

Retention Period

USPAP requires that appraisers retain the work file for "a period of at least five years after the preparation" of the report, or "at least two years after the final disposition of any judicial proceeding in which the appraiser provided testimony related to the assignment," whichever is later.[94]

CONCLUSION

Effective appraisal practice should be less concerned with the ultimate opinions of value and more concerned with developing and documenting the processes undertaken to arrive at those values. Valuation standards, including but not limited to USPAP and Revenue Ruling 59-60, provide a general template for drafting appraisal reports. Following the general framework outlined in this chapter will allow an appraiser to develop a systematic valuation process.

---

[93] *Id.*
[94] *Id.*

CHAPTER 10

Assessing the Quality of the Appraisal Report

SUMMARY

There are some steps, not necessarily required, that should be taken, that are desirable in any appraisal report. Chapter 9, *Expert Appraisal Reports*, detailed the items that must be included in an appraisal report to make it compliant with the Uniform Standards of Professional Appraisal Practice ("USPAP") and Revenue Ruling 59-60.[1] This chapter discusses some of the qualities found in top-tier reports, regardless of whether the report is used to support a tax reporting position or in connection with litigation.

REQUIRED ITEMS UNDER THE USPAP AND REVENUE RULING 59-60

Before we discuss the items to be included in an appraisal report, a word of caution is appropriate. We emphasize the importance of USPAP in controlling the items to be included in an appraisal report because USPAP is widely recognized and accepted as containing standards applicable to the appraisal profession. However, as noted in Chapter 9, *Expert Appraisal Reports*, USPAP is but one set of standards that may apply to a given appraisal assignment, and will not control all valuation assignments. In *Whitehouse Hotel Ltd. P'ship v. Commissioner*,[2] the Tax Court instructed that the failure to comply with USPAP in an appraisal assignment does not necessarily mean that an appraisal report is unreliable. Thus, while USPAP sets forth the items to be included in an appraisal report, other standards or considerations may bear on the items and substance to be included.

---

[1] Rev. Rul. 59-60, 1959-1 C.B. 237.
[2] *Whitehouse Hotel Ltd. P'ship v. Commissioner*, 131 T.C. 112, 126-127 (2008), *vacated on other grounds*, 615 F.3d 321 (5th Cir. 2010).

With these limitations in mind, appraisal reports should include the following items, each of which are discussed more fully in Chapter 9, *Expert Appraisal Reports*:

- Table of contents;
- Executive summary or cover letter;
- A body of the report, which should state:
  1. The retaining party and other intended users;
  2. The type of appraisal report (e.g., an appraisal report or a restricted appraisal report);
  3. The standard and source of value (e.g., fair market value as required for federal tax purposes);
  4. The effective date of the appraisal and the date of the report;
  5. The purpose of the appraisal and its intended use;
  6. A summary of the scope of work (i.e., the type and extent of research and analysis in a given assignment);
  7. A summary of the facts and data considered, including but not limited to: transactional documents; prior transactions; agreements affecting the current or future use of the property; specific rights, preferences, and privileges of interest affecting the property; and discussions with third parties, as appropriate;
  8. A description of the property to be valued and its condition, the type of asset to be valued, how title is held, the interest valued, the terms of any agreement relating to the property, and applicable geographic and economic data that bears on the valuation;
  9. Assumptions, extraordinary assumptions, hypothetical conditions, and limiting conditions;
  10. The highest and best use of the property;
  11. An explanation of the methodologies and analysis used to value the subject property (e.g., an explanation of the market, income, and asset-based approaches, as well as the different value indicated by each approach);
  12. A reconciliation of the different indicated values to determine value;
  13. The opinion of value;
  14. The appraiser's signature;
  15. A signed certification by the appraiser; and
- Appropriate addenda and exhibits, including but not limited to: the appraiser's curriculum vitae or statement of qualifications; any company financials reviewed in connection with valuing a business; any financial ratio comparisons (and the related computations) in connection with valuing a business; any documents related to the ownership of the property, contractual rights in the property, and preferences and privileges with respect to the property, as applicable.

To increase an appraisal report's overall reliability and defensibility, each appraiser should make sure that the report achieves the objectives set forth ahead.

MAKING THE REPORT UNDERSTANDABLE TO THE AUDIENCE

Remember, the audience for most appraisal reports is not another appraisal professional. Therefore, the report should be readable by a layperson. This means that any time financial jargon is used, it should be defined so that a layperson can understand it.

REPLICABILITY

Any report should be *replicable*. This means that the reader should be able to follow the same steps as the author and get the same answer. This requires that the sources of information be adequately identified so that the reader can access the same sources, including the issue and page for periodicals, the edition and page for books, and so forth. This also requires that the report include: a summary of conversations with third-parties and all documents analyzed in connection with the appraisal assignment, including but not limited to company financial statements and any agreements affecting the use of or the rights to the property.

COMPLETENESS

Another general quality is that the appraisal report be *complete*. This is especially important where the report will be used during litigation. For example, as discussed ahead, the United States Tax Court ("Tax Court") *requires* an appraisal report to include, among other items, a complete statement of all opinions the witness expresses and the basis and reasons therefor, the facts or data considered by the witness in forming them, and any exhibits used to summarize or support the opinions. The reason for this completeness requirement is relatively straightforward: the report is the expert's direct testimony.

For this reason, every detail should be contained within the four corners of the report. If a fact or exhibit is not included in the report, then it will not be included in the evidence the judge may consider unless the fact or exhibit is admitted into evidence through a stipulation or admission, each of which is discussed more fully in Chapter 8, *Discovery of Expert Material*. An expert may sometimes realize, after she submits her report to the Court, that a fact or exhibit was inadvertently omitted. In such cases, it is advisable for the expert to advise the trial attorney of the omission so that the trial attorney may seek to ask additional questions on this point. The judge may, but is not required to, allow the trial attorney to ask additional questions to allow the expert to clarify the items omitted from her report.

To avoid such issues at trial, it is generally advisable for the report to be as complete and unambiguous as possible.

INTERNAL CONSISTENCY

The report should be *internally consistent*, in both content and style. This is especially important when multiple appraisers contribute to creating the report.

With respect to content, the report should not say one thing in one place with a contradictory statement in another. Numbers in a table should agree with text that refers to the respective table, and numbers derived from one table should concur with the table from which they are derived.

With respect to style, spellings should be the same wherever they are used. If a word or phrase is hyphenated in one place, it should be hyphenated in each place that it is used. If a word or phrase is capitalized in one place, it should be capitalized each time that it appears. Punctuation should be consistent, and there should be a consistent style for footnotes.

Another category of internal inconsistency found in some reports is a discount rate applicable to one variable applied to some other variable. For example, discount rates are applicable to *net cash flow*. To apply such rates to net income or some other variable is not only inconsistent—it is *wrong*.

RECONCILIATION

Appraisers will invariably reach differing indicated values under the market approach, the income approach, and the asset-based approach. USPAP requires, and it is important from a defensibility position, for appraisal reports to include a reconciliation of the divergent values indicated under each method. As detailed more fully in Chapter 9, *Expert Appraisal Reports*, reconciliation requires the appraisal report to reconcile the different conclusions of value that may be indicated by the various methodologies employed. For example, appraisers tend to lend greater weight to the income approach than the cost or comparable sales methods.

It is advisable for appraisers to explain the decision to weight one method over others in a separate section of the appraisal report entitled "Reconciliation." Reconciliation is an important part of the appraisal process because it requires the appraiser to analyze alternative conclusions of value and select a final opinion of value from among two or more indicated values. Reconciliation also provides the appraiser with an opportunity to address shortcomings in his or her report, to draw upon his or her experience and expertise to determine which opinion of value is most reliable, and to resolve any differences between the values indicated by his or her various approaches.

REGRESSION ANALYSIS

A regression analysis is a useful tool that should be considered in appropriate appraisal assignments. A regression analysis is a statistical technique that can be used to determine the effect that one or more explanatory independent variables (e.g., the respective price paid to purchase the company with those earnings or revenues) has on a single dependent variable (e.g., the earnings or revenues of recently acquired companies). The regression analysis allows valuators to test the causal relationship, if any, between the independent and dependent variables. We discuss in Chapter 9, *Expert Appraisal Reports*, how to perform a regression analysis, its benefits, and how courts have perceived it to date.

FORECASTING FUTURE RESULTS

Past history does not always, or, in the case of business results, even usually, repeat itself. Yet, it is tempting when making forecasts to merely extrapolate from past results. This is usually wrong. When extrapolating, the analyst should at least make some attempt to explain why the future will or will not conform to the past.

Analysts usually get their forecasts from management. After all, who is in a better position to have a perspective on a company's future operations? However, managers are not all objective. There is a natural tendency for most managers to be optimistic; however, some are conservative by nature. The purpose of the valuation may have some bearing on management's tendency toward optimism or pessimism. The analyst should not accept management's forecasts without question. The analyst should at least ask enough questions to understand management's rationale for each forecasted number. The report should describe the analyst's efforts to evaluate the forecasts and explain the reasonableness of the conclusions reached.

ECONOMIC AND INDUSTRY SECTIONS

Most appraisal reports would include a section that discusses the economy and industry relating to the valued property. A good appraisal report connects this discussion to the appraisal assignment. Thus, the economic and industry sections should at least say something about the implications of the contents of those sections for the valuation, even if it is just a sentence at the end. Many analysts use one-size-fits-all boilerplate with a lot of material that has no bearing on the subject company and with no connection to the appraisal at hand. They leave the reader at the end of the respective sections compelled to ask the question, "So, what?" A top-tier appraisal explains the relevance of the statistics in these sections to the appraisal assignment.

SUPPORTING EXHIBITS

A few additional words are appropriate about supporting exhibits and addenda. Exhibits can include tables, charts, pictures, or other material that supports the text. All exhibits should be referenced and described in the text. Each exhibit should convey the contents of the exhibit as succinctly as possible without sacrificing thoroughness. There should not be any two exhibits with the same title.

Exhibits can be placed within the text as close as possible to the first time the exhibit is referenced or in an appendix at the back of the report. Keeping them with the text is more reader-friendly so the reader does not have to shuffle back and forth between the text and the exhibits. This probably provides more continuity and more impact.

On this point, *The Appraisal of Real Estate* says:

> *Ideally, illustrations should be integrated within the text or presented on pages that face the material being discussed. For example, a photograph of the subject property may be placed on the page facing the identification of the*

property. A neighborhood map could be included on a page facing the neigh-borhood description to show the location of the subject property. Charts and graphs should be presented where they are discussed, but illustrations that are not directly related to the narrative should be placed in the addenda.[3]

Exhibits and addenda are helpful to convey points, and as detailed ahead, they are often required to make the report compliant with court rules.

COMPLY WITH APPLICABLE COURT RULES

For expert reports prepared for litigation, it is important that the report comply with applicable court rules. These requirements are discussed in more detail in Chapter 13, *Attorney Involvement,* and are summarized in the following in the two sets of courts in which valuation is most likely to be litigated: the Tax Court and the U.S. district courts. The failure to comply with applicable court rules may altogether prevent the report from being admitted into evidence.

The Tax Court

The Tax Court's Rules of Practice and Procedure govern the practice and procedure in all cases and proceedings before the Tax Court.[4] Rule 143(g) of those rules sets forth various items that must be included in an expert report before the report can be admitted into evidence. Under those rules, an expert witness must prepare and submit a written report to the Court and to the opposing party no later than 30 days before trial. The Tax Court's Rules of Practice and Procedure require that the report set forth the following information:

(A) A complete statement of all opinions the witness expresses and the basis and reasons for them;
(B) The facts or data considered by the witness in forming them;
(C) Any exhibits used to summarize or support them;
(D) The witness' qualifications, including a list of all publications authored in the previous 10 years;
(E) A list of all other cases in which, during the previous 4 years, the witness testified as an expert at trial or by deposition; and
(F) A statement of the compensation to be paid for the study and testimony in the case.[5]

The Tax Court reviews the expert reports before trial. At trial, the report is marked as an exhibit, identified by the expert witness, and received in evidence as the expert witness's direct testimony upon the Court's finding that the witness is qualified as an expert. Additional direct testimony may be, but need not be, allowed to clarify or emphasize matters with respect to that expert's report.

---

[3] *The Appraisal of Real Estate*, 14th ed. (Chicago; The Appraisal Institute, 2013), p. 656.
[4] *Tax Ct. R.* 1(b).
[5] *Tax Ct. R.* 143(g)(1).

The District Courts

The Federal Rules of Civil Procedure generally govern the procedure in all civil actions and proceedings in the U.S. district courts.[6] Similar to Rule 143(g) of the Tax Court Rules of Practice and Procedure, Rule 26(a)(2) of the Federal Rules of Civil Procedure, entitled "Disclosure of Expert Testimony," provide as follows with respect to expert reports:

(**A**) *In General.* In addition to the disclosures required by Rule 26(a)(1), a party must disclose to the other parties the identity of any [expert] witness it may use at trial to present evidence . . . .
(**B**) *Witnesses Who Must Provide a Written Report.* Unless otherwise stipulated or ordered by the court, this disclosure must be accompanied by a written report—prepared and signed by the witness—if the witness is one retained or specially employed to provide expert testimony in the case or one whose duties as the party's employee regularly involve giving expert testimony. The report must contain:
   (**i**) a complete statement of all opinions the witness will express and the basis and reasons for them;
   (**ii**) the facts or data considered by the witness in forming them;
   (**iii**) any exhibits that will be used to summarize or support them;
   (**iv**) the witness's qualifications, including a list of all publications authored in the previous 10 years;
   (**v**) a list of all other cases in which, during the previous 4 years, the witness testified as an expert at trial or by deposition; and
   (**vi**) a statement of the compensation to be paid for the study and testimony in the case.

Some state courts have similar requirements. In any case, it is good practice to list the items set forth earlier, whether required by court rules or not.

CONCLUSION

A report must communicate information that is often complicated, highly technical, and that deals with concepts outside of the intended readers' expertise. A successful appraisal report, and the successful appraiser, will allow the complicated to be experienced as simple, the convoluted to appear straightforward, and the tedious to feel engaging.

---

[6]*Fed. R. Civ. P. 1.*

CHAPTER 11

Concurrent Evidence: A Novel Approach to Expert Testimony

SUMMARY

Our tax system inescapably creates many controversies, including complicated fair market valuation disputes. Accordingly, judges are routinely asked to decide fiercely contested factual valuation determinations. It should come as no surprise that, in the tenaciously adversarial judicial system found in the United States, our busy courts are often forced to analyze such valuation calculations in the face of significantly and fundamentally divergent appraisal models presented by the parties' expert witnesses.

Examples abound of these diametrically opposed expert opinions proffered in Tax Court litigation. In one case concerning the valuation of musician Michael Jackson's name and image for federal estate tax purposes, the taxpayer valued Mr. Jackson's name and image at $2,105, while the Internal Revenue Service (IRS) valued it at $434 million.[1] In another dispute concerning the valuation of artwork, which was the subject of a charitable contribution, the taxpayer, with expert support, valued a painting at $150,000, while the IRS, with expert support, valued it at only $2,000.[2]

---

[1] Eriq Gardner, "Michael Jackson Estate Faces Billion Dollar Tax Court Battle," *The Hollywood Reporter* (Apr. 20, 2016), available at http://www.hollywoodreporter.com/thr -esq/what-is-michael-jacksons-image-884963.

[2] *See* Andrew MacGregor Smith, "Using Impartial Experts in Valuations: A Forum-Specific Approach, 35 *Wm. & Mary L. Rev.* 1241, 1241 (1994) (citing *Farber v. Comm'r*), T.C. Memo. 1974-155, 33 T.C.M. (CCH) 673 (1974), *aff'd*, 535 F.2d 1241 (2d Cir.1975). *See also id.* (citing *Georgia-Pacific Corp. v. United States*), 640 F.2d 328, 339 (Ct. Cl. 1980) (a United States Court of Claims case, wherein the plaintiff's expert asserted the condemned property was valued at $51 million while the government's expert estimated the land to be worth only $1.4 million). *See also* a news report discussing a tax dispute relating to the valuation of the *Canyon*, a twentieth-century mixed-media art masterwork created by Robert Rauschenberg. This work includes a stuffed bald eagle (a federally protected creature). The taxpayers' experts claimed that, since the taxpayers cannot legally sell this work of art, the value must be discounted to zero. The Internal Revenue Service, on the other hand, valued this work of art at $65 million and demanded that the taxpayers pay $29.2 million in taxes. Patricia Cohen, "Art's Sale Value? Zero. The Tax Bill? $29 Million," *N.Y. Times*, July 22, 2012, available at http://www.nytimes.com/2012/07/22/arts/design/a-catch-22-of-art-and-taxes-starring -a-stuffed-eagle.html?hp.

Regrettably, the present routine of separately testifying government- and taxpayer-retained expert witnesses only serves to perpetuate the enduring concerns of trustworthiness, partiality, and litigation lethargy, while exacerbating the challenge of reaching the right results.[3] Concurrent expert witness testimony, in which experts meet under oath and on the record with the judge and engage in conversational, rather than adversarial, testimony, offers a fresh approach. This chapter discusses concurrent expert witness testimony as an alternative to the traditional adversarial process.[4]

A NEW APPROACH TO EXPERT TESTIMONY

Trying new things may very well have an element of discomfiting risk to it, but the never-ending folly of court-allowed partisan experts, producing diametrically different opinions that are routinely dumped in the laps of the fact finder for determination, calls for some novel judicial or statutory intervention.[5] Sure, there may be no "royal road to attain such accommodation concretely,"[6] but there is one mechanism that may help make our expert witnesses true contributors to the quest for truth. Such an approach would reject the pure lawyer-driven, adversarial nature of eliciting expert testimony and instead embrace methods that unite the conversational element of some alternative dispute resolution procedures and the inquisitorial element of some other legal systems' litigation models.

Accordingly, courts and legislators might consider uniformly mandating that expert trial testimony be initially presented concurrently, whereby the experts are simultaneously sworn and (on the record) engage in a dialogue with each other and the trial judge (more colloquially, the "hot tub" method).[7] Employing this concurrent evidence technique, as fully described ahead, will achieve increased reliability and efficiency in tax litigation as well as facilitate the trial judge's reasoned evaluation of competing expert testimony.

OUR LONG AND DEEP DISTRUST OF PARTISAN EXPERTS

Partisan experts are old news in American litigation, and have long been ridiculed. In 1891, the New York Court of Appeals went so far as to question the propriety of using party-appointed valuation experts.[8] The court's assessment was not a kind

---

[3] See generally N.S.W. Law Reform Commission, *Expert Witnesses*, Report No 109 (2005), ss 6.59-6.62, available at http://www.lawlink.nsw.gov.au/lawlink/lrc/ll_lrc.nsf/pages/LRC_r109toc; Nancy J. Fannon, "The Presumption of Advocacy: Why Experts Differ So Much and What Can Be Done About It," *Valuation Strategies* (Jan. 2007), at 2.

[4] This chapter was adapted from Michael R. Devitt, *A Dip in the Hot Tub: Concurrent Evidence Techniques for Expert Witnesses in Tax Court Cases*, 118 J. Tax'n 213 (2012). Reprinted with permission.

[5] The finders of fact in cases before the Tax Court and the U.S. Court of Federal Claims are judges, but the finder of fact in cases before the U.S. district courts can be either a judge or a jury.

[6] Judge Learned Hand quoted in Philip Hamburger, "The Great Judge," *Life*, Nov. 4, 1946.

[7] See, e.g., Marvin J. Garbis, "Aussie Inspired Musings on Technological Issues—Of Kangaroo Courts, Tutorials & Hot Tub Cross-Examination," 6 *Green Bag* 2d, 141, 148 (2003).

[8] *Roberts v. Elevated Ry. Co.*, 28 N.E. 486, 487 (N.Y. 1891).

one. In rejecting the use of such valuation experts, the court's contempt was evident in these pointed words:

> *Expert evidence, so-called, or in other words evidence of the mere opinion of witnesses, has been used to such an extent that the evidence given by them has come to be looked upon with great suspicion by both courts and juries; and the fact has become very plain that in any case where opinion evidence is admissible the particular kind of an opinion desired by any party to the investigation can be readily procured by paying the market price therefor.*[9]

Shortly thereafter, in applauding the virtues of this decision, one commentator was even more caustic:

> *Certainly every word of scathing criticism upon [the experts] and their methods was deserved, as anyone who has noted the absolute inconsistency of expert testimony in cases of late . . . . They have become as much counsel as the attorneys themselves.*[10]

The passage of more than a hundred years has not quieted these criticisms. Indeed, a querulous tone continues as it relates to the problems associated with bias and flimsily contrived expert opinions. Legal scholars, practitioners, and judges have lamented expert witnesses' incredibility and made bold articulations of promised changes. Some commentators have even called for eliminating adversarial experts and exclusively relying upon court-appointed experts, especially in valuation controversies.[11] But little has actually changed.[12] Most judges have just accepted fate that each party will present the expert witness most favorable to his or her client's position, regardless of whether it assists the judge.

Over the last three decades, financial instruments and other assets have become increasingly sophisticated and complex. It was not long ago that even a savvy businessperson would have given a quizzical look when asked for the definition of a credit default swap. As factual issues for trial become more complicated and problematic, the need for "true" expert witnesses to assist the court in sifting through these controversies abounds. Unfortunately, tempted by the confusion and uncertainty that surround complexity, litigants have oftentimes created and presented marginal expert

---

[9]*Id.*

[10]Frank Mackintosh, "Elevated Railroad Land-Damage Litigation," 2 *Yale L.J.* 106, 113 (1893).

[11]David E. Bernstein, "Expert Witnesses Adversarial Bias and the (Partial) Failure of the Daubert Revolution," 93 *Iowa L. Rev.* 451, 486–489 (2008); *see also* Hon. Justice Garry Downes, "Expert Evidence: The Value of Single or Court-Appointed Experts" (Nov. 11, 2005) (unpublished paper presented at the Australian Institute of Judicial Administration Expert Evidence Seminar, Melbourne).

[12]*See generally* Norman W. Spaulding, "The Rule of Law in Action: A Defense of Adversarial Values," 93 *Cornell L. Rev.* 1377 (2008); Gerald Walpin, "America's Adversarial and Jury Systems: More Likely to Do Justice," 26 *Harv. J.L. & Pub. Pol'y* 175, 177–178 (2003).

opinions that not only fail to assist the fact finder, but inject unnecessary costs and increased acrimony into the litigation process.

As detailed in Chapter 7, *From* Daubert *to* Boltar, both the Federal Rules of Evidence (Rule 702) and the U.S. Supreme Court have entrusted the trial judge with the power and responsibility as the gatekeeper to exclude unreliable expert testimony.[13] The hope was that with the help of the guiding factors set forth in *Daubert* and its progeny, judges would be better able to decipher unreliable expert valuations opinions while leaving intact sound valuation methodologies that produce predictably reliable results no matter what the given factual scenario.[14] Some jurists, including Chief Justice Rehnquist, expressed great skepticism as to whether federal judges would be able to fulfill their gatekeeping responsibility.[15] Such doubt is not without merit, especially in tax litigation where the benefits of *Daubert* have so far failed to materialize. Decades after the U.S. Supreme Court's decision in *Daubert*, we see that in all of the reported Tax Court opinions between 2010 and the present time, including memorandum opinions and summary opinions, only a few cases have reported meaningful *Daubert* analysis.[16] Indeed in the years since *Daubert* was decided, the Tax Court has as of the time of this writing cited *Daubert* only 31 times, most with only a passing reference.[17] This data suggests that it is not the Supreme Court's gatekeeping concept that is at fault, but it may be the litigants' and trial judges' unwillingness to put expert witnesses to the scrutiny of a *Daubert* analysis.

In the Tax Court, where there are no jury trials and the body of law is specialized, the trial judge can and should undertake an active role in the litigation process by utilizing all the procedural tools available in her legal arsenal to rein in faulty expert evidence and crack the partisan code of competing expert testimony.

---

[13] *Daubert v. Merrell Dow Pharms., Inc.*, 509 U.S. 579, 597 (1993); *Fed. R. Evid.* 702.

[14] *Daubert*, 509 U.S. at 597; *Gen. Elec. Co. v. Joiner*, 522 U.S. 136, 148 (1997); *Kumho Tire Co. v. Carmichael*, 526 U.S. 137, 141 (1998).

[15] *Daubert*, 509 U.S. at 597, 600.

[16] *Boltar, L.L.C. v. Comm'r*, 136 T.C. 326, 333-35 (2011); *Esgar Corp. v. Comm'r*, T.C. Memo. 2012-35, 11–13.

[17] *See, e.g., ADVO, Inc. v. Comm'r*, 141 T.C. 298, 308 n.8 (2013); *Boltar*, 136 T.C. at 333-35 (2011); *Whitehouse Hotel Ltd. P'ship v. Comm'r*, 131 T.C. 112, 126 n.5 (2008), *vacated and remanded*, 615 F.3d 321 (5th Cir. 2010); *Bank One Corp. v. Comm'r*, 120 T.C. 174, 278 (2003); *Caracci v. Comm'r*, 118 T.C. 379, 393 (2002), *rev'd*, 456 F.3d 444 (5th Cir. 2006); *Seagate Tech., Inc. v. Comm'r*, 102 T.C. 149, 321 (1994); *see also Davis v. Comm'r*, T.C. Memo. 2015-88, 109 T.C.M. (CCH) 1450 (2015); *Estate of Tanenblatt v. Comm'r*, T.C. Memo. 2013-263, 106 T.C.M. (CCH) 579 (2013); *Aries Commc'ns Inc. v. Comm'r*, T.C. Memo. 2013-97, 105 T.C.M. (CCH) 1585 (2013); *Crimi v. Comm'r*, T.C. Memo. 2013-51, 105 T.C.M. (CCH) 1330 (2013); *Estate of Giovacchini v. Comm'r*, T.C. Memo. 2013-27, 105 T.C.M. (CCH) 1179 (2013); *Esgar Corp.*, T.C. Memo. 2012-35, 103 T.C.M. (CCH) 1185 (2012); *Union Carbide Corp. v. Comm'r*, T.C. Memo. 2009-50, 97 T.C.M. (CCH) 1207 (2009); *Estate of Noble v. Comm'r*, T.C. Memo. 2005-2, 2005 WL 23303 (2005); *Santa Monica Pictures, LLC v. Comm'r*, T.C. Memo. 2005-104, 89 T.C.M. (CCH) 1157, 112-20 (2005); *Brewer Quality Homes, Inc. v. Comm'r*, T.C. Memo. 2003-300; 86 T.C.M. (CCH) 29, 9-15 (2003); *Seagate Tech., Inc. v. Comm'r*, T.C. Memo. 2000-388, 80 T.C.M. (CCH) 912 (2000); *Gross v. Comm'r*, T.C. Memo. 1999-254, 78 T.C.M. (CCH) 201 (1999); *Estate of Scanlan v. Comm'r*, T.C. Memo. 1996-331, 72 T.C.M. (CCH) 160 (1996); *Barrister-Equipment Assocs. Series #115 v. Comm'r*, T.C. Memo. 1994-205, 67 T.C.M. (CCH) 2932 (1994).

This exercise of power might come in the form of the trial judge *sua sponte* initiating a *Daubert* hearing on the expert's reliability or even the court ordering the retention of its own expert.[18]

More time and expense will be incurred as trial judges engage in the drudgery of weeding out unethical or unsupported expert testimony after trial.[19] For example, consider a case where the parties submitted expert stock valuation reports that differed by millions. The court could engage in the tedious, frustrating task of taking extensive trial expert testimony and then subsequently determining and documenting the testifying experts' credentials, methodologies, and analysis, ultimately concluding that the government expert's conclusions were not credible, entitled to zero weight, and valuing the estate's stock according to the taxpayer's expert report. Now imagine that instead of the time and energy the judge spent evaluating the government's flawed expert witness trial testimony, she reached the same conclusion with a *Daubert* pretrial hearing initiated by either the taxpayer or the judge herself. Think also about the message judges would be sending to litigants if they periodically forced parties to undergo a rigorous *Daubert* hearing to test expert opinion reliability. Once the word got out, litigants would likely be much more careful in providing reliable credible expert testimony that was useful to the fact finder.

Recently, one judge embraced her gatekeeping power and was able to resolve a case fully on a pretrial motion by excluding the taxpayer's expert report and testimony as "neither reliable nor relevant under the Federal Rules of Evidence and the *Daubert* factors."[20] As more fully detailed in Chapter 7, in *Boltar L.L.C. v. Commissioner*, the Tax Court conducted a full *Daubert* analysis and determined that the taxpayer's expert witness report was inadmissible because the report was "not the product of reliable methods," did not apply "principles and methods reliably to the facts of the case," and used assumptions that were "unrealistic in view of the facts of the case."[21] This judicial initiative was a strong warning to litigants and their lawyers to be much more prudent and discerning during expert selection and preparation.

COURT-APPOINTED EXPERTS

The Tax Court also appointed its own expert witness in *Bank One Corp. v. Commissioner*, a complicated tax litigation involving a financial institution's alleged improper accounting relating to numerous complex interest rate swaps.[22]

---

[18] Even though the Federal Rules of Evidence allow for the court appointment of experts, such authority is very sparingly utilized. Trial judges perceive difficulty in finding and selecting these experts and many maintain the faulty well-entrenched view that such court involvement would be an unwelcome departure from the adversarial process. *See* Federal Judicial Center, *Court-Appointed Experts: Defining the Role of Experts Appointed Under Federal Rule of Evidence 706* (1993) (detailed study found that "much of the uneasiness with court-appointed experts arises from the difficulty in accommodating such experts in a court system that values, and generally anticipates, adversarial presentations of evidence.").

[19] Joseph Sanders, "Expert Witness Ethics," 76 *Fordham L. Rev.* 1539, 1539 (2007).

[20] *Boltar*, 136 T.C. at 333–336.

[21] *Id*. at 340.

[22] *Bank One*, 120 T.C. at 174, 274–278, 331–334.

Despite the unequivocal power to do so, this was the first time the Tax Court appointed its own expert under Rule 706 of the Federal Rules of Evidence.[23]

A careful review of the opinion in *Bank One* evidences the Tax Courts' procedural construction for the use of trial judge's court-appointed experts to assist the judge in cutting through the partisanship of the party-hired experts. After completion of all party witness testimony, including experts, the court-appointed experts were given the then-existing trial record, and each prepared and submitted a written report.[24] Thereafter, the taxpayer and the IRS submitted rebuttal expert reports addressing the court-appointed experts' reports.[25] Lastly, the court-appointed experts were given an opportunity to submit replies to the parties' rebuttal reports. After all such reports were exchanged, the trial resumed, at which time the parties cross-examined the court-appointed experts and presented the rebuttal testimony of their own experts.[26] This procedure brought more neutral voices into the process. It is evident from the Tax Court opinion that the court-appointed expert played a critical role in assisting the Court to detect one expert's flawed valuation methodology as inconsistent with industry practice and in conflict with the court-appointed experts' findings.[27]

Bank One shows the frustration with the status quo of expert trial testimony and the need for change. It may be time to consider a doctrinal shift to the more novel "hot tub" approach to address this nagging expert witness distrust. The concurrent method is a procedural means to turn the parties' existing experts into more effective agents for truth, without undergoing the time and expense of court-appointed experts. As detailed ahead, United States Tax Court Judge Laro has challenged traditional partisan adversarial expert procedures by experimenting with the concurrent witness method.[28]

HEATING UP THE TUB: THE CONCURRENT EVIDENCE METHOD

As detailed more fully in Chapter 10, *Assessing the Quality of the Appraisal Report*, and Chapter 13, *Attorney Involvement*, the Tax Court's Rules of Practice and Procedure generally mandate that any party who intends to call an expert at trial must cause that expert witness to prepare a written report and submit that report to both the opposing party and the trial judge 30 days before trial.[29] In order to be acceptable, this written expert report must not only establish the qualifications of the expert witness, but it must also set forth the expert's opinions, the facts and data upon which these opinions rely, and the reasons for any conclusion reached by the expert.[30] If the trial judge determines the expert is qualified, the report is ultimately marked as an exhibit, identified by the expert witness, and received into evidence as the direct testimony of the expert.[31] The trial judge has the discretion

---

[23] *Id.* at 274.
[24] *Id.* at 278.
[25] *Id.*
[26] *Id.*
[27] *Id.* at 301–302.
[28] *Rovakat, LLC v. Comm'r*, T.C. Memo. 2011-225, *aff'd*, 529 Fed. Appx. 124 (3d Cir. 2013).
[29] *Tax Ct. R.* 143(g).
[30] *Id.*
[31] *Id.*

to allow additional direct testimony in order to clarify or emphasize matters in the report or to address other matters that may have arisen after the preparation of the report.[32] The opposing party is then routinely given the opportunity to fully cross-examine the expert in order to undermine or discredit her underlying reasoning and conclusions. This orchestrated dance is repeated, often at a later date, for the rival party's expert witnesses.

This profoundly fragmented procedure is disadvantageous for a number of reasons. First, it leaves the fact finder with an ineffective mechanism for a detailed analysis of opposing expert opinions. Traditional adversarial presentation of expert testimony does little to facilitate the fact finder's task of evaluating competing evidence and resolving the issue presented, especially when the presentation of evidence is conducted sequentially and with a lengthy time lapse separating the witnesses.

Second, under such traditional expert procedural methodology, since each party is empowered to select and present her own expert, such experts may not be fully held accountable at trial for the ineffectiveness of their opinions and the underlying bases for such opinions. In practice, some experts even ignore relevant information that bears on the outcome of the assignment because (1) the evidence does not advance the client's case, and/or (2) the expert thinks the other party's expert will not locate such information.

Third, where there is an imbalance between the parties' resources, the judge may be placed in a position of deciding a case without adequate information from both sides. For example, in the typical valuation case, one party may, if she can afford it, hire multiple experts and strategically use one (or more experts) to bolster that party's case while using the other expert (or experts) to discredit the other party's expert. While this may be advantageous to the lawyers and clients with the bigger purses, it can leave a judge without adequate evidence from both sides to decide the case.

Fourth, the traditional adversarial model is time-consuming, wasteful, and expensive as oftentimes many days (or weeks) are consumed in non-focused cross-examinations to test the knowledge and skill of the experts and their opinions.[33]

Fifth, the traditional disjointed adversarial process oftentimes fails to fully and effectively use an expert's scientific or other specialized knowledge.

Finally, another drawback of an expert fragmented adversarial system is that experts often provide faulty assumptions or render opinions based on facts that have not or will not be proven at trial (or found as fact by the trial judge). A search for

---

[32] *Id.*

[33] In *Winans v. New York & Erie R.R. Co.*, 62 U.S. 88 (1858), the Supreme Court observed:

Experience has shown that opposite opinions of persons professing to be experts may be obtained to any amount; and it often occurs that not only many days, but even weeks, are consumed in cross-examinations, to test the skill or knowledge of such witnesses and the correctness of their opinions, wasting the time and wearying the patience of both court and jury, and perplexing, instead of elucidating, the questions involved in the issue.

truth should flush out these expert opinion shortcomings, but are often missed in a disjointed expert presentation.[34] In light of these criticisms, it is surprising that the traditional adversarial method is still the preferred method for receiving expert witness testimony. Perhaps an analogy will help illustrate why current practice undermines the intended purpose of expert evidence: to "help the trier of fact to understand the evidence or to determine a fact in issue."[35] Picture a boxing match where the rules do not allow for a face-to-face slugfest but instead a procedure whereby the first boxer hits a punching bag before the judges for 36 minutes. A week later, in the same judges' presence, his opponent boxer hits the same bag for 36 minutes. Then months later, the group of judges who witnessed the bag punching declares a winner. Silly as it sounds, this is what our judges routinely do in complex tax litigation matters. Each party presents an expert who attacks the other side's position with no expert opponent in sight. Then later, the other side's expert does the same. Of course the possibility exists of having to recall experts to refute, explain, or otherwise qualify testimony made by opposing experts.[36] Days, weeks, or even months later, the judge is forced to recollect and reconcile all this complicated expert analysis. Judge Laro has described the frustrations of traditional expert testimony presentation as a procedure that leaves the Court with a "record that is not very satisfying in trying to get to the truth of the matter."[37]

Under the concurrent evidence method, the experts engage in a face-to-face discussion with each other and the trial judge about all relevant issues dealing with their expert opinions and the underlying bases for such opinions. These discussions take place on the record and under oath, so there is no confusion as to what is said. No longer is the process a disjointed mess. One foreign jurist lauds concurrent evidence for making it possible for judges to avoid "having to compare a witness giving evidence now with the half-remembered evidence of another expert given perhaps some weeks previously."[38] Not only does the basic premise of concurrent evidence better assist the trier of fact in highlighting and reconciling competing evidence, it results in an effective medium for reducing partisan bias as well as the time and expense of litigation.[39]

Sad as it may be, it is widely recognized that litigants can shop for accredited and experienced valuation expert witnesses in a bustling valuation expert litigation support industry that matches valuation experts and lawyers depending on the facts and needs of the case.[40] It is routine for many lawyers preparing for tax

---

[34] *Cf. United States v. Fogg*, 652 F.2d 551 (5th Cir. 1981) (recognizing expert testimony is "permissible in a tax evasion case, provided … that the expert testifies on the basis of facts in evidence." (internal citations and quotations omitted)).

[35] Fed. R. Evid. 702; Joseph Sanders, "Expert Witness Ethics," 76 *Fordham L. Rev.* 1539, 1540 (2007).

[36] *See generally* Megan A Yarnall, Comment, "Dueling Scientific Experts: Is Australia's Hot Tub Method a Viable Solution for the American Judiciary?" 88 *Or. L. Rev.* 311, 326 (2009).

[37] *Crimi v. Comm'r*, No. 13252-09 (U.S. Tax Ct. 2010) (transcript of proceedings at 15).

[38] Hon. Justice Peter Heerey, "Recent Australian Developments," *C.J.Q.* 2004 23(Oct.) 386, 390–391 (2004).

[39] Francis P. Kao et al., "Into the Hot Tub: A Practical Guide to Alternative Expert Witness Procedures in International Arbitration," 44 *Int'l Law.* 1035, 1043 (Fall 2010).

[40] Adam Liptak, "In U.S., Expert Witnesses Are Partisan," *N.Y. Times*, Aug. 11, 2008, http://www.nytimes.com/2008/08/12/us/12experts.html?_r=1&adxnnl=1&pagewanted=1&adxnnlx=1219680322-dzz9gNliSpXMJYrrdfwsSg.

litigation, or any complex litigation for that matter, to interview several potential expert witnesses in search of the expert who will most bolster their case or, more to the point, one who will use a valuation methodology that results in the most favorable valuation number.[41] Expert bias, whether conscious or unconscious, can result from the simple truth that experts are paid by the parties for the favorable opinions they render.[42]

Expert Bias

A 1992 poll conducted by the *National Law Journal* and Lexis found that over 30 percent of jurors polled in civil cases believed the experts presented in their cases were biased.[43] Similarly, a few years later a study by the American Bar Association found that an estimated 77 percent of party-hired experts believed attorneys manipulated them "to weaken unfavorable testimony and strengthen favorable testimony."[44] Current practices and procedures perpetuate this distrust by failing to address the built-in incentives for bias and continuing to allow extreme, sometimes outlandish, valuation concepts to be presented at trial.[45]

Foreign Court Experiences

In wrestling with similar problems of expert partiality, unreliability, and burgeoning litigation costs, some courts in our fellow common-law countries have adopted procedures instituting concurrent expert witness testimony.[46] In short, the hot tub method refers to contemporaneous expert witness presentation whereby all parties' expert witnesses proffered on the same or similar disputed issues are sworn in at the same time to testify before the fact finder. Instead of proceeding sequentially during a party's case, both sides' experts sit together at a table and discuss the relevant issues

---

[41] *Id.*

[42] *See* Professor Michael R. Devitt, address at the University of San Diego School of Law's *Business Valuation Conference: Summit on Lack of Marketability* (Sept. 18, 2008); address at Georgetown University School of Law's *Advanced Summit on Business Valuation: Resolving Tax and Legal Issues* (Nov. 10, 2010); *see generally* Elizabeth Reifert, Comment, "Getting into the Hot Tub: How the United States Could Benefit from Australia's Concept of 'Hot Tubbing' Expert Witnesses," 89 *U. Det. Mercy. L. Rev.* 103, (2011).

[43] Jeffery L. Harrison, "Reconceptualizing the Expert Witness: Social Costs, Current Controls and Proposed Responses," 18 *Yale J. on Reg.* 253, 255 (2001).

[44] Daniel W. Shuman, Elizabeth Whitaker, and Anthony Champagne, "An Empirical Examination of the Use of Expert Witnesses in the Courts—Part II: A Three City Study," 34 *Jurimetrics J.* 193, 201 (1994).

[45] *See, e.g.,* Nancy J. Fannon, "The Presumption of Advocacy: Why Experts Differ So Much and What Can Be Done About It," *Valuation Strategies* (Jan. 2007), at 2. *See also Wagner Construction, Inc. v. Commissioner,* T.C. Memo 2001-160 ("Although it is not unusual in valuation cases that two experts reach significantly different conclusions, the reports and testimony of the experts in this case are so dissimilar that the reliability of the experts is brought into question. In this case, the experts reached conclusions that patently favored their respective clients, and their reports were designed to support their conclusions").

[46] Federal Court Rules, O 34A r 3 (Austl.), as amended by Federal Court of Australia, *Practice Note CM 7— Expert Witnesses in Proceedings in the Federal Court of Australia* (June 4, 2013), available at <http://www.fedcourt.gov.au/pdfsrtfs_p/practice_notes_cm7.rtf>

with each other and the judge.[47] These combined expert sessions are much more informal and ideally proceed in a conversational tone[48] versus the more formal dictates of direct and cross-examinations present in traditional adversarial proceedings.

During the concurrent evidence process, experts are free from the constrictions of lawyer questioning. This method allows each expert to engage in more of a dialogue to express her opinions with extended statements and even to pose questions to the opposing expert.[49] One former Australian judge and leading proponent of this method describes the typical concurrent evidence procedure as follows:

> *The procedure involves the parties' experts giving evidence in the presence of each other after all the lay evidence on both sides has been given. The experts are sworn in and sit in the witness box or a suitably large table which is treated notionally as the witness box .... A day or so previously, each expert will have filed a brief summary of his or her position in the light of all the evidence so far. In the box, the plaintiff's expert will give a brief oral exposition, typically for ten minutes or so. Then the defendant's expert will ask the plaintiff's expert questions, that is to say directly, without the intervention of counsel. Then the process is reversed.... When all this is completed, counsel cross-examine[s] and re-examine[s] in the conventional way.[50]*

As reported by the New South Wales Law Reform Commission, the hot tub approach enables the presentation of expert testimony as a discussion rather than a series of questions and answers between a lawyer and a witness.[51] This method removes the lawyers from the process during this conversation stage of the trial testimony.

The concurrent witness procedure finds its roots in the Trade Practice Tribunals of Australia as early as 1985. Beginning in the mid-1990s, this evidential practice was formally incorporated into other Australian tribunals and the Australian federal courts by amendment to their Federal Court Rules in 1998.[52] In due course, the concurrent expert session procedure became the prevailing evidentiary approach in the Australian Land and Environmental Court. In 2005, the New South Wales

---

[47]*See generally* Gary Edmond, "Merton and the Hot Tub: Scientific Conventions and Expert Evidence in Australian Civil Procedure," 72 *Law & Contemp. Probs.* 159, 162 (2009).

[48]For example, Judge Laro explained to the expert witnesses that he would like them "to talk to [him] and to one another in a conversational tone" and should "feel free to interrupt as any conversation would happen, to probe, and to try to understand the strengths and weaknesses ... among your opinions." *Crimi v. Comm'r*, No. 13252-09 (U.S. Tax Ct. 2010) (transcript of proceedings at 328).

[49]Edmond, *supra* note 47, at 163.

[50]Heerey, *supra* note 38, at 390–391.

[51]*See* N.S.W. Law Reform Commission, *supra* note 3, at ss 4.12, 4.33, 4.50, 6.48, 6.56.

[52]Edmond, *supra* note 47, at 166; Federal Court Rules, O 34A r 3 (Austl.), as amended by Federal Court of Australia, *Practice Note CM 7—Expert Witnesses in Proceedings in the Federal Court of Australia* (June 4, 2013), available at <http://www.fedcourt.gov.au/pdfsrtfs_p/practice_notes_cm7.rtf>.

Law Reform Commission conducted a review of the use of the hot tub method and recommended its much wider implementation.[53]

As a result, within the last decade, hot tub expert evidence procedures have been formally adopted in the Australian Federal Court, the Administrative Appeals Tribunal, the Supreme Courts of New South Wales and the Australian Capital Territory, and the Land and Environmental Court of New South Wales.[54] Canada has now also codified expert concurrent evidence procedures into its Competition Tribunal Rules for use in contested antitrust proceedings.[55] In December 2009, during his comprehensive review of civil litigation costs in England and Wales, Lord Justice Jackson determined that: "A number of experts, practitioners and judges have expressed support for the use of concurrent evidence" and called for the creation of a pilot program, which would allow the use of concurrent witnesses in trials when all parties consent.[56]

American Experience with Concurrent Experts

So far, the concurrent evidence method is used infrequently in the United States. One federal District Court judge has used concurrent witness techniques in some non-jury cases in recent years.[57] Another federal District Court judge has used the hot tub method with counsel at oral argument, and described his use of this method as "terrific fun and productive."[58] Other judges have been supportive of hot tubbing, but have not used it in their courtroom.[59] Additionally, Judge Laro has now implemented the hot tub method in five Tax Court cases[60] and found that upon

---

[53]*See* N.S.W. Law Reform Commission, *supra* note 3, at s 6.58.

[54]*See* Edmond, *supra* note 47, at 166.

[55]Kao et al., *supra* note 39, at 1038; Lisa C. Wood, "Experts in the Tub," 21 *Antitrust* 95, 96–97 (2007); *Competition Tribunal Rules*, SOR/94-290, ss 48.1-48.2 (Can.); *see also Competition Tribunal Rules*, SOR/2008-141, s 75 (Can.) ("The Tribunal may require that some or all of the witnesses testify as a panel at any time that the Tribunal may determine.").

[56]Rt. Hon. Lord Justice Jackson, *Review of Civil Litigation Costs: Final Report* (Dec. 2009), available at http://www.judiciary.gov.uk/publications-and-reports/review-of-civil-litigation -costs/reports/civil-litigation-costs-review-final-report. *See also* recent reports of the concurrent evidence procedures being utilized in the Apple Inc. and Samsung Electronics Company patent litigation pending in Australia. Jane Wardell and Nick Macfie, "Apple and Samsung Take Australian Legal Battle to the 'Hot Tub,'" *Reuters*, Aug. 6, 2012, available at http:// www.reuters.com/article/2012/08/06/us-apple-samsung-experts-idUSBRE8750AN20120806.

[57]*See* Lisa C. Wood, "Experts in the Tub," 21 *Antitrust* 95, 96–97 (2007).

[58]*Id.* at 97 n.28.

[59]*See, e.g.*, Marvin J. Garbis, "Aussie Inspired Musings on Technological Issues—Of Kangaroo Courts, Tutorials & Hot Tub Cross-Examination," 6 *Green Bag* 2d 141, 148 (2003).

[60]*Green Gas Del. Statutory Trust v. Comm'r*, 147 T.C. 1 (2016); *Buyuk LLC v. Comm'r*, T.C. Memo. 2013-253, 106 T.C.M. (CCH) 502 (2013); *Crimi v. Comm'r*, T.C. Memo. 2013-51, 105 T.C.M. (CCH) 1330 (2013); *Rovakat, LLC v. Comm'r*, T.C. Memo. 2011-225, 102 T.C.M. (CCH) 264 (2011), *aff'd*, 529 Fed. Appx. 124 (3d Cir. 2013); *Exelon Corp. v. Comm'r*, 147 T.C. ___, 2016 WL 4992729 (T.C. Sept. 19, 2016), *appeal docketed*, No. 17-2964 (7th Cir. Sept. 22, 2017); *see also Estate of Pohlad v. Comm'r*, No. 12508-13 (T.C. filed June 6, 2013) (using concurrent witness testimony with nine experts, after which the case settled).

implementation of the concurrent evidence method, the expert discussion becomes "highly focused, highly structured, and directed by the Court."[61]

The first time the Tax Court used concurrent witness testimony was in *Rovakat, LLC v. Commissioner.*[62] A brief summary of the modified hot tub procedure that Judge Laro used in *Rovakat* may prove instructive to judges and practitioners as they consider the merits of this technique. Following the cross-examination and rebuttal of the expert witnesses, Judge Laro asked the parties if they would "be willing to engage in the technique whereby the experts would be sworn in and would talk to one another concurrently in the presence of the judge and in the presence of the attorneys."[63] With the parties' consent, Judge Laro held two successive hot tubs in which the petitioner's sole expert engaged in separate discussions with the government's two experts. The hot tubs occurred in the open courtroom, on the record, and with the parties' counsel present. The format was the same in both hot tub sessions; only the experts, with copies of their reports and any materials used during previous testimony, and the judge sat around a table.[64]

Acknowledging that this was the first time the hot tub had been used in the Tax Court, Judge Laro allowed counsel to make objections during the session.[65] Judge Laro then proceeded to engage the experts in "a conversation, [where] questions would be asked and answers would be provided with the hope that there would be clarity that would come out of that environment."[66] Throughout the process Judge Laro occasionally interjected to ask whether the opposing expert agreed or disagreed with what the other expert had just said, and asked if they could "talk directly to one another."[67] As a result, Judge Laro was able to narrow in on the specific points of divergence between the experts, especially in regard to the differences between book value and fair market value, as well as key variations in the experts' appraisal methodologies.[68] Aside from Judge Laro's intermittent direction, questions, and clarifications, the experts successfully engaged in a productive dialogue—asking each other questions and even changing the topic of discussion.[69] In the end, Judge Laro indicated that the conversation had been very helpful in assessing the strengths and weaknesses of all expert opinions.[70]

In his second implementation of the hot tub procedure in *Crimi v. Commissioner*, Judge Laro conducted a concurrent evidence session with all four testifying experts. He emphasized that the objective of the session was to have a "free-flowing" conversation whereby the experts "talk to one another and occasionally me and basically

---

[61] *Rovakat, LLC v. Comm'r*, T.C. Memo. 2011-225, *aff'd*, 529 Fed. Appx. 124 (3d Cir. 2013); *see also* N.S.W. Law Reform Commission, *supra* note 3, at s 6.48.

[62] *Rovakat, LLC v. Comm'r*, T.C. Memo. 2011-225, 102 T.C.M. (CCH) 264 (2011), *aff'd*, 529 Fed. Appx. 124 (3d Cir. 2013).

[63] *Rovakat, LLC v. Comm'r*, No. 3251-09 (U.S. Tax Ct. 2011 (transcript of proceeding at 706)).

[64] *Id.* at 713.

[65] *Id.* at 713–714.

[66] *Id.* at 706.

[67] *Id.* at 717, 718, 723, 744.

[68] *Id.* at 717–718, 816.

[69] *Id.* at 738.

[70] *Id.* at 762, 765, 767, 823.

point out on a professional basis why they think the opposing expert may be right or wrong and what rationale is appropriate and what is inappropriate."[71] Judge Laro encouraged the experts to "feel free to interrupt as any conversation would happen, to probe," and to delve into the strengths and weaknesses of the opinions rendered.[72] He stressed that, above all, the process "is designed to enlighten the Court as to what is the proper conclusion."[73] To that end, Judge Laro cautioned the experts that although "[e]ach of you have been hired by a party to be an expert witness in this case, ... the moment you walk through the door of this courtroom, as far as I'm concerned, now you belong to the Court."[74] Judge Laro also warned the experts not to be advocates and to instead act in a role "to help me understand the valuation issues here."[75] Judge Laro stated in his opinion that the importance of the concurrent testimony in *Crimi* could not be overstated.[76]

Judge Laro also implemented the hot tub procedure in *Buyuk LLC v. Commissioner* and *Green Gas Delaware Statutory Trust v. Commissioner* in substantially the same way as he did in *Rovakat* and *Crimi*.[77] Judge Laro describes the effectiveness of the procedure in *Buyuk* as follows:

> [W]e cannot overstate the importance of concurrent witness testimony in these cases. [T]hrough Mr. Burd's and Professor Bean's concurrent testimony, we were able to flesh out some of their reports' conclusions, reasonably reconcile the experts' varying conclusions when possible, and when reconciliation was impossible, understand the basis for their disagreeing opinions and decide which opinion to rely on.[78]

Judge Laro's admonition that the expert witnesses are "not advocates" goes to the heart of what the concurrent expert witness method is trying to achieve: reduced expert partisanship. As Judge Laro recognized, an expert's physical proximity to the judge and her peer in the hot tub may have a significant positive psychological effect on the credibility of expert witness testimony.[79]

SUGGESTED FOUR-STAGE HOT TUB APPROACH FOR TAX COURT JUDGES

Our Tax Court judges have the inherent power[80] to mandate that expert testimony at the time of trial be initially presented by the concurrent evidence method. In fact, Federal Rule of Evidence 611 goes one step further and directs that the trial

---

[71] *Crimi v. Comm'r*, No. 13252-09 (U.S. Tax Ct. 2010) (transcript of proceedings at 328, 329).
[72] *Id.* at 330.
[73] *Id.* at 329.
[74] *Id.* at 330.
[75] *Id.*
[76] *Crimi v. Comm'r*, T.C. Memo. 2013-51, 105 T.C.M. (CCH) 1330 (2013).
[77] *Buyuk LLC v. Comm'r*, T.C. Memo. 2013-253.
[78] *Id.* at *39-*40.
[79] *See also* Marvin J. Garbis, "Aussie Inspired Musings on Technological Issues—Of Kangaroo Courts, Tutorials & Hot Tub Cross-Examination," 6 *Green Bag* 2d 141, 148 (2003) ("The physical removal of the witness from his party's camp into the physical proximity of a (usually) respected professional colleague tends to reduce the level of partisanship.").
[80] *Fed. R. Evid.* 611(a)(1).

judge "should exercise reasonable control over the mode of examining witnesses and presenting evidence so as to make those procedures effective for determining the truth."[81] If a trial judge considers the hot tub method advantageous to assist the court in achieving a truthful result, the federal rule directs the court to implement its usage. One statistical assessment of trial evidence noted Federal Evidence Rule 611 as authority for the proposition that for expert witness reports that "go together, the judge might allow their presentations to be combined and the witnesses to be questioned as a panel discussion . . . ."[82] Although some judges cautiously seek the parties' consent to use the hot tub method, ample authority exists for a trial judge to mandate its implementation. Therefore, even though sequencing of evidence may be the traditional way to present expert trial testimony, neither the Federal Rules of Evidence nor reasoned thinking mandate the universal use of this antiquated method.[83]

Detailing the features of the hot tub method evidences why its many benefits lend themselves to Tax Court litigation. One thing to keep in mind, however, is that there is no single way to set up and administer the hot tub. Many variations of the technique exist and rightly so, since one of the most alluring attributes of the process is its flexibility "to accommodate different requirements and practices in different courts for different kinds of subject matter of varying degrees of complexity and importance."[84] Although there is no standardized procedure for concurrent evidence, the method will be most effective when separated into four distinct stages: the pretrial stage, the expert oath stage, the trial conversation stage, and the cross-examination stage.[85]

Stage One: Pretrial Expert Meeting and Joint Report

The Tax Court rules currently mandate expert witness reports be served on each other party and submitted to the trial judge no later than 30 days before the call of the trial calendar on which the case appears.[86] This rule could easily be amended to require the exchange of the expert reports 60 days prior to the call of the trial calendar. This would allow the rules to require the experts to meet face-to-face, without counsel present, and produce a joint expert report and still have this joint report submitted to the court within 30 days of trial. Forcing the experts to meet and report as to any remaining disagreements is entirely consistent with Tax Court rules, which already mandate "the parties to stipulate, to the fullest extent possible" as to all non-privileged relevant facts.[87]

---

[81] *Id.*

[82] *The Evolving Role of Statistical Assessments as Evidence in the Courts* 174 (Stephen E. Fienberg ed., 1989).

[83] *Id.*

[84] Hon. Justice Peter McClellan, Chief Judge of Supreme Court of New South Wales, Keynote Address at the Medicine and Law Conference at the Law Institute of Victoria: "Concurrent Expert Evidence" (Nov. 29, 2007), at 11. In one variation of the method, the experts do not give oral summaries of their evidence. *See also* Heerey, *supra* note 38, at 390–391.

[85] *See, e.g.,* Edmond, *supra* note 47, at 164.

[86] T.C.R. 143(g)(2).

[87] T.C.R. 91.

Many Australian courts also utilize an expanded joint pretrial meeting to require the expert witnesses to meet in person prior to trial with the goal of distilling down the areas of disagreement and reducing any remaining issues to writing in the form of a joint expert witness report to the court.[88] This joint report is intended to facilitate settlements and to focus any future litigation on only those points of contention while simultaneously addressing partisan issues.[89]

Our courts here in the United States are likewise routinely utilizing pretrial conferences to improve the quality of the trial. Tax Court rules allow the trial judge "to confer with the parties in pretrial conferences with a view to narrowing issues, stipulating facts, simplifying the presentation of evidence, or otherwise assisting in the preparation for trial or possible disposition of the case in whole or in part without trial."[90] This pretrial conference may serve as an additional opportunity for Tax Court judges to have the experts present themselves in a face-to-face meeting and endeavor to "limit the number of experts or the scope or subject matter of expert testimony" before the trial begins.[91]

Stage Two: The Expert Oath

Recognizing the reality of built-in expert witness bias, Australian lawmakers have not only mandated expert hot tub sessions, but also developed and drafted strict guidelines for experts to adhere to, including the following three important duties owed to the tribunal: (1) an expert witness has an overriding duty to assist the court; (2) an expert shall not act as an advocate; and (3) an expert's paramount duty is to the court, not to the party who hired her.[92] Just prior to the start of the hot tub conversation, all experts should be administered an oath under the penalty of perjury not only to tell the truth, but also to affirm compliance with each of these mandated guidelines. This procedure will hopefully awaken in the expert a sense of duty to the court and a stern reminder that no expert shall act as an advocate.

Stage Three: The Trial Hot Tub Conversation

The third stage departs from the conventional adversarial approach and instead focuses upon the development of a dialogue with the experts and judge.[93] Assume, for example, that there are only two experts in a tax controversy: one for the government and one for the taxpayer. During this stage, after both experts are simultaneously sworn, they will proceed to testify to their expert evidence at the same time by making presentations addressing their written opinions and the basis for such opinions and engage in a conversation with the trial judge and other expert.[94] No previous trial

---

[88] Edmond, *supra* note 47, at 165.

[89] *Id.*

[90] *See generally* T.C.R. 110(a).

[91] MacGregor Smith, *supra* note 2, at 1251.

[92] Federal Court of Australia, *Practice Note CM 7: Expert Witnesses in Proceedings in the Federal Court of Australia* (Austl.), available at http://www.fedcourt.gov.au/pdfsrtfs_p/ practice_notes_cm7.rtf.

[93] *NSW Law Reform Comm'n, supra* note 3, at §6.48.

[94] *Id.*

testimony should be received from these experts prior to the hot tub session. This way experts will not feel "locked in" to lawyer-elicited testimony. Of course experts may have that ego-protective instinct with respect to contents of reports, but having memories refreshed by friendly examination-in-chief would accentuate that problem.

The hot tub procedure will substantially replace the traditional expert testimony. Each expert should be given ample opportunity and time to comment upon the case, the issues, her conclusions, and her differences from the opinions of the other testifying experts.[95] And each expert should also be given the ability to ask pointed questions of the other expert.[96]

This format provides the opportunity for the experts to engage in an open forum, a "roundtable" interaction that invites each expert to probe, challenge, confer, and resolve their disagreements with each other.[97] Throughout this hot tub process, the trial judge should take an active role in leading and directing the conversation, which should include the trial judge asking pointed questions to clarify and flush out the areas of agreement and disagreement and the basis for such.[98] American trial judges should not be bashful in utilizing their already afforded power under the Federal Rules of Evidence to question expert witnesses during the hot tub session.[99]

Although some courts would allow counsel from either party to object or interject and supplement their expert's comments with questioning, during stage three of the hot tub, the conversation stage will work better if the court precludes all litigation attorney participation. Lawyers should remain silent and must save their objections and questioning for the fourth stage. A lawyer-free conversation among the judge and experts increases the integrity of all expert testimony by focusing the experts on the subject matter, not the lawsuit. This also helps the judge (the fact finder in Tax Court litigation) in assessing the experts on any given issue simultaneously and to have a learned conversation with the experts.[100] It is important to keep in mind that the real objective of these joint dialogues is to narrow down expert disagreement and not allow counsel to undermine and nitpick at the opposing party's expert testimony.[101] In order to have the most productive (and civilized) conversation, it is best to leave the lawyers out of it.

Face-to-face contact has been touted as one of the biggest contributors to mutual cooperation and conflict resolution.[102] Several studies have documented that

---

[95] Lisa C. Wood, "Experts in the Tub," 21 *Antitrust* 95, 95–96 (2007) (citing Competition Tribunal Rules (Competition Tribunal Act), SOR/94-290 §§ 48.1-48.2 (Can.)).

[96] *Id.*

[97] *See* Kao et al., *supra* note 39, at 1043.

[98] *See* Heerey, *supra* note 38, at 390–391; Edmond, *supra* note 47, at 164.

[99] *Fed. R. Evid.* 614 (Subsection (a) states that "the court may call a witness on its own … request" and subsection (b) allows the court to "examine a witness regardless of who calls the witness.").

[100] *See* NSW *Law Reform Comm'n, supra* note 3, at §6.56 (stating that "more importantly, the process moves somewhat away from lawyers interrogating experts towards a structured professional discussion between peers in the relevant field").

[101] Edmond, *supra* note 47, at 165.

[102] Aimee L. Drolet and Michael W. Morris, "Rapport in Conflict Resolution: Accounting for How Face-to-Face Contact Fosters Mutual Cooperation in Mixed-Motive Conflicts," *J. of Experimental Soc. Psychol.* (Jan. 2000), at 27.

the presence of face-to-face "communication, as opposed to its absence, facilitates mutual cooperation."[103] Indeed, behavioral experiments provide "evidence that the social psychological process of rapport accounts for facilitatory effects of face-to-face contact on cooperation in conflict resolution."[104] It really should come as no surprise that the chances of solving a dilemma are increased when those in conflict communicate.[105] Some social scientists have even shown that a group of strangers can elicit accommodating behavior from each if they have the opportunity to communicate with each other about a problem for just 10 minutes.[106] The psychological effect, therefore, on the adversarial experts when sitting side by side in a professional conversational setting before an active trial judge will lead to less controversy and a more focused approach to any remaining disputes. Such a procedure will have the dual effect of "improv[ing] the judge's understanding and reduc[ing] the tensions associated with the experts' adversarial role."[107]

Judge Laro cautiously allowed counsel to make objections during his hot tub discussions so that they could preserve the objection for appeal.[108] However, mandating objections be made at the conclusion of stage three of the hot tub is not only consistent with due process and the Federal Rules but also best serves the interests trying to be achieved by the lawyer-free dialogue.[109] Also, this way the issues are refined to their bare minimum, and the judge can hone in on the issues giving her the most difficulty without counsel intrusion.[110]

Stage Four: Cross-Examination and Rebuttal

Immediately following the conclusion of the third-stage conversation, counsel should be permitted to make whatever objections or offers of proof they so desire in order to preserve these issues for appeal.[111] After the third stage of the hot tub (the dialogue) is completed, no further expert direct examination should be allowed. The expert written reports combined with this hot tub discussion provide more than an ample opportunity for each party to present the direct examination of their expert testimony. An analogue is common in Tax Court litigation—qualified expert witness reports are routinely received into evidence as the direct testimony of the expert.[112]

---

[103] *Id.* at 28.

[104] *Id.* at 27.

[105] Robyn M Dawes, Jeanne McTavish, and Harriet Shaklee, "Behavior, Communication, and Assumptions About Other People's Behavior in A Commons Dilemma Situation," *J. of Personality and Soc. Psychol.* (Jan. 1977), at 6.

[106] *Id.*

[107] *The Evolving Role of Statistical Assessments as Evidence in the Courts* 174 (Stephen E. Fienberg ed., 1989).

[108] Transcript of Oral Argument at 715, *Rovakat, LLC v. Commissioner*, T.C. Memo. 2011-225 (U.S. Tax Ct. 2011); Transcript of Oral Argument at 328, *Crimi, et al. v. Commissioner*, No. 13252-09 (U.S. Tax Ct. Aug. 4, 2010).

[109] It is not uncommon to allow objections to postponed (for example, postponed until the "next opportunity when the jury is not present."). *Fed. R. Evid.* 614.

[110] Heerey, *supra* note 38, at 390–391.

[111] *See Fed. R. Evid.* 103(a)(1)(A), 103(a)(2).

[112] *Id.*

The fourth stage of the concurrent evidence session would proceed with a more conventional adversarial examination by allowing each party the opportunity to cross-examine opposition experts by use of leading questions.[113] Of course, redirection of a party's witness may still be allowed after this cross-examination at the discretion of the trial judge. Additionally, after such cross-examination questions are completed, the other expert should generally be permitted to remark upon the expert witness's cross-examination responses.[114] This fourth stage is intended to allow the adversarial process to bring out additional relevant testimony not previously discussed and to flow in harmony with the stage-three expert hot tub dialogue. It is here that the lawyers have a full opportunity to engage in thoughtful inquiry into the divergent opinions and reasoning of the expert witnesses expressed during the hot tub session.[115]

COMMON MISPERCEPTIONS OF THE CONCURRENT WITNESS MODEL

Much has been written about the use of the concurrent witness model in American courts, but a number of misconceptions persist. This section seeks to correct those misperceptions.

Myth 1: Concurrent Testimony Replaces the Traditional Model

Some practitioners think concurrent testimony replaces the traditional adversarial model. This is not true. The concurrent witness process, as proposed earlier, would allow for a traditional adversarial process to run its course during stage four. The concurrent witness process takes the traditional process one step further by also requiring the experts to testify concurrently.

Myth 2: The Consent of Both Parties Is Needed

Some practitioners think a judge can solicit concurrent evidence only with the consent of both parties. This is not true. As discussed earlier, there is ample authority for a trial court, in addition to its own inherent powers, to instruct witnesses to testify concurrently.

Myth 3: More Work Is Created for the Trier of Fact

Some judges are critical of the concurrent evidence model because they think more work will be created for them and their staff. This is not true. The concurrent evidence model requires judges to engage in extensive pretrial preparation to ensure that the evidence he or she believes is dispositive of the case makes it into the record. Counsel may, of course, develop that record during direct and cross-examination.

---

[113]Edmond, *supra* note 47, at 164.
[114]*Id.*
[115]*Id.*

The judge in turn is free to direct the concurrent testimony on the basis of her pretrial deliberation and the record as developed on direct and cross-examination. Thus, additional work is not created under the concurrent evidence model. Rather, the work is shifted from post-trial deliberation to pretrial preparation; that is, the work is front-loaded.

Myth 4: Concurrent Evidence Is Received Off the Record

Some attorneys believe that concurrent testimony is received off the record. This is also not true. All of the concurrent evidence (i.e., the joint dialogue of the parties) occurs in an open courtroom, on the record, and in the presence of the parties and their attorneys. While some judges initially believed that court reporters would have difficulty attributing testimony to the correct witness, in actuality the court reporters have kept a flawless record with, they say, relative ease.

Myth 5: The Concurrent Witness Model Is an Auction

Some valuators and lawyers are critical of concurrent testimony because they think the process turns into an auction in which their empirical evidence is ignored. This is not what is supposed to occur during a hot tub session, and this concern underscores the importance that the trier of fact be conversant in the expert's subject matter (usually valuation in tax cases).

Myth 6: The Lawyers Lose All Control in the Courtroom

Some practitioners are critical of the concurrent evidence model because, they claim, they lose control in the courtroom. This is mostly untrue. First, lawyers may lose control under the actual concurrent testimony session, but they still retain considerable control over the proposed findings of fact, the experts' direct report reports, the experts' rebuttal reports, the cross-examination of the expert, and the presentation of post-trial briefs. Any control a lawyer loses in the trial process is intended, and should be of no import to judges who implement the hot tub procedures. If we accept the premise that trials are ultimately about unearthing the truth, criticisms about loss of control in the courtroom are unwarranted because the very design of the concurrent evidence model is to get to the truth of the matter without the interference of counsel.

Myth 7: Hot Tubbing Is Prevalent in Tax Cases

Some believe that hot tubbing is prevalent and always advisable in tax cases. This is not true. Hot tubbing has been done several times, but it is not happening on a large scale. There are many reasons that might explain why hot tubbing is not more prevalent, but one reason judges may be reluctant to adopt the procedure is that not all judges have consented to using the procedure. Practitioners desiring to use hot tubbing in a case should make a written application to the Court to implement the hot tub procedures. The presiding judge is then free to decide whether he or she will implement the hot tub procedure.

PRACTICAL BENEFITS AND CLAIMED DRAWBACKS

The feedback from judges who have implemented concurrent evidence has been largely positive.[116] In fact, one jurist believes the method would "be particularly effective in valuation and similar disputes."[117] This comment is particularly enlightening because it further illustrates that the benefits of the hot tub method markedly lend themselves to the incessant stream of valuation controversies the Tax Court faces. Not only is the procedure well designed to highlight the discrepancies in valuation methodology and analysis, it also reduces the required time and expense for the court and the litigant.

These multidimensional benefits coincide with the overall purpose of Rule 102 of the Federal Rule of Evidence, which gives judges the discretion to use the rules "so as to administer every proceeding fairly, eliminate unjustifiable expense and delay, and promote the development of evidence law." As one litigation attorney succinctly put it, the concurrent evidence method "makes the expert evidence process more streamlined, less adversarial, and more useful."[118]

Proponents of concurrent witness evidence showcase the method's ability to considerably reduce the issues in dispute as well as provide the fact finder with a simultaneous look at each expert and her differing opinion.[119] One of the most frustrating problems with expert testimony in tax litigation is the presentation of diametrically opposed valuation methodologies and conclusions. The discrepancies between estimated valuations are often astonishing, and it is exactly these vast deviations that appear to have prompted a few judges to experiment with the concurrent evidence method.

The hot tub conversation focuses expert testimony by passing over the unimportant areas of agreement or disagreement and instead allows the judge to more readily identify the key, more nuanced issues in dispute. Tangential or superfluous testimony is easily identified and discarded when using this concurrent evidence method.

The hot tub procedure also allows new information to come to light as the experts explain why they think the opposing expert may be right or wrong and what rationale is appropriate or inappropriate. The contemporaneous nature of the expert testimony also disposes of time delays, which often put the trier of fact in the difficult position of having to recall opposing testimony or pore over extensive transcripts. It also eliminates the need for litigants to recall experts whenever counsel desires to dispute a particular aspect of a subsequent testifying expert. The ability to deal with expert testimony on a single issue in a single setting can expedite a process that is presently burdened with unnecessary delay and repetition.

Another potential advantage of concurrent expert witness testimony is the fundamental reduction in expert witness partisanship. Many commentators recognize

---

[116]*See* N.S.W. Report, *supra* note 3, at s 6.51; *Green Gas Del. Statutory Trust v. Comm'r*, 147 T.C.1(2016); *Buyuk LLC v. Comm'r*, T.C. Memo. 2013-253, 106 T.C.M. (CCH) 502 (2013); *Crimi v. Comm'r*, T.C. Memo. 2013-51, 105 T.C.M. (CCH) 1330 (2013); *Rovakat, LLC v. Comm'r*, T.C. Memo. 2011-225, 102 T.C.M. (CCH) 264 (2011), *aff'd*, 529 Fed. Appx. 124 (3d Cir. 2013).

[117]Jackson Report, *supra* note 56.

[118]Kao, et al., *supra* note 39, p. 1035.

[119]Heerey, *supra* note 38, pp. 390–391.

that all experts, at least to some extent, are "more or less aligned with and biased in favor of the side that hires them."[120] Not surprisingly, this expert bias results from the simple notion that the party who hires the expert is generally the same person who writes the checks.[121] More subtle forms of bias often also develop from the expert's sustained personal contact with the hiring lawyer.[122]

The physical proximity of the expert witnesses at the hot tub table with the trial judge and the expanded oath discussed earlier increase the likelihood that the experts will provide honest opinions. Anything an expert claims during the hot tub is subject to immediate challenge by a professional peer and questioning by the trial judge.[123] "Thus, having experts give testimony concurrently ... is likely to reduce embellishment, avoidance of tough issues, and harsh rhetoric, which, in turn, can reduce overall hostility in a contentious matter."[124] These rules endeavor to reduce expert bias in testimonial settings and provide a more pleasant dialogue that results in more accurate fact-finding.

The use of the concurrent evidence procedure also achieves increased judicial efficiency.[125] According to the New South Wales Land and Environmental Court, use of the concurrent evidence methods for expert testimony may take less than half of the time required by more traditional adversarial techniques.[126] The use of concurrent evidence would therefore radically reduce expenditures in complex litigation in which several experts are scheduled to testify.[127] Even in a more straight-forward legal proceeding, requiring the parties' experts to testify concurrently will likewise reduce the trial length and result in a cost savings to the litigants and the court system.[128]

Many practicing experts favor giving their testimony in the hot tub method over the traditional question-and-answer, lawyer-dominated procedure.[129] The concurrent evidence technique allows expert witnesses to express and defend their opinions and conclusions without restraint and their findings are not subject to possibly being distorted by opposing counsel's artful questioning during the hot tub session.[130] The hot tub procedure seeks to provide a forum of professional discussion led by the trial judge and jettison the acrimony often found when using a more customary adversarial approach to expert testimonial evidence.

---

[120]See, e.g., Edmond, *supra* note 47, p. 173 (citing Yearley, "The Relationship Between Epistemological and Sociological Cognitive Interests," 13 *Studies in History and Philosophy of Science* 353 (1982), p. 375).

[121]*Id.*

[122]*Id.*

[123]Kao, et al., *supra* note 39, p. 1043.

[124]*Id.*

[125]Wood, *supra* note 57, p. 96.

[126]Edmond, *supra* note 47, p. 167; *see also* Admin. Appeals Tribunal (Australia), *An Evaluation of the Use of Concurrent Evidence in the Administrative Appeals Tribunal* (2005) (hereinafter, "Admin Appeals"), p. 8.

[127]Edmond, *supra* note 47, p. 176.

[128]*Id.*

[129]*See* Admin. Appeals, *supra* note 126.

[130]*Id.*; *see also* N.S.W. Report, *supra* note 3, at § 6.51.

It is well understood that credible, honest, and articulate experts might not legitimately reach the same conclusion.[131] It would be naive to believe that "in fields of expert knowledge there is only one answer."[132] As such, in close situations, there already is an advantage (even in the traditional procedure of adversarial witness box testimony and cross-examination) favoring the more likeable and articulate experts.[133] Good lawyers have historically searched for and retained experts with good credentials, charisma, likeable personalities, and persuasive communication skills. At least under the concurrent evidence methods, experts will have to articulate their positions with instant peer review and comment by the other expert, and with judicial involvement that helps cut through any obfuscating showmanship. Charisma matters much less in the hot tub.

Under the concurrent evidence method, judges will also be in a better position to pierce the veil of excessive collusion between attorneys and experts. As such, the concurrent evidence method will restore some much-needed credibility to the process by requiring experts to be articulate in explaining their opinions and the reasoning supporting their conclusions without attorney manipulation.

Another Australian judicial critic of this procedure argues that "expert[s come] to the [h]ot [t]ub armed not merely as … expert witness[es] but as … expert advocate[s]."[134] Nevertheless, a procedure that requires an expert to demonstrate a profound understanding of the facts and issues in dispute, as well as to articulate his methodology, analysis, and conclusion in the hot tub, is not a drawback but a step forward. If the hot tub were mandatory for all parties in all Tax Court litigation, lawyers could not risk being intellectually lazy when presenting experts; they would have to endeavor to understand fully the underlying basis, data, and support for any expert opinions that they wished to submit. It is the trial attorney's responsibility to bring to the Tax Court thoughtful, candid, well-reasoned, concise, independent, relevant, and competent expert valuation testimony.

The lesson to be learned is that parties and their counsel must understand that the road to a successful valuation verdict will depend on the preparation of credible persuasive evidence in the form of lay and expert testimony necessary to determine the value of the property in dispute. The lawyers will need to assist in educating the experts as to the possible minefield of hot tub sessions and prepare them to ensure the experts "make all factual and technical points necessary to the case

---

[131] Rares, "Using the Hot Tub—How Concurrent Expert Evidence Aids Understanding Issues" (unpublished paper dated Aug. 25, 2010, presented at the New South Wales Bar Association, Continuing Professional Development Seminar, Sydney), ¶15.

[132] *Id.* (citing Hon. Justice Garry Downes, "Concurrent Expert Evidence in the Administrative Appeals Tribunal: The New South Wales Experience" (unpublished paper dated Feb. 27, 2004, presented at the Australasian Conference of Planning and Environment Courts and Tribunals, Hobart).

[133] Brodsky, "Credibility in the Courtroom: How Likeable Should an Expert Witness Be?," 37 *J. Amer. Acad. of Psychiatry and the Law* 4 (2009), pp. 525–526.

[134] *See, e.g.,* Fannon, *supra* note 3.

during the hot tubbing session."[135] In the end (and as hoped for all along), the emphasis of a good advocate will be on more thorough pretrial expert preparation leading to credible testimony that will assist the fact finder.

The concurrent witness process is especially appropriate for Tax Court litigation involving valuation. Tax Court judges are uniquely qualified to lead and direct such hot tub conversations. Without the aid of a jury, Tax Court judges are expected to take an active role in the fact-finding process and possess a deep understanding of the general legal principles. Trial judges need to challenge unsound expert opinions and experiment with alternative procedural devices if we are ever going to tackle the recurring deficiencies that plague our judicial system.

CONCLUSION

It may be time to depart from the perceived comfort of the traditional notion that witnesses have to be presented sequentially in the lawyer-controlled environment of direct and cross-examination. The concurrent evidence method is not a panacea for all the ills of the American judicial system. It is, however, a step in the right direction—one aimed at assisting Tax Court judges to determine the true fair market value of property for tax purposes. This hot tub technique has undeniable benefits when applied and should be considered as an alternative evidentiary expert witness procedure.

---

[135] *See* Devitt, address at the University of San Diego School of Law's Business Valuation Conference: "Summit on Lack of Marketability" (Sept. 2008), and address at Georgetown University School of Law's Advanced Summit on Business Valuation: "Resolving Tax and Legal Issues" (Nov. 2010). *See generally* Reifert, "Getting Into the Hot Tub: How the United States Could Benefit from Australia's Concept of 'Hot Tubbing' Expert Witnesses," 89 *U. Det. Mercy L. Rev.* 103 (2011).

CHAPTER 12

Penalties Associated with Faulty Appraisals

SUMMARY

Fundamental to modern appraisal practice is an appreciation of the civil penalties and professional sanctions that may be imposed upon an appraiser who authors a faulty appraisal in connection with the filing of a federal tax return. Similarly, a broad range of civil penalties may be imposed upon a client-taxpayer who uses a defective appraisal to support a position reported on a federal tax return. This chapter discusses the civil penalties and professional sanctions that may be imposed upon an appraiser, as well as those civil penalties that may be imposed upon a client-taxpayer, in connection with the filing of a federal tax return.

THE IMPORTANCE AND PREVALENCE OF PENALTIES IN MODERN-DAY APPRAISAL PRACTICE

Penalties for failure to comply with internal revenue laws are a necessary component of any self-reporting tax system, such as the one adopted in the United States.[1] From a tax policy perspective, penalties are the mechanism by which Congress encourages voluntary compliance with the tax laws, deters objectionable behavior by taxpayers and appraisers, and enables the Internal Revenue Service ("IRS") to fairly, efficiently, and effectively administer the internal revenue laws. Although penalties raise additional revenue for the government and, at least to an extent, indirectly fund the costs of enforcement, the IRS has advised its employees that revenue generation should not be a reason to impose penalties.[2]

The prevalence and importance of civil tax penalties in modern-day appraisal practice cannot be understated. At the time of this writing, the federal internal revenue laws authorize the imposition of more than 150 civil tax penalties, including those which may be imposed upon an appraiser under sections 6701 and 6695A of

---

[1] *See generally* Staff of J. Comm. on Taxation, *Study of Present-Law Penalty and Interest Provisions as Required by Section 3801 of the Internal Revenue Service Restructuring and Reform Act of 1998 (Including Provisions Relating to Corporate Tax Shelters)*, Vol. I at 30 (J. Comm. Print 1999); *see also Internal Revenue Manual* ("I.R.M."), pt. 20.1.1.2.1 (Nov. 25, 2011).
[2] I.R.M., pt. 20.1.2.20.1.1, Policy Statement 20-1 (June 29, 2004).

the Internal Revenue Code, upon a client-taxpayer under section 6662 of the Internal Revenue Code, and upon a paid return preparer under section 6694 of the Internal Revenue Code. As to the paid return preparer penalty under section 6694 of the Internal Revenue Code, an appraiser may be considered a paid return preparer for this purpose. Significantly, Congress has also given the IRS broad authority to regulate professionals who represent taxpayers before the agency. An appraiser who is shown to be technically incompetent or disreputable may, in addition to being subject to the foregoing penalties, also be disqualified from practice before the IRS. If an appraiser is disqualified from practicing before the IRS, he or she may also be barred from presenting evidence or testimony in any administrative proceeding before the U.S. Department of the Treasury, such as a hearing before the IRS's Office of Appeals.

FRAMEWORK FOR EXAMINATION

A thorough discussion of civil tax penalties as they relate to appraisal practice must begin with a discussion of the accuracy-related penalties that may be imposed upon a client-taxpayer because tax noncompliance is a condition precedent to the imposition of appraiser penalties. Thus, this chapter first discusses civil tax penalties for which a client-taxpayer may be held liable in connection with a defective appraisal; namely, accuracy-related penalties for substantial valuation misstatements, gross valuation misstatements, and estate or gift valuation misstatements under section 6662 of the Internal Revenue Code. Second, this chapter explores the broad range of civil tax penalties that may be imposed upon an appraiser under the Internal Revenue Code, including the section 6695A accuracy-related penalty, the section 6694 paid return preparer penalty, and the section 6701 penalty for aiding and abetting an understatement of income tax. Third, this chapter summarizes professional sanctions that may be imposed upon an appraiser under Circular 230 for failing to meet certain minimum standards of professional conduct.

ACCURACY-RELATED PENALTIES POSSIBLY APPLICABLE TO CLIENT–TAXPAYERS

As it relates to appraisals, section 6662 of the Internal Revenue Code authorizes the imposition of an accuracy-related penalty on any portion of an underpayment of tax that is attributable to the following types of misconduct:

- A substantial valuation misstatement;
- A substantial estate or gift tax valuation understatement; or
- A gross valuation misstatement.[3]

---

[3]I.R.C. § 6662(a), (b)(3), (5), (h). Section 6662 of the Internal Revenue Code also authorizes the imposition of an accuracy-related penalty for negligence or disregard of rules or regulations, any substantial understatement of income tax, any substantial overstatement of pension liabilities, any disallowance of claimed tax benefits by reason of a transaction lacking economic substance, or any undisclosed foreign financial asset understatement. *See* I.R.C. § 6662(a), (b)(1), (2), (4), (6), (7). A discussion of these additionally cited accuracy-related penalties is outside the scope of this book.

The amount of the accuracy-related penalty under section 6662 of the Internal Revenue Code is directly related to the type of misconduct. Generally, the amount of the penalty is equal to 20 percent on the portion of the underpayment of tax attributable to a substantial valuation misstatement or a substantial estate or gift tax valuation understatement.[4] In the case of a gross valuation misstatement penalty, which is discussed ahead, the amount of the penalty is increased to 40 percent on the portion of the underpayment of tax attributable to the valuation misstatement.[5] Notably, only one accuracy-related penalty may be imposed for a given portion of an underpayment of tax even though that portion implicates more than one form of misconduct described in section 6662 of the Internal Revenue Code.[6] The accuracy-related penalty under section 6662(a) of the Internal Revenue Code generally does not apply if it is shown that there was reasonable cause for, and that the taxpayer acted in good faith with respect to, any portion of the underpayment of tax.[7]

The Substantial Valuation Misstatement Penalty

Imposition of the Penalty   As noted, the Internal Revenue Code generally authorizes the IRS to impose a 20 percent accuracy-related penalty to any portion of an underpayment of tax that is attributable to a substantial valuation misstatement.[8] A substantial valuation misstatement generally occurs if a taxpayer files an income tax return on which:

- The value or adjusted basis of any property is reported as 150 percent or more of the value or adjusted basis of the property finally determined to be correct; or
- The price for any property or services reported on the return in connection with certain transfer pricing adjustments is 200 percent or more (or 50 percent or less) of the price finally determined to be correct, or if the net section 482 transfer price adjustment for the year exceeds the lesser of $5 million or 10 percent of the taxpayer's gross receipts.[9]

Substantial Valuation Misstatement Penalty Applies on a Property-by-Property Basis   For purposes of applying the substantial valuation misstatement penalty, the term *property* refers to both tangible property and intangible property.[10] Tangible property includes, but is not limited to, land, buildings, fixtures, inventory, and personal property. Intangible property includes, but is not limited to, goodwill, covenants not to compete, leasehold interests, patents, copyrights, trademarks, contract rights, and debts.

Notably, the substantial valuation misstatement penalty applies on a property-by-property basis.[11] Thus, if a taxpayer donates two items of property to a charitable

---

[4] I.R.C. § 6662(a), (b)(3), (5).
[5] I.R.C. § 6662(a), (h).
[6] Treas. Reg. § 1.6662-2(c).
[7] I.R.C. § 6664(c).
[8] I.R.C. § 6662(a), (b)(3).
[9] I.R.C. § 6662(e).
[10] Treas. Reg. § 1.6662-5(e)(3).
[11] Treas. Reg. § 1.6662-5(f)(1).

organization during a given year and files an income tax return claiming a charitable contribution deduction with respect to each item of property, the determination of whether a substantial valuation misstatement has occurred is made with respect to each item of property. The following example illustrates the application of the separate property rule:

EXAMPLE

Tom Taxpayer claims a charitable contribution deduction on his 2012 federal income tax return for two items of property: Property 1 with a claimed value of $75 and Property 2 with a claimed value of $100. During an audit of Tom's return, it is determined that the correct value of Property 1 is $60 and that the correct value of Property 2 is $40. The determination of whether there is a substantial valuation misstatement with respect to Property 1 or Property 2 is made on a property-by-property basis. Thus, there is not a substantial valuation misstatement with respect to Property 1 because the value claimed on Tom's 2012 return ($75) is 125 percent of the correct value ($60) (i.e., $75 divided by $60). There is, however, a substantial valuation misstatement with respect to Property 2 because the valued claimed on Tom's 2012 return ($100) is 250 percent of the correct value ($100) ($250 divided by $100). It is immaterial that the aggregate claimed values on the return ($175) are 150 percent or more than the correct values ($100).[12]

Dollar Limitation for Substantial Valuation Misstatements   The substantial valuation misstatement penalty may not be imposed for a given taxable year unless the portion of the tax underpayment for the year that is attributable to a substantial or gross valuation misstatement exceeds $5,000 (or $10,000 in the case of a non-Subchapter S corporation or a personal holding company).[13] This dollar limitation is applied separately to each taxable year for which there is a substantial or gross valuation misstatement.

Substantial Valuation Misstatements and Pass-Through Entities   In the case of a pass-through entity, such as a limited liability company, a partnership, or a trust, the determination of whether there is a substantial valuation misstatement is made at the entity level.[14] The dollar limitation, however, is applied at the individual taxpayer level.[15] Thus, whether the dollar limitation has been satisfied is determined at the individual taxpayer level by aggregating the portion of the underpayment attributable to the pass-through entity with all other underpayments on the individual taxpayer's return that are attributable to a substantial or gross valuation misstatement.[16]

---

[12]Treas. Reg. § 1.6662-5(f)(1).
[13]I.R.C. § 6662(e)(2).
[14]Treas. Reg. 1.6662-5(h)(1).
[15]*Id.*
[16]Treas. Reg. 1.6662-5(h)(2).

Increase in Penalty Rate for Gross Valuation Misstatements   As discussed more fully ahead, the amount of the accuracy-related penalty increases from 20 percent to 40 percent of the underpayment of tax in the case of a gross valuation misstatement.

Defenses

Reasonable Cause as a Defense to the Substantial Valuation Misstatement Penalty
The accuracy-related penalty under section 6662 of the Internal Revenue Code, including the penalty imposed for a substantial valuation misstatement, does not apply with respect to any portion of an underpayment of tax for which the taxpayer shows that there was reasonable cause and that the taxpayer acted in good faith.[17] The taxpayer bears the burden of proving that he or she acted with reasonable cause and in good faith, and to the extent the defense is raised in a judicial proceeding, the taxpayer must specifically plead reliance and good faith as an affirmative defense.[18] A taxpayer's reliance on the advice of a professional, including an attorney, an accountant, or an appraiser, may constitute reasonable cause and good faith where certain elements are specially proven.[19] The elements required to prove reasonable cause as an affirmative defense to the substantial valuation misstatement depends upon whether the property in question is charitable deduction property or non-charitable deduction property.

Charitable Deduction Property   The availability of reasonable cause as an affirmative defense to a substantial valuation misstatement is limited when applied to so-called charitable deduction property. The term *charitable deduction property* means any property, other than money and publicly traded securities, which the taxpayer contributes to a qualifying charitable organization and for which the taxpayer claimed a charitable contribution deduction under section 170 of the Internal Revenue Code.[20] A substantial valuation misstatement penalty with respect to charitable deduction property may be abated on grounds of reasonable cause only if:

- The claimed value of the property was based on a qualified appraisal made by a qualified appraiser; and
- In addition to obtaining such appraisal, the taxpayer also made a good-faith investigation of the contributed property.[21]

Two additional points are noteworthy. First, the terms *qualified appraisal* and *qualified appraiser* have the meanings set forth in section 170(f)(11)(E) of the Internal Revenue Code and are discussed more fully in Chapter 2, *Qualified Appraisal*, and Chapter 3, *Qualified Appraiser*, respectively.[22] Second, neither the statutes nor the related Treasury Regulations clarify the relationship between the

---

[17]I.R.C. § 6664(c)(1); Treas. Reg. § 1.6664-4(a).
[18]*See Higbee v. Comm'r*, 118 T.C. 438, 446-447 (2001); *see also* U.S. Tax Ct. R. 142(a), 39.
[19]*See Neonatology Associates, P.A. v. Comm'r*, 115 T.C. 43, 98-99 (2000), *aff'd* 299 F.3d 221 (3d Cir. 2002); *see also* Treas. Reg. § 1.6664-4(c)(1).
[20]I.R.C. § 6664(c)(4)(A); Treas. Reg. § 1.6664-4(h)(2).
[21]I.R.C. § 6664(c)(3), (4).
[22]I.R.C. § 6664(c)(4)(B), (C); *see also* Treas. Reg. § 1.6664-4(h).

good-faith and good-faith investigation requirements under sections 6664(c)(1) and 6664(c)(2)(B) of the Internal Revenue Code, but the United States Tax Court ("Tax Court") has stated that "it is clear that, with respect to any valuation misstatement or charitable deduction property, a taxpayer must act in good faith generally."[23]

Property Other than Charitable Deduction Property   The reasonable cause defense, with respect to a substantial valuation misstatement of property other than charitable deduction property, may be available under traditional reasonable cause affirmative defense principles. Specifically, the penalty imposed for a substantial valuation misstatement of property other than charitable deduction property will not be imposed with respect to any portion of an underpayment of tax if, with respect to that portion, the taxpayer establishes that there was reasonable cause for such position and that he or she acted in good faith.[24]

Whether a taxpayer acted with reasonable cause and good faith is made on a case-by-case basis, taking into account all pertinent facts and circumstances.[25] As a general rule, the most important factor in determining whether a taxpayer acted with reasonable cause and in good faith is "the extent of the taxpayer's efforts to assess the taxpayer's proper tax liability."[26] Commonly cited examples of circumstances that may constitute reasonable cause include:

- An honest misunderstanding of fact or law that is reasonable in light of the experience, knowledge, and education of the taxpayer;
- Reliance on facts that, unknown to the taxpayer, are incorrect; and
- Reliance by the taxpayer on a professional tax adviser or an appraiser.[27]

Reasonable cause and good faith do not exist merely because there is an appraisal of the value of property. Among the factors courts typically consider when deciding whether reliance on an appraisal justifies the reasonable cause exception are the methodology and assumptions underlying the appraisal, the appraised value, the relationship between the appraised value and the purchase price, the circumstances under which the appraisal was obtained, and the appraiser's relationship to the taxpayer or to the activity in which the property is or was used.[28]

Reliance on a Professional as a Basis for Reasonable Cause   A taxpayer's reliance on the advice of a professional, such as an attorney, an accountant, or an appraiser, may constitute reasonable cause and good faith sufficient to avoid the substantial valuation misstatement penalty. The taxpayer's education, sophistication, and business experience are also highly relevant in determining whether the taxpayer's reliance on the advice was reasonable and in good faith.[29] To avoid the imposition of the

---

[23]*Whitehouse Hotel Ltd. P'ship v. Comm'r*, 139 T.C. 304, 349-350 (2012).

[24]I.R.C. § 6664(c)(1).

[25]Treas. Reg. § 1.6664-4(b)(1).

[26]Treas. Reg. 1.6664-4(b)(1).

[27]*Id.*

[28]*Id.*

[29]Treas. Reg. § 1.6664-4(c)(1).

accuracy-related penalty for a substantial valuation misstatement, the taxpayer must prove that it is more likely than not (i.e., by a preponderance of the evidence) that each of the following three elements were present:

1. The taxpayer reasonably believed that the professional upon whom the reliance was placed was a competent tax adviser with sufficient expertise to justify reliance;
2. The taxpayer provided necessary and accurate information to the adviser; and
3. The taxpayer actually relied in good faith on the adviser's judgment.[30]

With respect to the third element, that the taxpayer actually relied in good faith on the adviser's judgment, relevant subfactors to this inquiry include (1) the taxpayer's business sophistication and experience, (2) the reasonableness of the advice solicited, and (3) whether the advice was obtained as part of a tax shelter.[31] Although tax opinion letters may help negate the imposition of accuracy-related penalties, courts have been skeptical of excusing the penalties where an opinion letter contains material misstatements of fact, does not properly explain the facts, or reaches improbable conclusions as to the tax and economic attributes of the items in question.[32]

Adequate Disclosure Not Available as an Affirmative Defense Unlike certain other accuracy-related penalties, which a taxpayer may avoid if he or she discloses the relevant facts affecting the tax treatment of the item and there is a reasonable basis for the tax treatment of such item by the taxpayer, the disclosure of the valuation overstatement on the tax return does not negate the substantial valuation misstatement penalty.[33]

The Gross Valuation Misstatement Penalty

The Internal Revenue Code generally authorizes the IRS to impose a 40 percent accuracy-related penalty with respect to any portion of an underpayment of tax that is attributable to a gross valuation misstatement.[34] A gross valuation misstatement generally occurs if a taxpayer files an income tax return on which:

- The value or adjusted basis of any property is reported as 200 percent or more of the value or adjusted basis of the property finally determined to be correct; or

---

[30]*Neonatology Associates, P.A. v. Comm'r*, 115 T.C. 43, 98-99 (2000), *aff'd* 299 F.3d 221 (3d Cir. 2002); see also Treas. Reg. § 1.6664-4(c)(1).
[31]*See, e.g.*, 106, *Ltd. v. Comm'r*, 136 T.C. 67, 77-78 (2011), *aff'd* 684 F.3d 84 (D.C. Cir. 2012); *see also* Treas. Reg. § 1.6664-4(b)(1).
[32]*See, e.g., Rovakat, LLC v. Comm'r*, T.C. Memo. 2011-225, 101 T.C.M. (CCH) 1087 (2012), *aff'd* 529 Fed. Appx. 124 (3d Cir. 2013); *Long Term Capital Holdings v. United States*, 330 F. Supp. 2d 122, 209 (D. Conn. 2004), *aff'd* 150 Fed. Appx 40 (2d Cir. 2005).
[33]Treas. Reg. § 1.6662-1.
[34]I.R.C. § 6662(a), (h).

■ The price for any property or services reported on the return in connection with certain transfer pricing adjustments is 400 percent or more (or 25 percent or less) of the price finally determined to be correct, or if the net section 482 transfer price adjustment for the year exceeds the lesser of $20 million or 20 percent of the taxpayer's gross receipts.

Where the value or adjusted basis claimed on a return of any property with a correct value or adjusted basis equal to zero, as may be the case in connection with a transaction determined to lack economic substance, the value or adjusted basis of the property is considered to be 400 percent or more of the correct amount.[35] Notwithstanding this regulation, as discussed in detail in this chapter, whether and how the gross valuation misstatement applies to a transaction determined to lack economic substance has been a subject of recent litigation.

Gross Valuation Misstatement Applies on a Property-by-Property Basis   The gross valuation misstatement applies on a property-by-property basis and operates in the same manner as described earlier with respect to a substantial valuation misstatement.[36] Also, the term *property* under the gross valuation misstatement rules again refers to any tangible or intangible property.[37]

Dollar Limitation for Gross Valuation Misstatements   The gross valuation misstatement penalty may not be imposed for a given year unless the portion of the tax underpayment for the tax year that is attributable to a gross valuation misstatement exceeds $5,000 (or $10,000 in the case of a non-Subchapter S corporation or a personal holding company).[38] This dollar limitation is again applied separately to each taxable year for which there is a substantial or gross valuation misstatement.

Gross Valuation Misstatements and Pass-Through Entities   Whether a substantial valuation misstatement occurred with respect to a tax return of a pass-through entity is made at the entity level.[39] However, the dollar limitation ($5,000 for taxpayers other than C corporations or $10,000 for C corporations, as the case may be) is applied at the individual taxpayer level (i.e., with respect to the return of the partner, shareholder, or beneficiary).[40]

This same rule applies to a gross valuation misstatement. Thus, whether the dollar limitation has been satisfied is determined at the individual taxpayer level by aggregating the portion of the underpayment attributable to the pass-through item with all other underpayments on the individual taxpayer's return that are attributable to a substantial or gross valuation misstatement.[41] To the extent the substantial or gross valuation misstatements exceed the dollar limitation ($5,000 for taxpayers other than C corporations and $10,000 for C corporations), the respective valuation misstatement penalty applies.

---

[35]Treas. Reg. § 1.6662-5(g).
[36]Treas. Reg. § 1.6662-5(f)(1).
[37]Treas. Reg. § 1.6662-5(e)(3).
[38]I.R.C. § 6662(e)(2).
[39]Treas. Reg. 1.6662-5(h)(1).
[40]*Id.*
[41]Treas. Reg. § 1.6662-5(h)(2).

Elimination of Reasonable Cause Exception   The reasonable cause exception discussed in detail in this chapter is not available for gross valuation misstatements reported on returns filed after August 17, 2006.[42] Also, adequate disclosure of the gross valuation misstatement is not available as a defense to the penalty.[43]

The Applicability of the Gross Valuation Misstatements to Transactions Determined to Lack Economic Substance

Introduction to the Economic Substance Doctrine   The Internal Revenue Code provides a set of rules for determining a taxpayer's tax liability, including the amount, timing, source, and character of items of income, gain, loss, and deduction. These rules are intended to provide taxpayers with a degree of certainty as to their tax liability if they undertake a particular course of action. Further, these rules ensure that similarly situated taxpayers will be treated equally and that taxpayers will be liable for comparable federal taxes when structuring the same transaction. Notwithstanding these well-established principles, taxpayers and their tax advisers repeatedly engineer transactions that allow taxpayers to avoid their tax obligations in a way that Congress did not intend.

In recent years, courts have applied the common law doctrine of economic substance with increased frequency to uncover sham transactions that have no purpose other than to generate tax benefits. Stated simply, the economic substance doctrine dictates that in order to receive a tax benefit, a transaction must result in a meaningful change to the taxpayer's economic position other than a purported reduction in federal income tax. The Tax Court has described the economic substance doctrine as follows:

> *The tax law * * * requires that the intended transactions have economic substance separate and distinct from economic benefit achieved solely by tax reduction. The doctrine of economic substance becomes applicable, and a judicial remedy is warranted, where a taxpayer seeks to claim tax benefits, unintended by Congress, by means of transactions that serve no economic purpose other than tax savings.*[44]

In 2010 Congress codified the economic substance doctrine as a two-part conjunctive test in which a transaction shall be respected as having economic substance only if:

- The transaction changes in a meaningful way (apart from federal income tax effects) the taxpayer's economic position, and
- The taxpayer has a substantial business purpose (apart from federal income tax effects) for entering into such transaction.[45]

---

[42]I.R.C. § 6664(c)(3); *see also Reisner v. Comm'r*, T.C. Memo. 2014-230 (holding as a matter of law that the reasonable cause defense is not available with respect to gross valuation misstatements on tax returns filed after August 17, 2006).

[43]Treas. Reg. § 1.6662-1.

[44]*ACM P'ship v. Comm'r*, T.C. Memo. 1997-115, 73 T.C.M. (CCH) 2189, 2215 (1997), *aff'd*, 157 F.3d 231 (3d Cir. 1998).

[45]I.R.C. § 7701(o).

While it is clear that economic substance may be applied to a transaction, it is less clear whether the gross valuation misstatement penalty applies to transactions determined to lack economic substance.

Competing Views as to Whether the Gross Valuation Misstatement Penalty Applies to Transactions Determined to Lack Economic Substance The Tax Court has long adhered to the view that the gross valuation misstatement penalty under section 6662(h) of the Internal Revenue Code applies when the Court determines that an underpayment of tax stems from a transaction lacking economic substance.[46] Two competing views, however, emerged among the judicial circuits as to the extent to which the gross valuation misstatement penalty applies to underpayments of tax that stem from any deductions or credits that are disallowed on grounds that the underlying transaction lacks economic substance. The majority view, endorsed by the United States Courts of Appeals for the First, Second, Third, Fourth, Sixth, Seventh, Eighth, Eleventh, and Federal Circuits, holds that the gross valuation misstatement penalty applies to an underpayment of tax that originates from a transaction lacking economic substance.[47] The minority view, espoused by the U.S. Courts of Appeals for the Fifth and Ninth Circuits, holds that the gross valuation misstatement penalty does not apply to an underpayment of tax that proceeds from a transaction lacking economic substance.[48]

On December 3, 2013, in a unanimous decision, the Supreme Court agreed with the majority view.[49] The Court further held that the outside basis of a partnership lacking economic substance was zero and that the gross valuation misstatement penalty therefore applied.[50] Thus, the law is now settled that the gross valuation misstatement penalty under section 6662(h) of the Internal Revenue Code applies where a court determines that an underpayment of tax stems from a transaction lacking economic substance.

---

[46]*See BLAK Investments*, T.C. Memo. 2012-273, 104 T.C.M. (CCH) 360 (2012) (and cases cited thereat).

[47]*See, e.g., Superior Trading, LLC v. Comm'r*, 728 F.3d 676 (7th Cir. 2013); *Rovakat, LLC v. Comm'r*, 529 Fed. Appx. 124 (3d Cir. 2013); *Crispin v. Comm'r*, 708 F.3d 507, 516 n.18 (3d Cir. 2013); *Gustashaw v. Comm'r*, 696 F.3d 1124, 1136–1137 (11th Cir. 2012); *Alpha I, L.P. v. United States*, 682 F.3d 1009, 1026–1031 (Fed. Cir. 2012); *Fid. Int'l Currency Advisor A Fund, LLC v. United States*, 661 F.3d 667, 671–675 (1st Cir. 2011); *Merino v. Comm'r*, 196 F.3d 147, 155 (3d Cir. 1999); *Zfass v. Comm'r*, 118 F.3d 184, 190–191 (4th Cir. 1997); *Illes v. Comm'r*, 982 F.2d 143, 149, 151 (2d Cir. 1991); *Massengill v. Comm'r*, 876 F.2d 616, 619–620 (8th Cir. 1989).

[48]*See, e.g., Keller v. Comm'r*, 556 F.3d 1056, 1060-1061 (9th Cir. 2009); *Heasley v. Comm'r*, 902 F.2d 380, 383 (5th Cir. 1990); *Todd v. Comm'r*, 862 F.2d 540 (5th Cir. 1988); *but see Bemont Invs., L.L.C. v. United States*, 679 F.3d 339, 351 (5th Cir. 2012); *Keller v. Comm'r*, 556 F.3d 1056, 1061 (9th Cir. 2009) (both questioning the soundness of their interpretation that the section 6662(h) gross valuation misstatement does not apply to a transaction determined to lack economic substance).

[49]*See United States v. Woods*, ___ U.S. ___, 134 S. Ct. 557 (2013).

[50]*Id.*

Estate or Gift Tax Valuation Understatements

The Internal Revenue Code generally authorizes the IRS to impose an accuracy-related penalty on any portion of an underpayment of tax that is attributable to an estate or gift tax valuation misstatement. Estate or gift tax valuation misstatements are of three varieties, the classification of which affects the amount of the accuracy-related penalty under section 6662 of the Internal Revenue Code: substantial estate or gift tax valuation understatements; gross estate or gift tax valuation understatements; and *de minimis* state or gift tax valuation understatements (i.e., understatements below a specified threshold).

An estate or gift tax valuation misstatement is substantial, and a 20 percent accuracy-related penalty may be imposed, where the taxpayer files an estate or gift tax return reporting a valuation of property that is 65 percent or less than the value finally determined to be correct.[51]

An estate or gift tax valuation misstatement is considered gross, and a 40 percent accuracy-related penalty may be imposed, where the taxpayer files an estate or gift tax return reporting a valuation of property that is 40 percent or less than the value finally determined to be correct.[52]

An estate or gift tax valuation misstatement is considered *de minimis*, and the accuracy-related penalty does not apply, where the portion of the underpayment attributable to substantial estate or gift tax valuation understatements for the taxable period is less than $5,000.[53]

CIVIL PENALTIES POTENTIALLY APPLICABLE TO APPRAISERS

In addition to the civil tax penalties that may be imposed upon a client-taxpayer, numerous civil penalties may also be imposed upon an appraiser in connection with an appraisal report used to support the filing of a federal tax return. Among the penalties for which an appraiser may be held liable are the accuracy-related penalty under section 6695A of the Internal Revenue Code, the paid preparer penalty under section 6694 of the Internal Revenue Code, and the penalty for aiding and abetting an understatement of tax under section 6701 of the Internal Revenue Code. The following section discusses the applicability of and affirmative defenses with respect to each type of penalty.

The Section 6695A Accuracy-Related Penalty

Enacted as part of the Pension Protection Act of 2006,[54] section 6695A of the Internal Revenue Code authorizes the IRS to impose an accuracy-related penalty upon a person who prepares an appraisal report and who knows, or should reasonably know, that the report will be used in connection with filing a return or a refund claim.[55] If the claimed value of the property based upon the appraisal results

---

[51]I.R.C. § 6662(a), (b)(5), (g).
[52]I.R.C. § 6662(g), (h)(2)(C).
[53]I.R.C. § 6662(g)(2).
[54]Pub. L. No. 109-280, 109th Cong., 2d Sess. (Aug. 17, 2006).
[55]I.R.C. § 6695A.

to the taxpayer in a substantial valuation misstatement under section 6662(e) of the Internal Revenue Code, a substantial estate or gift valuation overstatement under section 6662(g) of the Internal Revenue Code, or a gross valuation misstatement under section 6662(h) of the Internal Revenue Code, then there is imposed upon the appraiser a penalty equal to the lesser of:

- $1,000 or 10 percent of the amount of the taxpayer's underpayment of tax attributable to the misstatement, whichever is greater, or
- 125 percent of the gross income the appraiser derived from the preparation of the appraisal.[56]

The section 6695A penalty is in addition to any other penalty that may be imposed upon the appraiser, including but not limited to the penalty for aiding and abetting an understatement of tax under section 6701 of the Internal Revenue Code.[57] The IRS takes the position that it will not impose both the appraiser penalty under section 6695A of the Internal Revenue Code and the paid return preparer penalty under section 6694 of the Internal Revenue Code.[58] Unlike the section 6701 penalty, which is discussed more fully ahead, there is no requirement under section 6695A of the Internal Revenue Code that the appraiser know that the taxpayer's use of the appraisal will result in an understatement of tax.

The Statute   Section 6695A provides as follows:

Sec. 6695A. Substantial and gross valuation misstatements attributable to incorrect appraisals

a. Imposition of penalty. If—
   1. a person prepares an appraisal of the value of property and such person knows, or reasonably should have known, that the appraisal would be used in connection with a return or a claim for refund, and
   2. the claimed value of the property on a return or claim for refund which is based on such appraisal results in a substantial valuation misstatement under chapter 1 (within the meaning of section 6662(e)), a substantial estate or gift tax valuation understatement (within the meaning of section 6662(g)), or a gross valuation misstatement (within the meaning of section 6662(h)), with respect to such property, then such person shall pay a penalty in the amount determined under subsection (b).
b. AMOUNT OF PENALTY. The amount of the penalty imposed under subsection (a) on any person with respect to an appraisal shall be equal to the lesser of—
   1. the greater of—
      (A) 10 percent of the amount of the underpayment (as defined in section 6664(a)) attributable to the misstatement described in subsection (a)(2), or
      (B) $1,000, or

---

[56]I.R.C. § 6695A(a), (b).
[57]I.R.C. § 6696(a).
[58]T.D. 9436, 73 Fed. Reg. 78430 (Preamble).

2. 125 percent of the gross income received by the person described in subsection (a)(1) from the preparation of the appraisal.

c. EXCEPTION. No penalty shall be imposed under subsection (a) if the person establishes to the satisfaction of the Secretary that the value established in the appraisal was more likely than not the proper value.

Statute of Limitations and Collection of Penalty   The section 6695A penalty may be assessed at any time because the Internal Revenue Code does not specify a period of limitations on assessment with respect to such penalty.[59] The IRS, however, has stated that it will, to the extent practicable, assess such penalty within three years after the filing of the return or the claim for refund.[60] In addition, the section 6695A penalty can be assessed and collected immediately, and the deficiency procedures do not apply.[61] Thus, an appraiser's only ability to contest the penalty is to pay it and sue for a refund in the appropriate U.S. district court or the United States Court of Federal Claims.

Affirmative Defenses   The section 6695A penalty does not apply if the appraiser establishes that the value determined in the appraisal was more likely than not the proper value.[62] The reasonable cause exception of section 6664 does not apply to the section 6695A penalty.

Referral for Professional Sanctions   Significantly, if a section 6695A penalty is assessed against an appraiser, the appraiser may be referred to the IRS's Office of Professional Responsibility for the imposition of professional sanctions under Circular 230.[63] As discussed more fully ahead, among the permissible sanctions against an appraiser allowed by Circular 230 is the disqualification of the appraiser from appearing or presenting evidence or testimony before the U.S. Department of the Treasury or the IRS.

Paid Preparer Penalty—Section 6694

The Internal Revenue Code authorizes the IRS to impose a penalty on a tax return preparer, including appraisers in appropriate circumstances, who (1) prepare a tax return or refund claim that contains an unreasonable position that results in an understatement of tax liability, and (2) knew or reasonably should have known of the position.[64] A position is unreasonable unless the tax return preparer has "substantial

---

[59] *See* I.R.C. § 6696 (providing a three-year period of limitations on assessment of penalties under sections 6694 and 6695 of the Internal Revenue Code, but not specifying a period of limitations with respect to the penalty under section 6695A of the Internal Revenue Code).

[60] Chief Counsel Memorandum AM 2007-017 (Nov. 9, 2007); *but see* I.R.M. pt. 20.1.12.4 (Aug. 27, 2010) (stating that the statute of limitations on assessment for a penalty under section 6695A of the Internal Revenue Code expires three years from the later of the due date of the related return or the date on which the related return was filed).

[61] I.R.C. § 6696(b).

[62] I.R.C. § 6695A(c).

[63] I.R.M. pt. 20.1.12.7 (Aug. 27, 2010).

[64] I.R.C. § 6694(a).

authority" for that position, which means that the weight of the authorities supporting the treatment is substantial in relation to the weight of the authorities in support of contrary treatment.[65] The amount of the penalty with respect to each return or claim for refund is, with respect to an unreasonable position, equal to the greater of $1,000 or 50 percent of the income the preparer derives from the return or refund claim.[66] The amount of the penalty with respect to each return or claim for refund is, with respect to willful or reckless conduct, equal to the greater of (1) $5,000 or (2) 50 percent of the income the preparer derived from the return or claim for refund.[67]

The Statute   Section 6694 provides as follows:

Sec. 6694. Understatement of taxpayer's liability by tax return preparer

a. Understatements due to unreasonable positions.
   1. IN GENERAL. If a tax return preparer—
      (A) prepares any return or claim of refund with respect to which any part of an understatement of liability is due to a position described in paragraph (2), and
      (B) knew (or reasonably should have known) of the position, such tax return preparer shall pay a penalty with respect to each such return or claim in an amount equal to the greater of $1,000 or 50 percent of the income derived (or to be derived) by the tax return preparer with respect to the return or claim.
   2. Unreasonable position.
      (A) IN GENERAL. Except as otherwise provided in this paragraph, a position is described in this paragraph unless there is or was substantial authority for the position.
      (B) DISCLOSED POSITIONS. If the position was disclosed as provided in section 6662(d)(2)(B)(ii)(I) and is not a position to which subparagraph (C) applies, the position is described in this paragraph unless there is a reasonable basis for the position.
      (C) TAX SHELTERS AND REPORTABLE TRANSACTIONS. If the position is with respect to a tax shelter (as defined in section 6662(d)(2)(C)(ii)) or a reportable transaction to which section 6662A applies, the position is described in this paragraph unless it is reasonable to believe that the position would more likely than not be sustained on its merits.
   3. REASONABLE CAUSE EXCEPTION. No penalty shall be imposed under this subsection if it is shown that there is reasonable cause for the understatement and the tax return preparer acted in good faith.
b. Understatements due to willful or reckless conduct.
   1. IN GENERAL. Any tax return preparer who prepares any return or claim for refund with respect to which any part of an understatement of liability is due

---

[65]Treas. Reg. § 1.6662-4(d)(3)(i).
[66]I.R.C. § 6694(a).
[67]I.R.C. § 6694 (b).

to a conduct described in paragraph (2) shall pay a penalty with respect to each such return or claim in an amount equal to the greater of—

(A) $5,000, or

(B) 50 percent of the income derived (or to be derived) by the tax return preparer with respect to the return or claim.

2. WILLFUL OR RECKLESS CONDUCT. Conduct described in this paragraph is conduct by the tax return preparer which is—

(A) a willful attempt in any manner to understate the liability for tax on the return or claim, or

(B) a reckless or intentional disregard of rules or regulations.

3. REDUCTION IN PENALTY. The amount of any penalty payable by any person by reason of this subsection for any return or claim for refund shall be reduced by the amount of the penalty paid by such person by reason of subsection (a).

c. Extension of period of collection where preparer pays 15 percent penalty.

1. IN GENERAL. If, within 30 days after the day on which notice and demand of any penalty under subsection (a) or (b) is made against any person who is a tax return preparer, such person pays an amount which is not less than 15 percent of the amount of such penalty and files a claim for refund of the amount so paid, no levy or proceeding in court for the collection of the remainder of such penalty shall be made, begun, or prosecuted until the final resolution of a proceeding begun as provided in paragraph (2). Notwithstanding the provisions of section 7421(a), the beginning of such proceeding or levy during the time such prohibition is in force may be enjoined by a proceeding in the proper court. Nothing in this paragraph shall be construed to prohibit any counterclaim for the remainder of such penalty in a proceeding begun as provided in paragraph (2).

2. PREPARER MUST BRING SUIT IN DISTRICT COURT TO DETERMINE HIS LIABILITY FOR PENALTY. If, within 30 days after the day on which his claim for refund of any partial payment of any penalty under subsection (a) or (b) is denied (or, if earlier, within 30 days after the expiration of 6 months after the day on which he filed the claim for refund), the tax return preparer fails to begin a proceeding in the appropriate United States district court for the determination of his liability for such penalty, paragraph (1) shall cease to apply with respect to such penalty, effective on the day following the close of the applicable 30-day period referred to in this paragraph.

3. SUSPENSION OF RUNNING OF PERIOD OF LIMITATIONS ON COLLECTION. The running of the period of limitations provided in section 6502 on the collection by levy or by a proceeding in court in respect of any penalty described in paragraph (1) shall be suspended for the period during which the Secretary is prohibited from collecting by levy or a proceeding in court.

d. ABATEMENT OF PENALTY WHERE TAXPAYER'S LIABILITY NOT UNDERSTATED. If at any time there is a final administrative determination or a final judicial decision that there was no understatement of liability in the case of any return or claim for refund with respect to which a penalty under subsection (a) or (b) has been assessed, such assessment shall be abated, and if any portion of such penalty has been paid, the amount so paid shall be refunded to the person who made such payment as an overpayment of tax without regard to any period of limitations which, but for this subsection, would apply to the making of such refund.

e. UNDERSTATEMENT OF LIABILITY DEFINED. For purposes of this section, the term *understatement of liability* means any understatement of the net amount payable with respect to any tax imposed by this title or any overstatement of the net amount creditable or refundable with respect to any such tax. Except as otherwise provided in subsection (d), the determination of whether there is an understatement of liability shall be made without regard to any administrative or judicial action involving the taxpayer.

f. CROSS REFERENCE. For definition of tax return preparer, see section 7701(a)(36).

Appraisers as Paid Return Preparers Section 6694 of the Internal Revenue Code may also apply to appraisers in certain cases. For purposes of section 6694 of the Internal Revenue Code, the term *tax return preparer* means any person who prepares for compensation, or who employs one or more persons to prepare for compensation, all or a substantial portion of any tax return or claim for refund of tax under the Internal Revenue Code.[68] Paid return preparers are of two types: signing tax return preparers and non-signing tax return preparers.[69]

A signing tax return preparer is the individual tax return preparer who has the primary responsibility for the overall substantive accuracy of the preparation of the return or refund claim.[70] A non-signing tax return preparer is any tax return preparer who is not a signing tax return preparer but who prepares all or a substantial portion of a return or claim for refund with respect to events that have occurred at the time the advice is rendered.[71] U.S. Treasury Regulations expressly provide that an appraiser may be subject to penalties under section 6694 of the Internal Revenue Code as a non-signing tax return preparer if the appraisal is a substantial portion of the return or claim for refund and the applicable standards of care under section 6694 of the Internal Revenue Code have been breached.[72]

A single tax entry may constitute a substantial portion of a tax return or the claim for refund.[73] Whether a schedule, entry, or other portion of a return or claim for refund is a substantial portion of the return or the claim for refund is determined on the basis of whether the person knows or reasonably should know that the tax attributable to the schedule, entry, or other portion of a return or claim for refund is a substantial portion of the tax required to be shown on a return.[74] In this regard, an appraiser may be subject to the penalty under section 6694 of the Internal Revenue Code even though he or she did not sign or prepare the tax return in question.

De Minimis Exception U.S. Treasury Regulations provide for a *de minimis* exception that prevents a non-signing tax return preparer's work from being a substantial portion of the return if "the amounts of gross income, amounts of deductions, or amounts on the basis of which credits are determined are (1) less than $10,000, or (2) less than $400,000 if the items are also less than 20 percent of the taxpayer's

---

[68]I.R.C. § 7701(a)(36)(A).

[69]Treas. Reg. § 301.7701-15(b).

[70]Treas. Reg. § 301.7701-15(b)(1).

[71]Treas. Reg. § 301.7701-15(b)(2).

[72]T.D. 9436, 73 Fed. Reg. 78430 (Preamble).

[73]Treas. Reg. § 301.7701-15(b)(3)(i).

[74]Treas. Reg. § 301.7701-15(b)(3).

gross income."[75] In applying the *de minimis* rule, all schedules, entries, and other items on the return or claim for refund are aggregated.[76]

Affirmative Defenses   There are generally two affirmative defenses available to negate the imposition of a paid preparer penalty under section 6694 of the Internal Revenue Code. First, the appraiser might assert that there was "substantial authority" for the position taken.[77] The substantial authority standard is an objective standard that is met where there is a greater than 50 percent likelihood of the position being upheld.[78]

Second, the appraiser might assert that there was reasonable cause for the understatement and that the appraiser acted in good faith.[79] The following factors are typically examined to determine whether there was reasonable cause and good faith:

- The nature of the error causing the understatement (i.e., whether the error resulted from a complex, uncommon, or highly technical provision for which a competent paid preparer could have reasonably made the errors);
- The frequency of errors (i.e., whether the understatement was the result of an isolated error such as an inadvertent mathematical or clerical error or whether the understatement was the result of numerous errors);
- The materiality of the errors (i.e., whether the understatement was not material in relation to the correct tax liability);
- The paid return preparer's normal office practice (i.e., whether the paid return preparer's normal office practice indicates that the error in question would occur rarely and the normal office practice was followed in preparing the return or refund claim);
- The reliance in good faith on the advice of information or schedules provided by the taxpayer, another adviser, another tax return preparer, or another party; and
- The reliance on generally accepted administrative or industry practice.[80]

Aiding and Abetting an Understatement of Tax—The Section 6701 Penalty

The Internal Revenue Code authorizes the IRS to impose a $1,000 penalty on any individual, including an appraiser, who:

- Aids or assists, procures, or advises with respect to, the preparation or presentation of any portion of a return, affidavit, claim, or other document;
- Knows or has reason to believe that such portion will be used in connection with any material matter arising under the internal revenue laws; and

---

[75]Treas. Reg. § 301.7701-15(b)(3)(ii)(A).
[76]Treas. Reg. § 301.7701-15(b)(3)(ii)(B).
[77]I.R.C. § 6694(a)(1), (2).
[78]Treas. Reg. § 1.6662-4(d)(2).
[79]I.R.C. § 6694(a)(3).
[80]Treas. Reg. § 1.6694-2(e).

■ Knows that such portion, if so used, would result in an understatement of the tax liability of another person.[81]

Only one penalty may be imposed under section 6701 of the Internal Revenue Code for any false document relating to any taxpayer for any tax period. Thus, the amount of the penalty imposed under section 6701 of the Internal Revenue Code is equal to $1,000 for each false document.

The Statute Section 6701 provides as follows:

Sec. 6701. Penalties for aiding and abetting understatement of tax liability

a. Understatements due to unreasonable positions. Any person—
   1. who aids or assists in, procures, or advises with respect to, the preparation or presentation of any portion of a return, affidavit, claim, or other document,
   2. who knows (or has reason to believe) that such portion will be used in connection with any material matter arising under the internal revenue laws, and
   3. who knows that such portion (if so used) would result in an understatement of the liability for tax of another person, shall pay a penalty with respect to each such document in the amount determined under subsection (b).
b. Amount of penalty.
   1. IN GENERAL. Except as provided in paragraph (2), the amount of the penalty imposed by subsection (a) shall be $1,000.
   2. CORPORATIONS. If the return, affidavit, claim, or other document relates to the tax liability of a corporation, the amount of the penalty imposed by subsection (a) shall be $10,000.
   3. ONLY 1 PENALTY PER PERSON PER PERIOD. If any person is subject to a penalty under subsection (a) with respect to any document relating to any taxpayer for any taxable period (or where there is no taxable period, any taxable event), such person shall not be subject to a penalty under subsection (a) with respect to any other document relating to such taxpayer for such taxable period (or event).
c. Activities of subordinates.
   1. IN GENERAL. For purposes of subsection (a), the term *procures* includes—
      (A) ordering (or otherwise causing) a subordinate to do an act, and
      (B) knowing of, and not attempting to prevent, participation by a subordinate in an act.
   2. SUBORDINATE. For purposes of paragraph (1), the term *subordinate* means any other person (whether or not a director, officer, employee, or agent of the taxpayer involved) over whose activities the person has direction, supervision, or control.
d. TAXPAYER NOT REQUIRED TO HAVE KNOWLEDGE. Subsection (a) shall apply whether or not the understatement is with the knowledge or consent of the persons authorized or required to present the return, affidavit, claim, or other document.

---

[81]I.R.C. § 6701(a) and (b); *see also* Chief Counsel Memorandum 2005-12016 (Mar. 25, 2005) (discussing the applicability of the penalty under section 6701 of the Internal Revenue Code to appraisers).

    e. CERTAIN ACTIONS NOT TREATED AS AID OR ASSISTANCE. For purposes of subsection (a)(1), a person furnishing typing, reproducing, or other mechanical assistance with respect to a document shall not be treated as having aided or assisted in the preparation of such document by reason of such assistance.

    f. PENALTY IN ADDITION TO OTHER PENALTIES.

        1. IN GENERAL. Except as provided by paragraphs (2) and (3), the penalty imposed by this section shall be in addition to any other penalty provided by law.

        2. COORDINATION WITH RETURN PREPARER PENALTIES. No penalty shall be assessed under subsection (a) or (b) of section 6694 on any person with respect to any document for which a penalty is assessed on such person under subsection (a).

        3. COORDINATION WITH SECTION 6700. No penalty shall be assessed under section 6700 on any person with respect to any document for which a penalty is assessed on such person under subsection (a).

Coordination with Other Penalties   The penalty for aiding and abetting an understatement of tax under section 6701 of the Internal Revenue Code is coordinated with other penalties imposed upon parties other than the taxpayer whose liability is at issue. The IRS may not assess a penalty for aiding and abetting an understatement of tax liability under section 6701 of the Internal Revenue Code and a paid return preparer penalty under section 6694 of the Internal Revenue Code.[82] Similarly, the IRS cannot assess the penalty for aiding and abetting an understatement of tax liability under section 6701 of the Internal Revenue Code and the penalty for promoting a tax shelter under section 6700 of the Internal Revenue Code with respect to the same document.[83]

Injunctions against Appraisers   The IRS is also authorized to bring a civil action to enjoin an individual, including an appraiser, from engaging in prohibited conduct such as the type of conduct that is subject to a penalty under section 6701 of the Internal Revenue Code.[84] Thus, an appraiser who is assessed a penalty under section 6701 of the Internal Revenue Code faces the additional risk of the U.S. government enjoining his or her preparation of appraisals in the future. To obtain an injunction, the government must establish that (1) the person is engaged in conduct subject to a penalty under section 6701 of the Internal Revenue Code, and (2) the injunctive relief is appropriate to prevent the recurrence of such conduct.[85]

Effect of Imposition of the Section 6701 Penalty   After a penalty is imposed upon an appraiser under section 6701 of the Internal Revenue Code, the IRS may also provide that appraisals by the appraiser shall have no probative effect in any administrative proceeding before the U.S. Department of the Treasury or the IRS.[86] In addition, the appraiser may be barred from presenting evidence or testimony in any such proceeding.[87]

---

[82]I.R.C. § 6701(f)(2).
[83]I.R.C. § 6701(f)(3).
[84]I.R.C. § 7408(a) and (c).
[85]I.R.C. § 7408(b).
[86]31 U.S.C. § 330(c)(1).
[87]31 U.S.C. § 330(c)(2).

PROFESSIONAL SANCTIONS

Circular 230 Generally

Section 330 of title 31 of the United States Code generally authorizes the IRS to regulate attorneys, certified public accountants, enrolled agents, and other individuals who practice before the IRS, including appraisers. Regulations under section 330 of title 31 of the United States Code are set forth in title 31 of the Code of Federal Regulations, and are reprinted as Treasury Department Circular No. 230 (commonly known as "Circular 230").[88] Through Circular 230, the U.S. Department of the Treasury sets forth its view of the minimum standard of care for attorneys, accountants, and other tax professionals practicing before the IRS. Regulations promulgated in May 2005 added strict requirements for practitioners, including appraisers.

Disqualification of Appraisers under Circular 230

Circular 230 authorizes the IRS to disqualify an appraiser from practice for various reasons. Specifically, an appraiser may be disqualified from practicing before the IRS if the appraiser:

- Is shown to be technically incompetent;
- Is shown to be disreputable (within the meaning of section 10.51 of Circular 230);
- Fails to comply with any regulation under Circular 230; or
- Willfully and knowingly misleads or threatens a client or prospective client with the intent to defraud.[89]

An appraiser who is disqualified under Circular 230 is barred from presenting evidence or testimony in any proceeding before the U.S. Department of the Treasury and the IRS regardless of whether the evidence or testimony pertains to an appraisal made prior to or after the effective date of the disqualification.[90] An appraisal made by a disqualified appraiser after the effective date of disqualification will have no probative effect in any administrative proceeding before the U.S. Treasury Department and/or the IRS, and any such appraisal may be admitted into evidence solely for purposes of determining whether a taxpayer relied in good faith on such appraisal.[91]

Monetary Penalty

The IRS may also impose a monetary penalty on any practitioner who engages or has engaged in conduct subject to sanction under Circular 230.[92]

---

[88]Notice 2007-39, 1 C.B. 1243. We generally refer to these requirements as existing in Circular 230, though they are also codified at 31 C.F.R. § 10.0, et seq.
[89]31 C.F.R. §§ 10.50(a), (b).
[90]31 C.F.R. § 10.50(b)(1).
[91]31 C.F.R. § 10.50(b)(2).
[92]31 C.F.R. § 10.50(c).

CONCLUSION

The civil tax penalties and professional sanctions that may be imposed upon an appraiser who authors a faulty appraisal, as well as the civil tax penalties that may be imposed upon a client-taxpayer to support a federal tax reporting position, are costly and have proven to apply strictly in favor of the government. Numerous affirmative defenses may be available to negate the accuracy-related penalties, but the applicability of such affirmative defenses has proven to be the exception and not the norm. Appraisers, taxpayers, and practitioners alike should be mindful of the penalties and professional sanctions when obtaining an appraisal to support a federal tax reporting position.

CHAPTER 13

Attorney Involvement

SUMMARY

Before an appraisal report can be considered a qualified appraisal, the Internal Revenue Code and U.S. Treasury Regulations impose strict requirements that must be met, dictating who may prepare a qualified appraisal and the items to be included in an appraisal report. Appraisers, lawyers, and accountants potentially face the imposition of civil penalties and professional sanctions for failing to comply with these requirements, as well as potential malpractice claims from jilted client-taxpayers. Notably, the Internal Revenue Service ("IRS") regularly audits (and litigates) charitable contribution deductions and the issue of whether an appraisal is in fact "qualified."[1] Noncompliance is costly, time-consuming, and ill-advised in the increasingly litigious environment surrounding modern appraisal practice.

In light of the high stakes associated with using an appraisal to claim a tax benefit, clients and appraisers should include an attorney well-versed in modern appraisal practice in many stages of the appraisal preparation process. At the same time, however, the appraiser must take preventive measures to ensure that the attorney's involvement does not jeopardize the integrity of the appraisal process. Experience has proven that involving an attorney early and often can be invaluable for fact-gathering, for reviewing the appraisal for weaknesses and accuracy, and for ensuring compliance with the statutory and regulatory requirements. In sum, direct and consistent communication between the appraiser and an attorney can greatly improve the quality, effectiveness, and defensibility of an appraisal report.

FRAMEWORK FOR EXAMINATION

This chapter examines the role of the attorney in the appraisal process, from preparation of the report to litigation concerning a taxpayer's entitlement to a claimed tax benefit. This chapter first discusses the role of an attorney in selecting an appraiser, including the importance of ensuring that the selected appraiser can withstand a

---

[1]In her annual report to Congress, the National Taxpayer Advocate regularly identifies charitable contribution deductions, including the issue of whether an appraisal report is qualified, as among the most litigated issues. *See, e.g.,* 1 *Nat'l Taxpayer Advocate, 2015 Annual Report to Congress,* 517–521 (2015); 1 *Nat'l Taxpayer Advocate, 2013 Annual Report to Congress,* 396 (2013).

Daubert challenge in the context of litigation. Next, the chapter explains the extent to which an attorney can be involved in the appraisal process without jeopardizing the integrity of that process. Third, the chapter highlights the importance of involving an attorney in the appraisal review process to ensure the appraisal's effectiveness, defensibility, and general compliance with statutory and regulatory requirements. Lastly, the chapter examines the function attorneys serve in litigation surrounding appraisals before the United States Tax Court ("Tax Court"). This final section details the requirements that must be met before an appraisal can be admitted into evidence as an expert report and discusses, in addition to the discussion in Chapter 11, *Concurrent Evidence: A Novel Approach to Expert Testimony*, the concurrent witness testimony or "hot-tubbing" procedure as a procedure being used with increased frequency in trials before the Tax Court.

ATTORNEY INVOLVEMENT IN SELECTING THE APPRAISER

The first task of any attorney or client-taxpayer in connection with obtaining an appraisal is to select an appraiser. A number of factors may bear on the appraiser to be selected, including:

- Whether the appraiser is experienced in appraising property of the type to be valued (e.g., closely held businesses, real estate in a specific geographic region or for a particular use, conservation easements);
- Whether the appraiser is certified in the correct area of valuation (note, appraisers are generally certified in the following six areas: business valuation; personal property; machinery and technical specialties; real property; gems and jewelry; or appraisal review and management);
- Whether the appraiser is sufficiently credentialed with designations from an accredited professional organization (e.g., Member of the Appraisal Institute (MAI), Senior Real Property Appraiser (SRPA), Accredited in Business Valuation (ABV), Accredited Senior Appraiser (ASA), Accredited Valuation Analyst (CVA), Accredited Member (AM), and Accredited by the Institute of Business Appraisers (AIB));
- Whether the appraiser is a member of an accredited professional organization, such as the American Society of Appraisers (ASA), the Appraisal Institute (AI), the National Association of Certified Valuators and Analysts (NACVA), the Institute of Business Appraisers (IBA), the Society of Real Estate Appraisers, the American Institute of Real Estate Appraisers, and the American Institute of Certified Public Accountants (AICPA), among others;
- Whether the appraiser is neutrally detached from the property to be valued and the transaction at issue so as to offer an unbiased opinion of value;
- How long the individual has been performing valuations;
- How much time the appraiser spends valuing property of the type to be valued;
- The resources the appraiser or appraiser's firm have available to perform relevant economic and industry research;
- The academic and professional qualifications of the appraiser;
- The appraiser's track record for withstanding challenges to his or her appraisals;

- Whether the appraiser has previously been used, and whether he or she has provided a favorable opinion of value;
- Whether the appraiser is being recommended by a trusted adviser such as an attorney or an accountant; and
- Whether the cost of the appraisal is warranted in the light of the complexity of the assignment.

An Appraiser's Ability to Withstand a *Daubert* Challenge

One of the most important factors to consider when selecting an appraiser, and one not considered enough, is whether the appraiser can withstand a *Daubert* challenge if the appraisal (and by extension the appraiser) is the subject of future litigation. As discussed more fully in Chapter 7, *From* Daubert *to* Boltar, a *Daubert* challenge is made at trial by a party who challenges the qualification of an individual (the purported expert) to testify as an expert witness rather than as a lay witness. The party offering the potential expert witness bears the burden of establishing the admissibility of the expert's testimony by a preponderance of the evidence.[2] This requires the moving party to establish that it is more likely than not that the witness possesses the requisite scientific, technical, or other specialized knowledge that will assist the trier of fact in understanding the evidence or to determining a fact at issue.[3] As discussed in Chapter 7, *From* Daubert *to* Boltar, the Tax Court has reconfirmed the importance of making timely and appropriate *Daubert* challenges. Lawyers, by virtue of their specialized legal knowledge and training, are especially well suited to aid a client-taxpayer to ensure that the potential appraiser can survive a *Daubert* challenge.

The Importance of Having the Attorney Engage the Appraiser

A second factor to consider is who should engage the appraiser: the attorney; the client-taxpayer; or the tax professional. The answer to this question depends upon the purpose for which the appraisal is procured. Tax law has long recognized that the presence of a professional, such as an accountant or appraiser, may be "necessary, or at least highly useful, for the effective consultation between the client and the lawyer."[4] For this reason, the attorney–client privilege and the work product doctrine have been extended to protect communications between the lawyer and professionals so that the attorney can give legal advice to the client.[5] No similar privilege has been recognized for communications and draft reports exchanged between the expert and the client-taxpayer.

As detailed in Chapter 8, *Discovery of Expert Material*, if an appraisal report is obtained to support a federal tax reporting position, the IRS is authorized to summons documents related to the appraisal report, including draft appraisal reports and communications between the appraiser and the client. If the report is obtained in connection with litigation, draft appraisal reports and communications

---

[2]*Daubert v. Merrell Dow Pharmaceuticals, Inc.*, 509 U.S. 579, 592 n.10 (1993).
[3]*See Fed. R. Evid.* 702.
[4]*United States v. Kovel*, 296 F.2d 918, 921-922 (2d Cir. 1961).
[5]*See, e.g., id.*

between the attorney and the expert used in connection with litigation are generally privileged from disclosure. Practitioners should keep in mind that when a client sends a confidential communication to an attorney, and the attorney then sends that correspondence to the expert, privilege has been broken, and the expert may be called to testify as to that communication. The inadvertent waiver of privilege can be altogether avoided if the attorney engages the appraiser and all correspondence between the client and the attorney is sent through the attorney.

ATTORNEY INVOLVEMENT IN THE APPRAISAL PROCESS

After an appraiser has been selected and an engagement letter has been signed, the core appraisal process begins. The appraisal process, as it relates to appraisals used to support a federal tax reporting position, generally consists of the following four stages: the fact-gathering process; the report-preparation process; the review process; and the tax-reporting process. Attorneys who are well versed in modern appraisal practice can improve the overall accuracy, efficiency, and defensibility of the report at each stage of the process. Regular and open communication between the client, the appraiser, and the attorney is of paramount importance when securing a reliable appraisal. Counsel may assist expert witnesses to understand the requirements of admissibility for an expert witness report under the respective court's rules of practice and procedure, and doing so will increase the likelihood that the report complies with the minimum standards to be received as the expert's direct testimony.

The Fact-Gathering Process

Professional appraisal practice necessarily begins with the appraiser researching the property to be appraised. Attorneys can be an indispensable resource in the fact-gathering process as they are often intimately familiar with the client, the property to be valued, how the property was acquired (e.g., purchase, gift, bequest, or formation), the terms of any offers with respect to the property in question, and any restrictions, ordinances, or similar items that may affect the property to be valued. Among the information that will undoubtedly need to be collected in connection with an appraisal, and that may be garnered from an attorney, are the following items:

- The valuation date (i.e., as of what date is an opinion of value required);
- The property to be appraised;
- The client and the intended users of the appraisal;
- The purpose of the appraisal (e.g., for federal income, estate, or gift tax purposes); and
- The standard of value to be used in the appraisal (e.g., fair market value (as required for federal tax purposes), market value, or some other measure of value).

Lawyers also keep various formational documents that, when valuing a closely-held business, must be examined. As discussed in Chapter 9, *Expert Appraisal Reports*, the appraisal report must analyze those restrictions that are imposed upon the property as a result of the contractual claims of all potential users of the property to be valued. Among the documents to be examined, when evaluating said contractual rights, preferences, and privileges of interest, are the following:

- Articles of incorporation;
- Corporate bylaws;
- Operating agreement;
- Buy–sell agreements;
- Rights of first refusal; and
- Leases, including any options associated therewith.

Attorneys must, as a matter of ethics, professionalism, and liability management, receive client approval before releasing any such documents.

The Report Preparation Process

The Tax Court's Rules of Practice and Procedure requires an expert witness to prepare and submit a written report to the Court at least 30 days before trial.[6] An attorney must limit his or her involvement in the preparation of the appraisal report to comply with the literal requirements of those Rules and to preserve the integrity of the appraisal process. At the same time, the Tax Court's Rules of Practice and Procedure, which parallel the Federal Rules of Civil Procedure in many material respects, recognizes that counsel will normally need to assist experts in preparing their reports. The Advisory Committee Notes to Rule 26(a)(2)(B) of the Federal Rules of Civil Procedure provides as follows:

> *Rule 26(a)(2)(B) does not preclude counsel from providing assistance to experts in preparing the reports, and indeed, * * * this assistance may be needed. Nevertheless, the report which is intended to set forth the substance of the direct examination should be written in a manner that reflects the testimony to be given by the witness and it must be signed by the witness.*[7]

This naturally leads to the question: To what extent, if at all, should an attorney be involved in the drafting and review of the expert witness's report? Attorney involvement during the report preparation stage should generally be limited to answering questions that the appraiser believes may affect the ultimate opinion of value and ensuring that the appraiser has all relevant information and documents. Additionally, lawyers may wish to provide the appraiser with an overview of the specific statutory or regulatory requirements that must be included in the appraisal. Apart from this support function, an attorney's involvement in the report preparation process should be focused on giving the appraiser sufficient autonomy to complete his or her job without influence.[8] In no event should an attorney seek to change the opinions of expert witnesses.

---

[6] *Tax Ct. R.* 143(g)(1).

[7] *Fed. R. Civ. P.* 26(a)(2)(B).

[8] *See* Stuart M. Hurwitz and Richard Carpenter, "Can an Attorney Participate in the Writing of an Expert Witness' Report in the Tax Court?," 100 *J. Tax'n* 358 (2004) (discussing the extent to which an attorney may be involved in the drafting of an expert witness report).

An attorney's overreach during the appraisal preparation process can jeopardize the admissibility of an expert's report. For example, in *Bank One Corp. v. Commissioner*,[9] the Tax Court heard testimony from various expert witnesses as to the tax treatment of interest rate swaps. At trial, a question arose with regard to the extent to which the taxpayer's counsel participated in the writing of the taxpayer's expert witness's rebuttal report. The government argued that the taxpayer's rebuttal report was inadmissible because its preparation was tainted by significant participation of the taxpayer's counsel. The Court ruled that the expert's rebuttal report was excluded from evidence because it was never clear to the Court that the words, analysis, and opinions in the rebuttal report were that of the taxpayer's expert and not that of the taxpayer's lawyer. The Court went on to note that the report was not reliable and therefore not admissible because the witness lacked familiarity with portions of the report that were purported to be his testimony. *Bank One* does not stand for the proposition that an attorney may never assist an expert in writing his or her report; however, the attorney should not significantly participate in the writing of an expert witness's report and the expert should always understand, be able to explain, and own the thoughts and opinions therein as his or her own.

The Review Process

Once the initial report has been circulated to the client and his or her attorney, the review process begins. At this stage, the attorney, the appraiser, and the client should engage in regular and open communications with respect to the report. An attorney's responsibility during the review process is threefold. First, the lawyer should ensure that the appraisal is legally and procedurally correct. This entails the attorney communicating to the appraiser the correct standard of value to be used as well as the statutory and regulatory requirements. It also entails familiarizing the expert witness with the requirements of Rule 143(g) of the Tax Court's Rules of Practice and Procedure to ensure the admissibility of the report into evidence.

Second, the lawyer should confirm that the appraisal is factually and empirically sound, that the computations therein are correct, and that the assumptions underlying the appraised value are reasonable and appropriate. To the extent the attorney disagrees with any assumptions relied upon in the appraisal, the attorney should help the appraiser to understand why the assumptions may be unreasonable. The attorney should never simply instruct the appraiser to change his or her conclusions.

Third, the lawyer should check that the appraiser considered all relevant facts in reaching his or her ultimate conclusion of value, regardless of the impact of those facts on the ultimate opinion of value. To the extent the appraisal is deficient in its consideration of such facts, then the attorney should help the appraiser to understand how other facts may affect the report. Again, the attorney should not commandeer

---

[9] *Bank One Corp. v. Commissioner*, 120 T.C. 174 (2003), *aff'd in part and vacated in part sub nom. J.P. Morgan Chase & Co. v. Comm'r*, 458 F.3d 564 (7th Cir. 2006).

the appraisal process but ensure that all facts that should be considered are in fact considered and made clear in the report.

In *Trigon Ins. Co. v. United States*,[10] the U.S. District Court for the Eastern District of Virginia found significant evidence of teamwork and collaboration among a litigation consultant employed by the government and the government's testifying experts. The depositions of testifying experts indicated that the litigation consultant had participated extensively in the drafting of the expert witness report. The Court declined to bar the government's expert from testifying, but barred the consulting firm from further participating in the case and sanctioned the faulting party for allowing the expert's report to be ghost written.[11] It is imperative that attorneys keep in mind that the review process must preserve the objectivity of the appraisal process and ensure that it is the appraiser's opinions reflected in the report, not the attorney's.

Early involvement by an attorney who appropriately questions and tests the validity of underlying assumptions improves the defensibility of an appraisal report that is challenged by a tax authority or reviewed by a court. By way of example, and not by way of limitation, valuation discounts are one area of appraisal practice where attorneys may create value for both the client and the appraiser, given the role of case law in determining appropriate discounts. Attorneys should question the applicability of various discounts in the light of jurisprudential developments, including but not limited to:

- Lack of marketability discount;
- Lack of control discount;
- Fractional interest or partition discount;
- Blockage or market absorption discount; and
- S corporation premiums.

Sanctions for Improper Attorney Assistance

The Supreme Court has given trial courts broad discretion to determine the reliability and the admissibility of expert witness testimony. An attorney who oversteps the permissible boundaries of assistance to an appraiser risks various sanctions, including but not limited to:

- Denying the admissibility of the expert witness's report;
- Denying the witness the opportunity to testify;
- Disqualifying the expert;
- Disregarding all or a portion of the witness's report or testimony;
- Imposing monetary sanctions against the faulting party and/or that party's counsel;

---

[10] *Trigon Ins. Co. v. United States*, 204 F.R.D. 277 (E.D. Va. 2001).
[11] The Court described the ghost writing of an expert's report as "the preparation of the substance writing of the report by someone other than the expert purporting to have written it." *Id.* at 291.

- Granting a new trial;
- Dismissing the petition;
- Entering a default judgment; or
- Contempt.[12]

Improper attorney assistance during the appraisal process can taint a taxpayer's reliance on an appraiser to avoid an accuracy-related penalty. For example, in *Exelon Corp. v. Commissioner*,[13] which involved alleged sale-in/lease-out tax shelters, the taxpayer claimed to rely upon a law firm's opinion, which in turn was based on an accounting firm's appraisal. The Tax Court found that the law firm "interfered with the integrity and independence of the appraisal process by providing [the accounting firm] with a list of conclusions it expected to see in the appraisal to be able to issue tax opinions at the 'will' and 'should' level." The Tax Court held that "[s]uch interference improperly tainted the [accounting firm's appraisal], rendering it useless." *Exelon* confirms that attorneys should defer to the expertise of their clients and not become improperly entangled in the appraisal process.

The Tax Preparation Process

After the appraisal review process has been finalized, the final report may be delivered to the client and his or her accountants and lawyers for use in filing the related tax return. Again, the attorney should see that all legal and ministerial requirements have been met, including that the appraisal is submitted with the return when required. For example, as discussed in Chapter 2, *Qualified Appraisal*, a qualified appraisal must be submitted with a federal income tax return claiming a charitable contribution deduction of $500,000 or more. The attorney should also ensure that the appraisal submitted complies with both the statutory and regulatory requirements for a qualified appraisal.

COORDINATING THE ATTORNEY'S AND THE APPRAISER'S INVOLVEMENT IN NEGOTIATIONS WITH TAX AUTHORITIES

When an appraisal report is challenged as part of an audit, it may be useful for the tax professional to have an appraiser or engineer join the parties at any settlement conferences or Appeals meetings. Doing so allows the appraiser to explain, and the tax authority to understand, the appraiser's rationale, methodology, or underlying assumptions. Additionally, if the tax authority has its appraiser or engineer present at the conference, the appraisers may be able to come to an agreement among themselves as to certain material issues affecting the valuation.

Trials are a vital part of tax controversy. Though sometimes necessary, they usually result from a failure of imagination and are rarely in the client's best interest.

---

[12]*See* Stuart M. Hurwitz and Richard Carpenter, "Can an Attorney Participate in the Writing of an Expert Witness' Report in the Tax Court?," 100 *J. Tax'n* 358 (2004).
[13]*Exelon Corp. v. Comm'r*, 147 T.C. ___, ___, 2016 WL 4992729 (T.C. Sept. 19, 2016) (slip op. at 158–169), *appeal docketed*, No. 17-2964 (7th Cir. Sept. 22, 2017).

Alternative dispute resolution is a legitimate alternative to a trial that is advisable in almost all valuation cases. In connection with full- or partially-agreed cases, there are many alternatives to trial offered by the IRS, including:

1. Fast Track Settlement;[14] and
2. Post-Appeals Mediation.[15,16]

The concurrent witness procedure discussed in Chapter 11, *Concurrent Evidence: A Novel Approach to Expert Testimony*, is another tool that parties may want to use to help resolve a case without litigation. This procedure is especially well suited for the Fast Track Settlement, Fast Track Mediation, or Post-Appeals Mediation procedures, where the mediator serves as the judge. Notwithstanding the various alternative dispute resolution programs offered by tax authorities, appraisers and their client-taxpayers may nevertheless find that administrative remedies have failed and that litigation is necessary.

ATTORNEY INVOLVEMENT IN LITIGATION WHERE EXPERT REPORTS WILL BE SUBMITTED

The attorney's litigation function, as it relates to modern appraisal practice, may include pretrial discovery, submitting the expert witness's report to the Court, preparing and filing motions *in limine* with respect to the opposing party's expert witness reports, submitting the expert witness's rebuttal report to the Court, examining the client's expert witness on direct examination, and cross-examining the adverse party's expert witness on cross-examination. Each topic is discussed more fully throughout this book, though this chapter summarizes the most relevant points and notes where a more thorough discussion of the topic may be found. Before we discuss the various functions that a lawyer may need to perform when litigating a case in which an appraisal is at issue, we first discuss the backdrop against which these appraisals are received and reviewed.

---

[14]Fast Track Settlement ("FTS") is a jointly administered program offered by the Service's Small Business/Self-Employed Unit ("SBSE") and Appeals to expedite case resolution at the earliest opportunity. Internal Revenue Manual ("I.R.M."), pt. 4.25.13.2 (Aug. 6, 2015). FTS is intended to enable taxpayers and the Service to work together in resolving disputed issues while the case remains in SBSE jurisdiction. *Id.* FTS is designed to streamline the settlement process of cases because the taxpayer, the taxpayer's representative, the examiner, the manager, and an Appeals mediator actively participate in the outcome. *Id.* FTS is generally available for all non-docketed SBSE cases with no regard to dollar amount.

[15]Post-Appeals Mediation ("PAM") is a formal mediation procedure for cases in the Appeals administrative process that is conducted by third parties. I.R.M., pt. 8.26.5.1 (Aug. 27, 2015). PAM is a nonbinding process that uses the service of a mediator or mediators, as neutral third parties, to help Appeals and the taxpayer reach a negotiated settlement. *Id.*

[16]The IRS previously offered a Fast Track Mediation ("FTM") program, which was eliminated in late-2016. *See* Rev. Proc. 2016-57, 2016-49 I.R.B. 707. The IRS replaced FTM with a Fast Track Mediation Collection program in which valuation may be mediated in certain collection cases. The Service also offered an Appeals Arbitration Program beginning in 2006, but that program was discontinued in September 2015. *See* Rev. Proc. 2015-44, 2015-38 I.R.B. 354.

Trials in the Tax Court are nonjury trials conducted in accordance with the Federal Rules of Evidence.[17] Not surprisingly, matters before the Tax Court in which valuation, accounting, and finance are central issues may require specialized knowledge, experience, training, or judgment to assist the judge (the trier of fact) in understanding complex or novel issues. Sometimes judges possess the requisite skill, knowledge, and experience to adjudicate the specialized issues; other times judges do not. Expert witnesses, including appraisers and engineers, play an indispensable role in the adjudication of these issues. Judge Learned Hand stated that "[n]o one will deny that the law should in some way effectively use expert knowledge wherever it will aid in settling disputes. The only real question is as to how it can do so best."[18] Deciding how best to utilize an expert's knowledge, experience, and education is the ultimate task of the lawyer who handles a case in which valuation is a central issue.

Discovery and the Expert Appraiser

Lawyers routinely must discover information, opinions, and conclusions of the opposing party's expert witness. This pretrial phase of litigation, known as discovery, allows one party to obtain evidence and other information from an opposing party by using various discovery devices, including but not limited to interrogatories, requests for production of documents, requests for admissions, and depositions. The importance of the lawyer's role in discovery cannot be understated as discovery may encourage settlement of cases, help narrow the issues to be decided, prevent false claims from going to trial, prevent the concealment of evidence relevant to the case, and allow attorneys to prepare for effective cross-examination.

SUBMITTING THE EXPERT APPRAISAL REPORT TO THE COURT

An attorney seeking to have a witness offer expert testimony before the Tax Court must have his or her expert witness prepare and submit a written report to the Court and the opposing party. More specifically, the Tax Court's Rules of Practice and

---

[17] *See* I.R.C. § 7453; *Tax Ct. R.* 143(a). Until December 18, 2015, trials before the Tax Court were conducted in accordance with the rules of evidence that apply to nonjury trials in the United States District Court for the District of Columbia. The statutory language was recently amended to provide that trials before the Tax Court are conducted in accordance with the Federal Rules of Evidence. *See* I.R.C. § 7453; *see also* Protecting Americans from Tax Hikes Act of 2015, Pub. L. 114-113, § 425, 129 Stat. 2242. On March 28, 2016, the Tax Court adopted interim amendments to its Rules of Practice and Procedure to implement this change. *See* Press Release, Tax Court, *Interim Amendments to the Tax Court Rules of Practice and Procedure Relating to the Bipartisan Budget Act of 2015, the Fixing America's Surface Transportation Act, and the Protecting Americans from Tax Hikes Act of 2015* (Mar. 28, 2016), available at http://www.ustaxcourt.gov/press/032816.pdf. Under the old rule, the Tax Court followed the rules of evidence as determined by the U.S. Court of Appeals for the District of Columbia Circuit. Under the new rule, the Tax Court will follow the rules of evidence as determined by the Court of Appeals for the circuit in which the appeal in that case will be filed (i.e., it applies the *Golsen* rule with respect to evidentiary rulings). *See Golsen v. Comm'r*, 54 T.C. 742, 756-757 (1970).

[18] Judge Learned Hand, "Historical and Practical Considerations Regarding Expert Testimony," 15 *Harv. L. Rev.* 40 (1901).

Procedure provides a specific set of rules that must be followed before an appraisal can be admitted into evidence. Those rules require an expert witness to prepare and submit a written report to the Court and to the opposing party no later than 30 days before trial.[19] The Tax Court's Rules of Practice and Procedure require that the report set forth the following information:

(A) A complete statement of all opinions the witness expresses and the basis and reasons for them;
(B) The facts or data considered by the witness in forming them;
(C) Any exhibits used to summarize or support them;
(D) The witness's qualifications, including a list of all publications authored in the previous 10 years;
(E) A list of all other cases in which, during the previous 4 years, the witness testified as an expert at trial or by deposition; and
(F) A statement of the compensation to be paid for the study and testimony in the case.[20]

The presiding judge usually reviews the parties' expert witness reports before trial. At trial, the report is marked as an exhibit, identified by the expert witness, and received in evidence as the expert witness's direct testimony upon the Court's finding that the witness is qualified as an expert. Additional direct testimony may be allowed to clarify or emphasize matters with respect to that expert's report. Following the additional direct testimony, if any, the witness is tendered for cross-examination by the opposing party.

It is imperative that an attorney ensure that his client's expert is compliant with the procedural requirements for submitting an appraisal report. The failure to comply with the procedural or substantive requirements may result in an expert witness's testimony being altogether excluded.[21] The Tax Court will not ordinarily grant a request to permit an expert witness to testify without a written report where the expert witness's testimony is based upon third-party contacts, comparable sales, statistical data, or other detailed, technical information.[22] As part of their standing pretrial order, many judges require that such expert witness reports be prepared and submitted to the Court and the opposing party within 30 days of trial.

Motions *in Limine*

An attorney may wish to move the Court *in limine* after receiving the opposing party's expert witness report to have such report excluded from evidence on various grounds.

---

[19] *Tax Ct. R.* 143(g)(1).
[20] *See id.* On July 6, 2012, the Tax Court amended Rule 143(g) of its Rules of Practice and Procedure to require that an expert witness report contain the same information required under Rule 26(a)(2)(B) of the Federal Rules of Civil Procedure. *See* Press Release dated July 6, 2012, pp. 9–10.
[21] *Tax Ct. R.* 143(g)(2).
[22] *Tax Ct. R.* 143(g)(3); *see also Estate of Tannenblatt v. Comm'r*, T.C. Memo. 2013-263 (excluding the taxpayer's expert report because the taxpayer's expert did not appear at trial to lay the required foundation).

A motion *in limine* is a motion filed in advance of trial that requests from the Court a pretrial ruling as to the admissibility of certain evidence. Among the reasons most often cited for excluding an appraiser's report *in limine* are:

- The report does not comply with the literal requirements of the Rules of Practice and Procedure (i.e., it does not state the expert witness's qualifications and/or does not contain the opinions and facts on which the appraiser based his or her opinion);
- The appraisal offers impermissible legal conclusions rather than conclusion as to ultimate issues of fact; or
- The expert is being proffered as an expert in an area outside of his or her area of expertise.

Lawyers who are served with a motion *in limine* should zealously defend against the motion, especially in cases in which valuation is a dispositive issue.

Rebuttal Reports

The Tax Court may allow the submission of a rebuttal report with respect to the opposing party's expert witness reports.[23] The judge's standing pretrial order, which is a directive issued at the direction of the trial judge to facilitate an orderly and efficient disposition of a case, may permit parties to exchange such reports. As a practical matter, a rebuttal report should focus on identifying factual misstatements in the opposing party's expert report, revealing unsound assumptions, and providing a direct and concise response to the expert's conclusions. An attorney involved in the preparation of a rebuttal report must, however, exercise great caution so as to not impugn the valuation process or jeopardize the admissibility of the report as was the case in *Bank One*.

An attorney's responsibilities with respect to rebuttal reports are threefold. First, the lawyer should advise the expert to ensure that the rebuttal report is legally and procedurally correct. Second, the lawyer should confirm that the rebuttal report is factually and empirically sound, that the computations therein are correct, and that the underlying assumptions are reasonable and appropriate. Third, the lawyer should confirm that the expert considered all relevant facts in reaching his or her opinion, regardless of the impact of those facts on the ultimate opinion of value. To the extent the rebuttal report is deficient in any of these areas, the attorney should help the expert to remediate the rebuttal report. As is true for expert reports generally, the attorney should not supplant his or her own analysis and conclusions for the expert's in the rebuttal report.

---

[23]The Tax Court does not currently have a rule that provides for the automatic exchange of rebuttal reports, and the rules regarding the exchange of such reports are typically set forth in the judge's standing pretrial order.

QUALIFYING THE APPRAISER AS AN EXPERT AND SATISFYING *DAUBERT*

As discussed more fully in Chapter 7, *From* Daubert *to* Boltar, the Federal Rules of Evidence prescribe a specific set of rules as to when an expert witness may testify. Rule 702 of the Federal Rules of Evidence provides that a qualified expert may testify:

> *If scientific, technical, or other specialized knowledge will assist the trier of fact to understand the evidence or to determine a fact in issue, a witness qualified as an expert by knowledge, skill, experience, training, or education may testify thereto in the form of an opinion or otherwise, if (1) the testimony is based upon sufficient facts or data, (2) the testimony is the product of reliable principles and methods, and (3) the witness has applied the principles and methods reliably to the facts of the case.*

Denying experts the right to testify if they do not satisfy *Daubert* is both appropriate and necessary in trials before the Tax Court. Therefore, lawyers are well advised to challenge the opposing party's expert witnesses under the standards set forth in *Daubert* and to prepare their own expert witnesses for a vigorous *voir dire* under the standards as set forth in *Daubert*.

CROSS-EXAMINATION AND REHABILITATION

Cross-Examination

As mentioned earlier, the expert witness's direct testimony is generally received by the Tax Court in the form of his or her written report. At trial, if the Court finds that the witness is qualified as an expert, the expert is then typically tendered for cross-examination. In the traditional adversarial process, the opposing party may cross-examine the expert witness for purposes of elucidating the disputed findings, but also ostensibly to discredit the witness's reasoning, conclusions, and opinions. The cross-examination is intended to allow the truth to prevail. In Chapter 8, *Discovery of Expert Material*, we discuss strategies by which an attorney may use information obtained in the discovery phase of litigation to impeach and discredit the opposing party's expert witness under the traditional adversarial model. In Chapter 11, *Concurrent Evidence: A Novel Approach to Expert Testimony*, we offer two alternatives to the traditional cross-examination process: (1) concurrent witness testimony, and (2) court-appointed experts. Attorneys should be mindful of these alternative approaches and, where appropriate, request from the trial judge that such procedures be implemented. It is worth noting that concurrent witness testimony is especially well suited for cases in which valuation is an ultimate issue of fact.

Rehabilitating the Expert Witness

After the opposing party has concluded his or her cross-examination of the expert witness, the expert witness may be rehabilitated by his client's counsel. The rehabilitation should focus on accrediting the expert's testimony and allowing the expert to explain his or her conclusions. Attorneys who can successfully rehabilitate an expert witness can avoid any adverse effect of cross-examination on the reasonableness and reliability of the expert witness's opinion.

CONCLUSION

An effective and defensible appraisal report results from the coordinated efforts of the appraiser, the client, and the client's advisors. Attorneys must be sufficiently involved in the appraisal process to ensure that the appraisal is procedurally correct and reasonable, yet must remain sufficiently detached so as not to jeopardize the trustworthiness of the appraisal. Appraisers must likewise be careful to ensure that a client's attorney does not impugn the integrity of the appraisal process.

CHAPTER 14

Common Errors with Appraisal Reports and How to Avoid Them

SUMMARY

The qualified appraisal requirements are undeniably complex, and it is often the case that defects in an appraisal report may jeopardize the very tax benefits the report is intended to confer. As detailed in Chapter 4, *Substantial Compliance vs. Strict Compliance*, the substantial compliance doctrine may apply in limited circumstances to excuse such defects, but the infrequency with which courts apply that doctrine requires appraisers and tax professionals to recognize (and proactively seek to limit the effect of) defects with appraisal reports at the earliest possible time. This chapter discusses nine common defects, and a tenth potential defect with appraisal reports, primarily emphasizing how these defects can jeopardize the status of an appraisal report as a qualified appraisal for federal tax purposes. This chapter also provides practical tips practitioners can use to avoid such errors altogether or remedy them in administrative proceedings before the Internal Revenue Service (IRS) and the IRS's Office of Appeals, as well as in litigation before the courts.

COMMON DEFECTS WITH APPRAISALS

For the purpose of this book, there are two types of defects with appraisal reports: those that threaten the report's status as a qualified appraisal, and those that hurt the report's reliability and usefulness. Either type of defect can be fatal to a litigant's success in a tax case. On the one hand, defects with a purported qualified appraisal may result in disallowance of a taxpayer's charitable contribution deduction of non-cash property with a claimed fair market value greater than $5,000. On the other hand, defects with appraisal reports can also cause a litigant to be unable to prove the value of "something" for tax purposes, whether that "something" is the value of property donated to a charitable organization, real property, intangibles, a business, inventory, compensation, goodwill, or any one of a number of other items that are routinely valued in tax cases. For this reason, it is important that practitioners understand common defects with appraisal reports and proactively limit the adverse effect that the defects can have in a tax case. The listed defects are not exclusive, and readers should keep in mind other potential defects, such as the failure to include a regression analysis.

Defect 1: Untimely Appraisal Report

Requirement and Error   Recall from Chapter 2, *Qualified Appraisal*, that section 1.170A-13(c)(3)(i) of the Treasury Regulations imposes a temporal requirement that a qualified appraisal generally be made no earlier than 60 days before the contribution date and no later than the extended due date of the federal income tax return on which the charitable contribution deduction is first claimed.[1] Appraisal reports are sometimes not made within the required 60-day period or before the extended due date of the requisite return, the effect of which may be to jeopardize the status of the appraisal report as a qualified appraisal and in turn the taxpayer's eligibility for a charitable contribution deduction.

Remedy   To the extent the appraisal was untimely, if the facts of a particular case permit such a claim, practitioners should rely upon the reasonable cause exception found in section 170(f)(11)(A)(ii)(II) of the Internal Revenue Code to argue that the untimeliness is excusable with respect to charitable contribution deductions claimed after August 17, 2006.[2] The United States Tax Court ("Tax Court") accepted this argument in *Crimi v. Commissioner*.[3]

In *Crimi*, the taxpayers relied upon an appraisal report prepared in 2000 to support the value of a $2.95M charitable contribution deduction claimed with respect to a part-sale, part-gift of 65 acres of undeveloped land in New Jersey. The IRS argued that the 2000 appraisal was not a qualified appraisal because, among other things, it was not prepared within the 60-day period specified in section 1.170A-13(c)(3)(i) of the Treasury Regulations. The primary argument in the taxpayers' response was that the untimeliness of the appraisal should not affect the taxpayers' right to the deduction because the 2000 appraisal substantially complied with the qualified appraisal regulation.

The Tax Court declined to decide whether the 2000 appraisal substantially complied with the qualified appraisal regulation because, as the Court held, any noncompliance with the qualified appraisal regulation was excused by the taxpayers' good-faith reliance on their accountant's advice that the 2000 appraisal was a qualified appraisal. The Tax Court ruled that reliance on the advice of a professional, such as an attorney or an accountant, may constitute reasonable cause to the extent the taxpayer (1) reasonably believed the professional was a competent tax adviser with sufficient expertise to justify reliance, (2) the taxpayer provided necessary and accurate information to the advising professional, and (3) the taxpayer actually relied in good faith on the professional's advice. The Court concluded that each of these requirements was met, and therefore, that it was not unreasonable for the taxpayers to rely on the accountant's advice that an untimely appraisal was "qualified" because it was not "stale in substance."

---

[1] In the case of a charitable contribution deduction first claimed on an amended return, the qualified appraisal must be secured no later than the date on which the amended return is filed. *See* Treas. Reg. § 1.170A-13(c)(3)(iv)(B).

[2] Recall that, specifically for returns filed after August 17, 2006, a deduction will not be disallowed if the failure to obtain a qualified appraisal was due to reasonable cause and not to willful neglect. *See* I.R.C. § 170(f)(11)(A)(ii)(II).

[3] T.C. Memo. 2013-51, 105 T.C.M. (CCH) 1330 (2013).

Importantly, the reasonable cause exception codified at section 170(f)(11)(A)(ii)(II) of the Internal Revenue Code is expressly made effective for charitable contribution deductions claimed after August 17, 2006. However, this does not mean that the exception may not also be available with respect to charitable contribution deductions claimed on or before August 17, 2006. Thus, regardless of the date on which the charitable contribution is made and so long as the facts of the case support such a claim, it is advisable for taxpayers to assert a reasonable cause defense for the failure to satisfy the temporal requirement in section 1.170A-13(c)(3)(i) of the Treasury Regulations.

Defect 2: Inadequate Description of Property

Requirement and Error   Recall from Chapter 2, *Qualified Appraisal*, that section 1.170A-13(c)(3)(ii) of the Treasury Regulations provides that an appraisal report will be regarded as a qualified appraisal only if the report includes a description of the property in sufficient detail for a person who is not generally familiar with the type of property to ascertain that the appraised property is the property that was (or will be) contributed.[4] Where the qualified appraisal relates to a group of properties, as opposed to one item of property, a group description rather than a specific description of each will satisfy the description requirement set forth in section 1.170A-13(c)(3)(ii)(A) of the Treasury Regulations.[5] The purpose of the description requirement is to allow a revenue agent who audits the return to understand that the appraisal report relates to the item for which a charitable contribution deduction is claimed.

Appraisal reports sometimes inadequately (or incorrectly) describe the donated property, the effect of which can negate an appraisal report's status as a qualified appraisal. For example, in *Rothman v. Commissioner* the Tax Court concluded that an appraisal report that incorrectly described a façade easement (the donated property) as a single-family residence and office (the property to which the easement related) did not adequately describe the donated property for purposes of section 1.170A-13(c)(3)(ii)(A) of the Treasury Regulations.[6] For this reason, the Tax Court found that this defect (among others) negated the status of the appraisal report as a qualified appraisal. Similarly, in *Costello v. Commissioner*,[7] the Tax Court held that an appraisal report valuing an easement was not qualified because the failure of the report to include the words "conservation easement" or "land preservation easement" did not adequately identify the property within the meaning of section 1.170A-13(c)(3)(ii)(A) of the Treasury Regulations.

Remedy   It is important for the appraiser and tax professional who review an appraisal report to review the description of the donated property for both accuracy and sufficiency. To the extent this review occurs after the filing of the return and the

---

[4]Treas. Reg. § 1.170A-13(c)(3)(ii)(A).
[5]T.D. 8199, 53 Fed. Reg. 16076 (May 5, 1988).
[6]*See Rothman v. Comm'r*, T.C. Memo. 2012-163, 103 T.C.M. (CCH) 1864 (2012), *vacated in part on reconsideration*, T.C. Memo. 2012-218, 104 T.C.M. (CCH) 126 (2012).
[7]T.C. Memo. 2015-87.

incorrectness (or inadequacy) of the description is not discovered until the IRS raises the issue (either administratively or in litigation), practitioners should rely upon the reasonable cause defense discussed earlier to excuse the defect to the extent the facts of the case warrant such a defense. This defense may support a ruling that the failure to obtain a qualified appraisal is justified on grounds of reasonable cause.

Defect 3: Failing to Analyze Agreements and Restrictions with Respect to the Property

Requirement and Error   Recall from Chapter 2, *Qualified Appraisal*, that section 1.170A-13(c)(3)(ii)(D) of the Treasury Regulations requires a qualified appraisal to disclose the terms of any agreement or understanding entered into (or expected to be entered into) between the donor and the donee that affects the use, sale, or other disposition of the donated property. Thus, in formulating a value opinion, the appraiser must "identify and analyze any known restrictions, ordinances, or similar items, and the likelihood of any modifications to those restrictions."[8] As noted in Chapter 2, *Qualified Appraisal*, this requirement exists to create parity between the qualified appraisal regulations and the principles of the Uniform Standards of Professional Appraisal Practice ("USPAP"), which require an appraisal report to take into account "any known easements, restrictions, encumbrances, leases, reservations, covenants, contracts, declarations, special assessments, ordinances, or other items of a similar nature."[9] Appraisers sometimes fail to identify or analyze in their appraisal reports existing agreements, restrictions, and ordinances that affect the use of the subject property. Where an appraisal report fails to identify and analyze these items, the report may be deemed not a qualified appraisal. For example, in *Costello v. Commissioner*,[10] the Tax Court held that an appraisal report was not a qualified appraisal because it failed to disclose the existence of an easement on the property, which was an agreement or understanding between the donor and the donee that affected the use, sale, or other disposition of the property.

Remedy   An appraisal report that does not analyze how agreements, restrictions, and local ordinances affect the value of the property in question is suspect and inherently unreliable. First, in connection with real property, leases, options, and rights of first refusal (among other types of agreements affecting the property) should be disclosed and analyzed to understand how those agreements affect the value of the property in question. Second, where local ordinances could arguably overlap with the restrictions contained in an agreement, as may be the case with local preservation laws and conservation deeds of easement, any additional restrictions conferred by the deed of easement should be critically analyzed to understand how (if at all) those additional restrictions affect the value of the property. Thus, it is advisable for practitioners to disclose to the appraiser, and for the appraiser to disclose in the appraisal report, all relevant agreements, restrictions, and ordinances that affect the use of the property.

---

[8] *See* Internal Revenue Bulletin (Oct. 6, 2008), Notice of Proposed Rulemaking Substantiation and Reporting Requirements for Cash and Noncash Charitable Contributions, available at http://www.irs.gov/irb/2008-40_IRB/ar13.html#d0e6635.
[9] *Id.; see also* USPAP, Standards Rules 1-2(e)(iv) and 1-3(a) (2014-2015).
[10] T.C. Memo. 2015-87.

Of equal importance is that practitioners should analyze how, if at all, those existing restrictions, agreements, and local ordinances affect the use and value of the property in question. To the extent an agreement, restriction, or ordinance is deemed to be irrelevant to the question of value, the basis for that conclusion should also be stated. If, subsequent to the procurement of the putative qualified appraisal and before litigation has begun, it is determined that existing restrictions, agreements, and local ordinances were not disclosed or analyzed in the original report, it is generally advisable for the taxpayer to (1) obtain a revised appraisal report that analyzes the effect of these agreements on the value of the property, and (2) submit that revised appraisal report to the IRS on an amended tax return.[11] If the error is not realized until litigation has ensued, an expert report that considers the effect of these agreements on the value of the property should be submitted to the Court as the parties' expert report in accordance with the procedure discussed in Chapters 8, *Discovery of Expert Material*, and 13, *Attorney Involvement*, respectively. In cases where litigation has already begun, it may be advisable for the taxpayer to call as an expert witness the valuator who prepared the original putative qualified appraisal, the purpose of which is to allow the valuator, now qualified as an expert, to explain how the originally omitted agreements and restrictions would affect the appraiser's original opinion of value.

Defect 4: Qualifications Not Disclosed

Requirement and Error   Recall from Chapter 2, *Qualified Appraisal*, that section 1.170A-13(c)(3)(ii)(F) of the Treasury Regulations requires a qualified appraisal to disclose the qualifications of the qualified appraiser who prepared the appraisal, including the appraiser's background, experience, education, and membership in professional appraisal associations. The purpose of this requirement is to allow a revenue agent who examines the appraisal report to determine whether the appraiser is qualified to prepare appraisals of the type of property valued. Appraisal reports often fail to disclose these requirements, which can lead to unwelcome scrutiny to the qualified appraisal and, perhaps, cause the appraisal report to fail to be a qualified appraisal.

Remedy   Practitioners should ensure that the appraisal report includes a copy of the appraiser's curriculum vitae that specifies the appraiser's background, experience, education, and membership in any professional appraisal associations. It is important for practitioners to ensure that the statement of qualifications shows that the appraiser is qualified to prepare appraisals of the type of property being valued. Where the appraisal report concerns a novel issue or an appraiser's first attempt at valuing the type of property in question, this does not necessarily mean that the appraiser is unqualified to perform the appraisal. Rather, the appraisal report should

---

[11]In *Costello v. Comm'r*, T.C. Memo. 2015-247, the Tax Court held that addendums to an appraisal submitted to the Service five months after the extended due date of the taxpayer's return, and before litigation commenced, would not be considered in deciding whether the taxpayers obtained a qualified appraisal. In practice, however, the Service may be willing to accept revised appraisal reports for purposes of resolving a case without litigation.

detail the appraiser's qualifications and what additional steps the appraiser took to become qualified to perform the appraisal. Examples of such steps may include: taking continuing education courses, with a reference to the courses taken; consulting books, periodicals, and articles, with a reference to the publications consulted; conferring with third parties who are qualified to appraise the property in question, with a reference to the individuals consulted; and any other relevant facts that show that the appraiser's qualifications in a particular area are directly transferable to appraise the property in question.

Defect 5: No Statement That Appraisal Was Prepared for Federal Tax Purposes

Requirement and Error   Recall from Chapter 2, *Qualified Appraisal*, that section 1.170A-13(c)(3)(ii)(G) of the Treasury Regulations requires a qualified appraisal to disclose that the appraisal report was prepared for income tax purposes. The Tax Court recognized in *Rothman v. Commissioner* that "[a]cknowledging that the appraisal was made for federal income tax purposes is not insignificant. Such a statement serves as notice to the appraiser that he or she may be subject to a civil penalty under section 6701 for aiding and abetting an understatement of tax liability, and as a result, that appraisals he or she prepared may be disregarded pursuant to 31 U.S.C. [§] 330(c)."[12] Thus, the Tax Court in *Rothman* found that the failure to include a statement that the report was prepared for federal income tax purposes (among many other defects) negated the status of the report as a qualified appraisal.

Remedy   Practitioners should ensure that the appraisal report complies with this straightforward requirement in clear and unequivocal terms. To the extent it is discovered after the tax return was filed that this statement was not included in the report, and to the extent the facts of the case warrant such a defense, practitioners should rely upon the reasonable cause defense discussed earlier to excuse the defect. Again, practitioners should rely upon the reasonable cause defense discussed earlier to save the appraisal from classification as not a qualified appraisal.

Defect 6: Wrong Measure of Value

Requirement and Error   Recall from Chapter 2, *Qualified Appraisal*, that section 1.170A-13(c)(3)(ii)(I) of the Treasury Regulations requires a qualified appraisal to use fair market value as its measure of value. As set forth in Chapter 1, *Tax Valuation and the Necessity for Expert Appraisals*, there are many different measures

---

[12]*Rothman v. Comm'r*, T.C. Memo. 2012-163, 103 T.C.M. (CCH) 1864 (2012) (comparing Treas. Reg. § 1.170A-13(c)(5)(i), which requires a qualified appraiser to declare on the appraisal summary that he or she understands that intentionally false or fraudulent overstatements of the property valued may result in civil penalties and disciplinary action), *vacated in part on reconsideration*, T.C. Memo. 2012-218, 104 T.C.M. (CCH) 126 (2012).

of value, some of which are appropriate for federal tax purposes, and some of which are not.[13] The standard of value for federal tax purposes, and the one that section 1.170A-13(c)(3)(ii) of the Treasury Regulations requires appraisers to use, is "fair market value."

As noted elsewhere in this book, fair market value is "the price at which the property would change hands between a willing buyer and a willing seller, neither being under any compulsion to buy or sell and both having reasonable knowledge of relevant facts."[14] Appraisers, who generally speak in terms of the USPAP, often use market value as the appropriate measure of value. USPAP Advisory Opinion 22 defines *market value* as:

> *the most probable price which a property should bring in a competitive and open market under all conditions requisite to a fair sale, the buyer and seller each acting prudently and knowledgeably, and assuming the price is not affected by undue stimulus. Implicit in this definition are the consummation of a sale as of a specified date and the passing of title from seller to buyer under conditions whereby:*

> 1. *Buyer and seller are typically motivated;*
> 2. *Both parties are well informed or well advised and acting in what they consider their best interests;*
> 3. *A reasonable time is allowed for exposure in the open market;*
> 4. *Payment is made in terms of cash in U.S. dollars or in terms of financial arrangements comparable thereto; and*
> 5. *The price represents the normal consideration for the property sold unaffected by special or creative financing or sales concessions granted by anyone associated with the sale.*[15]

In *Crimi v. Commissioner*, the Tax Court observed that *market value* is "an approximate value for fair market value" and the "two terms are not necessarily synonymous depending on how they are defined."[16] The Tax Court's statement was not a mere exercise in semantics. A complete discussion of the ways in which market

---

[13]Different measures of value include but are not limited to market value, fair market value, fair value, appraised value, replacement value, orderly liquidation value, forced liquidation value, investment value, and intrinsic value.

[14]*United States v. Cartwright*, 411 U.S. 546, 551 (1973); *see also* Rev. Rul. 59-60, 1959-1 C.B. 237; Treas. Reg. § 1.170A-1(c)(2).

[15]USPAP, Advisory Opinion 22 (2014-2015).

[16]T.C. Memo. 2013-51, 105 T.C.M. (CCH) 1330 (2013); *see also Alli v. Comm'r*, T.C. Memo. 2014-15 n.17, 107 T.C.M. (CCH) 1082 (2014); *Rothman v. Comm'r*, T.C. Memo. 2012-163, 103 T.C.M. (CCH) 1864 (2012) (comparing Treas. Reg. § 1.170A-1(c)(c) (defining fair market value) with USPAP, Advisory Opinion 22 (2008) (defining market value)), *vacated in part on reconsideration*, T.C. Memo. 2012-218, 104 T.C.M. (CCH) 126 (2012); *DiDonato v. Comm'r*, T.C. Memo. 2011-153 n.8, 101 T.C.M. (CCH) 1739 (2011).

value and fair market value differ is outside the scope of this book, but the following points help to explain the key differences between the terms:

- Fair market value contemplates a transaction between a hypothetical willing buyer and a hypothetical willing seller; market value contemplates a transaction between an actual buyer and an actual seller;
- Fair market value assumes a hypothetical transfer of title; market value assumes an actual transfer of title;
- Fair market value requires the buyer and the seller to have "reasonable knowledge of relevant facts"; market value requires only that the buyer and seller are well informed and well advised; and
- Fair market value does not require an actual date on which the title changes hands; market value requires an actual transfer of title on a date certain.[17]

Market value is an approximate measure for fair market value, and because the two measures of value are not necessarily the same, depending upon how the terms are defined and used, an appraiser's insistence on using market value could mean that the appraisal does not comply with section 1.170A-13(c)(3)(ii)(I) of the Treasury Regulations.

Remedy   Practitioners should ensure that the appraisal report uses fair market value, not market value, as the measure of value. Some appraisers may resist deviating from use of the term *market value* because USPAP expresses a clear preference for using market value rather than fair market value as its measure of value. These concerns are unfounded.

USPAP recognizes that there are times, such as when property is valued for federal tax purposes, that it is not possible to use market value as the appropriate measure of value. For example, in USPAP Advisory Opinion 29, the Appraisal Foundation observes that fair market value is the appropriate standard of value to use when valuing a 25 percent minority interest in the equity of a small privately held company for estate tax reporting purposes.[18] Thus, USPAP provides for a jurisdictional exception rule that allows the appraiser to use the measure of value required by controlling law without violating USPAP.

Under the USPAP jurisdictional exception rule, where any applicable law or regulation precludes compliance with another part of USPAP, then that portion of USPAP is void for purposes of the assignment, and the law or regulation controls.[19] At the same time, USPAP requires the appraiser to disclose the variance between that which is required by USPAP and that which is required by the controlling law or regulation. Consequently, the attorney should counsel the appraiser to invoke the jurisdictional exception requirement. Neither the government nor a reviewing court

---

[17]For a comprehensive discussion of the differences between market value and fair market value, *see Alli v. Comm'r*, T.C. Memo. 2014-15 n.17, 107 T.C.M. (CCH) 1082 (2014); David Maloney, "Market Value vs. Fair Market Value: What's the Difference?," available at http://www.appraisalcourseassociates.com/2012/10/01/1265/ (last visited Sept. 17, 2017).

[18]USPAP, Advisory Opinion 29 (2014–2015).

[19]*See* USPAP, Jurisdictional Exception Rule, U-15 (2014–2015).

should be surprised to find a statement in a qualified appraisal that compliance with USPAP is not possible. USPAP is clear that, when an appraiser properly invokes the jurisdictional exception requirement and discloses it in the appraisal report, USPAP is not violated.[20]

If it is not discovered until after the return is filed that the purported qualified appraisal used the wrong measure of value, and to the extent the facts support such a claim, the practitioner (through an affidavit of the appraiser for the IRS or the sworn testimony of the appraiser for a court) should explain the reasons that market value as used in the appraisal report is the same as fair market value as expressed in sections 1.170A-1(c)(2) and 1.170A-13(c)(3)(ii)(I) of the Treasury Regulations. Practitioners may proactively bring this issue to a head before trial and briefing by filing with the Court a motion for partial summary judgment that the appraisal report in question is a qualified appraisal. The issue of whether the appraisal report is a qualified appraisal can be determined before litigation has progressed too far.

Defect 7: Lack of Reconciliation

Requirement and Error   Recall from Chapter 2, *Qualified Appraisal*, that sections 1.170A-13(c)(3)(ii)(J) and (K) of the Treasury Regulations require a qualified appraisal to disclose the method of value and the specific basis therefor in the report. Appraisers sometimes exclude (or more often inadequately describe) the method of value and specific basis for the valuation from an appraisal report. As explained ahead, such omissions may not necessarily cause an appraisal report to be not a qualified appraisal, but they may call into question the reliability and usefulness of the appraisal report.

In *Scheidelman v. Commissioner*,[21] the Court of Appeals for the Second Circuit held that sections 1.170A-13(c)(3)(ii)(J) and (K) of the Treasury Regulations do not require an appraisal report to include a "reasoned analysis" to support the proffered value. Rather, the Second Circuit stated that the purpose of the method of value and specific basis requirements is for the appraiser to provide the information and analysis informing the opinion of value, not necessarily that the method of value or the specific basis be persuasive. It is now well settled that an appraisal report's failure to apply the method of value and specific facts in a reasoned analysis does not necessarily mean that the report is not a qualified appraisal.[22] However, to the extent an appraisal report does not reconcile a range of values indicated by different valuation methods, the reasonableness, reliability, and effectiveness of the appraisal report may be called into question. In addition, USPAP may be violated because appraisers are

---

[20]*See* USPAP, Statement on Appraisal Standards No. 3 (2014–2015).

[21]682 F.3d 189, 195–199 (2d Cir. 2012), *rev'g*, T.C. Memo. 2010-151, 100 T.C.M. (CCH) 24 (2010).

[22]*Accord Rothman v. Comm'r*, T.C. Memo. 2012-218, 104 T.C.M. (CCH) 126 (2012) (concluding that an appraisal report which was in all material respects identical to the one at issue in *Scheidelman* would not be disregarded as a qualified appraisal because the appraisal report lacked a method of value or a specific basis for the valuation), *vacating in part on reconsideration*, T.C. Memo. 2012-163, 103 T.C.M. (CCH) 1864 (2012).

required to "provide sufficient information to enable the client and intended users to understand the rationale for the opinions and conclusions, including reconciliation of the data and approaches."[23]

Remedy   USPAP requires, and it is important from a defensibility position in litigation, appraisal reports to include a reconciliation of the divergent values indicated under different valuation methods. As detailed more fully in Chapter 9, *Expert Appraisal Reports*, reconciliation requires the appraisal report to reconcile the different conclusions of value that may be indicated by the various methodologies employed. For example, appraisers tend to lend greater weight to the income approach than the cost or comparable sales methods. Disproportionately weighting the income approach may be (and often is) justified, but the reason for such a conclusion needs to be explained in the appraisal report.

It is advisable for appraisers to explain the decision to weigh one method over others in a separate section of the appraisal report entitled "Reconciliation." Reconciliation is an important part of the appraisal process because it requires the appraiser to analyze alternative conclusions of value and to select a final opinion of value from among two or more indicated values. Reconciliation also provides the appraiser with an opportunity to address shortcomings in his or her report, to draw upon his or her experience and expertise to determine which opinion of value is most reliable, and to resolve any differences between the values indicated by his or her various approaches.

When viewed in this light, reconciliation may increase the likelihood that the appraisal report is recognized as a qualified appraisal. Specifically, when a proper reconciliation is included in the appraisal report, it is more likely that the requirements of sections 1.170A-13(c)(3)(ii)(J) and (K) of the Treasury Regulations are met because reconciliation requires the appraiser to (1) value the property under multiple appropriate valuation methods, (2) explain any differences in the indicated values, and (3) state his or her conclusion as to the specific basis that informs the appraiser's opinion of value. Finally, if litigation ensues, reconciliation generally increases the reliability, reasonableness, effectiveness, and defensibility of the appraisal report. In sum, including a reconciliation in an appraisal report not only increases the likelihood that the report will be recognized as a qualified appraisal but it is sound valuation practice.

---

[23]USPAP, Standards Rule 2-2(a)(viii); *see also* USPAP, Standards Rules 1-6 (requiring an appraiser in a real property appraisal to reconcile the applicability and relevance of the approaches, methods, and techniques used to arrive at the value conclusion); 6-7 (requiring an appraiser in a mass appraisal to reconcile the quality and quantity of data available and analyzed within the approaches used and the applicability and relevance of the approaches, methods, and techniques used); 8-2(a)(viii) (requiring that an appraisal report include, among other things, "the information analyzed, the appraisal methods and techniques employed, and the reasoning that supports the analyses, opinions, and conclusions; exclusion of the sales comparison approach, cost approach, or income approach must be explained"); 9-5 (requiring an appraisal of an interest in a business enterprise or intangible asset to reconcile the applicability and relevance of the approaches, methods, and procedures used to arrive at the value conclusion).

Defect 8: Consideration of Subsequent Events

Requirement and Error   An issue that is not outcome-determinative with respect to whether an appraisal report is a qualified appraisal, but which is important to the appraisal's reliability, is the extent to which events occurring after the valuation date may be considered in a retrospective appraisal report. This issue arises due to a potential tension in how appraisers treat post–valuation date events for USPAP and federal tax purposes. The following background helps explain this tension.

USPAP provides as follows with respect to whether subsequent events may be considered in a retrospective appraisal:

> *A retrospective appraisal is complicated by the fact that the appraiser already knows what occurred in the market after the effective date of the appraisal. Data subsequent to the effective date may be considered in developing a retrospective value as a confirmation of trends that would reasonably be considered by a buyer or seller as of that date. The appraiser should determine a logical cut-off because at some point distant from the effective date, the subsequent data will not reflect the relevant market. This is a difficult determination to make. Studying the market conditions as of the date of the appraisal assists the appraiser in judging where he or she should make this cut-off. In the absence of evidence in the market that data subsequent to the effective date were consistent with and confirmed market expectations as of the effective date, the effective date should be used as the cut-off date for data considered by the appraiser.*[24]

Thus, USPAP permits appraisers to consider post-valuation data, but only to confirm trends and market expectations in effect as of the valuation date.

For federal tax purposes, events occurring after the valuation date may generally not be considered in determining fair market value because such evidence is usually irrelevant and inadmissible.[25] However, depending upon the federal judicial circuit court to which the case is ultimately appealable, events occurring after the valuation date may be considered for federal tax purposes to the extent the events were reasonably foreseeable on the valuation date.[26] Appraisers sometimes include in their appraisal reports events occurring after the valuation date, but they do not clarify

---

[24]USPAP, Statement on Appraisal Standards No. 3 (2014–2015).

[25]*Ithaca Trust Co. v. United States*, 279 U.S. 151, 155 (1929); *Estate of Giovacchini v. Comm'r*, T.C. Memo. 2013-27, 105 T.C.M. (CCH) 1179 (2013).

[26]*See, e.g., Trout Ranch, LLC v. Comm'r*, 493 Fed. Appx. 944, 952–954 (10th Cir. 2012), *aff'g*, T.C. Memo. 2010-283, 100 T.C.M. (CCH) 581 (2010). There is a split among the Circuit Courts of Appeals in estate tax cases as to whether facts occurring after the date of death (the valuation date) may be considered in valuing claims against the estate. These cases have been interpreted to stand for the broader proposition that some federal circuit courts allow appraisers to consider subsequent events and some do not. In *Propstra v. United States*, 680 F.2d 1248, 1253–1256 (9th Cir. 1982), the U.S. Court of Appeals for the Ninth Circuit held, as a matter of law, that post-death events are not relevant in computing a permissible deduction where the claims are for sums certain and are legally enforceable as of the date of death. The U.S. Courts of Appeals for the Fifth agreed with the Ninth Circuit in *Estate of Smith v. Comm'r*, 198 F.3d 515, 517 (5th Cir. 1999) (holding that claims against an estate must be valued as of the

the extent to which (if at all) these events were considered in forming their opinion of value. It is rarely clear from these appraisal reports whether the events are included in the report to (1) as USPAP permits, confirm market expectations or historical trends, or (2) as federal tax law may prohibit, consider subsequent events that were not reasonably foreseeable on the valuation date.

In practice, some appraisers decline to state an opinion as to whether a post–valuation date event was reasonably foreseeable as of the valuation date because, they claim, such a determination is for the trier of fact to make. These appraisers instead choose to leave the appraisal report intentionally ambiguous as to the extent to which (if at all) these subsequent events were considered in forming their value opinion. This practice is ill advised because it may be inferred that the appraiser impermissibly considered subsequent events (potentially in violation of the valuation principles that apply for federal tax purposes).

Remedy   Appraisers facing a post–valuation date event that may affect the value of the property in question should confer with counsel to determine the extent to which (if at all) the subsequent event may be considered in the report. Where an appraiser uses a subsequent event in a retrospective appraisal to confirm historical trends or market expectations on the valuation date, the appraiser should state so and note for the intended user the specific USPAP provision that authorizes such an analysis. However, if the federal judicial circuit court to which the case is ultimately appealable prohibits consideration of such subsequent events, the appraiser should refrain from considering those events in forming his or her opinion value. More importantly, the appraiser should make clear the extent to which (if at all) the post–valuation date event affected his or her opinion of value.

Defect 9: Tax-Affecting S Corporations

Requirement and Opportunity for Error   Another issue that is not outcome-determinative with respect to whether an appraisal report is a qualified appraisal, but that appraisers may face in valuing a small business corporation ("S corporation"), is whether the value of the S corporation should be tax-affected. It has been argued that shares of an S corporation, by virtue of the fact that an S corporation does not pay an entity-level

---

decedent's date of death and therefore must be appraised on information known or available up to (but not after) that date), *rev'g*, 108 T.C. 412 (1997). On the other hand, in *Estate of Sachs v. Comm'r*, 856 F.2d 1158, 1160 (8th Cir. 1988), *rev'g*, 88 T.C. 769 (1987), the U.S. Court of Appeals for the Eighth Circuit held that events occurring after the date of death may be considered in determining whether the estate is entitled to a deduction for a claim against the estate. The U.S. Court of Appeals for the Second Circuit endorses the view of the Eighth Circuit, though it measures the relevant date for testing the foreseeability of the subsequent events as the date the estate tax return is filed, not the date of death. *See Comm'r v. Estate of Shively*, 276 F.2d 372, 375 (2d Cir. 1959) ("We hold that where, *prior to the date on which the estate tax return is filed*, the total amount of a claim against the estate is clearly established under state law, the estate may obtain under … no greater deduction than the established sum, irrespective of whether this amount is established through events occurring before or after the decedent's death."). Thus, appraisers who value claims against an estate must be mindful of governing case law for the assignment.

tax, are more valuable than C corporation shares. It is common practice for many appraisers to "tax-affect" an S corporation's earnings by reducing the corporation's earnings by a hypothetical corporate tax rate. The theory for this approach is that tax-affecting is necessary to reflect the risk a hypothetical buyer assumes that the corporation would lose (or reverse) its status as an S corporation.

In some cases, the Tax Court has been critical of tax-affecting S corporations and rejects the practice as unsound.[27] In other cases, the Tax Court has endorsed tax-affecting as the correct approach.[28] Some appraisers insist that tax-affecting is appropriate, that the Tax Court's opinions that reject tax-affecting are wrong, and that the Tax Court's opinions approving of tax-affecting are correct.[29] An appraiser's insistence on tax-affecting may, depending upon whether the appraisal report is presented to a IRS's appraiser or a judge who disagrees with tax-affecting, constitute an error that impugns the report's reliability. How should a practitioner handle an appraisal report written by an appraiser who insists that tax-affecting is appropriate to value an S corporation?

Remedy   If an appraiser believes it is appropriate to tax-affect an S corporation's earnings, the practitioner should defer to the appraiser's judgment. However, the practitioner should also counsel the appraiser to: (1) reconcile his or her valuation to explain why tax-affecting is appropriate under the assignment; and (2) if the case may be litigated in Tax Court, state the appraiser's awareness of the Tax Court's precedent against tax-affecting and the appraiser's opinion of value as if the value of the S corporation is not tax-affected. The appraisal report protects the client's interests regardless of whether the reviewing party agrees or disagrees with tax-affecting. It is important for the tax practitioner and the appraiser to remember that the appropriate valuation method (i.e., whether or not to tax-affect) is a legal conclusion reserved to the trier of fact (i.e., the judge in the Tax Court). The practitioner and the appraiser should also remember that the purpose of the expert is to assist the trier of fact. An appraiser who states separate opinions of value, one tax-affecting and one not, stands a greater chance of the Court recognizing him or her as a credible expert.

Potential Defect 10: Failure to Include a Regression Analysis

An item that is technically not required to be included in an appraisal report, but that may be helpful nonetheless, is a regression analysis. As detailed more fully in

---

[27]*See, e.g., Estate of Gallagher v. Comm'r*, T.C. Memo. 2011-148, 101 T.C.M. (CCH) 1702 (2011); *Estate of Adams v. Comm'r*, T.C. Memo. 2002-80, 83 T.C.M. (CCH) 1421 (2002); *Gross v. Comm'r*, T.C. Memo. 1999-254, 78 T.C.M. (CCH) 201 (1999), *aff'd*, 272 F.3d 333 (6th Cir. 2001).

[28]*See, e.g., Wall v. Comm'r*, T.C. Memo. 2001-75, n.19, 81 T.C.M. (CCH) 1425 (2001) (holding that tax-affecting is appropriate).

[29]*See, e.g.*, Shannon P. Pratt and Roger J. Grabowski, *Cost of Capital in Litigation: Applications and Examples*, 77 (John Wiley & Sons, 2d ed. 2010) (expressing the opinion that cases rejecting tax-affecting "represent bad case law and a misinterpretation of fair market value"); Charles J. Russo, Lasse Mertins, and Charles L. Martin, Jr., *Business Valuation Transaction Prices and Tax-Affecting S Corporations*, available at http://russophdcpa.com/uploads/3/1/2/9/3129429/bus_valuation_premiums_s_corporations_2012.pdf (discussing empirical evidence to support tax-affecting).

Chapter 9, *Expert Appraisal Reports*, a regression analysis is a statistical technique that can be used to determine the effect that one or more explanatory independent variables (e.g., the respective price paid to purchase the company with those earnings or revenues) have on a single dependent variable (e.g., the earnings or revenues of recently acquired companies). The regression analysis allows valuators to test the causal relationship, if any, between the independent and dependent variables.

Courts have viewed regression analyses with mixed fervor. In *Crimi v. Commissioner*, the Tax Court relied upon a regression analysis that used polynomial curve fitting to derive an indicated per-lot value for developable land.[30] In so ruling, the Court observed that "[t]he benefit of a regression analysis is its ability to draw a wider range of data to produce a better approximation of the dependent variable ... as a function of the independent variable." By contrast, where valuators have based their regression analyses on a small sample, courts have been skeptical. For example, in *Estate of Giovacchini v. Commissioner* and *Karlin v. Commissioner*,[31] the Tax Court faulted a taxpayer for limiting his regression analysis to "an extremely small sample." Similarly, where valuators did not effectively communicate the basis for the regression analysis, courts have rejected it.[32]

Valuators should consider whether a regression analysis would benefit the appraisal assignment. The regression analysis should use a broad sample, and it should explain in simple and understandable terms how the calculation was performed, what the results indicate, and why the approach is reliable.

CONCLUSION

Defects with appraisal reports can threaten the status of an appraisal report as a qualified appraisal and in turn jeopardize taxpayers-clients' entitlement to otherwise allowable tax benefits. These defects can also cause a reviewing court to disregard the ultimate opinion of value as unreliable. Tax practitioners must proactively and skeptically review purported qualified appraisal reports to ensure compliance with the qualified appraisal requirements. To the extent the defects are not realized until after the return claiming the tax benefit was filed, practitioners are well advised to rely upon the remedies cited throughout this chapter to counteract those defects.

---

[30] *Crimi v. Comm'r*, T.C. Memo. 2013-51, 105 T.C.M. (CCH) 1330 (2013).

[31] *Estate of Giovacchini v. Comm'r*, T.C. Memo. 2013-27, 105 T.C.M. (CCH) 1179 (20103); *Karin v. Comm'r*, T.C. Memo. 1987-552, 54 T.C.M. (CCH) 909 (1987).

[32] *See e.g.*, *Vitamin Village, Inc. v. Comm'r*, T.C. Memo. 2007-272, 94 T.C.M. (CCH) 278 (2007).

Table of Cases

106, Ltd. v. Comm'r, 136 T.C. 67 (2011), *aff'd* 684 F.3d 84 (D.C. Cir. 2012)

1982 East, LLC v. Comm'r, T.C. Memo. 2011-84, 101 T.C.M. (CCH) 1380 (2011)

ACM P'ship v. Comm'r, T.C. Memo. 1997-115, 73 T.C.M. (CCH) 2189 (1997), *aff'd*, 157 F.3d 231 (3d Cir. 1998)

Addis v. Comm'r, 118 T.C. 528 (2002), *aff'd*, 374 F.3d 881 (9th Cir. 2004)

ADVO, Inc. v. Comm'r, 141 T.C. 298 (2013)

Alli v. Comm'r, T.C. Memo. 2014-15, 107 T.C.M. (CCH) 1082 (2014)

Alltmont v. United States, 177 F.2d 971 (3d Cir. 1949), *cert. denied*, 339 U.S. 967 (1950)

Alpha I, L.P. v. United States, 682 F.3d 1009 (Fed. Cir. 2012)

Am. Air Filter Co. v. Comm'r, 81 T.C. 709 (1983)

Ambrosini v. Labarraque, 101 F.3d 129 (D.C. Cir. 1996)

Aries Commc'ns Inc. v. Comm'r, T.C. Memo. 2013-97, 105 T.C.M. (CCH) 1585 (2013)

Armstrong v. Comm'r, 139 T.C. 468 (2012)

Auto Indus. Supplier Emp. Stock Ownership Plan v. Ford Motor Co., 435 Fed. Appx. 430 (6th Cir. 2011)

Bank One Corp. v. Commissioner, 120 T.C. 174 (2003), *aff'd in part and vacated in part sub nom. J.P. Morgan Chase & Co. v. Comm'r*, 458 F.3d 564 (7th Cir. 2006)

BarristerEquipment Assocs. Series #115 v. Comm'r, T.C. Memo. 1994-205, 67 T.C.M. (CCH) 2932 (1994)

Bemont Invs., L.L.C. v. United States, 679 F.3d 339 (5th Cir. 2012)

Black Indus., Inc. v. Comm'r, 38 T.C.M. (CCH) 242 (1979)

BLAK Investments, T.C. Memo. 2012-273, 104 T.C.M. (CCH) 360 (2012)

Boltar, L.L.C. v. Comm'r, 136 T.C. 326 (2011)

Bond v. Comm'r, 100 T.C. 32 (1993)

Bone Care Intern. LLC v. Pentech Pharm., Inc., No. 08–CV–1083, 2010 WL 3928598 (N.D. Ill. Oct. 1, 2010)

Brewer Quality Homes, Inc. v. Comm'r, T.C. Memo. 2003-300; 86 T.C.M. (CCH) 29 (2003)

Brusewicz v. United States, 604 F. Supp. 2d 1197 (N.D. Ill. 2009)

Buyuk LLC v. Comm'r, T.C. Memo. 2013-253, 106 T.C.M. (CCH) 502 (2013)

Cabrera v. Cordis Corp., 134 F.3d 1418 (9th Cir. 1998)

Capitol Market, Ltd. v. United States, 207 F. Supp. 376 (D. Haw. 1962)

Caracci v. Comm'r, 118 T.C. 379 (2002), *rev'd*, 456 F.3d 444 (5th Cir. 2006)

Cave Buttes, L.L.C. v. Commissioner, 147 T.C. ___, ___, 2016 WL 5107038 (2016)

Champagne Metals v. Ken-Mac Metals, Inc., No. CIV-02-0528-HE, 2008 WL 5205204 (W.D. Okla. Dec. 11, 2008)

Chartwell Litig. Trust v. Addus Healthcare, Inc. (In re Med Diversified, Inc.), 334 B.R. 89 (Bankr. E.D.N.Y. 2005)

Claar v. Burlington N. R.R., 29 F.3d 499 (9th Cir. 1994)

Clear-View Techs., Inc. v. Rasnick, No. 13-cv-02744-BLF, 2015 WL 3505003 (N.D. Cal. July 2, 2015)

Colton v. United States, 306 F.2d 633 (2d Cir. 1962), *cert. denied*, 371 U.S. 951 (1963)

Comm'r v. Estate of Shively, 276 F.2d 372 (2d Cir. 1959)

Consol. Investors Group v. Comm'r, T.C. Memo. 2009-290, 98 T.C.M. (CCH) 601 (2009)

Costello v. Comm'r, T.C. Memo. 2015-87, 109 T.C.M. (CCH) 1441 (2015)

Cowan v. Treetop Enters., Inc., 120 F. Supp. 2d 672 (M.D. Tenn. 1999)

Crimi v. Comm'r, T.C. Memo. 2013-51, 105 T.C.M. (CCH) 1330 (2013)

Crispin v. Comm'r, 708 F.3d 507 (3d Cir. 2013)

D'Arcangelo v. Comm'r, T.C. Memo. 1994-572, 68 T.C.M. (CCH) 1223 (1994)

Daubert v. Merrell Dow Pharmaceuticals, Inc., 509 U.S. 597 (1993)

Davis v. Comm'r, T.C. Memo. 2015-88, 109 T.C.M. (CCH) 1450 (2015)

DiDonato v. Comm'r, T.C. Memo. 2011-153, 101 T.C.M. (CCH) 1739 (2011)

Dunaway v. Comm'r, 124 T.C. 80 (2005)

Dunlap v. Comm'r, 103 T.C.M. (CCH) 1689 (2012)

Dunn v. Comm'r, 301 F.3d 339 (5th Cir. 2002)

E.E.O.C. v. Bloomberg L.P., No. 07 Civ. 8383 (LAP), 2010 WL 3466370 (S.D.N.Y. Aug. 31, 2010)

Embroidery Express, LLC v. Comm'r, T.C. Memo. 2016-136, 112 T.C.M. (CCH) 76 (2016)

Esgar Corp. v. Comm'r, T.C. Memo. 2012-35, 103 T.C.M. (CCH) 1185 (2012)

Estate of Adams v. Comm'r, T.C. Memo. 2002-80, 83 T.C.M. (CCH) 1421 (2002)

Estate of Chamberlain v. Comm'r, T.C. Memo. 1999-181, 77 T.C.M. (CCH) 2080 (1999), *aff'd*, 9 Fed. Appx. 713 (9th Cir. 2001)

Estate of Elkins v. Comm'r, 140 T.C. 86 (2013), *rev'd in part*, 767 F.3d 443 (5th Cir. 2014)

Estate of Gallagher v. Comm'r, T.C. Memo. 2011-148, 101 T.C.M. (CCH) 1702 (2011)

Estate of Gilford v. Comm'r, 88 T.C. 38 (1987)

Estate of Giovacchini v. Comm'r, T.C. Memo. 2013-27, 105 T.C.M. (CCH) 1179 (2013)

Estate of Kirkpatrick v. Comm'r, 34 T.C.M. (CCH) 1490 (1975)

Estate of Noble v. Comm'r, T.C. Memo. 2005-2, 89 T.C.M. (CCH) 649 (2005)

Estate of Pohlad v. Comm'r, No. 12508-13 (T.C. filed June 6, 2013)

Estate of Renier v. Comm'r, T.C. Memo. 2000-298, 80 T.C.M. (CCH) 401 (2000)

Estate of Sachs v. Comm'r, 856 F.2d 1158 (8th Cir. 1988), *rev'g*, 88 T.C. 769 (1987)

Estate of Scanlan v. Comm'r, T.C. Memo. 1996-331, 72 T.C.M. (CCH) 160 (1996)

Estate of Smith v. Comm'r, 198 F.3d 515 (5th Cir. 1999), *rev'g*, 108 T.C. 412 (1997)

Estate of Tanenblatt v. Comm'r, T.C. Memo. 2013-263, 106 T.C.M. (CCH) 579 (2013)

Exelon Corp. v. Comm'r, No. 29183-13 (T.C. filed Dec. 13, 2013)

Farber v. Comm'r, T.C. Memo. 1974-155, 33 T.C.M. (CCH) 673 (1974), *aff'd*, 535 F.2d 1241 (2d Cir.1975)

Fid. Int'l Currency Advisor A Fund, LLC v. United States, 661 F.3d 667 (1st Cir. 2011)

French v. Comm'r, T.C. Memo. 2016-53, 111 T.C.M. (CCH) 1241 (2016)

Frye v. United States, 54 App. D.C. 46 (D.C. Cir. 1923)

Frymire-Brinati v. KPMG Peat Marwick, 2 F.3d 183 (7th Cir. 1993)

Gemperlee v. Comm'r, T.C. Memo. 2016-1, 111 T.C.M. (CCH) 1001 (2016)

Gen. Elec. Co. v. Joiner, 522 U.S. 136 (1997)

Georgia-Pacific Corp. v. United States, 640 F.2d 328 (Ct. Cl. 1980)

Golsen v. Comm'r, 54 T.C. 742 (1970)

Goodfriend v. Comm'r, 52 T.C.M. (CCH) 845 (1986)

Gow v. Comm'r, 79 T.C.M. (CCH) 1680 (2000)

Green Gas Del. Statutory Trust v. Comm'r, 147 T.C. 1 (2016)

Gross v. Comm'r, T.C. Memo. 1999-254, 78 T.C.M. (CCH) 201 (1999), *aff'd*, 272 F.3d 333 (6th Cir. 2001)

Gustashaw v. Comm'r, 696 F.3d 1124 (11th Cir. 2012)

Hall v. United States, 353 F.2d 500 (7th Cir. 1965)

Harris v. United States, No. 06–0412 JP/KBM., 2008 WL 5600225 (D.N.M. July 31, 2008)

Heasley v. Comm'r, 902 F.2d 380 (5th Cir. 1990)

Hein v. Merck & Co., 868 F. Supp. 230 (M.D. Tenn. 1994)

Heller v. Shaw Indus., Inc., 167 F.3d 146 (3rd Cir. 1999)

Hendrix v. United States, 2010 WL 2900391 (S.D. Oh. 2010)

Hewitt v. Comm'r, 109 T.C. 258 (1997)

Hickman v. Taylor, 329 U.S. 495 (1947)

Higbee v. Comm'r, 118 T.C. 438 (2001)

Hilborn v. Comm'r, 85 T.C. 677 (1985)

Hill v. Comm'r, T.C. Memo. 2004-156, 87 T.C.M. (CCH) 156 (2004)

Huffman v. Comm'r, 126 T.C. 322 (2006)

Hutchison v. Parent, No. 3:12 cv 320, 2015 WL 1914794 (N.D. Ohio Apr. 27, 2015)

Illes v. Comm'r, 982 F.2d 143 (2d Cir. 1991)

In re Kearney, 227 F. Supp. 174 (S.D.N.Y. 1964)

In re Med Diversified, 334 B.R. 89 (Bankr. E.D.N.Y. 2005)

In re Nellson Nutraceutical, Inc., 356 B.R. 364 (Bankr. D. Del. 2006)

Isaacs v. Comm'r, T.C. Memo. 2015-121, 109 T.C.M. (CCH) 1624 (2015)

Ithaca Trust Co. v. United States, 279 U.S. 151 (1929)

Izen v. Comm'r, 148 T.C. ___, ___, 2017 WL 809946 (2017)

James River Ins. Co. v. Rapid Funding, LLC, No. 07CV01146CMABNB, 2009 WL 481688 (D. Colo. Feb. 24, 2009)

Jorgenson v. Comm'r, T.C. Memo. 2000-38, 79 T.C.M. (CCH) 1444 (2000)

Karin v. Comm'r, T.C. Memo. 1987-552, 54 T.C.M. (CCH) 909 (1987)

Kaufman v. Comm'r, 77 T.C.M. (CCH) 1779 (1999), *rev'd on other grounds sub. nom. Morrissey v. Comm'r*, 243 F.3d 1145 (9th Cir. 2001)

Kaufman v. Motorola, Inc., No. 95 C 1069, 2000 WL 1506892 (N.D. Ill. Sept. 21, 2000)

Kaufman v. Schulman, 687 F.3d 21 (1st Cir. 2012), *aff'g in part, vacating in part, and remanding in part*, 134 T.C. 182 (2010)

Keller v. Comm'r, 556 F.3d 1056 (9th Cir. 2009)

Kohler v. Comm'r, T.C. Memo. 2006-152, 92 T.C.M. (CCH) 48 (2006)

Kohli v. Comm'r, T.C. Memo. 2009-287, 98 T.C.M. (CCH) 572 (2009)

Kumho Tire Co. v. Carmichael, 526 U.S. 137 (1999)

Lippe v. Bairnco Corp., 288 B.R. 678 (S.D.N.Y. 2003)

Lockheed Martin Corp. v. United States, 210 F.3d 1366 (Fed. Cir. 2000)

Long Term Capital Holdings v. United States, 330 F. Supp. 2d 122 (D. Conn. 2004), *aff'd* 150 Fed. Appx 40 (2d Cir. 2005)

Massengill v. Comm'r, 876 F.2d 616 (8th Cir. 1989)

McAlpin v. United States, No. EC81-156-LS-P, 1982 WL 1714 (N.D. Miss. Aug. 27, 1982)

MDG Int'l, Inc. v. Austl. Gold, Inc., No. 1:07–cv–1096–SEB–TAB, 2009 WL 1916728 (S.D. Ind. June 29, 2009)

Merino v. Comm'r, 196 F.3d 147 (3d Cir. 1999)

Mohamed v. Comm'r, T.C. Memo. 2012-152, 103 T.C.M. (CCH) 1814 (2012)

Multimatic, Inc. v. Faurecia Interior Sys. USA, Inc., 358 Fed. Appx. 643 (6th Cir. 2009)

Neonatology Associates, P.A. v. Comm'r, 115 T.C. 43 (2000), *aff'd* 299 F.3d 221 (3d Cir. 2002)

Nicoladis v. Comm'r, 55 T.C.M. (CCH) 624 (1988)

Okerlund v. United States, 53 Fed. Cl. 341 (2002)

Oughton v. Comm'r, 67 T.C.M. (CCH) 2271 (1994)

Pabst Brewing Co. v. Comm'r, T.C. Memo. 1996-506, 72 T.C.M. (CCH) 1236 (1996)

Propstra v. United States, 680 F.2d 1248 (9th Cir. 1982)

Prussner v. United States, 896 F.2d 218 (7th Cir. 1990)

Quad City Bank & Trust v. Elderkin & Pirnie, P.L.C., 863 N.W.2d 35 (Iowa Ct. Appeals 2015)

Raleigh Props., Inc. v. Comm'r, 21 T.C.M. (CCH) 812 (1962)

Ralston v. Mortg. Inv'rs Grp., Inc., No. 08–536–JF (PSG), 2011 WL 6002640 (N.D. Cal. Nov. 30, 2011)

Reisner v. Comm'r, T.C. Memo. 2014-230

RERI Holdings I, LLC v. Comm'r, 149 T.C. ___, ___ , 2017 WL 2839773 (2017)

Riether v. United States, 2012 WL 6934116 (N.M. 2012)

Roberts v. Elevated Ry. Co., 28 N.E. 486 (N.Y. 1891)

Rothman v. Comm'r, T.C. Memo. 2012-163, *vacated in part on other grounds*, T.C. Memo. 2012-218

Rovakat, LLC v. Comm'r, T.C. Memo. 2011-225, *aff'd*, 529 Fed. Appx. 124 (3d Cir. 2013)

Santa Monica Pictures, LLC v. Comm'r, T.C. Memo. 2005-104, 89 T.C.M. (CCH) 1157, 112-20 (2005)

Scheidelman v. Comm'r, 755 F.3d 148 (2d Cir. 2014)

Scheidelman v. Comm'r, T.C. Memo. 2010-151, 100 T.C.M. (CCH) 24 (2010), *vacated and remanded by* 682 F.3d 189 (2d Cir. 2012)

Seagate Tech., Inc. v. Comm'r, 102 T.C. 149 (1994)

Sheehan v. Daily Racing Form, Inc., 104 F.3d 940 (7th Cir. 1997)

Sherman Concrete Pipe, Co. v. United States, No. 3542, 1978 WL 4511 (M.D. Tenn. 1978)

Simmons v. Comm'r, T.C. Memo. 2009-208, 98 T.C.M. (CCH) 211 (2009)

Smith v. Comm'r, T.C. Memo. 2007-368, 94 T.C.M. (CCH) 574 (2007), *aff'd*, 364 Fed. Appx. 317 (9th Cir. 2009)

Superior Trading, LLC v. Comm'r, 728 F.3d 676 (7th Cir. 2013)

Tamraz v. Lincoln Elec. Co., 620 F.3d 665 (6th Cir. 2010)

Taylor v. Comm'r, 67 T.C. 1071 (1977)

Tech. Licensing Corp. v. Gennum Corp., No. 3:01–cv–4204–RS, 2004 WL 1274391 (N.D. Cal. Mar. 26, 2004)

Todd v. Comm'r, 862 F.2d 540 (5th Cir. 1988)

Trigon Ins. Co. v. United States, 204 F.R.D. 277 (E.D. Va. 2001)

Trout Ranch, LLC v. Comm'r, 100 T.C.M. (CCH) 581 (2010), *aff'd* 493 Fed. Appx. 944, 949-50 (10th Cir. 2012)

U.S. ex rel. Loughren v. UnumProvident Corp., 604 F. Supp. 2d 259 (D. Mass. 2009)

Union Carbide Corp. v. Comm'r, T.C. Memo. 2009-50, 97 T.C.M. (CCH) 1207 (2009)

United States v. 23.76 Acres of Land, 32 F.R.D. 593 (D. Md. 1963)

United States v. Cartwright, 411 U.S. 546 (1973)

United States v. Fogg, 652 F.2d 551 (5th Cir. 1981)

United States v. Kovel, 296 F.2d 918 (2d Cir. 1961)

United States v. McKay, 372 F.2d 174 (5th Cir. 1967)

United States v. Summe, 208 F. Supp. 925 (E.D. Ky. 1962)

United States v. Woods, ___ U.S. ___, 134 S. Ct. 557 (2013)

Upjohn Co. v. United States, 449 U.S. 383 (1981)

Vitamin Village, Inc. v. Comm'r, T.C. Memo. 2007-272, 94 T.C.M. (CCH) 278 (2007)

Wagner Construction, Inc. v. Comm'r, T.C. Memo. 2001-160, 2001 WL 739234 (2016)

Wall v. Comm'r, T.C. Memo. 2001-75, 81 T.C.M. (CCH) 1425 (2001)

Walsh v. Reynolds Metals Co., 15 F.R.D. 376 (D.N.J. 1954)

Weiner v. Snapple Beverage Corp., No. 07 Civ. 8742(DLC), 2010 WL 3119452 (S.D.N.Y. Aug. 5, 2010)

Weiss v. Comm'r, 65 T.C.M. (CCH) 2768 (1993)

Welch v. Helvering, 290 U.S. 111 (1933)

Whitehouse Hotel Ltd. P'ship v. Comm'r, 131 T.C. 112 (2008), *vacated and remanded on other grounds*, 615 F.3d 321 (5th Cir. 2010)

Whitehurst v. Comm'r, T.C. Summ. Op. 2003-7 (2003)

Winans v. New York & Erie R.R. Co., 62 U.S. 88 (1858)

Zarlengo v. Comm'r, T.C. Memo. 2014-161, 108 T.C.M. (CCH) 155 (2014)

Zeropack Co. v. Comm'r, 47 T.C.M. (CCH) 181 (1983)

Zfass v. Comm'r, 118 F.3d 184 (4th Cir. 1997)

About the Authors

This book is authored by two people, each of whom approaches the subject matter of valuation and qualified appraisals from a different perspective but with overlapping commonality. This is the virtue and strength of this book. By combining and integrating diverse concepts and ideas on valuation, the authors hope the reader will gain valuable insight into the practicalities and technicalities of the valuation process.

Michael R. Devitt is both an accomplished lawyer and a *Professor of Law* who teaches trial evidentiary rules and advocacy. Professor Devitt's perspective is based on over 30 years of teaching and practicing law. Professor Devitt's research and scholarship has brought the subject of concurrent witness testimony to the forefront in the United States judiciary.

Lawrence A. Sannicandro is a skilled practicing attorney in New Jersey with the law firm of McCarter & English, LLP. Mr. Sannicandro brings to the task a wealth of practical experience, including his former employment as counsel for the IRS and his service as a law clerk with the Tax Court. He has written extensively on valuation issues and has chaired national conferences dealing with valuation.

Together, the authors offer to the readers experience and knowledge that will serve appraisers, attorneys, certified public accountants, and other professionals in this dynamic field of valuation appraisals.

Accredited Member (A.M.), 70, 192
Accredited Senior Member (A.S.A.), 70
Admissions
  Court of Claims, 119
  District Courts, 119
  Tax Court, 113
American Institute of Certified Public
  Accountants
  Accredited in Business Valuation
    (ABV), 33, 71, 192
  CPA designation, 71
American Society of Appraisers (ASA),
  33, 62, 69, 120, 192
  Accredited Member (A.M.), 70
  Accredited Senior Member (A.S.A.),
    70
  Member of the ASA College
    of Fellows (FASA), 70
Appraisal fees
  effect on objectivity, 40
  exception to general prohibition on
    contingent fee arrangements, 40
  general prohibition on contingent fee
    arrangements, 40
Appraisal Institute, 70
  Appraisal Institute, General Review
    Specialist (AI-GRS), 70
  Appraisal Institute, Residential
    Review Specialist (AI-RRS), 70
  Member of the Appraisal Institute
    (MAI), 70
  Residential Member (RM), 70
  Senior Real Estate Analysis
    (SREA), 70
  Senior Real Property Appraiser
    (SRPA), 70
  Senior Residential Appraiser
    (SRA), 70
Appraisal Institute, General Review
  Specialist (AI-GRS), 70

Appraisal Institute, Residential Review
  Specialist (AI-RRS), 70
Appraisal reports
  addenda, 144
  attorney involvement generally, 191
  attorney involvement in engaging the
    appraiser, 193
  attorney involvement in selecting an
    appraiser, 192
  attorney involvement in the appraisal
    process, 194
  attorney involvement in the
    fact-gathering process, 194
  attorney involvement in the report
    preparation process, 195
  attorney involvement in the review
    process, 196
  defined, 122
  generally, 122
  internally consistent, 142
  multiple authors, 40
  reconciliation, 143
Appraisal summary, 12, 19, 20, 24,
  28, 29, 35, 38–40, 44, 48, 50,
  51, 210
Appraisers and tax authorities, 124,
  197, 198
Attorney-client privilege, 100–102,
  106, 193

Bank One Corp. v. Commissioner, 151,
  196
Boltar, L.L.C. v. Commissioner,
  see Daubert, 81
Book value, 121, 125, 133, 158
Burden of proof, 58, 66
  deductions, 58
  preponderance of the evidence, 56,
    58, 176, 193
Buy-sell agreement, 4

Certified Business Appraiser
  (CBA), 70
Charitable contribution deduction
  disallowance of tax benefit for lack
    of qualified appraisal, 14, 15
  reasonable cause exception, 55
  statutory purpose, 47
Charitable deduction property
  gross valuation misstatement
    penalty, 174
  property other than charitable
    deduction property, 175
  substantial valuation misstatement
    penalty, 174
Circular, 230
  disqualification of appraisers,
    189
  generally, 189
  monetary penalty, 189
  professional sanctions, 189
Comparable properties, 8, 36, 129
Conclusion of value, 124, 136, 196
Concurrent expert witness testimony
  advantages, 166
  attorney objections, 163
  consent of the parties, 164
  cross-examination, 163, 164
  disadvantages, 166
  expert bias, 155
  expert dialogue, 162, 163
  expert oath, 161
  expert report, 160, 161
  foreign court experiences, 155–157
  frequency, 165
  generally, 148, 157–159
  lawyers' involvement, 165
  myths and misconceptions, 164, 165
  on the record requirement, 165
  partisan experts, 148
  process, 152, 154
  rebuttal, 164
  suggested approach, 159, 160
Concurrent witness testimony
  use in alternative dispute resolution,
    199
  use in negotiations with tax
    authorities, 199
Condition of the property, 20, 21,
  28, 131

Contents of appraisal report
  addenda, 138
  body of report, 124
  cover letter, 123
  executive summary, 123
  signature, 124, 136
  table of contents, 123
Contents of appraisal signed
  certification, 136
Contractual rights, preferences, and
  privileges of interest, 130, 134, 195
Control over property, 124
Coordinated industry cases, 63
Court-appointed experts, 149, 151
Criminal tax
  generally, 1, 3, 4
  tax loss, 4
Cross-examination, 4, 59, 72, 103, 110,
  160, 164, 165, 200, 201, 203, 204
Current appraisal, 126

Date of the appraisal report, 123
Daubert
  discretion to trial judges, 79, 80, 105,
    107, 116, 117, 152, 164, 166, 197
  discussion of case, 78, 79
  factor, whether the potential rate
    of error is known, 80, 86–88
  factor, whether the theory or
    technique has been subject to peer
    review and publication, 80, 84–86
  factor, whether the theory or
    technique has gained general
    acceptance, 80, 88–90
  factors, accounting for alternative
    explanations, 81, 95, 96
  factors, degree of care, 81, 96, 97
  factors, degree of reliability in field
    generally, 81, 97
  factors, does the conclusion square
    with common sense, 81, 97, 98
  factors, generally, 80
  factors, non-judicial use of theory
    or method, 81, 97
  factors, unfounded conclusions, 80,
    93–95
  factors, whether the proposed theory
    or technique can and has been
    tested, 80, 83, 84

factors, whether the theory is the result of litigation, 80, 91, 92
generally, 77, 78
legal opinions, 93
progeny, 58, 76, 79, 83, 150
PwC Study, 83
Daubert challenges, 73, 76, 82, 83, 98, 151, 193
Daubert illustration, 83
Daubert trial court discretion, 82
De minimis estate or gift tax valuation misstatement, 180
De minimis exceptions for preparer penalties under section 6694, 186
Defects with qualified appraisals
    failing to analyze agreements, 208
    inadequate description of property, 207
    lack of reconciliation, 213
    lack of regression analysis, 217
    qualifications not disclosed, 209
    reliance on subsequent events, 215
    statement for federal tax purposes, 210
    untimely report, 206
    wrong measure of value, 210
Defects with qualified generally, 205
Deficit Reduction Act of 1984, 17, 18, 31
Description of the property, 17, 20, 21, 28, 30, 130, 131, 138, 141, 207
Description of the subject property, 123
Discounts
    blockage, 9, 134, 197
    built-in capital gain, 9
    contingent liabilities, 9
    fractional interest, 9, 66, 134, 197
    key person, 9, 134
    lack of control, 9, 134, 197
    lack of marketability, 9, 65, 88, 134, 197
    lack of voting rights, 9
    partition, 9, 134, 197
    portfolio, 9
Discovery
    attorney-client privilege, 100
    Court of Claims, generally, 119
    Depositions of opposing experts, 119
    District Courts, depositions, 118

District Courts, discovery of experts, 116
District Courts, generally, 113
District Courts, interrogatories generally, 117
District Courts, limitations on discovery, 116
District Courts, limitations on discovery of experts, 117
District Courts, production of documents pursuant to a request, 118
District Courts, production of documents pursuant to a subpoena, 118
District Courts, scope of discovery, 116
District Courts, time for discovery, 115
experts, generally, 103
generally, 99, 103
limitations, 100
Tax Court, attorney-client privilege extended to experts, 107
Tax Court, depositions generally, 110
Tax Court, depositions with the consent of the parties, 110–112
Tax Court, depositions without the consent of the parties, 111, 112
Tax Court, discovery of experts, 105
Tax Court, document production, 108, 109
Tax Court, document production concerning experts, 109
Tax Court, draft appraisal reports, 109, 110
Tax Court, generally, 104
Tax Court, interrogatories concerning experts, 107, 108
Tax Court, interrogatories generally, 107
Tax Court, limitations on discovery, 105
Tax Court, scope of discovery, 105
Tax Court, time for discovery, 105
Tax Court, work files, 109, 110
Tax Court, work product limitation on expert discovery, 106
unfairness doctrine, 102
work product doctrine, 101

Dissenting shareholders, 4
District Courts
  Disclosures within 30 days of trial,
    115
  Initial disclosures concerning experts,
    114
  Initial disclosures, generally, 114
  Rule 26 plan, 113
  Rule 26(f) conference, 113
Divorce, 4
Doctrine of variance, 115

Economic conditions, 133
Economic substance common law
  doctrine, 178
Economic substance, codification,
  178
Effective date of the appraisal report,
  123, 126, 127, 141, 215
Employee Stock Ownership Plans
  (ESOPs), 3, 4
Engaging the appraiser and *Kovel*, 193
Estate or gift tax valuation
  misstatement, 180
Expert reports in litigation
  District Court requirements, 146
  process to receive report, 103
  Rule 143(g), 10, 101, 103, 105–108,
    145, 146, 196, 201
  Tax Court requirements, 145
Expert witness testimony
  standards of admissibility, 76
Expert witnesses
  allocation of time and resources, 74
  availability, 73
  bias, generally and mitigation, 71
  communication ability, 71
  correcting errors in report, 73
  credibility, 4, 67, 72, 87, 88, 110,
    159, 168
  duty to client, 74
  duty to court, 74
  early involvement in engagement,
    72
  education, 69
  experience, 69
  knowledge, 69
  legal issues v. factual issues, 74

neutrality, 71
practice tips in selection, 68
preparation, 74
sample appraiser used for tax return,
  72
scheduling, 73
selection, 68
skeletons in the closet, 73
skills, 69
training, 69

Fair market value
  arm's length, 6
  cash value, compared, 7
  compared with market value, 25,
    125, 211
  compulsion, 6
  defined, 5, 123
  equation, *see also* net asset value
    and valuation discounts, 7
  highest and best use, 6, 10, 87, 132,
    141
  hypothetical transfer of title, 26, 212
  hypothetical willing buyer, 6, 26, 212
  hypothetical willing seller, 6, 26, 212
  market value, compared, 7
  reaasonable knowledge, 6, 25, 26,
    211, 212
  reasonable knowledge, 6
  subsequent events, 6, 127, 215, 216
Fast Track Settlement, 199
Federal Rules of Evidence
  Rule 701, 13, 76
  Rule 702, 3, 69, 77, 79, 87, 122,
    150, 203
  Rule 703, 77
Fee simple, 124
Financial analysis, 133
Financial ratios, 138, 141
Forecasting, 144
Frye v. United States, 78

Geographic data, 131, 132
Ghost writing
  generally, 196–198
  sanctions for improper attorney
    assistance, 196–198
Going concern value, 125

Government experts
  advantages, 63
  Appeals employees as experts, 60
  Appeals Quality Measurement
    System, 63
  bias problem, 63, 64
  Chief Counsel library, 59
  decision to forego expert testimony,
    66
  disadvantages, 63
  evaluation, 63
  hiring, 62
  in-house appraisers, 60
  IRS policy, 63
  IRS policy regarding valuations, 61
  IRS specialist as an expert witness, 64
  LB&I Quality Measurement System,
    63
  management oversight, 63
  performance, 63
  procurement process, 59
  quality asurance system, 63
  selection, 59
  survey of cases, 64
  third-party expert, 60
  training, 62
Gross estate or gift tax valuation
  misstatement, 180
Gross valuation misstatement and
  transactions without economic
  substance, 179
Gross valuation misstatement penalty,
  35, 38, 171–174, 176, 177, 179, 181
Gross valuation misstatement penalty
  and reasonable cause defense, 178

Hypotheticals and or limiting
  conditions, 124, 132

Industry cases, 63
Influence, 134
Information considered, 123, 133
Institute of Business Appraisers, 33, 70,
  121, 192
  Certified Business Appraiser (CBA),
    70
  Master of Certified Business
    Appraiser (MCBA), 70

Intended use, 128
Intended user, 120, 122–125, 128–130,
  138, 141, 194, 214
Intrinsic value, 125, 211
Investment value, 125, 211
IRS Art Appraisal Service, 60, 61
IRS Economist Program, 60, 61
IRS Engineering Program, 60, 62
Ithaca Trust Co. v. United States,
  127, 215

Joint tenancy property, 124
Jurisdictional exception rule, 126,
  212

Kumho Tire Co. v. Carmichael, 80,
  81, 97, 150

Lay witnesses, 76, 78
Linear regression analysis, 135
Liquidation value, 125, 128, 211
Liquidity constraints with respect to
  property, 124

Market value
  defined, 7
  exposure, 7
  generally, 25
  knowledge, 7
  payment, 7
  USPAP Advisory Opinion 22, 7
Master Certified Business Appraiser
  (MCBA), 70
Measures of value
  fair market value, *see* fair market
    value, 5
  fair value, 5
  investment value, 5
  Market value, *see also* fair market
    value, 5
  quick sale value, 5
  salvage value, 5
Member of the Appraisal Institute
  (MAI), 70, 192
Member of the ASA College of Fellows
  (FASA), 70
Motions *in limine*, 82, 199, 201, 202
Multiple appraisers, 40, 42, 128

National Association of Certified
Valuators and Analysts, 33, 192
National Association of Valuers and
Analysts, 71
Accredited in Business Appraisal
Review (ABAR), 71
Certified Valuation Analyst (CVA), 71
National Association of Valuers and
Analysts, 71
Net asset value
asset-based approach, cost approach,
8, 214
income approach, 8, 10, 26, 134,
135, 143, 214
market approach, 8, 134, 143

Penalties
accuracy-related penalties, 2, 14, 32,
55, 171, 176, 190
accuracy-related penalties under
section 6662, 2, 14, 171–174,
176–181, 183, 186
adequate disclosure defense, 176
appraiser penalties under section
6695A, 32, 170, 180–182
good faith, 176
gross valuation misstatement, 3
misunderstanding of fact or law, 175
preparer penalties under section
6694, 171, 180–183, 185, 186, 188
preparer penalties under section 6694
and appraisers as preparers, 185
reliance defense, 175
section 6694 and appraisers as
preparers, 185
section 6694 and defenses, 186
section 6695A, 32, 35, 38, 171,
180–182
section 6695A and defenses, 182
section 6695A and referral for
professional sanctions, 182
section 6695A and the statute
of limitations, 182
section 6701, 187, 188
section 6701 and aiding and abetting
an understatement of tax, 20, 24,
35, 38, 170, 171, 180, 181,
186–188, 210
substantial valuation misstatement, 3

Pension Protection Act of 2006, 17, 18,
32, 180
Post-Appeals Mediation, 199
Premiums, 124
control premium, 9
Prior transactions, 130
Property Taxes, 4
Prospective appraisals, 127
Purpose of appraisal, 123, 128

Qualified appraisal
basis of value requirement under
Treas. Reg. § 1.170A-13(c)(3)(ii)(K),
20, 26, 27, 51, 213, 214
charitable contribution deduction,
more than §5,000, 2, 9, 12, 13,
15–17, 28, 31, 46, 55, 109, 173,
177, 180, 183, 184, 205
charitable remainder trusts, 2, 9, 14
counterclaims against an estate, 2, 9,
14
date of contribution requirement
under Treas. Reg.
§ 1.170A-13(c)(3)(ii)(C), 21
date(s) of appraisal requirement
under Treas. Reg.
§ 1.170A-13(c)(3)(ii)(H), 25
defined by regulation, 18
defined by statute, 18
disallowance of tax benefits, 14, 43
easement litigation, 10, 12, 21, 23,
48, 51, 52, 81, 87, 130, 207, 208
fair market value requirement under
Treas. Reg. § 1.170A-13(c)(3)(ii)(I),
25
identifying information of the
appraiser requirement under Treas.
Reg. § 1.170A-13(c)(3)(ii)(E),
23, 24, 29
interplay with appraisal summary, 28
legislative history, 17
method of value requirement under
Treas. Reg. § 1.170A-13(c)(3)(ii)(J),
20, 26, 27, 51, 213, 214
no prohibited fee arrangement
requirement under Treas. Reg.
§ 1.170A-13(c)(3)(i)(D), 27
pass-thru entities, 27
policy, 15, 29, 48, 100, 101, 170

property description requirement
under Treas. Reg.
§ 1.170A-13(c)(3)(ii)(A), 20
qualifications of the appraiser
requirement under Treas. Reg.
§ 1.170A-13(c)(3)(ii)(E), 24
qualified appraiser requirement under
The 60 Day Requirement Treas.
Reg. § 1.170A-13(c)(3)(i)(A), 19
qualified settlement fund, 2, 9, 14
reasons for enactment, 15
regulatory requirements, 20
statement of preparation for income
tax purposes requirement under
Treas. Reg. § 1.170A-13(c)(3)(ii)(G),
17, 20, 24, 48, 210
statutory requirements, 15
substantiation requirements,
generally, 15
tangible property description under
Treas. Reg. § 1.170A-13(c)(3)(ii)(B),
21
terms of agreement requirement
under Treas. Reg.
§ 1.170A-13(c)(3)(ii)(D), 22, 131,
208
timing requirement under Treas. Reg.
§ 1.170A-13(c)(3)(i)(A), 19, 206
Qualified appraiser
appraisal designation requirement,
32, 33
appraiser understands consequences
of fraudulent violation requirement
under Treas. Reg.
§ 1.170A-13(c)(5)(i)(D), 38
declaration requirement under Treas.
Reg. § 1.170A-13(c)(5)(i), 35
declaration requirement under Treas.
Reg. § 1.170A-13(c)(5)(i)(A), 36
defined, 19
defined by statute, 31, 32
denial of qualified appraiser status, 39
disallowance of tax benefits, 14, 43
education and experience
requirement, 32–34
excluded persons, 36–38
legislative history, 31
litigation generally, 41
litigation, excluded persons, 42

litigation, multiple parties, 42
litigation, scrutiny of qualifications,
42
litigation, sufficiency of
documentation, 41
not an excluded person requirement
under Treas. Reg.
§ 1.170A-13(c)(5)(i)(C), 35, 36
not prohibited from practice
requirement under 31 U.S.C.
§ 330(c), 34
Notice 2006–96, 19, 32–35, 38
qualification requirement under
Treas. Reg. § 1.170A-13(c)(5)(i)(B),
36
regularly perform appraisals for
compensation requirement, 34
regulatory requirements, 35
verifiable education and experience
requirement, 33, 34
Qualifying the expert, 203

Reason for which the appraisal was
prepared, 123
Reasonableness, 21, 58, 64, 144, 176,
204, 213, 214
Rebuttal testimony, 59, 74, 99, 152,
158, 165, 196, 199, 202
Reconciliation, 135, 143, 213, 214
Regression analysis, 135, 136, 143,
205, 217, 218
Rehabilitation, 84, 94, 203
Replicability, 13, 15, 142
Residential Member (RM), 70
Restrictions under contract claims, 134
Restrictions under law, 134
Retaining party, 123, 141
Retention period, 139
Retrospective appraisal, 127, 215, 216
Revenue Ruling 59–60, 120, 121, 134,
139, 140

Scope of work, 123, 125, 128, 141
Senior Real Estate Analyst (SREA), 70
Senior Real Property Appraiser (SRPA),
70, 192
Senior Residential Appraiser (SRA), 70
Standard of value, 5, 11, 25, 49, 123,
125, 126, 194, 196, 211, 212

Strict compliance doctrine
  bright-line test, 56
  generally, 43
  judicial approaches, 53
Substantial compliance doctrine
  appellate courts, 54
  Bond v. Commissioner, 46, 50
  current trend, 49
  draft appraisal reports, 49
  flawed appraisal reports, 50
  generally, 43
  judicial approaches, 45
  relevance of Form 8283, 48
  role of contemporaneousness,
    50
  specific basis, 51
  sufficiency of information, 48
  Taylor test, 47
  valuation methodology, 51
  when it applies, 44
Substantial estate or gift tax valuation
  misstatement, 180
Substantial estate or gift tax valuation
  understatement penalty, 171, 172,
  181
Substantial valuation misstatement
  penalty, 171–177, 181
Substantial valuation misstatement
  penalty and pass-through entity,
  173
Substantial valuation misstatement
  penalty, property-by-property
  determination, 172, 177
Substantial valuation misstatements
  dollar limitations, 173
Summary of information considered,
  129
Summary witnesses, 76
Summonses, 102, 104

Table of contents, 141
Tax-affecting S corporations, 9, 134,
  216, 217
Tenants-in-common property, 124, 132
Terms of agreement affecting property,
  22, 124, 141, 208
Title to property, 124, 132
Traditional adversarial process
  advantages, 153, 154
  disadvantages, 153, 154
Transactional documents, 130, 133,
  134, 141
Trends, 83, 132, 135
Types of appraisals, 123, 125, 141

Unfairness doctrine, 102
Unintended users, 124
United States v. Kovel, 101, 193
USPAP
  assumption, 132
  client defined, 124
  compliance with USPAP, 122
  generally, 122
  hypothetical condition, 132
  in Tax Court, 121
  intended user defined, 124
  jurisdictional exception rule, 126
  limiting condition, 132
  noncompliance with USPAP, 122
  retention period, 139
  types of appraisal reports, 125
  work file, 138

Valuation standards, 5, 120, 121
Voir dire, 82, 203

Work file, 109, 110, 138, 139
Work product doctrine, 101, 102, 106,
  112, 117, 193